Arya Sura

The Gâtakamâlâ; or, Garland of Birth-stories

Arya Sura

The Gâtakamâlâ; or, Garland of Birth-stories

ISBN/EAN: 9783337007713

Printed in Europe, USA, Canada, Australia, Japan

Cover: Foto ©Lupo / pixelio.de

More available books at **www.hansebooks.com**

OR

GARLAND OF BIRTH-STORIES

BY

ÂRYA SÛRA

TRANSLATED FROM THE SANSKRIT

BY

J. S. SPEYER

London

HENRY FROWDE

OXFORD UNIVERSITY PRESS WAREHOUSE

AMEN CORNER, E.C.

1895

EDITOR'S PREFACE.

AFTER all the necessary preparations for the first and second series of the *Sacred Books of the East*, consisting in all of forty-nine volumes, with two volumes of *General Index*, had been completed, I still received several offers of translations of important texts which I felt reluctant to leave unpublished. As they were chiefly translations of Buddhist texts, I mentioned the fact to several of my Buddhist friends, and I was highly gratified when I was informed that H. M. the King of Siam, being desirous that the true teaching of the Buddha should become more widely known in Europe, had been graciously pleased to promise that material support without which the publication of these translations would have been impossible.

I therefore resolved to do what I could for helping to spread a more correct knowledge of the religion of Buddha: but after the first three volumes of this new Series of the Sacred Books of the Buddhists is published, it will mainly depend on the interest which the public may take in this work, whether it can be continued or not.

As long as my health allows me to do so I shall be quite willing to continue what has been a labour of love to me during many years of my life. It was not always an easy task. The constant correspondence with my fellow-workers has taxed my time and my strength far more than I expected. The difficulty was not only to select from the very large mass of Sacred Books those that seemed most important

and most likely to be useful for enabling us to gain
a correct view of the great religions of the East, but
to find scholars competent and willing to undertake
the labour of translation. I can perfectly understand
the unwillingness of most scholars to devote their time
to mere translations. With every year the translation
of such works as the Veda or the Avesta, instead of
becoming easier, becomes really more perplexing and
more difficult. Difficulties of which we formerly had
no suspicion have been brought to light by the ever-
increasing number of fresh students, and precautions
have now to be taken against dangers the very
existence of which was never dreamt of in former
years. I do not exaggerate when I say that the
translation of some of the hymns of the Veda, often
clearly corrupt in the original, has become as difficult
as the deciphering of hieroglyphic or cuneiform in-
scriptions, where at all events the text may be
depended on. What critical scholars like is to translate
a verse here and a verse there, possibly a hymn or
a whole chapter with various readings, critical notes
and brilliant conjectures; but to translate a whole
book without shirking a single line is a task from
which most of them recoil. Nor have the labours of
those who have hitherto ventured on a more complete
translation of the Rig-veda, such as Wilson, Grassmann,
Ludwig and Griffith, been received as they ought to
have been, with gratitude for what they have achieved,
and with allowances for what they failed to achieve.
I therefore remarked in the Preface to the first volume
of this collection, p. xlii:

'Oriental scholars have been blamed for not having as yet supplied
a want so generally felt, and so frequently expressed, as a complete,
trustworthy, and readable translation of the principal Sacred Books
of the Eastern Religions. The reasons, however, why hitherto they
have shrunk from such an undertaking are clear enough. The
difficulties in many cases of giving complete translations, and not
selections only, are very great. There is still much work to be done
for a critical restoration of the original texts, for an examination of
their grammar and metres, and for determining the exact meaning
of many words and passages. That kind of work is naturally far

more attractive to scholars than a mere translation, particularly when they cannot but feel that, with the progress of our knowledge, many a passage which now seems clear and easy, may, on being re-examined, assume a new import. Thus while scholars who would be most competent to undertake a translation prefer to devote their time to more special researches, the work of a complete translation is deferred to the future, and historians are left under the impression that Oriental scholarship is still in so unsatisfactory a state as to make any reliance on translations of the Veda, the Avesta, or the Tâo-te king extremely hazardous.

'It is clear, therefore, that a translation of the principal Sacred Books of the East can be carried out only at a certain sacrifice. Scholars must leave for a time their own special researches in order to render the general results already obtained accessible to the public at large. And even then, useful results can be achieved *viribus unitis* only.'

My expectations, however, have not been deceived. My appeal was most generously responded to by the best Oriental scholars in England, France, Germany, Holland and America. Nor have these scholars, who were not afraid to come forward with translations which they knew to be far from final, had to regret their courage and their public spirit. The most competent judges have accepted what we had to offer in a grateful and indulgent spirit. There has only been one painful exception in the case of a scholar who has himself never ventured on the translation of a sacred text, and who seems to have imagined that he could render more useful service by finding fault with the translation of certain words and passages, or by suggesting an entirely different and, in his eyes, a far more excellent method of translation. All scholars know how easy it is to glean a few straws, and how laborious to mow a whole field. There are passages in every one of the Sacred Books, even in such carefully edited texts as the Old and New Testaments, on which interpreters will always differ; and we know how, after centuries of constant labour bestowed on those texts, the most learned and careful scholars have not been able to agree, or to avoid oversights in their Revised Version of the Bible. Could we expect anything different in the first attempts at translating the Sacred Books of other religions? Valuable emendations, offered in a scholarlike spirit, would have been most gratefully accepted by myself and by my fellow-workers. But seldom, nay hardly ever, have emendations been proposed that would essentially alter the *textus receptus* or throw new light on really obscure passages, while the offensive tone adopted by our critic made it impossible to answer him. As he is no longer among the living, I shall say no more. I feel bound, however, for the sake of those who do not know me, to correct one remark, as invidious as it was groundless, made by the same departed scholar, namely that I had received an excessive *honorarium* as Editor of the Sacred Books of the East, nay, as he expressed it, that I had levied tribute of my fellow-workers. The fact is that during all the years which I devoted to the superintending of the publication of the fifty volumes of the Sacred Books of the East, I have not had the smallest addition to my income. I was relieved by the University of Oxford from the duty of delivering my public lectures, so that I might devote my time to this large literary undertaking brought out by our University Press. My labour, even the mere official correspondence with my many contributors, was certainly not less than that of delivering lectures which I had been in the habit of delivering for twenty-five years. My private lectures were continued all the same, and the publications of my pupils are there to show how ungrudgingly I gave them my time and my assistance in their literary labours. It is difficult to see of what interest such matters can be to other people, or with what object they are dragged before the public. I should have felt ashamed to notice such an accusation, if the accuser had not been a man whose scholarship deserved respect. I have never claimed any credit for the sacrifices which I have made both in time and in money, for objects which were near and dear to my heart. It has been, as I said, a labour of love, and I shall always feel most grateful to the University of Oxford, and to my fellow-translators, for having enabled me to realise this long cherished plan of making the world better acquainted with the Sacred Books of the principal religions of mankind, a work which has borne fruit already, and will, I hope, bear still richer fruit in the future.

If the members of the principal religions of the world wish to understand one another, to bear with one another, and possibly to recognise certain great truths which, without being aware of it, they share in common with one another, the only solid and sound foundation for such a religious peace-movement will be supplied by a study of the Sacred Books of each religion.

One such religious Peace-Congress has been held already in America. Preparations for another are now being made; and it is certainly a sign of the times when we see Cardinal Gibbons, after conferring with Pope Leo XIII at Rome, assuring those who are organising this new Congress : 'The Pope will be with you, I know it. Write, agitate, and do not be timid [1].'

The *Gâtakamâlâ*, of which Prof. Speyer has given us an English translation in this volume, is a work well known to students of Buddhism. The edition of the Sanskrit text by Prof. Kern is not only an *editio princeps*, but the text as restored by him will probably remain the final text, and Prof. Speyer in translating has had but seldom to depart from it.

*G*âtaka has generally been translated by Birth-story or Tale of Anterior Births, and it would be difficult to find a better rendering. This class of stories is peculiar to Buddhism; for although the idea that every man had passed through many existences before his birth on earth and will pass through many more after his death was, like most Buddhist theories, borrowed from the Brâhmans, yet its employment for teaching the great lessons of morality seems to have been the work of Buddha and his pupils. In addition to this there was another theory, likewise Brahmanic in its origin, but again more fully developed for practical purposes by the Buddhists, that of Karma, a firm belief that an

---

[1] *Le Pape sera avec vous, je le sais. Écrivez, agissez, ne soyez pas timides.* Revue de Paris, Sept. 1, 1895, p. 136.

unbroken chain of cause and effect binds all existences together. The great problems of the justice of the government of the world, of the earthly sufferings of the innocent, and the apparent happiness of the wicked, were to the Indian mind solved once for all by the firm conviction that what we experience here is the result of something that has happened before, that there is an unbroken heredity in the world, and that we not only benefit by, but also suffer from our ancestors. In order fully to understand the drift of the *G*âtakas we must, however, bear in mind one more article of the Buddhist faith, namely that, though ordinary mortals remember nothing of their former existences beyond the fact that they did exist, which is involved in the very fact of their self-consciousness, highly enlightened beings have the gift of recalling their former vicissitudes. It is well known that Pythagoras claimed the same gift of remembering his former lives, or at all events is reported to have claimed it. A Buddha is supposed to know whatever has happened to him in every existence through which he has passed: and it seems to have been the constant habit of the historical Buddha, Buddha *S*âkya-muni, to explain to his disciples things that were happening by things that had happened countless ages before. Those lessons seem certainly to have impressed his hearers, after they once believed that what they had to suffer here on earth was not the result of mere chance, but the result of their own former deeds or of the deeds of their fellow-creatures, that they were in fact paying off a debt which they had contracted long ago. It was an equally impressive lesson that whatever good they might do on earth would be placed to their account in a future life, because the whole world was one large system in which nothing could ever be lost, though many of the links of the chain of cause and effect might escape human observation or recollection.

The Buddha, in telling these stories of his former births or existences, speaks of himself, not exactly as the same individual, but rather as the enlightened one, the Buddha as he existed at any and at every time; and from a moral point of view, the enlightened meant the good, the perfect man. We must not suppose that his hearers were expected to believe, in our sense of the word, all the circumstances of his former existences as told by Buddha *S*âkya-muni. Even for an Indian imagination it would have been hard to accept them as matters of fact. A *G*âtaka was not much more than what a parable is with us, and as little as Christians are expected to accept the story of Lazarus resting in Abraham's bosom as a matter of fact (though, I believe, the house of *Dives* is shown at Jerusalem) were the Buddhists bound to believe that Buddha as an individual or as an historical person, had formerly been a crow or a hare. The views of the Buddhists on the world and its temporary tenants, whether men, animals, or trees, are totally different from our own, though we know how even among ourselves the theories of heredity have led some philosophers to hold that we, or our ancestors, existed at one time in an animal, and why not in a vegetable or mineral state. It is difficult for us to enter fully into the Buddhist views of the world; I would only warn my readers that they must not imagine that highly educated men among the Buddhists were so silly as to accept the *G*âtakas as ancient history.

It would be more correct, I believe, to look upon these Birth-stories as homilies used for educational purposes and for inculcating the moral lessons of Buddhism. This is clearly implied in the remarks at the end of certain *G*âtakas, such as 'This story is also to be used when discoursing on the Buddha' (p. 148), or 'This story may be used with the object of showing the difficulty of finding companions for a religious life' (p. 172). We know that Christian divines also made use of popular stories for similar purposes. In India many of these stories must have existed long before the rise of Buddhism, as they exist even now, in the memory of the people. It is known how some of them reached Greece and Rome and the Western world through various well-ascertained channels[1], and how they still supply our nurseries with the earliest lessons of morality, good sense, and good manners.

It may be said that the lessons of morality inculcated in these homilies are too exaggerated to be of any practical usefulness. Still this *modus docendi* is very common in Sacred Books, where we often find an extreme standard held up in the hope of producing an impression that may be useful in less extreme cases. To offer the other cheek to whosoever shall strike our right cheek, to give up our cloak to him who takes away our coat, to declare that it is easier for a camel to go through the eye of a needle than for a rich man to enter into the kingdom of God, are all lessons which we also take *cum grano salis*. They ask for much in the hope that something may be given. That there is danger too in this mode of teaching cannot be denied. We are told that Ârya Sûra, in order to follow the example of Buddha in a former birth, threw himself in this life before a starving tigress to be devoured. Let us hope that this too was only a *G*âtaka.

When once a taste for these moralising stories had arisen, probably owing to Buddha's daily intercourse with the common people, their number grew most rapidly. The supply was unlimited, all that was required was the moral application, the *Hacc fabula docet*. The Buddhists give their number as 550. The earliest are probably those which are found in different parts of the Buddhist Canon. In the *K*ariyâ-pi*t*aka there is a collection of thirty-five stories of the former lives of Buddha, in each of which he acquired one of the ten Pâramitâs or Great Perfections which fit a human being for Buddhahood[2]. A similar collection is found in the Buddhava*m*sa[3], which contains an account of the life of the coming Buddha, the Bodhisat, in the various

---

[1] Migration of Fables, in Chips from a German Workshop, vol. iv, p. 412.
[2] See Buddhist Birth-stories, translated by Rhys Davids, p. lv.
[3] Some doubt attaches to the canonicity of the *K*ariyâ-pi*t*aka and the Buddhava*m*sa (see Childers, s. v. Nikâya).

characters which he filled during the periods of the twenty-four previous Buddhas.

The Gâtaka stories are therefore at least as old as the compilation of the Buddhist Canon at the Council of Vesâli, about 377 B.C.[1] It was at that Council that the great schism took place, and that the ancient Canon was rearranged or disarranged. Among the books thus tampered with is mentioned the Gâtaka, which therefore must be considered as having existed, and formed part of the old Canon before the Council of Vesâli. This is what the Dipavamsa (V, 32) says on the subject:

'The Bhikkhus of the Great Council settled a doctrine contrary (to the true Faith). Altering the original text they made another text. They transposed Suttas which belonged to one place (of the collection) to another place; they destroyed the true meaning of the Faith, in the Vinaya and in the five collections (of the Suttas). . . . Rejecting single passages of the Suttas and of the proposed Vinaya, they composed other Suttas and another Vinaya which had (only) the appearance (of the genuine ones). Rejecting the following texts, viz. the Parivâra, which is the abstract of the contents (of the Vinaya), the six sections of the Abhidhamma, the Patisambhidâ, the Niddesa, and *some portions of the Gâtaka*, they composed new ones.'

Whatever else this may prove with regard to the way in which the ancient Canon was preserved, it shows at all events that Gâtakas existed before the Vesâli Council as an integral portion of the sacred Canon, and we learn at the same time that it was possible even then to compose new chapters of that canon, and probably also to add new Gâtaka stories.

Whether we possess the text of the Gâtaka in exactly that form in which it existed previous to the Council of Vesâli in 377 B.C. is another question. Strictly speaking we must be satisfied with the time of Vattagâmani in whose reign, 88-76 B.C., writing for literary purposes seems to have become more general in India, and the Buddhist Canon was for the first time reduced to writing.

What we possess is the Pâli text of the Gâtaka as

---

[1] Dhammapada, p. xxx, S. B. E., vol. x.

it has been preserved in Ceylon. The tradition is that these 550 *G*âtaka stories, composed in Pâli, were taken to Ceylon by Mahinda, about 250 B.C., that the commentary was there translated into Singhalese, and that the commentary was retranslated into Pâli by Buddhaghosha, in the fifth century A.D. It is in this commentary alone that the text of the *G*âtakas has come down to us. This text has been edited by Dr. Fausböll. He has distinguished in his edition between three component elements, the tale, the frame, and the verbal interpretation. This text, of which the beginning was translated in 1880 by Prof. Rhys Davids, is now being translated by Mr. R. Chalmers, Mr. W. R. D. Rouse, Mr. H. T. Francis and Mr. R. A. Neil, and the first volume of their translation has appeared in 1895 under the able editorship of Professor Cowell.

As Professor Speyer has explained, the *G*âtakamâlâ, the Garland of Birth-stories, which he has translated, is a totally different work. It is a Sanskrit rendering of only thirty-four *G*âtakas ascribed to Ârya *S*ûra. While the Pâli *G*âtaka is written in the plainest prose style, the work of Ârya *S*ûra has higher pretensions, and is in fact a kind of kâvya, a work of art. It was used by the Northern Buddhists, while the Pâli *G*âtaka belongs to the Canon of the Southern Buddhists. The date of Ârya *S*ûra is difficult to fix. Târanâtha (p. 90) states that *S*ûra was known by many names, such as A*s*vaghosha, Mât*ri*ke*t*a, Pit*ri*ke*t*a, Durdar*sh*a (*sic*), Dharmika-subhûti, Mati*k*itra. He also states that towards the end of his life *S*ûra was in correspondence with king Kanika (Kanishka?), and that he began to write the hundred *G*âtakas illustrating Buddha's acquirement of the ten Pâramitâs (see p. xiv), but died when he had finished only thirty-four. It is certainly curious that our *G*âtakamâlâ contains thirty-four *G*âtakas[1]. If therefore we could rely on Târanâtha,

---

[1] The same is also the number of Avadânas in the Bodhisattva-Avadâna, and the stories seem to be the same as those of our *G*âtakamâlâ.—Rajendralal Mitra, Sanskrit Buddhist Literature, p. 49.

Ârya Sûra, being identical with Asvaghosha, the author of the Buddhakarita, would have lived in the first century of our era. He is mentioned as a great authority on metres (Târanâtha, p. 181), and he certainly handles his metres with great skill. But dates are always the weak point in the history of Indian Literature. Possibly the study of Tibetan Literature, and a knowledge of the authorities on which Târanâtha relied, may throw more light hereafter on the date of Sûra and Asvaghosha.

F. MAX MÜLLER.

OXFORD, *October*, 1895.

CONTENTS.

	PAGE.
INTRODUCTION	xxi
Introductory Stanzas	1
I The Story of the Tigress	2
II. The Story of the King of the Sibis	8
III. The Story of the Small Portion of Gruel	20
IV. The Story of the Head of a Guild	25
V. The Story of Avishahya, the Head of a Guild	30
VI. The Story of the Hare	37
VII. The Story of Agastya	46
VIII. The Story of Maitrîbala	55
IX. The Story of Viśvantara	71
X. The Story of the Sacrifice	93
XI. The Story of Śakra	104
XII. The Story of the Brâhman	109
XIII. The Story of Unmâdayantî	114
XIV. The Story of Supâraga	124
XV. The Story of the Fish	134
XVI. The Story of the Quail's Young	138
XVII. The Story of the Jar	141
XVIII. The Story of the Childless One	148
XIX. The Story of the Lotus-Stalks	154
XX. The Story of the Treasurer	164
XXI. The Story of Kuddabodhi	172
XXII. The Story of the Holy Swans	181
XXIII. The Story of Mahâbodhi	200
XXIV. The Story of the Great Ape	218

		PAG
XXV. The Story of the Sarabha		227
XXVI. The Story of the Ruru-Deer .		234
XXVII. The Story of the Great Monkey		244
XXVIII. The Story of Kshântivâdin . . .		253
XXIX. The Story of the Inhabitant of the Brahmaloka		268
XXX. The Story of the Elephant		281
XXXI. The Story of Sutasoma .		291
XXXII. The Story of Ayogr*i*ha .		314
XXXIII. The Story of the Buffalo .		324
XXXIV. The Story of the Woodpecker . .		329
Synoptical Table of the Correspondence between the Stanzas of the Gâtakamâlâ and the Scripture Verses of the Pâli Gâtaka		337
Index . .		341

Transliteration of Oriental Alphabets adopted for the Translations of the Sacred Books of the Buddhists . . . 347

INTRODUCTION.

THE 'Garland of Birth-stories' belongs to the Canon of the Northern Buddhists. For the discovery of this work we are indebted to Mr. Brian H. Hodgson, who as early as 1828 mentioned it among the interesting specimens of Bauddha scriptures communicated to him by his old Patan monk, and also procured copies of it. One of these was deposited in the library of the college of Fort William, now belonging to the Bengal Asiatic Society, and was described, in 1882, by Râgendralâla Mitra. Another was forwarded to the Paris library. Burnouf, who thoroughly studied other works belonging to the Sûtra and Avadâna classes, which form part of the Hodgson MSS. in Paris, seems to have had a merely superficial acquaintance with the Gâtakamâlâ, if we may judge from the terms with which he deals with it in his 'Introduction à l'histoire du Bouddhisme indien,' p. 54 of the second edition: 'Je dis les livres, quoiqu'il n'en existe qu'un seul dans la liste népalaise et dans la collection de M. Hodgson, qui porte et qui mérite le titre de *Djâtaka* (naissance); c'est le volume intitulé *Djâtakamâlâ* ou la Guirlande des naissances, qui passe pour [1] un récit des diverses actions méritoires de Çâkya antérieurement à l'époque où il devint Buddha.' In fact, he has never given a summary, still less a detailed account of its contents. It was not until 1875 that M. Féer gave such an account in the Journal Asiatique, VIIe Sér., t. 5, p. 413.

Moreover, Burnouf's statement is not quite correct with respect to the Nepal list. Not one, but three Gâtaka works are named there[2], the Gâtakâvadâna (No. 32), the Gâtakamâlâ (No. 33), and the Mahâgâtakamâlâ (No. 34). Of these only one, indeed, is extant, viz. No. 33, our 'Garland of Birth-stories.' No. 34 may be the work, containing 550 or 565 Gâtakas, spoken of by the Bauddha monk who imparted so much valuable

---

[1] I have spaced the words that prove my statement.
[2] See Hodgson, Essays on the Languages &c. of Nepal and Tibet, 1874, p. 37.

information to Hodgson [1], or, perhaps, the original of the Tibetan collection of 101 tales, including also our Gâtakamâlâ, to which two Russian scholars, Serge d'Oldenburg and Ivanovski, have of late drawn the attention of the public [2]. As to No. 32, its title, Gâtakâvadâna, allows the supposition that it is either a collection of Gâtakas and avadânas, or that it contains 'great religious exploits' (avadâna) performed by the Bodhisattva, who afterwards became Buddha, the Lord. Nothing is more common than the use of both terms in a nearly synonymous manner. Our Gâtakamâlâ bears also the appellation of Bodhisattvâvadânamâlâ [3]. In translating Gâtaka by 'birth-story,' I comply with the general use and official interpretation of that term by the Buddhist Church. The original meaning must have been simply ' tale, story,' as Prof. Kern has demonstrated in his ' History of Buddhism in India [4].' Additional evidence of this statement may be drawn from the fact, that in several of the old and traditional headings of these stories the former part of the compound denotes not the Bodhisattva, but some other person of the tale, as Vyâghrigâtaka, 'the Story of the Tigress,' or a thing, as Kumbhagâtaka, 'the Story of the Jar;' Bisagâtaka, 'the Story of the Lotus-stalks,' which are respectively Nos. I, XVII, and XIX of this collection; or an action, as Silavima*m*sa(ka)-gâtaka, the common heading of Nos. 86, 290, 305, and 330 in Fausböll's Pâli Gâtaka, Nak*k*agâtaka, ibid., No. 32, or a quality, as Silânisa*m*sagâtaka, ibid., No. 190.

Some time after M. Féer's compte-rendu of the Paris MS. was published two new MSS. of the Gâtakamâlâ came to Europe. They belong to the valuable set of Sanskrit Buddhist works which Dr. Wright acquired for the Cambridge University Library, and are described by Prof. Cecil Bendall in his excellent Catalogue (1883). Prof. Kern was the first to appreciate the great literary merits of the Gâtakamâlâ, and soon planned an edition, availing himself of the two Cambridge MSS. (Add. 1328 and 1415) and the Paris one [5]. This editio princeps was published at the end of 1891 as the first volume of the Harvard Oriental Series of Prof. Lanman. It has every right to bear the name of ' princeps,' not only because Ârya Sûra's work has never been edited before, but on account of

---

[1] See Hodgson, Essays, pp. 17 and 37.
[2] See the paper of d'Oldenburg, translated by Dr. Wenzel in the Journ. Roy. As. Soc. of 1893, p. 304.
[3] Also cp. the passage of the Avadânakalpalatâ, quoted infra, p. xxiii.
[4] See I, p. 257 of the original (Dutch) edition.
[5] Dr. d'Oldenburg mentions two more copies; they are at St. Petersburg. See his paper in the Journ. Roy. As. Soc., p. 306.

the critical acumen and the untiring care of the editor, whose exertions have almost purged the text from the clerical errors and blunders which greatly encumber the Nepal manuscripts[1]. Thus, thanks to Prof. Kern, this masterpiece of Sanskrit Buddhist literature is now accessible to Sanskritists in an excellent edition. I have undertaken to translate it, as I consider it a most valuable document for the knowledge of Buddhism.

Properly speaking, *Gâtakamâlâ* is a class-name. It has been pointed out above that in the Northern Buddhist Canon several writings of that name have been made known, and though, so far as I know, this appellation does not occur in the book-titles of the Pâli Tripi*t*aka, such texts as the Pâli *G*âtaka and the *K*ariyâpi*t*aka may have some right to be thus designated. That it is a generic appellation is made plain from Somendra's Introduction to the Avadânakalpalatâ of his father Kshemendra. It is said there, verses 7 and 8:—

'â*k*âryaGopadattâdyair avadânakramo*ggh*itâ*h* u*kk*ityo*kk*itya vihitâ gadyapadyavi*sr*iṅkhalâ*h*, ekamârgânusâri*n*ya*h* para*m* gâmbhîryakarka*sâh* vistîr*n*avar*n*anâ*h* santi *G*ina*g*âtakamâlikâ*h*.'

'There exist many "Garlands of Birth-stories of the *G*ina" by Gopadatta and other teachers, who, discarding the usual order of the Avadânas, gathered tales *carptim*, and told them at length in elaborate prose (gadya) interspersed with verse, holding themselves free as to the proportions of the two styles, which they made interchange. They all treat of the praise of the Right Path, but, owing to their profoundness, are hard to understand.'

This definition of that class exactly suits the work, the translation of which is here published. This composition consists, indeed, of verse intermingled with flowery prose built up according to the rules and methods of Sanskrit rhetoric; it claims to be a florilegium, a selection of *G*âtakas, with the avowed object of rousing or invigorating the true faith in the minds of the reader; and the stories are told at length. It has perhaps been the most perfect writing of its kind. It is distinguished no less by the superiority of its style than by the loftiness of its thoughts. Its verses and artful prose are written in the purest Sanskrit[2], and charm the reader by the

---
[1] Compare the complaint of Prof. Cowell, p. xii of the Introduction to his translation of the Buddha*k*arita (Sacred Books, vol. xlix).
[2] The peculiarities of our author are not many, and bear chiefly on lexicology, not on grammar or style, which show the most intimate acquaintance with the classic language. His subject-matter and his faith, of course, necessitate the use of a number of terms, found in Buddhist writings only; yet he avoids several of

elegance of their form and the skill displayed in the handling of a great variety of metres, some of which are rarely to be met with elsewhere[1], and are sometimes adorned with the additional qualities of difficult and refined rhymes, and the like. Apparently Sûra, to whom the Gâtakamâlâ is ascribed, was a poet richly gifted by Nature, whose talent must have been developed by thorough and extensive literary studies. Above all, I admire his moderation. Unlike so many other Indian masters in the art of literary composition, he does not allow himself the use of embellishing apparel and the whole luxuriant *mise en scène* of Sanskrit alamkâra beyond what is necessary for his subject. His flowery descriptions, his long and elaborate sermons, his elegant manner of narration, are always in harmony with the scheme of the whole or the nature of the contents. Similarly, in the choice of his metres he was guided by stylistic motives in accordance with the tone and sentiment required at a given point of the narrative. It is a pity that most of these excellencies are lost in the translation.

Thus much for the philologist and the lover of Oriental literature. To the student of Buddhism it is the peculiar character of the Gâtakamâlâ which constitutes its great importance. Although it is styled 'a garland of stories,' it is really a collection of homilies. Each Gâtaka is introduced by a simple prose sentence of ethical and religious purport, which is to be illustrated by the story. The whole treatment of the tale bears the character of a religious discourse. Prof. Cowell, in his preface to the translation of the Pâli Gâtaka, observes that the Gâtaka-legends are 'continually introduced into the religious discourses .... whether to magnify the glory of the Buddha or to illustrate Buddhist doctrines and

---

them, which are not good Sanskrit, as vigita and most of those signalized by Cowell and Neil in p. ix of their edition of the Divyâvadâna. He often employs uddhava = Pâli utthava [which itself is = Skt. utsava], sumukha = 'propense,' sâtmîbhavati, °karoti, °bhâva, a term to express the imbibing of qualities into one's nature, adhyâsaya = âsaya, vitâna and vaitânya = 'dejected' and 'dejection,' vimanah = durmanah 'sad,' pratipat and pratipatti = '(good) conduct' and so on. Likewise he uses such words as vanîpaka, pratisammodana, (ahorâtram atinâmayâm âsa, XXVI, 27 ârabhya [= Pâli ârabbha] in the meaning of 'concerning' = adhikrr̥tya, âsritya and VIII, 20 pratyâham = pratyaham. On the other hand, instances of old words and expressions, and of such as were hitherto only known from the Dictionaries, are found in his work. So e. g. addhâ IX, 60 and elsewhere, âkumbha XVII, 5, XXVIII, 31, dândâginika in XXVIII, 37.

[1] Among the less common metres I notice the Mattamayûra V, 22-24, XXIX, 4 and 32; the Pramitâkshara XVII, 17, XVIII, 20, XXIII, 25; the Bhujaṅgaprayâta XXIX, 26; the Praharanakalitâ or Kalikâ XVII, 20; some metre akin to the Sumânikâ—cp. Colebrooke, Misc. Ess. II, 141—XXIII, 34-39, for it does not suit the scheme taught by Colebrooke, in verses 35-39 each pâda consisting of two trochees and a bacchius, whereas verse 34 is made up of two trochees and a molossus.

precepts by appropriate examples[1].' Our *Gâtakamâlâ* has a right to be called a choice collection of such sermons, distinguished by their lofty conception and their artistic elaboration. It is a document of the first rank for the study of ancient Buddhist homiletics, and is for this reason entitled to a place among the Sacred Books of the East.

*Sû*ra took his thirty-four holy legends from the old and traditional store of *G*âtaka-tales. Almost all of them have been identified with corresponding ones in other collections, both of Northern and Southern Buddhism. So far as I could control those parallels or add to them, I have taken care to notice them at the beginning or at the end of each story. The author himself in his introductory stanzas declares his strict conformity with scripture and tradition; and, however much he has done for the adornment and embellishment of the outer form of his tales, we may trust him, when he implies that he has nowhere changed their outlines or their essential features, but has narrated them as they were handed down to him by writing or by oral tradition. Wherever his account differs from that preserved in other sources, we may infer that he followed some different version. Sometimes he passes over details of minor importance. For instance, in the second story he avoids the hideous particulars of the eye-operation, dwelt upon in the Pâli *G*âtaka. The same good taste will be appreciated in Story XXVIII, when the cruel act of the wicked king against the monk Kshântivâdin has to be told, and in Story VIII. Stories XVII, XXII, XXXI are much simpler than their parallels in the holy Pâli book, which are unwieldy, encumbered as they are by exuberance of details. I cannot help thinking that *Sû*ra omitted such particulars purposely. For the rest, he does not pretend to tell stories new or unknown to his readers. He acknowledges their popularity; he puts the story of the tigress at the beginning, in order to honour his teacher, who had celebrated that *G*âtaka. He often neglects to give proper names to the actors in his tales. For instance, of Agastya, Ayog*ri*ha, *K*u*dd*abodhi, the heroes of the *G*âtakas thus named, it is nowhere said that they were so called. *G*ûgaka, the Brâhman who begged the children from Vi*s*vantara, consequently a well-known figure in the legend, is only named 'a Brâhman.' In the same story (IX) Madrî, the wife of the hero, is introduced as a well-known person, although her name had not been mentioned before.

That he closely adheres to the traditional stock of legends

---

[1] See The Jātaka, translated from the Pāli by various hands under the editorship of Prof. E. B. Cowell, Cambridge, 1895, I, p. vi.

is also shown by a good number of his verses. Generally speaking, the metrical part of the *Gâtakamâlâ* admits of a fourfold division. There are laudatory verses, praising and pointing out the virtues of the hero; these are commonly found in the first part or preamble of the tale. There are descriptive verses, containing pictures of fine scenery or of phenomena. Further, there are religious discourses, sometimes of considerable length, put in the mouth of the Bodhisattva ; they have their place mostly at the end [1]. The rest consists in verses treating of facts in the story, and it is chiefly there that we find again the gâthâs of the corresponding Pâli *Gâtakas*. It is incontestable that in a great many cases *Sûra* worked on the same or a very similar stock of gâthâs as are contained in the Sacred Canon of the Southern Buddhists. For the sake of reference I have registered those parallel verses in a Synoptical Table, which is placed at the end of this book (pp. 337–340). Sometimes the affinity is so striking that one text will assist the interpretation and critical restitution of the other. *Sûra's* stanza, V, 11, for example, has not been invented by the author himself; it is a refined paraphrase in Sanskrit of some Prâkrit gâthâ of exactly the same purport as that which in Fausböll's *Gâtaka* III, p. 131, bears the number 158. By comparing pâda c in both, it is plain that in the Pâli text no ought to be read instead of vo[2]. It must have been sacred texts in some popular dialect, not in Sanskrit, that underly the elaborate and high-flown verses of *Sûra*. This is proved, among other things, by the mistake in XIX, 17, pointed out by Prof. Kern in the Various Readings he has appended to his edition.

As I have already remarked, each story is introduced by a leading sentence, expressing some religious maxim, which, according to Indian usage, is repeated again at the end as

---

[1] It is but seldom that the verses contain a mere repetition or development of what has just been told in the prose immediately preceding. Of this kind are XIII, 16; XIX, 5; XXV, 1; XXX, 5.

[2] Here are some other instances. In the Bhisagâtaka, Fausb. IV, 309, 11, read puttî... sabbakâmî, cp. *Gâtakamâlâ* XIX, 13, ibid. l. 22 sabbasamatta-vedam and l. 24 pûgentu, cp. *Gâtakamâlâ* XIX, 16; ibid. p. 310, 3 lattha, not alattha, cp. XIX, 18.—In the *K*ullaha*m*sagâtaka, F. V, 340, 12 kha*nd*am the reading of *B*[u] and *S*[dr] is confirmed by *Sû*ra, XXII, 37 ûna*m*. Ibid. 343, 16 I read tâvad eva *k*a te lâbho kat' assa yâ*k*anâ *k*a me, comparing *Sû*ra XXII, 50, and from XXII, 80 I infer that F. V, 350, 16 mama is to be read for dhamma*m*, vasu for vaso, sabbatth' instead of sabb' atth'.—In F. I, 213, 13 a prose passage may be corrected from the parallel prose of *Gâtakamâlâ* (p. 98, 8 of the edition); divide the words thus, ku*kkh*ito gâto a*nd*akosam padâletvâ.

On the other hand the Pâli text is of use to correct a passage of *Sû*ra. XXII, 33 c we should read dharmo hy apa*k*ita*h* samyag &c., cp. Fausb. V, 339, 22.

a conclusion to the story, being preceded by evam or tathâ, 'in this manner.' But, as a rule [1], the epilogues are not limited to that simple repetition. They often contain more, the practical usefulness of the story thus told being enhanced by the addition of other moral lessons, which may be illustrated by it, or by pointing out different subjects of religious discourses, in connection with which our tale may be of use. Most of these epilogues, in my opinion, are posterior to Sûra. Apart from the argument offered by some remarkable discrepancies in style and language and the monkish spirit pervading them, I think it highly improbable that, after the author had put at the head and at the end of each Gâtaka the moral maxim he desires to inculcate upon the minds of his readers by means of the account of a certain marvellous deed of the Bodhisattva, he should himself add different indications for other employments to serve homiletical purposes. It is more likely that these accessories are of later origin, and were added when the discourses of Sûra had gained so great a reputation as to be admitted to the Canon of Sacred Writings, and had come to be employed by the monks as a store of holy and edifying sermons for the purposes of religious instruction.

On account of these considerations, I have bracketed in my translation such part of the epilogues as seemed to me later interpolations. Yet I did not think it advisable to omit them. They are not without importance in themselves. They allow us an insight into the interior of the monasteries and to witness the monks preparing for preaching. Moreover, some of them contain precious information about holy texts of the Northern Buddhists, which are either lost or have not yet been discovered. In the epilogue of VIII there is even a textual quotation; likewise in that of XXX, where we find the words spoken by the Lord at the time of his Complete Extinction. As to XI, see my note on that epilogue. In XII and XXI similar sayings of holy books are hinted at.

Concerning the person of the author and his time, nothing certain is known. That he was called Ârya Sûra is told in the manuscripts, and is corroborated by Chinese tradition; the Chinese translation of the Gâtakamâlâ, made between 960 and 1127 A.D., bears Ârya Sûra on its title as the author's name (see Bunyiu Nanjio's Catalogue, No. 1312). Tibetan tradition, too, knows Sûra as a famous teacher, and as the author of our collection of stories. Târanâtha identifies him

---

[1] With the exception of V and XV. In the conclusion of III and XIII the leading text is repeated, and then more fully developed; in that of the ninth Gâtaka it is repeated in an abridged form.

with Asvaghosha, and adds many more names by which the same great man should be known. It is, however, impossible that two works so entirely different in style and spirit as the Buddhakarita and the Gâtakamâlâ should be ascribed to one and the same author.

As to his time, Dr. d'Oldenburg observes that the terminus ante quem is the end of the 7th century A.D., since it seems that the Chinese traveller I-tsing speaks of our 'Garland of Birth-stories.' If No. 1349 of Bunyiu Nanjio's Catalogue of the Chinese Tripitaka, being a Sûtra on the fruits of Karma briefly explained by Ârya Sûra, is written by our author—and there seems to be no reasonable objection to this—Sûra must have lived before 434 A.D., when the latter work is said to have been translated into Chinese. This conclusion is supported by the purity and elegance of the language, which necessarily point to a period of a high standard of literary taste and a flourishing state of letters. Prof. Kern was induced by this reason to place Sûra approximately in the century of Kâlidâsa and Varâhamihira, but equally favourable circumstances may be supposed to have existed a couple of centuries earlier. I think, however, he is posterior to the author of the Buddha-karita. For other questions concerning the Gâtakamâlâ, which it would be too long to dwell upon here, I refer to Prof. Kern's preface and d'Oldenburg in Journ. Roy. As. Soc. 1893, pp. 306-309.

Târanâtha, the historian of Tibetan Buddhism, has preserved a legend which shows the high esteem in which the Gâtakamâlâ stands with the followers of the Buddha's Law. 'Pondering on the Bodhisattva's gift of his own body to the tigress, he [viz. Sûra] thought he could do the same, as it was not so very difficult. Once he, as in the tale, saw a tigress followed by her young, near starvation; at first he could not resolve on the self-sacrifice, but, calling forth a stronger faith in the Buddha, and writing with his own blood a prayer of seventy Slokas, he first gave the tigers his blood to drink, and, when their bodies had taken a little force, offered himself[1].' In this legend I recognise the sediment, so to speak, of the stream of emotion caused by the stimulating eloquence of that gifted Mahâyânist preacher on the minds of his co-religionists. Any one who could compose discourses such as these must have been capable of himself performing the extraordinary exploits of a Bodhisattva. In fact, something of the religious enthusiasm of those ancient apostles of the Mahâyâna who

---

[1] I quote the very words, with which Dr. Wenzel translates d'Oldenburg's quotation from the Russian. See Journ. Roy. As. Soc., l. l. p. 307.

brought the Saddharma to China and Tibet pervades the work of Sûra, and it is not difficult to understand that in the memory of posterity he should have been represented as a saint who professed the ethics of his religion, *non disputandi causa*, as Cicero says of Cato, *ut magna pars, sed ita vivendi*.

It was no easy task to translate a work of so refined a composition, still less because there is no help to be had from any commentary. The Sanskrit text has none, and the Chinese commentary mentioned by Bunyiu Nanjio is not translated. Repeated and careful study of the original has led me to change a few passages of the translation I formerly published in the Bijdragen voor Taal-Land-en Volkenkunde van Ned. Indië, vols. viii and x of the fifth 'Volgreeks.' Moreover, I have adapted this, which may almost be styled a second edition, to the wants and the arrangements of the 'Sacred Books of the East.'

J. S. SPEYER.

GRONINGEN, *April* 16, 1895.

GÂTAKAMÂLÂ

OR

GARLAND OF BIRTH-STORIES

BY

ÂRYA SÛRA.

—··—

Om! Adoration to all Buddhas and Bodhisattvas!

INTRODUCTORY STANZAS.

1[1]. Grand and glorious, of inexhaustible praise and charm, comprising excellent virtues and thereby auspicious, are the wonderful exploits which the Muni performed in previous births. Them will I devoutly worship with the handful of flowers of my poem.

2, 3. 'By those praiseworthy deeds the way is taught that is leading to Buddhahood; they are the landmarks on that way. Further even the hard-hearted may be softened by them. The holy stories may also obtain a greater attractiveness.' So I considered, and for the benefit of men the attempt will be made to find a favourable audience for my own genius, by treating of the extraordinary facts of the Highest One in the world in a manner which is in accordance with the course of facts as recorded by Scripture and Tradition.

4. Him, whose beautiful practice of virtues, while acting for the sake of others, no one could imitate, though bent on self-interest; Him, the blaze of whose glory is involved in his true name of the All-Knowing One; Him, the Incomparable One together with the Law and the Congregation I venerate with bowed head.

---

[1] The cipher on the left denotes the number of the stanza. The prose parts of the original are indicated by the absence of the cipher.

I. The Story of the Tigress.

Even in former births the Lord showed His innate, disinterested, and immense love towards all creatures, and identified himself with all beings. For this reason we ought to have the utmost faith in Buddha, the Lord. This will be instanced by the following great performance of the Lord in a previous birth, which has been celebrated by my guru, a venerator of the Three Jewels, an authority because of his thorough study of virtues, and beloved by his own guru by virtue of his religious practices.

In the time that the Bodhisattva, who afterwards became our Lord, benefited the world by manifold outpourings of his compassion: gifts, kind words, succour, and similar blameless deeds of a wisdom-cultivating mind, quite in accordance with the excessive engagements to which he had bound himself, he took his birth in a most eminent and mighty family of Brâhmans, distinguished by the purity of their conduct owing to their attachment to their (religious) duties. Being purified by the *gâtakarma* and the other sacraments in due order, he grew up and in a short time, owing to the innate quickness of his understanding, the excellent aid in his studies, his eagerness for learning and his zeal, he obtained the mastership in the eighteen branches of science and in all the arts (kalâs) which were not incompatible with the custom of his family.

5. To the Brâhmans he was (an authority) like the Holy Writ; to the Kshatriyas as venerable as a king; to the masses he appeared like the embodied Thousand-eyed One[1]; to those who longed for knowledge he was a helpful father.

In consequence of his prosperous destiny (the result of merits formerly earned), a large store of wealth, distinction, and fame fell to his share. But the Bodhisattva took no delight in such things. His thoughts had been purified by his constant study of

---

[1] Viz. Sakra, the Indra or Lord of the Devas.

the Law, and he had become familiar with world-renunciation.

6. His former behaviour had wholly cleared his mind, he saw the many kinds of sin which beset (worldly) pleasures. So he shook off the householder's state, as if it were an illness, and retired to some plateau, which he adorned by his presence.

7. There, both by his detachment from the world and by his wisdom-brightened tranquillity, he confounded, as it were, the people in the world, who by attachment to bad occupations are disinclined for the calmness of the wise.

8. His calmness full of friendliness spread about, it seems, and penetrated into the hearts of the ferocious animals so as to make them cease injuring one another and live like ascetics.

9. By dint of the pureness of his conduct, his self-control, his contentment, and his compassion, he was no less a friend even to the people in the world, who were unknown to him, than all creatures were friends to him.

10. As he wanted little, he did not know the art of hypocrisy, and he had abandoned the desire for gain, glory, and pleasures. So he caused even the deities to be propitious and worshipful towards him.

11. On the other hand, those whose affection he had gained (in his former state) by his virtues, hearing of his ascetic life, left their families and their relations and went up to him as to the embodied Salvation, in order to become his disciples.

12. He taught his disciples, as best he could, good conduct (sila), chastity, purification of the organs of sense, constant attentiveness, detachment from the world, and the concentration of the mind to the meditation on friendliness (maitri) and the rest[1].

Most of his numerous disciples attained perfection in consequence of his teaching, by which this holy road (to salvation) was established and people were put on

---

[1] The four, or five, bhâvanâs or 'meditative rites' are meant.

the excellent path of world-renunciation. Now, the doors of evils being shut, as it were, but the ways of happiness widely opened like high roads, it once happened that the Great-minded One (mahâtman) was rambling along the shrubby caverns of the mountain well adapted to the practices of meditation (yoga), in order to enjoy at his ease this existing order of things. Agita, his disciple at that time, accompanied him.

13–15. Now, below in a cavern of the mountain, he beheld a young tigress that could scarcely move from the place, her strength being exhausted by the labour of whelping. Her sunken eyes and her emaciated belly betokened her hunger, and she was regarding her own offspring as food, who thirsting for the milk of her udders, had come near her, trusting their mother and fearless; but she brawled at them, as if they were strange to her, with prolonged harsh roarings.

16, 17. On seeing her, the Bodhisattva, though composed in mind, was shaken with compassion by the suffering of his fellow-creature, as the lord of the mountains (Meru) is by an earthquake. It is a wonder, how the compassionate, be their constancy ever so evident in the greatest sufferings of their own, are touched by the grief, however small, of another!

And his powerful pity made him utter, agitation made him repeat to his pupil, the following words manifesting his excellent nature: 'My dear, my dear,' he exclaimed,

18. 'Behold the worthlessness of Samsâra! This animal seeks to feed on her very own young ones. Hunger causes her to transgress love's law.

19. 'Alas! Fie upon the ferocity of self-love, that makes a mother wish to make her meal with the bodies of her own offspring!

20. 'Who ought to foster the foe, whose name is self-love, by whom one may be compelled to actions like this?

'Go, then, quickly and look about for some means of appeasing her hunger, that she may not injure her young ones and herself. I too shall endeavour to avert her from that rash act.' The disciple promised to do so, and went off in search of food. Yet the Bodhisattva had but used a pretext to turn him off. He considered thus:

21. 'Why should I search after meat from the body of another, whilst the whole of my own body is available? Not only is the getting of the meat in itself a matter of chance, but I should also lose the opportunity of doing my duty.

'Further,

22–24. 'This body being brute, frail, pithless, ungrateful, always impure, and a source of suffering, he is not wise who should not rejoice at its being spent for the benefit of another. There are but two things that make one disregard the grief of another: attachment to one's own pleasure and the absence of the power of helping. But I cannot have pleasure, whilst another grieves, and I have the power to help; why should I be indifferent? And if, while being able to succour, I were to show indifference even to an evildoer immersed in grief, my mind, I suppose, would feel the remorse for an evil deed, burning like shrubs caught by a great fire.

25. 'Therefore, I will kill my miserable body by casting it down into the precipice, and with my corpse I shall preserve the tigress from killing her young ones and the young ones from dying by the teeth of their mother.

'Even more, by so doing

26–29. 'I set an example to those who long for the good of the world; I encourage the feeble; I rejoice those who understand the meaning of charity; I stimulate the virtuous; I cause disappointment to the great hosts of Māra, but gladness to those who love the Buddha-virtues; I confound the people who are absorbed in selfishness and subdued by egotism and lusts; I give a token of faith to the adherents of the most excellent of vehicles[1], but I fill with astonishment

---

[1] This best of vehicles (yânavara) is the Buddhayâna, the

those who sneer at deeds of charity; I clear the highway to Heaven in a manner pleasing to the charitable among men; and finally that wish I yearned for, "When may I have the opportunity of benefiting others with the offering of my own limbs?"—I shall accomplish it now, and so acquire erelong Complete Wisdom.

30, 31. 'Verily, as surely as this determination does not proceed from ambition, nor from thirst of glory, nor is a means of gaining Heaven or royal dignity, as surely as I do not care even for supreme and everlasting bliss for myself, but for securing the benefit of others[1]: as surely may I gain by it the power of taking away and imparting for ever at the same time the world's sorrow and the world's happiness, just as the sun takes away darkness and imparts light!

32. 'Whether I shall be remembered, when virtue is seen to be practised, or made conspicuous, when the tale of my exploit is told; in every way may I constantly benefit the world and promote its happiness!'

33. After so making up his mind, delighted at the thought that he was to destroy even his life for securing the benefit of others, to the amazement even of the calm minds of the deities—he gave up his body.

The sound of the Bodhisattva's body falling down stirred the curiosity and the anger of the tigress. She desisted from her disposition of making a slaughter of her whelps, and cast her eyes all around. As soon as she perceived the lifeless body of the Bodhisattva, she rushed hastily upon it and commenced to devour it.

But his disciple, coming back without meat, as he had got none, not seeing his teacher, looked about for

---

vehicle by which Buddhahood may be reached, or mahâyâna, for both appellations cover nearly the same ground. The other two are the Srâvakayâna and the Pratyekabuddhayâna. See Dharmasamgraha II, with the annotation of Kenjiu Kasawara.

[1] Parârthasiddhi here and in st. 33 is a rather ambiguous term, as it may also convey this meaning: 'the attainment of the highest object.' Apparently this ambiguity is intentional. Cp. Story XXX, verse 17.

him. Then he beheld that young tigress feeding on the lifeless body of the Bodhisattva. And the admiration of the extraordinary greatness of his performance driving back his emotions of sorrow and pain, he probably gave a fair utterance[1] to his veneration for his teacher's attachment to virtues by this monologue :

34-37. 'Oh, how merciful the Great-minded One was to people afflicted by distress! How indifferent He was to His own welfare! How He has brought to perfection the virtuous conduct of the pious, and dashed to pieces the splendid glory of their adversaries! How He has displayed, clinging to virtues, His heroic, fearless, and immense love! How His body, which was already precious for its virtues, has now forcibly been turned into a vessel of the highest veneration! And although by His innate kindness He was as patient as Earth, how intolerant He was of the suffering of others! And how my own roughness of mind is evidenced by the contrast of this splendid act of heroism of His! Verily, the creatures are not to be commiserated now, having got Him as their Protector, and Manmatha[2], forsooth, is now sighing away, being disturbed and in dread of defeat.

'In every way, veneration be to that illustrious Great Being (mahāsattva), of exuberant compassion, of boundless goodness, the refuge of all creatures, yea, that Bodhisattva for the sake of the creatures.' And he told the matter over to his fellow-disciples.

38. Then his disciples and also the Gandharvas, the Yakshas, the snakes, and the chiefs of the Devas, expressing by their countenance their admiration for his deed, covered the ground that held the treasure of his bones, with a profusion of wreaths, clothes, jewel ornaments, and sandal powder.

---

[1] The text has *sobheta*, not *asobhata*, as might have been expected.
[2] Manmatha, Kâma, Kandarpa and the other names of the god of sensual love and pleasure are common equivalents of Mâra. Cp. Buddha*k*arita XIII, 2.

So, then, even in former births the Lord showed His innate, disinterested, and immense love towards all creatures, and identified Himself with all creatures. For this reason we ought to have the utmost faith in Buddha, the Lord. [And also this is to be propounded: 'And having obtained this faith in Buddha the Lord, we ought to strive for feeling the highest gladness; in this manner our faith will have its sanctuary.'—Likewise we must listen with attention to the preaching of the Law, since it has been brought to us by means of hundreds of difficult hardships[1].—And in sermons on the subject of compassion, thus is to be said: 'in this manner compassion, moving us to act for the benefit of others, is productive of an exceedingly excellent nature[2].']

The story of the tigress, which does not appear either in the Pâli Gâtaka or in the Kariyâpi/aka, is alluded to in the Bodhisattvâvadânâkalpalatâ of Kshemendra II, 108. There the Bodhisattva, on the occasion of a similar fact of self-denial and heroism in a later birth, says: 'Formerly, on seeing a hungry tigress preparing to eat her whelps, I gave her my body, in order to avert this, without hesitation.' And in the fifty-first pallava the story is narrated at length, verses 28–50. It differs in some points from ours. So does also the redaction of the Southern Buddhists, told by Spence Hardy, Manual, p. 94 of the 2nd ed.

II. THE STORY OF THE KING OF THE SIBIS.

(Comp. the Pâli Gâtaka, No. 499, Fausb. IV, 401–412; Kariyâpi/aka I, 8.)

The preaching of the excellent Law must be listened to with attention. For it is by means of hundreds of difficult hardships that the Lord obtained this excellent Law for our sake. This is shown by the following.

In the time, when this our Lord was still a Bodhisattva, in consequence of his possessing a store of

---

[1] Dushkara*s*atasamudânîtatvât, cp. Divyâvadâna, ed. Cowell, p. 490.
[2] Viz. as far as gathering merit, the consequence of good actions, improves our nature.

meritorious actions collected by a practice from time immemorial, he once was a king of the Sibis. By his deference to the elders whom he was wont to honour from his very childhood, and by his attachment to a modest behaviour, he gained the affection of his subjects; owing to his natural quickness of intellect, he enlarged his mind by learning many sciences; he was distinguished by energy, discretion, majesty and power, and favoured by fortune. He ruled his subjects as if they were his own children.

1. The different sets of virtues, that accompany each member of the triad (of dharma, artha, and kâma) all together gladly took their residence, it seems, with him; and yet they did not lose any of their splendour in spite of the disturbance which might occur from their contrasts.

2. And felicity, that is like a mockery to those who have attained a high rank by wrong means, like a grievous calamity to the fool, like an intoxicating liquor to the feeble-minded—to him it was, as is indicated by its name, real happiness.

3. Noble-hearted, full of compassion, and wealthy, this best of kings rejoiced at seeing the faces of the mendicants beaming with satisfaction and joy at the attainment of the wished-for objects.

Now this king, in accordance with his propensity for charity, had caused alms-halls, provided with every kind of utensils, goods, and grains, to be constructed in all parts of the town. In this way he poured out the rain of his gifts, not unlike a cloud of the Kr*i*ta Yuga. And he distributed them in such a manner, as well became the loftiness of his mind, supplying the wants of each according to his desire, with lovely deference and kind speed, whereby he enhanced the benefit of his gifts. He bestowed food and drink on those who were in need of food and drink; likewise he dispensed couches, seats, dwellings, meals, perfumes, wreaths, silver, gold, &c., to those who wanted them. Then, the fame of the king's sublime munificence spreading abroad, people who lived in different regions and parts of the world went to that country, with surprise and joy in their hearts.

4. The mendicants, when letting the whole world of men pass before their mind's eye, did not find in others an opportunity of putting forth their requests; to him it was that they went up in crowds with glad faces, just as wild elephants go up to a great lake.

The king, on the other hand, when beholding them, whose minds were rejoiced with the hope of gain, flocking together from all directions, though the outward appearance of that mendicant people in travelling dress was anything but handsome,—

5. Nevertheless he received them, as if they were friends come back from abroad, his eyes wide-opened with joy; he listened to their requests, as if good news were reported to him, and after giving, his contentment surpassed that of the recipients.

6. The voices of the beggars spread about the perfume of the fame of his munificence, and so abated the pride of the other kings. In a similar way, the scent of the juice that runs out of the temples of the scent-elephant in rut, being scattered by the wind, causes the bees to neglect the like fluid of the other elephants [1].

One day the king, making the tour of his alms-halls, noticed the very small number of supplicants staying there, in consequence of the wants of the mendicant people being supplied. When he considered this, he was uneasy, because his habit of almsgiving could not well proceed.

7. The indigent, when coming to him, quenched their thirst (for the desired boons), not he his (thirst for giving), when meeting with them. His passion for charity was so great, that no requester by the extent of his request could outdo his determination of giving.

Then this thought arose within him: 'Oh, very blessed are those most excellent among the pious, to

---

[1] In the original this simile is expressed by the rhetorical figure, called *slesha*.

whom the mendicants utter their desires with confidence and without restraint, so as to ask even their limbs! But to me, as if they were terrified by harsh words of refusal, they show only boldness in requesting my wealth.'

8. Now Earth, becoming aware of that exceedingly lofty thought, how her lord holding on to charity, had stopped the very attachment to his own flesh, trembled as a wife would, who loves her husband.

The surface of the earth being shaken, Sumeru, the lord of mountains, radiant with the shine of its manifold gems, began to waver. Sakra, the Lord of the Devas (Devendra), inquiring into the cause of this wavering, understood that it was the sublime thought of that king which produced the shivering of Earth's surface; and as he was taken up with amazement, he entered into this reflection:

9. 'How is this? Does this king bear his mind so high and feel so great a rejoicing at giving away in charity as to conceive the thought of girding his resolution to give with the strong determination of parting with his own limbs?

'Well, I will try him.'

Now the king, surrounded by his officials, was sitting (on his throne, in his hall) in the midst of the assembly. The usual summons by proclamation had been given, inviting anybody who was in need of anything; stores of wealth, silver, gold, jewels, were being disclosed by the care of the treasurer; boxes filled to the top with various kinds of clothes, were being uncovered; various excellent carriages, the yokes of which enclosed the necks of different well-trained beasts of draught, were being made to advance; and the mendicants were crowding in. Among them Sakra, the Lord of the Devas, having assumed the shape of an old and blind Brâhman, drew the attention of the king. On him the king fixed his firm, placid, and mild looks expressive of compassion and friendliness, and he seemed with them to go to his encounter and to embrace him. The royal attendants requested him to say what he was wanting, but he drew near the king, and after uttering his hail and blessing, addressed him with these words:

10. 'A blind, old man I have come hither from afar begging thy eye, O highest of kings. For the purpose of ruling the world's regular course one eye may be sufficient, O lotus-eyed monarch.'

Though the Bodhisattva experienced an extreme delight at his heart's desire being realised, a doubt arose within him as to whether the Brâhman had really said so or, this thought being always present to his mind, himself had fancied so, and since he longed to hear the very sweet words of the eye being asked, he thus spoke to the eye-asker:

11. 'Who has instructed thee, illustrious Brâhman, to come here and to ask from me one eye? No one, it is said, will easily part with his eye. Who is he that thinks the contrary of me?'

Sakra, the Lord of the Devas in the disguise of a Brâhman, knowing the intention of the king, answered:

12. 'It is Sakra. His statue, instructing me to ask thee for thy eye, has caused me to come here. Now make real his opinion and my hope by giving me thy eye.'

Hearing the name of Sakra, the king thought: 'Surely, through divine power this Brâhman shall regain his eyesight in this way,' and he spoke in a voice, the clear sound of which manifested his joy:

13. 'Brâhman, I will fulfil thy wish, which has prompted thee to come here. Thou desirest one eye from me, I shall give thee both.

14. 'After I have adorned thy face with a pair of bright lotus-like eyes, go thy way, putting the bystanders first into doubt's swing as to thy identity, but soon amazing them by the certainty of it.'

The king's counsellors, understanding that he had decided to part with his eyes, were perplexed and agitated, and sadness afflicted their minds. They said to the king:

15, 16. 'Majesty, Your too great fondness for charity makes you overlook that this is mismanagement leading to evil. Be propitious, then, desist from your purpose; do not give up your eyesight! For the sake of one twice-born man you must not disregard all of us. Do not burn with the fire of sorrow your subjects, to whom you have hitherto ensured comfort and prosperity.

17, 18. 'Money, the source of opulence; brilliant gems; milch cows; carriages and trained beasts of draught; vigorous elephants of graceful beauty; dwellings fit for all seasons, resounding with the noise of the anklets[1], and by their brightness surpassing the autumn-clouds: such are boons fit to be bestowed. Give those, and not your eyesight, O you who are the only eye of the world.

'Moreover, great king, you must but consider this:

19. '.How can the eye of one person be put in the face of another? If, however, divine power may effect this, why should your eye be wanted for it?

'Further, Your Majesty,

20. 'Of what use is eyesight to a poor man? That he might witness the abundance of others? Well then, give him money; do not commit an act of rashness!'

Then the king addressed his ministers in soft and conciliating terms:

21. 'He who after promising to give, makes up his mind to withhold his gift, such a one puts on again the bond of cupidity which he had cast off before.

22. 'He who after promising to give, does not keep his promise, being driven from his resolution by avarice, should he not be held for the worst of men?

23. 'He who, having strengthened the hope of the mendicants by engaging himself to give, pays them with the harsh disappointment of a refusal, for him there is no expiation.

'And with respect to your asserting "is divine

---

[1] Not only the houses, therefore, are meant, but also the (female) attendance; in other words, the epithet is indicative of the richness and magnificence of the habitations.

power of itself not sufficient to restore the eyesight to that man?" you should be taught this.

24. 'That different means are wanted to carry out purposes, is well known, indeed. For this reason even Destiny (Vidhi), though a deity, needs some means or other.

'Therefore, you must not exert yourselves to obstruct my determination to accomplish an extraordinary deed of charity.'

The ministers answered: 'We have only ventured to observe to Your Majesty that you ought to give away goods and grains and jewels, not your eye; when saying this, we do not entice Your Majesty to wickedness.'

The king said:

25. 'The very thing asked for must be given. A gift not wished for does not afford pleasure. Of what use is water to one carried off by the stream? For this reason, I shall give to this man the object he requests.'

After this, the first minister who more than the others had got into the intimate confidence of the king, overlooking, owing to his solicitude, the respect due to the king, spoke thus: 'Pray, do it not.

26. 'You are holding an empire, which is vying with the riches of Sakra, to the attainment of which no one can aspire without a large amount of penance and meditation, and the possession of which may pave with numerous sacrifices the way to glory and Heaven, and you care not for it! and you are willing to give away both your eyes! With what aim do you wish so? Where on earth has there been seen such a way of proceeding?

27. 'By your sacrifices you have gained a place among the celestial gods, your fame is shining far and wide, your feet reflect the splendour of the head-ornaments of the kings (your vassals)—what then is it that you long for to give up your eyesight?'

But the king answered that minister in a gentle tone:

28. 'It is not the realm of the whole earth for which

I am striving in this manner, nor is it Heaven, nor final extinction, nor glory, but with the intention of becoming a Saviour of the World I now provide that this man's labour of asking be not fruitless.'

Then the king ordered one eye of his, the lovely brightness of which appeared like a petal of a blue lotus, to be extirpated after the precepts of the physicians gradually and intact, and with the greatest gladness he had it handed over to the beggar, who asked it. Now Sakra, the Lord of the Devas, by the power of magic produced an illusion of such a kind that the king and his bystanders saw that eye filling up the eye-hole of the old Brâhman. When the king beheld the eye-asker in the possession of one unclosed eye, his heart expanded with the utmost delight, and he presented him with the other eye too.

29. The eyes being given away, the king's visage looked like a lotus-pond without lotuses, yet it bore the expression of satisfaction, not shared however by the citizens. On the other hand, the Brâhman was seen with sound eyes

30. In the inner apartments of the palace as well as in the town, everywhere tears of sorrow moistened the ground. But Sakra was transported with admiration and satisfaction, seeing the king's unshaken intention of attaining Supreme Wisdom (Sambodhi).

And in this state of mind he entered into this reflection :

31. 'What a constancy! What a goodness and a longing for the good of the creatures! Though I witnessed the fact, I can scarcely believe it.

'It is not right, then, that this person of marvellous goodness should endure this great hardship for a long time. I will try to render him his eyesight by showing him the way for it.'

Afterwards, when time had healed the wounds caused by the operation, and lessened and almost lulled the sorrow of the inhabitants of the palace, the town, and the country, it happened one day that the king, desirous of solitary retirement, was sitting with crossed legs in his garden on the border of a pond of lotuses. That spot was beset by fair and fine trees bent down by the weight of their flowers; swarms of bees were humming; a gentle, fresh, and odoriferous wind was blowing agreeably. Suddenly *S*akra, the Lord of the Devas, presented himself before the king. Being asked who he was, he answered:

32 a. 'I am *S*akra, the Lord of the Devas, I have come to you.'

Thereupon the king welcomed him and said that he waited for his orders. After being thus complimented, he again addressed the king:

32 b. 'Choose some boon, holy prince (râ*g*arshi); say on what thou desirest.'

Now the king being ever wont to give, and having never trodden the way of miserable begging, in conformity with his astonishment and his lofty mind spoke to him:

33, 34. 'Great is my wealth, *S*akra, my army is large and strong; my blindness, however, makes death welcome to me. It is impossible for me, after supplying the wants of the mendicants, to see their faces brightened by gladness and joy; for this reason, O Indra, I love death now.'

*S*akra said: 'No more of that resolution! Only virtuous persons come in such a state as thine. But this thou must tell me:

35. 'It is the mendicants who have caused thee to come in this state; how is it that thy mind is occupied with them even now? Say on! do not hide the truth from me and thou mayst take the way to immediate cure [1].'

The king replied: 'Why dost thou insist upon my boasting myself? Hear, however, Lord of the Devas.

---

[1] This way is the Act of Truth, as Hardy, Manual of Buddhism [2], 197, calls it. In the Pâli *G*âtaka, Sakka invites the king to it in plain terms. Other instances of the sa*kk*akiriyâ, as it is styled in Pâli, will occur in Stories XIV, XV, XVI.

36. 'As surely as the supplicatory language of begging people both now and before is as pleasing to my ears as the sound of benedictions, so surely may one eye appear to me!'

No sooner had the king pronounced these words than by the power of his firm veracity and his excellent store of meritorious actions one eye appeared to him, resembling a piece of a lotus-petal, encompassing a pupil like sapphire. Rejoiced at this miraculous appearance of his eye, the king again spoke to Sakra:

37. 'And as surely as, after giving away both eyes to him who asked but one, my mind knew no other feeling but the utmost delight, so surely may I obtain also the other eye!'

The king had hardly finished, when there appeared to him another eye, the rival, as it were, of the first one.

38-40. Upon this the earth was shaken with its mountains; the ocean flowed over its borders; the drums of the celestials spontaneously uttered deep-toned and pleasing sounds; the sky in all directions looked placid and lovely; the sun shone with pure brightness as it does in autumn[1]; a great number of various flowers, tinged by the sandal powder which was whirling around, fell down from heaven; the celestials, including Apsarasas and Ga*n*as, came to the spot, their eyes wide opened with amazement; there blew an agreeable wind of extreme loveliness; gladness expanded in the minds of the creatures.

41-43. From all parts were heard voices of praise, uttered by crowds of beings endowed with great magic power. Filled with joy and admiration, they glorified the great exploit of the king in such exclamations: 'Oh, what loftiness! what compassion! see the purity of his heart, how great it is! oh, how little he cares for his own pleasures! Hail to thee, renowned one, for thy constancy and valour!

---

[1] It was spring when the miracle happened, as is to be inferred from the flowers being mentioned above.

'The world of creatures has recovered their protector in thee, of a truth, as the lustre of thy eye-lotuses has again expanded! Surely, the stores of merit are solid treasures! After a long time Righteousness has, indeed, obtained an immense victory!'

Then Sakra applauded him, 'Very well, very well!' and spoke again:

44, 45. 'Thy true feeling was not hidden from me, pure-hearted king; so I have but rendered thee these eyes of thine. And by means of them thou wilt have the unencumbered power of seeing in all directions over one hundred of yoganas, even beyond mountains.'

Having said these words, Sakra disappeared on the spot.

Then the Bodhisattva, followed by his officials[1], whose wide-opened and scarcely winking eyes indicated the astonishment that filled their minds, went up in procession to his capital. That town exhibited a festival attire, being adorned with hoisted flags and manifold banners, the citizens looking on and the Brâhmans praising the monarch with hails and benedictions. When he had seated himself in his audience-hall, in the midst of a great crowd, made up of the ministers in the first place, of Brâhmans and elders, townsmen and countrymen, all of whom had come to express their respectful congratulations; he preached the Law to them, taking for his text the account of his own experience.

46-48. 'Who in the world, then, should be slow in satisfying the wants of the mendicants with his wealth, who has beheld how I have obtained these eyes of mine, endowed with divine power, in consequence of charity-gathered merit? In the circumference of one hundred of yoganas I see everything, though hidden by many mountains, as distinctly as if it were

---

[1] The sudden appearance of these officials and ministers is somewhat strange here. The Pâli Gâtaka may account for it. 'At the same time, it is said there (IV, p. 411) that [the eyes] reappeared, the whole attendance of the king (sabbâ râgaparisâ) was present by the power of Sakka.'

near. What means of attaining bliss is superior to charity, distinguished by commiseration with others and modesty? since I, by giving away my human eyesight, have got already in this world a superhuman and divine vision.

49. 'Understanding this, *S*ibis, make your riches fruitful by gifts and by spending[1]. This is the path leading to glory and future happiness both in this world and in the next.

50. 'Wealth is a contemptible thing, because it is pithless; yet it has one virtue, that it can be given away by him who aims at the welfare of the creatures; for if given away, it becomes a treasure (nidhâna), otherwise its ultimate object is only death (nidhana).'

So, then, it is by means of hundreds of difficult hardships that the Lord obtained this excellent Law for our sake; for this reason its preaching is to be heard with attention. [This story is also to be told on account of the high-mindedness of the Tathâgata, just as the foregoing[2]. Likewise when discoursing of compassion, and when demonstrating the result of meritorious actions appearing already in this world: 'in this manner the merit, gathered by good actions, shows already here (in this world) something like the blossom of its power, the charming flowers of increasing glory.']

In the list of the contents of the Avadânakalpalatâ which Somendra added to that poem of his father Kshemendra, I do not find our avadâna, unless it should happen to be included in No. 91, which deals with a king of the *S*ibis. But the edition which is being published in the Bibl. Indica is not yet so far advanced. For the rest, like the story of the tigress, it is alluded to in the second pallava, verse 108: 'And in my *S*ibi-birth I gave away both my eyes to a blind man, and with (the gift of) my body preserved a pigeon from the danger caused by a falcon.'

---

[1] The purport of this royal precept may be illustrated by the corresponding parts of the narrative in the Pâli *G*âtaka. The precept is there given twice, in prose and in verse, see Fausböll's *G*âtaka IV, p. 411, 22, and p. 412, 7.
[2] Viz. the story of the tigress.

III. THE STORY OF THE SMALL PORTION OF GRUEL.

(Comp. the Pâli *G*âtaka, No. 415. Fausb. III, 406-414; Divyâvadâna VII, p. 88, Cowell's ed.; Kathâsarits. XXVII, 79-105.)

Any gift that proceeds from faith of the heart and is bestowed on a worthy recipient produces a great result; there does not exist at all anything like a trifling gift of that nature, as will be taught by the following.

In the time, when our Lord was still a Bodhisattva, he was a king of Ko*s*ala. Though he displayed his royal virtues, such as energy, discretion, majesty, power, and the rest in an exceedingly high degree, the brilliancy of one virtue, his great felicity, surpassed the others.

1. His virtues, being embellished by his felicity, shone the more; as the moonbeams do, when autumn makes their splendour expand.

2. Fortune, who dwelt with him, distributed her wrath and favour to the other kings in such a manner, that she abandoned his enemies, however proud, but like an amorous woman cherished his vassals.

3. His righteousness, however, prevented his mind from doing ill; so he did not oppress at all his adversaries. But his dependents displayed their affection for him in such a degree, that Fortune would not stay with his foes.

Now one day this king recollected his last previous existence. In consequence of remembering this he felt greatly moved. He bestowed still greater gifts in charity—the motive and essential cause of happiness—on *S*rama*n*as and Brâhmans, the wretched and the beggars; he fostered unceasingly his observance of good conduct (*s*îla); and he kept strictly the poshadha[1]-restrictions on sabbath-days. Moreover, as he was desirous of bringing his people into the way of salvation by magnifying the power of meritorious actions, he was in the habit of uttering with a believing

---

[1] Poshadha in Buddhistic Sanskrit=Pâli uposatha, which is of course the same word as Sanskrit upavasatha. A fuller form uposhadha occurs in the Avadânakalpalatâ VI, 76.

heart in his audience-hall as well as in the inner apartments of his palace these two stanzas, full of import:

4. 'Attending on Buddhas[1] by paying them honour, howsoever little, cannot produce a trifling fruit. This has been taught before only by words, now it may be seen. Look at the rich affluence of the fruit, produced by a small portion of saltless, dry, coarse, reddish-brown gruel.

5. 'This mighty army of mine with its beautiful chariots and horses and its dark-blue masses of fierce elephants; the sovereignty of the whole earth; great wealth; Fortune's favour; my noble wife: behold the beauty of this store of fruit, produced by a small portion of coarse gruel.'

Neither his ministers nor the worthiest among the Bráhmans nor the foremost among the townsmen, though tormented with curiosity, ventured to question the king as to what he meant by these two stanzas which he was in the habit of reciting every moment. Now by the king's incessant repeating of them the queen also grew curious; and as she felt less embarrassment in putting forth her request, one day, the opportunity of entering into conversation upon this subject pre-

---

[1] The text has na Sugataparikaryâ vidyate svalpikâpi, the parallel passage in the Páli Gâtaka may serve as its commentary:
Na kir' atthi anomadassisu
Párikariyâ Buddhesu appikâ.
In stanza 18 of this Gâtaka the purport of these words of the king is thus expressed: kshinâsraveshu na kritam tanu nâma kimkit; therefore, kshinâsrava = Páli khinâsavo, 'who has extinguished his passions,' is here synonymous with buddha. Speaking properly, then, all wandering monks, who are earnestly performing their duties as such, may be styled 'buddhas,' cp. for instance, Suttanipâta, Sammâparibbâganiyasutta, verse 12; in other terms, buddha may sometimes be an equivalent of muni. So it is used in chapter xiv of the Dhammapada; see the note of Prof. Max Müller on verses 179 and 180 in Sacred Books, vol. x, p. 50, and the verses pointed out by Weber, Ind. Streifen, I, p. 147. It is also plain that the Pratyekabuddhas are considered to belong to the general class of the Buddhas. Though they are different from the Supreme Buddhas (Samyaksambuddha), they are nevertheless also sugatas or buddhas. Cp. Spence Hardy, Manual, pp. 37-39; Kern, Het Buddhisme, I, pp. 294-296.

senting itself, she put this question in full audience to him:

6, 7. 'Verily, at all times, my lord, you are reciting, as if you were giving vent to the gladness which is within your heart. But my heart is troubled by curiosity at your speaking so. If my person is allowed to hear it, say on, then, what you mean by this utterance, sir. A secret is nowhere proclaimed in this manner; therefore, it must be a matter of public knowledge, and I may ask you about it.'

Then the king cast a mild look of gladness on his queen, and with a smile-blooming face he spoke:

8, 9. 'When hearing this utterance of mine without perceiving its cause, it is not only you, that are excited by curiosity, but also the whole of my officials, my town, and my zenana are troubled and disturbed by the desire of knowing the meaning of it. Listen, then, to what I am going to say.

10. 'Just as one who awakes from sleep, I remember my existence, when I lived a servant in this very town. Although I was keeping good conduct, I earned a sorry livelihood by performing hired labour for people elevated only because of their wealth.

11. 'So one day I was about to begin my service for hire, that abode of toil, contempt, and sorrow, striving to support (my family) and fearing, lest I should lack the means of sustenance myself; when I saw four *Srama*n*as with subdued senses, accompanied as it were by the bliss of monkhood, going about for alms.

12. 'After bowing to them with a mind softened by faith, I reverentially entertained them in my house with a small dish of gruel. Out of that sprout has sprung this tree of greatness, that the glitterings of the crest-jewels of other kings are now reflected in the dust on my feet.

13. 'Thinking of this, I recite these stanzas, my queen, and for this reason I find satisfaction in doing meritorious actions and receiving Arhats.'

Then the queen's face expanded with gladness and

surprise. She raised her eyes respectfully to the king, saying: 'Highly probable, indeed, is it that such very great prosperity is the fruit produced by meritorious actions, since you, great king, being yourself a witness of the result of meritorious actions, are so anxious for (gathering) merit. For this very reason you are disinclined to evil actions, disposed to protect your subjects duly like a father, and intent on earning plenty of merit.

14. 'Shining with illustrious glory enhanced by charity, vanquisher of your rival kings waiting with bent heads for your orders, may you for a long time with a righteous management rule the earth up to its wind-wrinkled ocean-border!'

The king said: 'Why should this not be? my queen!

15. 'In fact, I will endeavour to keep once more the path leading to salvation, of which I have noted the lovely marks. People will love giving, having heard the fruit of charity; how should not I be liberal, having experienced it in myself?'

Now the king, tenderly looking on his queen, beheld her shining with almost divine splendour, and desiring to know the reason of that brightness, said again:

16. 'Like the crescent amidst the stars you shine in the midst of the women. Say, what deed have you done, my dear, having this very sweet result?'

The queen replied: 'O yes, my lord, I too have some remembrance of my life in my former birth.' Now, as the king gently entreated her to tell it, she spoke:

17, 18. 'Like something experienced in my childhood I recollect that being a slave, after giving with devotion to a Muni with extinguished passions the remnants of one dish, I fell asleep there, as it were, and arose from sleep here. By this wholesome action, my prince, I remember, I have obtained you for my lord, sharing you with the earth. What you said: "surely, no benefit given to holy persons who have extinguished their passions, can be a small one"— these very words were then spoken by that Muni.'

Then the king, perceiving that the assembly was overcome by feelings of piety and amazement, and that the manifestation of the result of merit had roused in their minds a high esteem for meritorious actions, earnestly pressed on the audience something like this:

19. 'How is it possible, then, that anybody should not devote himself to performing meritorious actions by practising charity and good conduct, after seeing this large and splendid result of a good action however small? No, that man is not even worth looking at, who inwrapt in the darkness of avarice, should decline to make himself renowned for his gifts, though being wealthy enough to do so.

20. 'If by abandoning in the right manner wealth, once necessarily to be left and so of no use at all, any good quality may be acquired: who, then, knowing the charm of virtues, would follow in this matter the path of selfishness? And different virtues, in truth, gladness, &c., being followed by good renown, are founded on charity.

21. 'Almsgiving is a great treasure, indeed, a treasure which is always with us and is inaccessible to thieves and the rest[1]. Almsgiving cleanses the mind from the dirt of the sins of selfishness and cupidity; it is an easy vehicle by which to relieve the fatigue of the travel through Sa*m*sâra; it is our best and constant friend, that seeks to procure manifold pleasure and comfort for us.

22. 'All is obtained by almsgiving, whatever may be wished for, whether it be abundance of riches or brilliant domination, or a residence in the city of the Devas, or beauty of the body. Who, considering this matter so, should not practise almsgiving?

23. 'Almsgiving, it is said, constitutes the worth of riches; it is also called the essential cause of dominations, the grand performance of piety. Even rags for

---

[1] That is: to fire, water, seizure from the part of the king. Cp. Story V, stanza 8.

dress, given away by the simple-minded, are a well-bestowed gift.'
The audience respectfully approved this persuasive discourse of the king, and felt inclined to the exercise of charity and the like.

So any gift that proceeds from faith of the heart, and is bestowed on a worthy recipient, produces a great result; there does not exist at all anything like a trifling gift of that nature. [For this reason, by giving with a faithful heart to the Congregation of the Holy[1]—that most excellent ground fit for (sowing) meritorious actions—one may obtain the utmost gladness, considering thus: 'such blessings, and even greater than these, may erelong occur to me too.']

IV. THE STORY OF THE HEAD OF A GUILD.

(Comp. the Pâli Gâtaka, No. 40, Fausb. I, 231–234.)

The pious wish to exercise almsgiving even in spite of imminent peril; who, then, should not be charitable when safe? This will be taught as follows.

In the time, when our Lord was still a Bodhisattva, he was a head of a guild. In consequence of the excessive favour of his destiny, and owing to his own great activity, he had acquired a large estate. His fairness and integrity in commercial transactions procured him the highest esteem among the people; he was born of an illustrious family; he had acquainted himself with various branches of learning and art, and by them purified his mind. These qualities and his noble virtues caused him to be honoured by the king. As he was always keeping the precept of almsgiving, he shared his opulence with the people.

1. The mendicants loving him, praised his name far and wide, so as to fill all parts of the horizon with the high reputation of his prowess as an almsgiver.

---

[1] Âryasamghe.

2. With him, no one indigent was floating on the swing of doubt as to whether he would give or not. Trusting in this benefactor of renowned exploits, the mendicants were bold enough to put forth their wants freely.

3. And he, for his part, did not keep his wealth from them, neither for his own pleasures, nor striving to emulate others, nor overcome by avarice. It was impossible for him to see the suffering of the mendicants, and for this reason he avoided saying 'no' to them.

One day, at meal-time, when the Great Being had just bathed and anointed himself, and a complete dinner made up of various dishes of hard and soft food and the rest, dressed by skilled and excellent cooks, and so prepared as to please by their colour, smell, taste, touch, &c., was served up, a mendicant came near his house. It was a Pratyekabuddha, who by the fire of his knowledge had burned away all the fuel of innate evil passions, and now desired to increase the merit of the Bodhisattva. He placed himself in the gateway.

4. There he stood without apprehension, without agitation, looking firmly and quietly[1] to no greater distance before him than the length of a yoke[2], in a quiet attitude, holding his lotus-white fingers clasped on his almsbowl.

Now Mâra, the Wicked One, could not bear the Bodhisattva to enjoy that bliss of almsgiving. In order to put an obstacle in his way, he created by magic between the Reverend and the threshold of the entrance-door a very deep hell measuring several fathoms in width. It offered a dreadful sight, accompanied with terrible sounds; tremulous flames were burning awfully within; it contained many hundreds of men in great agony.

---

[1] Read prasama° instead of praṇama°, an error of print of course.
[2] Cp. Lalitavistara (Bibl. Ind.), p. 230 infra, Buddhakarita X, 13.

In the meanwhile the Bodhisattva, seeing the Pratyekabuddha come in search of alms, said to his wife: 'My dear, go yourself and give an abundant portion of food to the holy man.' She said she would do so, and went off with excellent hard and soft food; but beholding the hell near the gateway, she suddenly turned on her heels, terror-stricken and with bewildered looks. When her husband asked her what was the matter, she could hardly tell; the sudden fright had almost barred her throat. As the Bodhisattva, however, was uneasy at the thought that this holy man might turn back from his house without receiving his begged meal, he did not heed what she told him, but taking the excellent hard and soft food, came himself, desiring to fill with it the almsbowl of the Great-Minded One. When he arrived near the gateway, he saw that most dreadful hell between. And whilst he considered what could be the meaning of this, Mâra, the Wicked One, went out of the house-wall, and showing his divine and marvellous shape, stood in the air, and, as if he wished to do good to the Bodhisattva, spoke: 'Householder, this is the great hell, named Mahâraurava.

5. 'Here is the abode—an abode, out of which it is difficult to escape—of those who, greedy of the praising voices of the beggars, desire to give away wealth, indulging in the vicious passion for charity. In this hell they must stay for many thousands of autumns.

6. 'Material prosperity (artha) is the principal cause of the world's regular striving after the triad of objects. Whoso injures artha, injures righteousness (dharma) too[1]. How is it possible, then, that the injurer of righteousness by destroying material prosperity, should not stay in hell?

---

[1] The idea which underlies this assertion is often met with in Brâhmanical literature. If practising dharma is the same thing as performing the sacrifices to the deities, material prosperity may be justly styled the foundation-ground or substratum of dharma; for the right performance of sacrifices requires the possession of goods.

7. 'Thou hast sinned, being attached to charity and destroying thy wealth, which is the root of dharma. For this reason this flame-tongued hell, that looks like the face of Narakântaka[1], has come to thy encounter in order to devour thee.

8. 'Well then, desist from giving, lest thou immediately fall down and share the fate of those almsgivers, who shrink away from pain and are weeping piteously.

9. 'The recipients, on the other hand, who have ceased from the bad custom of giving, obtain the rank of Devas. Therefore, desist from thy effort for charity, which obstructs the way to Heaven, and rather apply thyself to restraint[2].'

The Bodhisattva, however, knew him: 'Surely, this is an attempt of the Evil One to thwart my almsgiving.' And understanding so, he made, in truth, a vigorous reply, yet in accordance with his firm attachment to virtue, without breaking modesty and kindness of words. He spoke thus to him:

10–12. 'It is with respect to my welfare, that thou hast had the kindness to show me the path of the pious. Indeed, it is most proper for divine beings to show by their actions their skill in feeling compassion for others. Nevertheless, it would have been wise to use that way of stopping the illness before its appearance, or immediately after its first symptoms. For if a sickness have already made progress[3] by the fault of bad treatment, the desire for cure will but tend to calamity. So this passion of mine for charity has already spread, I fear, beyond the compass of medical

---

[1] See Vishṇupurâṇa IV, chapter xxix (Wilson, p. 581).
[2] The Evil One uses ambiguous expressions purposely. The worthy recipients of the gifts are indeed on the way that leads to salvation; and the 'restraint' saṃyama he recommends, may imply the meaning of the self-restraint of the monks. The Bodhisattva in his well-turned answer takes care to keep the same ambiguous word (see stanza 15, saṃyamayishyatâpi).
[3] The reading prayâmam, proposed by Prof. Kern in the various readings of his edition, is undoubtedly right. Cp. pp. 78, 2; 96, 23; 111, 16; 171, 15; 182, 3; 238, 11 of his edition.

cure, inasmuch as my mind will never shrink from almsgiving, notwithstanding thy well-wishing counsel.

13, 14. 'As for what thou saidst about unrighteousness arising from charity and wealth being the principal cause of righteousness, my weak human understanding cannot grasp how wealth without charity can be called the path of virtue. Why, tell me, please, at what time is it that wealth produces virtue? whether when laid up as a treasure, or when robbed violently by thieves, or when sunk away to the bottom of the sea, or when having become fuel for fire?

15, 16. 'Further, thou saidst, "the giver goes to hell and the receiver to the celestial abodes." Speaking so, however, thou hast increased my longing for works of charity, though endeavouring to restrain me. Yea, may that word of thine be fulfilled, and those who beg from me rise to heaven! For it is not as a means of procuring my own happiness that I give in charity, but I love charity that I may do good to the world.'

Then Mâra, the Wicked One, once more addressed the Bodhisattva, speaking earnestly as though he were a well-meaning friend.

17. 'Decide thyself, whether I have spoken for thy good or idle talk, and afterwards go as thou desirest. Thou shalt remember me with high regard—either happy or remorseful.'

The Bodhisattva said : 'Sir, thou must excuse me.

18. 'I will fall of my own accord into this fiercely blazing hell headlong, a prey to the flames, that will lick at me, rather than at the due time of honouring the mendicants, who show me their affection by requesting from me, incur the guilt of neglecting them.'

After so speaking, the Bodhisattva—relying on the power of his destiny and knowing that almsgiving cannot at any rate entail evil—stepped forth across the hell without heeding his family and his attendants, who were eager to withhold him; his mind was not overcome by terror, and his desire of giving was still increased.

19. Then, owing to the power of his merit, in the midst of the hell a lotus sprang up, not rooted in mud like other lotuses[1]. With its row of stamen-teeth[2] it seemed to laugh contemptuously at Mâra. And with the aid of the lotus, produced out of the large amount of his merit, the Bodhisattva having reached the Pratyekabuddha, filled his bowl with food, while his heart was expanding with gladness and joy.

20. The monk, in order to show his satisfaction, rose into the air. There he displayed his splendour, raining and flaming with as great a majesty as a cloud from which appear flashes of lightning.

21. Mâra, on the other hand, seeing his design overturned, was in low spirits and lost accordingly his splendour. He dared no longer look in the face of the Bodhisattva, and soon he disappeared with his hell.

Why has this been taught? (For this purpose): in this manner the pious wish to exercise almsgiving even in spite of imminent peril; who, then, should not be charitable when safe? [Further this too is to be propounded: 'the virtuous cannot be induced even by fear to take the wrong way.']

V. THE STORY OF AVISHAHYA, THE HEAD OF A GUILD.

(Comp. the Pâli Gâtaka, No. 340, Fausb. III, 128-132.)[3]

The virtuous do not allow themselves to be deficient in the virtue of charity either from respect to the loss of their fortune, or from the prospect of riches, as will be taught in the following.

---

[1] In the original there is a pun, pamkaga, 'originating in mud, born from mud,' being a common word for 'lotus.'

[2] Instead of danti° I read danta°.

[3] In the Pâli redaction the story is told of the se*tthi* Visayha, not Avisayha, in consequence, it seems, of the misinterpretation of the first pâda of the first gâthâ in this story; that line should be read adâsi dânâni pure 'visayha. Likewise in the Nidânakathâ (Fausb. I, p. 45, l. 14) we must read *K*andakumârakâle 'vishah-yase*tthi*kâle.

V. THE STORY OF AVISHAHYA.

In the time, when our Lord was yet a Bodhisattva, he was the head of a guild, born of an illustrious family. He possessed many virtues: liberality, modesty, morals, sacred learning, spiritual knowledge [1], humility, &c. His affluent riches made him appear another Kubera. He spent them by admitting everybody as his guest and practising charity like an everlasting sacrifice (sattra). In short, he was the best of almsgivers and lived for the good of mankind. On account of his being invincible by vices, selfishness, and the rest, he was known under the name of Avishahya (that is, 'the Invincible One').

1. The sight of the mendicants had the same effect on him, as he had on the mendicants. On both sides it was a principal cause of gladness, since it destroyed the uncertainty as to the attainment of the object wished for.

2. When requested to give, he was not capable of saying 'no.' His great compassion had left no room in his heart for attachment to wealth.

3. His joy rose to the highest pitch, when mendicants carried away the best things out of his house. For he knew those so-called goods to be the source of violent and heavy calamities, and therefore to cause dissatisfaction in a short time and without any apparent reason.

4. As a rule, indeed, riches, being joined with covetousness, may be called caravans on the road towards wretchedness. With him, on the contrary, they conduced to the bliss of both himself and others; his goods appeared to be what is signified by their name.

So then, that Great Being bestowed large gifts on the mendicant people all around, and satisfied them wholly, giving to each according to his desire and generously, and adorning his bounty by paying a pious

---

[1] The 'sacred learning' is *sruta*, knowledge of Vaidik texts, &c., the 'spiritual knowledge,' *gñâna*, to be learnt from the Upanishads, the philosophical Darsanas and the like.

respect to the requesters. When Sakra, the Lord of the Devas, heard of his lofty munificence, he was transported with amazement; and wishing to try the firmness of his resolution, he caused the every-day provisions of money, grains, jewels, clothes to disappear day after day; 'perhaps, so he thought, his apprehension at least of the loss of his goods may entice him to self-interest.' Nevertheless, the Great Being remained intent on the virtue of charity.

5. As often as his goods disappeared, like waterdrops hit by the sun-darts, so often did he order them to be fetched again from his house, as if it were on fire, and continued his large gifts.

Sakra, the Lord of the Devas, understanding the Great Being to be bent as intently as ever on deeds of charity, although his riches always went on decreasing, his amazement grew. Now he concealed the whole of his wealth in one night, except a coil of rope and a sickle. When the Bodhisattva, as usual, awoke at daybreak, he nowhere saw his household goods, neither furniture, nor money, nor grains, nor clothes, nor even his attendants. His house looked quite empty, desolate, and sad, as if it were plundered by Râkshasas; in short, it offered an afflicting aspect. Then he began to reflect upon the matter; and searching about, he found nothing left but that coil of rope and that sickle. And he considered thus: 'Perhaps somebody, not accustomed to begging, but wont to get his livelihood by his own energy, has in this manner shown a favour to my house. In that case, my goods are well spent. If, however, by the fault of my destiny, some person whom my high rank has made envious, has caused them to run away without being of use to any one, it is a great pity.

6. 'The fickleness of Fortune's friendship was known to me long before; but that the indigent have come to grief by it, on this account my heart aches.

7. 'When coming to my empty house, how will they feel, my mendicants, who for a long time were accustomed to the enjoyment of my gifts and my

V. THE STORY OF AVISHAHYA.

hospitality? Will they not be like thirsty people coming to a dried-up pond?'

Nevertheless, the Bodhisattva did not yield to the feeling of affliction and sadness, but kept the constancy of his mind, and though, being in this condition, he was not capable of asking others, not even his intimates, as he never had followed the course of getting his livelihood by begging. Moreover, since he experienced himself that it is hard to beg, his compassion for the begging people became still greater. Then that High-minded One, still with the disposition to earn, from those who lived by begging their food, kind words of welcome and the like, took that coil of rope and that sickle, and went out to weed grass day after day. With the little money he earned by selling the grass, he attended to the wants of the mendicants.

But Sakra, the Lord of the Devas, seeing his imperturbable calmness and his devotion to almsgiving even in a state of extreme poverty, was filled not only with astonishment, but also with admiration. Showing his wonderful celestial body, he stood in the air and spoke to the Great Being to dissuade him from giving: 'Householder,

8-10. 'Neither thieves have robbed thee of thy wealth, nor water, nor fire, nor princes. It is thy own largesses, that have brought thee into this condition, which alarms thy friends. For this reason I tell thee for thy own good: restrain thy passionate love of charity. Though being as poor as thou art now, if thou dost not give, thou mayst recover thy former beautiful riches. By constant consuming of however little at a time, possessions fade; by gathering ant-hills become high. For him who sees this, the only way of increasing his property is self-restraint.'

The Bodhisattva, however, displayed his high-mindedness and his constant practice of charity, when he answered Sakra in this manner:

11. 'A gentleman (ârya), however distressed, will scarcely do anything ignoble (anârya), O thou Thousand-eyed One! Never let such wealth be mine,

O Sakra, to obtain which I should have to live as a miser.

12, 13. 'Who, thinking himself to belong to an honest family, would strike with the clear-sky thunderbolt of his refusal the wretched men who desire to find a remedy for their misery by death-like begging? Is it possible, then, that such a one as I am, should accept any jewel, or wealth, or even the realm among the Celestials, and not use it for the purpose of gladdening the faces of the beggars, grown pale by the pain of asking?

14. 'Such receiving as would only tend to increase the vice of selfishness, not to strengthen the propensity to give away, must be entirely abandoned by such as me; for it is a calamity in disguise.

15. 'Wealth is as fickle as a flash of lightning; it may come to every one, and it is the cause of many calamities; but almsgiving is a source of happiness. This being so, how may a nobleman cling to selfishness?

16. 'Therefore, Sakra, thou hast shown me thy good nature, I thank thee also for thy commiseration and well-wishing words; yet my heart is too much accustomed to the gladness caused by deeds of charity. How, then, can it take delight in the wrong way?

17. 'Do not, however, bend thy mind to anger on this account, I pray thee! Indeed, it is impossible to assault the hostile fortress of my native character with small forces.'

Sakra spoke: 'Householder, what thou describest is the line of conduct for a wealthy man, whose treasury and granary are full to the top, for whom manifold and abundant work is well-performed (by his servants), who has assured his future, and has gained domination among men, but that conduct does not suit thy condition. See,

18-20. 'Thou must, before all, through honest business either carried on by exerting thy own sagacity, or by following the traditional line of trade of thy family, in so far as it be compatible with thy fame, gather riches surpassing, like the sun, the splendour of thy rivals; then on proper occasions, display thy opulence to the people, and rejoice by it thy relations and friends. Afterwards, having obtained due honour even from the part of the king and enjoying Fortune's favour, like the embrace of a loving sweetheart, if then there may arise in thee the inclination for charity or worldly pleasures, nobody will blame thee. But the sole love of charity without means makes a man come to calamity and resemble a bird desiring to rise in the air with wings not yet full-grown.

21. 'Therefore, thou must acquire wealth by practising restraint and pursuing humble aims, and meanwhile give up the longing for almsgiving. And what meanness can there be in this after all, if thou dost not give, possessing nothing?'

The Bodhisattva replied: 'Pray, thy Highness must not urge me.

22, 23. 'Even he who cares more for his own interest than for the benefit of others, ought to give in charity, not caring for riches. For great opulence affords him no such gladness, as is caused by the satisfaction he enjoys by subduing covetousness with charitable deeds. Add to this, that mere riches do not lead to Heaven, but charity alone is sufficient to obtain a holy reputation; further, that riches are an impediment to the subduing of selfishness and the other vices. Who, then, should not observe charity?

24. 'He, however, who in order to protect the creatures surrounded by old age and death, desires to give away his very self in alms, moved by compassion; he whom the sufferings of others forbid to enjoy the relish of pleasures; say, of what use will be to him the very great bliss, possessed by thee?

' Hear also this, Lord of the Devas.

25. 'The duration of our life is as uncertain as the prosperity of our wealth. Thus reflecting, we must not care for riches, when getting a mendicant.

26. 'If one carriage has beaten a track on the ground, a second goes by that track with some confi-

dence, and so on. For this reason I will not spurn this first good road, nor prefer conducting my carriage on the wrong path.

27. 'And should I once more come to great wealth, it shall to a certainty enrapture the minds of the mendicants; and for the present, even in this condition, I will give alms according to my means. And may I never be careless in keeping my vow of charity, *S*akra!'

On these words *S*akra, the Lord of the Devas, being wholly propitiated, exclaimed with praise: 'Excellent, excellent,' and looking at him with admiration and kindness, spoke:

28, 29. '(Other) people run after riches by every trade, be it low and rough and prejudicial to their reputation, not minding danger, since they are attached to their own pleasures and misguided by their inconsiderateness. Thou, on the contrary, dost not mind the loss of thy wealth, nor the deficiency of thy pleasures, nor my temptation; keeping thy mind firmly intent on promoting the welfare of others, thou hast manifested the greatness of thy excellent nature!

30. 'Ah! how thy heart shines with the lustre of exceeding loftiness, and how it has wiped off entirely the darkness of selfish feelings, that even after the loss of thy riches the hope for recovering them cannot spoil it by bringing about reduction of its charitableness!

31. 'Yet, since thou sufferest at the suffering of others, and moved by compassion strivest for the good of the world, it is no wonder after all, that I have not been able to deter thee from almsgiving. As little is the Snow-bright Mountain shaken by the wind.

32. 'But it is in order to enhance thy fame by trial, that I have hidden that wealth of thine. Not otherwise than by trial can a gem, though beautiful, reach the great value of a renowned jewel.

33. 'Well then, pour thy gifts down on the mendicants, satisfy them as a great rain-cloud fills the pools. By my favour thou shalt never experience the loss of

thy wealth, and thou must forgive me my behaviour towards thee.'

After praising him so, Sakra restored his large estate to him, and obtained his pardon, then he disappeared on the spot.

In this manner, then, the virtuous do not allow themselves to be deficient in the virtue of charity either through regard to the loss of their fortune, or through the prospect of riches.

VI. THE STORY OF THE HARE.

(Comp. the Pâli *G*âtaka, No. 316, Fausb. III, 51–56; *K*ariyâpi*t*aka I, 10; Avadânasataka in Féer's transl. Ann. du Musée Guimet, XVIII, 142 [1].)

The practice of charity according to their power by the Great-minded, even when in the state of beasts, is a demonstrated fact; who then, being a man, should not be charitable? This is taught by the following.

In some inhabited region of a forest there was a spot frequented by ascetics. It was beset with thickets made up of lovely creepers, grasses, and trees; abounding in flowers and fruits; adorned on its boundary with a river, the stream of which was as blue and as pure as lapis lazuli; its ground, covered with a carpet of tender grass, was soft to the touch and handsome to look at. There the Bodhisattva lived a hare.

1. In consequence of his goodness, his splendid figure, his superior strength, and his great vigour, not suspected by the small animals nor fearing others, he behaved like the king of animals in that part of the forest.

2. Satisfying his wants with blades of grass, he bore

---

[1] In the Avadânakalpalatâ the hare that gave up his body is No. 104. It is much akin to the version of the Avadânasataka, as I ascertained from the two Cambridge MSS. of the Avadânakalpalatâ.

the handsome appearance of a Muni. For the ascetic's skin he wore his own, his bark-garment was the hairs of his body.

3. As everything he did in thought, speech, and action was purified by his friendliness, most of the animals given to wickedness were like his pupils and friends [1].
But more especially he had caught the hearts of an otter, a jackal, and an ape. They became his companions, attracted by the love and respect which his eminent virtues inspired in them. Like relations whose affection is founded on mutual relationship, like friends whose friendship has grown by the compliance to each other's wishes, they passed their time rejoicing together. Opposed to the nature of the brutes, they showed compassion to living beings, and their cupidity being extinguished, they forgot to practise theft. By this behaviour and by their having regard to good renown conformably to (the precepts of) righteousness (dharma), by their keen understanding and, owing to this, by their close observance of religious obligations in the manner approved by the pious, they roused even the surprise of the deities.

4, 5. If out of the two lines of conduct—that which complies with pleasures and checks virtue, and that which is in accordance with virtue and obstructs pleasures—a man applies himself to the virtuous side, he is already illustrious, how much more a being that has the shape of a beast! But among them, he who bore the figure of a hare and was their teacher, was so pious, he esteemed the practice of compassion for others so highly, and his excellent native character was accompanied by such a set of virtues, that their renown reached even the world of the Devas.

One day at evening-time, the Great-minded One

---

[1] The text is slightly corrupt here. The MSS. have 'sukhâ*h*, the printed text 'mukhâ*h*, but in the various readings the editor again adopts the reading of the MSS. But now Prof. Kern tells me he should rather suppose that the original reading was 'sakhâ*h*, which suits the sense better.

was in the company of his friends, who had come to him to hear him preach the Law and reverentially sat down at his feet. The moon, then being at a great distance from the sun, showed its orb almost full and resembling by its bright beauty a silver mirror without handle. When the Bodhisattva beheld it showing its disc not fully rounded on one side [1], and considered that it was the moon of the fourteenth of the bright half, that had risen, he said to his comrades:

6. 'See! The moon by the beauty of its almost complete orb is announcing with a laughing face as it were the holyday of sabbath (poshadha) to the pious.

'Surely, to-morrow is the fifteenth. Ye must perform accordingly the religious duties which are prescribed for the sabbath, and not satisfy the want of sustaining your body before honouring some guest at the time appearing with excellent food obtained in a right manner. Ye must consider thus:

7, 8. 'Every union has separation at its end, of high rank the conclusion is dreary downfall; life is as frail and fickle as a flash of lightning. It is for this very reason, that ye must be upon your guard against carelessness (in the fulfilment of your duties), and also endeavour to increase your merit by charity, which has good conduct (sila) for its ornament. Meritorious actions, indeed, are the strongest support for the creatures moving round in the troublesome succession of births.

9, 10. 'That the moon by its lovely brightness outdoes the lustre of the host of stars, that the sun's splendour overpowers the (other) luminaries, is due to the sublimity of the qualities produced by merit. It is also by the power of their merit that mighty kings cause presumptuous high officials and princes to bear, like excellent horses, willingly and with abated pride the yoke of their command.

---

[1] Instead of ishatpârsvâpavrittabimba*m*, the reading of the MSS., I think we should read 'âpakrittabimba*m*. In the evening before full-moon's day the disc of the moon is not completely round, presenting one side so as to seem a little flattened.

11. 'But if they are devoid of merit, misfortune goes after them, be they ever moving about on the road of political wisdom (nîti)¹. For that unhappiness, being rebuffed by the excess of merit, hovers, as if moved by wrath, round the possessors of demerit.

12. 'Leave then that path of demerit; suffering is underlying it, and it is connected with dishonour. But merit being the illustrious source and instrument of happiness, ye must keep your mind intent on all opportunities of gathering it.'

The others, after listening to his teaching, said amen, and saluting him with respect circumambulated him from left to right, then they went off each to his dwelling. When his comrades were not far off, the Great-minded One entered upon this reflection:

13-15. 'They are able to honour with some food or other the guest that may happen to arrive, but I am here in a pitiful condition. It is in no way possible to present a guest with the very bitter blades of grass I cut off with my teeth. Alas! how helpless I am! My powerlessness afflicts me. Of what use, then, is life to me, since a guest that ought to be a matter of joy to me, must in this manner become a matter of sorrow!

'On what occasion, then, may this worthless body, which is not even able to attend on a guest, be given up so as to conduce to the profit of anybody?' When his reflection had come to that point, the Great-minded One recovered his keenness of thought. 'Well!

16. 'The property which will suit the purpose of honouring any guest is easy to be got; for it is in my power; it is unobjectionable; it belongs to none but me; indeed, it is the property of my body.

'Why, then, should I be in trouble?

---

[1] The political wisdom, which aims at attaining worldly ends by worldly means, and makes morals subordinate to self-interest, is taught in such books as Kâmandaki's Nîtisâstra, Sukra's Nîtisâra, in the Pañkatantra and the Hitopadesa. It is considered sinful by Buddhistic lore. The Gâtakamâlâ often reproves it, see for instance, IX, 10; XXIII, 51.

17. 'Yes, I have found proper food for my guest; now, my heart, abandon thy grief and thy sadness! With this vile body of mine I will practise hospitality and satisfy the want of my guest.'

Having thus resolved, the Great Being felt an extreme delight as though he had obtained a very great gain, and remained there (in his dwelling, waiting for some guest).

18. Now, when that sublime reflection had presented itself to the Great Being's mind, the Celestials manifested their propitiousness and their power.

19–21. Earth shook with her mountains, as if from joy, nor was her garment, the Ocean, quiet[1]; divine drums resounded in the sky; the regions of the horizon were ornamented with a placid sheen; all around clouds of a pleasant aspect, which were girded with lightnings and gave forth prolonged soft rattlings of thunder, strewed on him a shower of flowers falling close together, so as to spread the pollen through the air by their contact. The god of wind, too, showed him his esteem; blowing steadily he bore to him the fragrant flower-dust from various trees, as if out of gladness he presented him with gauzy veils, bearing them up and so disarranging the figures interwoven in them.

As the deities, rejoiced and astonished, were praising everywhere the marvellous resolution of the Great Being, Sakra, the Lord of the Devas, became aware of it; and curiosity and surprise overtaking his mind, he was desirous of knowing the truth about his disposition. On the next day at noon-tide, when the sun, ascending in the midst of the sky, darts his sharpest beams; when the horizon, clothed in a net of trembling rays of light and veiled with the outburst of radiant heat, does not suffer itself to be looked upon; when shadows are contracting; when the interior of the woods resounds with the loud shrieks of the cicadae; when birds cease to

---

[1] Read babhûvânibhr*i*tâ°. Cp. supra, II, 38, and Bodhisattvâvadânakalpalatâ II, 52.

show themselves and the vigour of travelling people is exhausted by heat and fatigue: in that time of the day, then, Sakra, the chief (adhipati) of the Devas having assumed the figure of a Brâhman, cried out not far from the spot where the four animals were living. He wept and wailed aloud, like one who has lost his way, and as one worn out with hunger and thirst, weariness and sorrow.

22. 'Alone and astray, having lost my caravan, I am roaming through the deep forest, exhausted by hunger and lassitude. Help me, ye pious!

23. 'Not knowing the right way nor the wrong, having lost my faculty of orientation, wandering at random, alone in this wilderness, I suffer from heat, from thirst, from fatigue. Who will rejoice me by friendly words of hospitality?'

The Great Beings, touched in their heart and alarmed by the sound of his piteous outcries for help, quickly went to that spot, and beholding him who offered the miserable appearance of a traveller gone astray, approached him and in a respectful manner spoke to him these words of comfort:

24, 25. 'Be no more disturbed, thinking thou art astray in the wilderness; with us thou art altogether as if thou wert with thine own disciples. Therefore, grant us the favour of accepting to-day our attendance, gentle sir; to-morrow thou mayst go thy way according to thy wish.'

Then the otter, understanding from his silence that he accepted the invitation, went off hastily; joy and agitation quickened his pace. He came back with seven rohita-fishes, which he offered him, saying:

26. 'These seven fishes I found on the dry ground, where they were lying motionless, as if asleep through lassitude; either they have been left there by fishermen who forgot them, or they have jumped upon the shore through fear. Feed on them, and stay here.'

Then the jackal also brought to him such food as he happened to have at that time, and after bowing reverentially, he spoke with deference thus:

27. 'Here, traveller, is one lizard and a vessel of sour milk, left by somebody; grant me the benefit of thy enjoying them, and take thy abode in this forest this night, O thou who art an abode of virtues!'

So speaking he handed them over to him with an extreme gladness of mind.

Then the monkey drew near. He brought mango-fruits, ripe and consequently distinguished by their softness, their strong orange colour, as if they were dyed with red orpiment, their very red stalk-ends, and their roundness; and performing the reverence of the añgali, he spoke:

28. 'Ripe mangos, delicious water, shadow refreshing like the pleasure of good society, these things, O best of those who know the brahma, I have for thee. Enjoy them, and stay this night here.'

Then the hare approached, and as soon as he had made his reverence, he bade him accept the offer of his own body. Thus he spoke, looking up to him with great regard:

29. 'A hare, who has grown up in the forest, has no beans nor sesamum seeds nor grains of rice to offer, but prepare this body of mine with fire, and having fed upon it stay over this night in this hermitage.

30. 'On the holiday of a mendicant's arrival every one provides him with whatever of his goods may be a means of supplying his wants. But my wealth is limited to my body; take it, then, this whole of my possessions.'

Sakra answered:

31. 'How is it possible that anybody like me should kill another living being? And how much less a being like thee, who hast shown friendship to me?'

The hare said: 'Verily, this becomes well a Brâhman, inclined to compassion. Well then, thou must grant me at least the favour of resting here in this place; in the mean while I think I shall find in some way or other the means of showing my favour to thee.' Now Sakra, the Lord of the Devas, understanding his intention, created by magic a heap of charcoal burning without smoke; this mass had the colour of purified gold, very thin flames shot forth out of it, and a multitude of sparks were scattered about. The hare, who was looking around on all sides, perceived that fire. On seeing it, he said, rejoiced, to Sakra : ' I have found that means of showing thee my favour. Thou, then, must fulfil the hope with which I give thee this boon, and enjoy my body. See, great Bráhman,

32. ' It is my duty to give in charity, and my heart is inclined to do so, and in a person like thee I have met with a worthy guest; such an opportunity for giving cannot be easily obtained. Let then my charity not be useless, inasmuch as it depends on thee.'

So saying the Great-minded One persuaded him, and after showing him by his salutation his esteem, his respect, and his hospitable mind—

33. Then, with the utmost gladness, like one desirous of wealth on suddenly beholding a treasure, he threw himself in that blazing fire, as the supreme ha*m*sa plunges into a pond with laughing lotuses.

When the chief of the Devas saw this deed, he was affected with the highest admiration. Reassuming his own shape, he praised the Great Being with words both agreeable to the mind and the ears and preceded by a shower of celestial flowers. Then with his delicate hands of a rich lustre, like that of the petal of the white lotus, and embellished with their fingers resplendent like jewel ornaments, he took him up himself and showed him to the Celestials. ' Behold, ye Devas, inhabitants of the celestial residence, behold and rejoice at this astonishing deed, this heroic exploit of this Great Being.

34. ' Oh, how he has given away his body without hesitation to-day, to be charitable to his guest! But the fickle-minded[1] are not even able to give up, with-

---

[1] Strength of mind, constancy, earnestness, wisdom and virtue are all

out trembling, faded flowers, the remainder of a sacrifice.

35. 'What a contrast between the animal species, which he belongs to, and the loftiness of his self-sacrifice, the sharpness of his mind! Indeed, he confounds all such as are slow in striving for meritorious actions, deities as well as men.

36. 'Oh, how his mind is impregnated with the fragrance of a constant practice of virtues! How he loves good conduct, as he manifested by his sublime deed!'

Then, in order to glorify that extraordinary fact, and having in view the good of the world, Sakra adorned with the image of the hare as a distinctive mark both peaks on the top of the belvederes—one on his most excellent palace Vaigayanta and the other on Sudharmâ, the hall of the Devas—and likewise the disc of the moon.

37, 38. At full-moon even now that image of the hare (*sasa*) appears in the moon's disc in the sky, as a reflected image shines in a silver mirror. From that time onward *K*andra (the Moon), named also the Ornament of the Night and the Cause of the Brilliancy of the Night-waterlilies, is famous in the world as the Hare-marked (*Sasânka*).

And the others, the otter, the jackal, and the ape, disappeared thereafter (from the earth) and arrived in the world of the Devas, thanks to their possessing such a holy friend.

So then the practice of charity according to their power by Great Beings, even when in the state of beasts, is a demonstrated fact; who, then, being a man, should not be charitable? [Moreover, this too is to be propounded: 'Even beasts are honoured by the pious for their attachment to virtues; for this reason one must be intent on virtues.']

---

implied by the Buddhistic term dhîra; its opposite, adhîra, denotes therefore those who possess the opposed qualities, the 'fickle-minded.'

VII. THE STORY OF AGASTYA.

(Comp. the Páli *Gâ*taka, No. 480, Fausb. IV, 236–242; and *K*ariyâ-pi*t*aka I, 1.)

A heroic practice of liberality is an ornament even to ascetics, how much more to householders; as is taught by the following.

In the time, when our Lord, still being a Bodhisattva, was moving on his road through Sa*m*sâra for the good of the world, he was born of an illustrious family of Brâhmans, which being distinguished by great purity of conduct might pass for an ornament of the earth. His birth enhanced the lustre of this family in the same way as the moon rising in autumn with full and spotless orb, beautifies the firmament. He had in due order obtained the different sacraments ordained by the sacred texts and the tradition: *g*âtakarma and the rest; he had studied the Vedas with their Aṅgas and the whole ritual, and the fame of his learning filled the world of men. By the large gifts which he received, begging from charitable people who were lovers of virtues, he amassed considerable wealth.

1. Like a big cloud showering over the fields, he gladdened with his wealth his relations, his friends, his clients, his guests, his teachers, in short the distressed as well as those who are to be honoured.

2. Owing to his grand munificence, the bright glory which he had obtained by his learning shone the more. So the complete beauty of the moon's full disc is still augmented with loveliness, when autumn makes it shine brightly.

Yet the Great-minded One soon understood that the state of a householder is a source of sorrow, and affords but meagre comfort; for by its close connection with wrong business, it is thronged with noxious qualities, it is the abode of carelessness (about religious duties), it is a troublesome state, being connected with occupations for gathering wealth and guarding it, it affords a scope for hundreds of arrows made up of calamities and evil habits obstructive of tranquillity, and is accompanied with toil, inasmuch as it implies the necessity of accomplishing numberless tasks. On the other hand, he became convinced that renunciation of the world brings about comfort by its freedom from those evils, that it is a state favourable to the performance of religious duties, and that it may be called the proper basis for undertaking the religious practices required for salvation. So casting away, as if it were a straw, that great abundance of wealth which he had obtained without trouble, and which must have possessed charms for him because of the high regard which he enjoyed among the people, he gave himself up to the observance of the discipline and the self-restraint of world-renouncing ascetics. But also, after his leaving the world—owing to his celebrated fame, the remembrance of former intercourse, the respect for his virtues, and the tranquillity by which he was distinguished—the Great Being was frequented as before by people longing for salvation, whose affection he had gained by the multitude of his virtues. Yet, disliking that contact with householders, as prejudicial to the happiness that arises from entire detachment from the world, and an obstacle to throwing away the bonds by which he had held to it, he repaired to the island of Kârâ, aspiring to solitude. That island is situated in the Southern Ocean. Its outskirts are moistened by the play of the wanton waves, which moved by the wind have the blue colour of pieces of sapphire; white sand covers its ground; various trees, the branches of which are adorned with twigs, flowers and fruits, enhance its beauty; near its shore there is a lake of pure water. This lovely country he embellished with the splendour of his hermitage.

3. There he lived, manifesting the lustre of his heavy penance by the emaciation of his body, as the crescent appears in the sky, joining great loveliness to a small size.

4. That this man living in the forest, absorbed in vows and penances, and whose modest actions and sensations attested his tranquillity of mind, was a Muni, even the wild quadrupeds and birds of the forest did understand, even their small intellect became aware of it, and they imitated his behaviour.

While staying in the grove of penance, the Great-minded One, being in the habit of giving, continued also honouring the guests that happened to arrive, with such roots and fruits as he had just gathered, with fresh water and such hearty and kind words of welcome and blessings as are appropriate to ascetics, and himself lived on as much of his forest-produced food as his guests had left, strictly limiting his meals to the sustenance of his body.

Now, the glory of his excessive penance having spread about, Sakra, the Lord of the Devas, touched by it, desired to prove his constancy. In that part of the forest where the Great Being dwelt, he caused to disappear successively all roots and fruits fit for the food of ascetics. But the Bodhisattva, absorbed in meditation and being accustomed to the feeling of contentment, insensible to the perplexing influence of stupefaction, and indifferent concerning his food and his body, did not direct his thoughts to the cause of that disappearance[1]. And having dressed young leaves on the fire, he accomplished with these the action of taking his meal, without any feeling of discontent, nor longing for a better meal, but calm as ever he went on living in the same way.

5. The livelihood of those who in earnest practise continence is nowhere difficult to be obtained. Say, where are not found grass and leaves and ponds?

Yet Sakra, the Lord of the Devas, though his astonishment increased, in consequence of the Bodhisattva's behaviour in that situation, and his high opinion of his virtues grew stronger, resorted to another

---

[1] For, if he had, he would have discovered it, owing to the transcendent power he had obtained by his penance.

VII. THE STORY OF AGASTYA. 49

trial. Like the wind at summer-time he stripped of their leaves the whole number of trees, shrubs and grasses, that were in that grove. Then the Bodhisattva, taking such fallen leaves as were still fresh, and boiling them in water, lived on them without feeling any uneasiness; rejoiced by the happiness of meditation, he stayed there as if he had feasted upon ambrosia.

6. Modesty in the learned, disinterestedness in the wealthy, and contentment in the ascetics: each of these splendid virtues is the highest treasure of each of them [1].

Now that very marvellous constancy of his contentment increased the surprise of Sakra, and as if he were angry on account of it, having assumed the shape of a Brâhman, that he might be a guest, of course, he appeared before the eyes of the Great Being, when at the time prescribed by his vow, after performing the Agnihotra-sacrifice and repeating his prayers, he was just looking about for some guest. And the Bodhisattva rejoiced went to meet him, and welcoming him and addressing kind words to him, invited him to take his meal by announcing to him that it was mealtime. Understanding by his silence that he accepted, the Great-minded One,

7. Manifesting by his expanding eyes and his blooming face the gladness he experienced in practising charity, and rejoicing his guest with gentle words both pleasant to the mind and to the ears, entertained him with the whole of his boiled leaves, which he had had so much trouble to procure, and himself was satisfied with joy alone.

And even so he entered his home of meditation [2], and passed that day and night in the very ecstasy of gladness.

Now Sakra reappeared to him in the same

---

[1] Instead of guṇasobhâvidhiḥ paraḥ I read ᵒnidhiḥ paraḥ, comp. p. 51, l. 11 of the edited text guṇâbhyâsanidher udâratâ.

[2] In other words, his hut. Both Pâli redactions mention here his paṇṇasâlâ, 'hut of leaves.'

E

manner the next day at the time destined for (the accomplishment of) his vow (of hospitality). So he did also on the third, fourth, and fifth day. And the other received him as his guest in the same way, and with still more joy.

8. No suffering, indeed, not even peril of life, is able to compel the virtuous to a miserable infringement of their love for giving, a love fostered by their practice of commiseration.

Then Sakra, whose mind was overcome by the utmost amazement, knowing him to be enabled by his excess of penance to get into the possession of (his own) brilliant realm of the gods[1], if he did but ask for it, began to feel uneasy, and fear arose within him. Having assumed the wonderful beauty of his own celestial shape, he questioned him as to the purpose for which he performed his penance.

9, 10. 'Say, on what hast thou set thy hopes, that they could impel thee to leave thy beloved relations, who shed tears at thy departure, thy household and possessions that had been a source of happiness to thee, and to resort to this toilsome life of penance? For it is not for a trifling motive that the wise despise enjoyments easily obtained, and afflict their relations with grief, leaving them to go to the penance-forest destructive of pleasures.

11. 'If thou thinkest it may be told me, please, satisfy my curiosity. What may be the object of thy wishes, the penetration into the excellent qualities of which fascinated to this point a mind like thine?'

The Bodhisattva replied: 'Hearken, sir, what I am exerting myself for.

12. 'Repeated births tend to great sorrow; so do calamitous old age and illnesses, those dismal

---

[1] This fear of the Lord of the Devas rests on the belief in the transcendent power of penance, which enables great ascetics to aspire even to that dignity. Sakra, afraid of human tapas and trying to prevent its earning by every means, is a well-known figure in Indian mythology.

plagues; and the necessity of death is a disturbance to the mind. From those evils I am resolved to save the creatures.'

Then Sakra, the Lord of the Devas, understanding that it was not his own celestial splendour that was claimed by the Bodhisattva, was set at rest, and as he was very pleased with that well-said sentence, he honoured it by exclaiming 'Very well!' and requested him to accept some boon.

13. 'Ascetic, Kâsyapa[1], for this right and well-said sentence I give thee some boon; choose then what thou desirest.'

The Bodhisattva, being not at all desirous of pleasures and rejoicings connected with existence, and thinking it painful even to ask for anything, since he had attained the state of contentment, said to Sakra:

14. 'If thou wishest to give me some boon, that may please me, I ask the foremost of the Devas this boon,

15. 'May that fire of covetousness, which after obtaining a beloved wife, children, power, riches more abundant than had been longed for, still goes on heating the mind of men never to be satisfied—may that fire never enter my heart!'

The propensity to contentment declared by this well-turned saying delighted Sakra in a still higher degree. He praised the Bodhisattva again, saying: 'Excellent, excellent!' and once more he urged him to choose some boon.

16. 'Muni, also for this right and well-said sentence I offer thee gladly as a present in return a second boon.'

Then the Bodhisattva, in order to show him the difficulty of getting rid entirely of the innate evil passions[2], preached him the Law once more under the guise of asking a boon,

---

[1] In the metrical part of the Pâli redaction of this story in the Gâtaka, Akitti (=Agastya) is likewise called Kassapa and addressed by that name.

[2] Viz. the klesâs, cp. Dharmasamgraha LXVII with Kenjiu Kasawara's explanatory note on p. 49 and the literature quoted there.

17. 'If thou givest me some boon, thou Vâsava, abode of excellent qualities, then I ask thee another boon, and no mean one, Lord of the Devas.

18. 'May that fire of hatred, subdued by which the creatures come to [1] loss of wealth, loss of caste and of good reputation, as if they were vanquished by a hostile attack—may that fire be far from me!'

On hearing this, Sakra, the chief of the Devas, highly admiring him, praised him: 'Excellent, excellent!' and again he said:

19. 'Justly Fame, like a loving woman, attends upon those who have renounced the world. Well, accept some other boon from me for this well-said sentence.'

Then the Bodhisattva, induced by his hostility to innate evil passions to blame the intercourse with such creatures as are not free from those passions, under the guise of accepting the boon [2], said this:

20. 'May I never hear a fool, nor get the sight of such a one, nor speak to such a one, nor endure the annoyance and the pain of staying with such a one! This is the boon I ask thee for.'

Sakra spoke:

21, 22. 'What dost thou say? Anybody being in distress is most deserving of the commiseration of the pious. Now, foolishness being the root of calamities, is held to be the vilest condition. How is this that thou, though compassionate, abhorrest the sight of a fool, a person especially fit for commiseration?'

The Bodhisattva answered: 'Because there is no help for him, sir. Do but consider this:

23. 'If a fool were at any rate curable by treatment, how would anybody like me be wanting in effort to bring about his good?

'But such a one, thou must understand, can derive no profit at all from medical treatment.

---

[1] In order to correct the fault against the metre in the first pâda of this stanza, I think we should read arthâd api bhra*m*sam avâpnuvanti.
[2] Instead of vrati, which is here almost meaningless, Prof. Kern suggests v*r*iti = vara.

24, 25. 'He follows the wrong course of conduct, as if it were the right one, and desires to put also his neighbour in that way, and not having been accustomed to a decent and upright behaviour, becomes even angry when admonished for his good. Now, then, to such a person, who burns with the infatuation of self-conceit, thinking himself wise, whose harsh anger is provoked by those who speak for his good, and whose impetuousness has not been softened because of the deficiency of his moral education—say, what means does there exist to bring profit to him?

26. 'For this reason, then, O most excellent of the Devas, because there is no help for him, not even in the power of the compassionate, I do not want to see a fool, since he is the most unfit object.'

On hearing this, Sakra praised him, exclaiming 'Very well! very well!' and charmed by his right sayings, spoke again:

27. 'The invaluable jewels of well-said sentences cannot be rewarded by any equivalent. But as a handful of flowers to worship thee, I gladly offer thee some boon for these too.'

Then the Bodhisattva, in order to show that the virtuous are welcome in every circumstance, spoke:

28. 'May I see a wise man, and hear a wise man, dwell with such a one, Sakra, and converse with such a one! This boon, best of the Devas, do grant me.'

Sakra said: 'Thou seemest, indeed, to be a warm partisan of the wise. Why, tell me then,

29. 'What have the wise done for thee? Say, Kâsyapa, what is the reason that thou showest this rather foolish greediness for the sight of a wise man?'

Then the Bodhisattva, in order to show him the magnanimity of the virtuous, spoke: 'Hearken, sir, for what reason my mind longs for the sight of a wise man.

30, 31. 'He walks in the path of virtue himself, and brings also others into that way, and words said for his good, even if they be harsh, do not rouse his impatience. Being adorned by uprightness and decency, it is always possible to make him accept what is said for his good. For this reason my mind, adhering to virtue, is inclined to the partisan of virtue.'

Then Sakra praised him, exclaiming: 'Well said! very excellent!' and with still increased satisfaction again summoned him to ask some boon.

32, 33. 'Surely, thou hast already obtained everything, since thou art wholly satisfied, yet thou shouldst take some boon from me, considering it as a means of gratifying me. For a favour offered out of reverence, from abundance of power, and with the hope of affording a benefit, becomes a cause of great pain, if not accepted.'

Then the Bodhisattva, seeing his utmost desire for doing good, and wishing to please him and to benefit him, answered so as to declare to him the superiority of the strong desire of almsgiving.

34. 'May thy food, which is free from destruction and corruption, thy mind, which is lovely because of its practice of charity, and mendicants adorned by the pureness of their good conduct, be mine! This most blessed boon I ask.'

Sakra said: 'Thy Reverence is a mine of jewels of well-said sentences. Further,

35. 'Not only will everything thou hast requested be accomplished, but on account of this well-said sentence I give thee some other boon.'

The Bodhisattva said:

36. 'If thou wilt give me a boon which incloses the highest favour for me, O most excellent of all Celestials, do not come to me again in this thy blazing splendour. For this boon I ask the destroyer of the Daityas.'

Upon this Sakra was somewhat irritated, and highly astonished he thus spoke to him : ' Do not speak so, sir.

37. 'By every kind of ritual: prayers, vows, sacrifices, with penances and toilsome exertions, people on earth seek to obtain the sight of me. But thou dost not desire so. For what reason then? I came up to thee, wishing to bestow my boons on thee.'

The Bodhisattva said: 'Do not yield to thy anger. I will pacify Thy Highness, king of the Devas. It is not for want of courtesy, that I ask so, nor is it a deed of irreverence, nor do I aim at showing lack of devotion towards Thy Majesty. Not at all, but,

38. 'Contemplating thy superhuman wonderful shape, which though shining gently, is still blazing with brilliancy, I fear the sight of thee, however mildly shining, lest it should cause any want of strictness in the fulfilment of my penance.'

Then Sakra bowed to him, circumambulated him from left to right, and disappeared on the spot. And lo, at daybreak the Bodhisattva perceived plenty of divine food and drink, brought thither by the power of Sakra, and many hundreds of Pratyekabuddhas called by the invitation of Sakra, also many angels (devaputras) high girded, ready to wait on them.

39. Supplying in this way with food and drink the wants of those most holy sages, the Muni obtained a sublime joy; and he delighted in living after the manner suitable for ascetics, in performing his boundless vow of meditation (dhyâna), and in tranquillity.

In this manner, then, a heroic practice of liberality is an ornament even in ascetics, how much more in householders.

[So considering, a virtuous man must adorn himself with heroic constancy of giving. This (story) must also be adduced, when treating of the gladness caused to a liberal and charitable man; when blaming covetousness, hatred, infatuation, and foolishness; when preaching on the virtue of the intercourse with a pious friend, or on contentment. Likewise in discourses on the magnanimity of the Tathâgata: 'So our Lord was an inexhaustible mine of jewels of excellent sayings, when still in his former existences, how much more so was he after attaining Complete Wisdom.']

VIII. THE STORY OF MAITRÎBALA.

Being afflicted by the sufferings of others, the intensely compassionate do not mind their own pleasure. This will be taught as follows.

At the time when the Bodhisattva, always having in view his purpose of saving the creatures, had fixed upon (the exercise of the pâramitâ of) compassion, as became his high-mindedness, and was always increasing in matchless virtues—charity, humility, self-restraint, tenderness, and the like, suitable for the benefit of the world, he was, it is said, a king kind-hearted towards all creatures, named Maitrîbala[1].

1, 2. This king felt the weal and the woe of his subjects as his own, and being skilled in the art of protecting them, he handled both his sword and his law in accordance with this feeling. Yet his sword was only an ornament to him, since the (other) kings waited for his orders, respectfully bowing their head-crests; his law, on the contrary, showed itself most openly in the measures he took for promoting the welfare of his people.

3. He dealt out punishments and rewards without infringing righteousness. In consequence of his goodness of heart and his political wisdom, he inquired into his subjects like a father.

So he ruled with righteousness, and while directing his veracity, his liberality, his tranquillity, his wisdom, and his other virtues to conduce to the welfare of others, he increased his store of exceedingly lofty actions, which are the due requisites for the attainment of Buddhahood. Now one day, five Yakshas, whom for some offence or other (Kubera) the Lord of the Yakshas had exiled from his dominions, came to his realm. These goblins were Ogohâras [that is, vigour-bereaving spirits], skilled in the art of killing others[2]. When they saw the kingdom exhibiting the aspect of the utmost prosperity, and became aware that the absence of every kind of calamity made the people

---

[1] This name signifies, 'he whose strength is kindness,' cp. stanza 14. The edition has here Maitrabalo, by a misprint, it seems.
[2] It is likely, those Yakshas were thought to possess the power of causing consumptive diseases; consumption is called in Sanskrit yakshma or râgayakshma. In the Divyâvadâna (295, 6) a râkshasa o*g*ohâra*h* is mentioned.

VIII. THE STORY OF MAITRÎBALA.

rejoiced, satisfied, thriving, and in the habit of having merriment and manifold festivals, the desire of taking away the vigour from the inhabitants of that region arose within them.

4. But, though they did their usual work with the greatest effort, they were still not able to take away the vigour of the inhabitants of that country.

5. The power of that king was so excessive that his very intention of shielding proved the highest protection. For this reason those Yakshas were powerless to take away the vigour of his subjects.

And as they were not able to debilitate any one, living in that kingdom, however much they exerted themselves, they deliberated among themselves and said: 'How may this be, sirs?

6. 'They do not possess such superiorities of learning, penance, or magic as to enable them to obstruct our power, and yet all of us are reduced to impotency, so as to bear our appellation (of O*g*ohâras) in vain.'

And they assumed the shape of men of the Brâhman class, and going about, they saw a certain cowherd of those who live in the forest-region, who was sitting upon a grass-plot at the foot of a shady tree. He had shoes on his feet, and on his head he wore a garland, made of flowers and opening buds of forest-trees. His stick and his hatchet he had laid on the earth on his right. He was alone and occupied with twisting a rope, diverting himself meanwhile with singing and humming. Him they approached and imitating human voice [1], they said to him: 'Well, friend, thou who art charged with guarding the cows, how is it that staying thus alone in this lonely forest where no man is to be seen, thou are not afraid?' And he, looking at them, spoke: 'Of what should I be afraid?' The Yakshas said: 'Hast thou never before heard that such goblins as Yakshas, Râkshasas, or Pisâ*k*as are cruel by nature?

---

[1] In the original the Yakshas utter some inarticulate sounds before succeeding in speaking Sanskrit.

7, 8. 'If men are in company and endowed with learning, penance, and svastyayana-charms[1], even then, be they never so brave and contemptuous of fear, they will but narrowly escape those Râkshasas who feed on the flesh and fat of men. How, then, is it that thou art not afraid of them, thou who stayest without any comrade amidst these solitary, remote, and frightful forests?'

On hearing this, the cowherd laughed heartily, and said to them:

9, 10. 'Well, the people of this country are protected by a mighty svastyayana, so that even the Lord of the Devas himself has no power over them, how much less the flesh-eating goblins. So it happens that I wander fearless through the wilderness as if I stayed at home, at night as if it were day, and alone as if I were in a crowd.'

Upon this the Yakshas became very curious, and said to him respectfully, as if to encourage him: 'Why, you must tell us, gentle sir, you must tell us, of what kind this extraordinary svastyayana of yours is.' He answered them, laughing once more: 'Hear, then, of what kind this very wonderful excellent svastyayana of ours is.

11. 'It is he whose broad breast is equal to a plate of the Golden Mountain (Meru), he whose face displays the lovely beauty of the spotless moon in autumn, he whose long and full arms are like golden clubs, he who has the eyes of a bull and the gait of a bull. In short, it is our king.

'Of this kind our excellent svastyayana is.' And after saying these words, looking with resentment and astonishment in the face of the Yakshas, he continued: 'Ah! this is rather a wonder, is not it?

12. 'So renowned is the power of our king, and it has not come to your hearing! How has this happened? Or have you perhaps heard of it, but dis-

---

[1] Viz. spells and charms, effective of bliss and happiness and obstructive of the contrary.

VIII. THE STORY OF MAITRÎBALA. 59

trusting the excessive marvel of that fame, not minded it?

13. 'I suppose, the people of the country, from whence you have come hither, are either disinclined to search after virtue or indifferent about it; it may also be that, the store of their good fortune[1] being exhausted, the great renown of our king has shunned them.

'At all events, for you there is still some remnant of good fortune, since you are come here from such a savage country.'

The Yakshas said: 'Gentle sir, tell us, of what nature is this power of that king, that spirits are by no means able to hurt the inhabitants of his realm?' The cowherd replied: 'Our monarch has obtained this power through his high-mindedness. See, noble Brâhmans.

14. 'On friendliness does his strength rest, not on his motley-bannered army, which he keeps only to comply with custom. He knows no anger, nor does he speak harsh words. He protects his land in the proper manner. Righteousness is the rule of his actions, not political wisdom, that base science. His wealth serves to honour the virtuous. And endowed with those marvellous qualities, still he does not take unto himself either the wealth of the wicked, or pride.

'Such and many, many more virtues are to be found in our master. For this reason no calamities have the power to hurt the inhabitants of his realm. But how little is the information you may get from me! If you are curious to learn the excellent qualities of our king, it would rather be suitable for you to enter the capital. There you will behold the people in their every-day life; you will see how firm they stand in the (moral) bounds of the âryas, loving each the peculiar duties proper to him; how merry and thriving they are, in consequence of a constant abundance of

---

[1] Every one's good fortune is the result of his merit, and lasts until that store of good actions is exhausted.

food and uninterrupted welfare; how splendidly they are dressed, yet not presumptuously; how kind they are to worthy strangers who come to them as guests; how enraptured they are with the virtues of their king, the praises of whose glory they never cease to proclaim with gladness, as if they were uttering some auspicious and evil-averting charm. When beholding all this, you will obtain the standard for measuring the multitude of virtues possessed by our lord. And if you once begin to feel something like reverence for his virtues, you will witness them, for you will not fail to feel the desire for getting the sight of him.'

The Yakshas, being already moved with anger against the king on account of his obstructing the manifestation of their power, were in no way softened by this affectionate and well-deserved eulogy of his virtues.

15. Verily, as a rule the mind of fools[1] becomes inflamed the more by the praise of the object which has excited their fervent wrath.

Now considering that king's love of charity and wishing to do harm to him, they approached him at the time of his audience, and asked him for a meal. The king rejoiced, ordered his officers who stood in charge of such matters: 'Go and quickly present the Brâhmans with a delicious meal.' The Yakshas, however, were not ready to accept the meal served to them, though it might have suited the royal table, but spurning it, as tigers would green grass, said they did not feed on such dishes. On hearing which, the king went to them saying: 'But what sort of repast will agree with your digestion, that something of the kind may be fetched?'

The Yakshas answered:

---

[1] In the original they are not called bâla, as above, Story VII, stanza 22, but by the nearly synonymous term of manda. Still there may be a slight difference between both appellations. Bâla meant at the outset 'child, childish, ignorant;' manda, 'slow, feeble, sick, dull, lazy.' Cp. Suttanipâta, verses 666, 728, 820, and 1051.

16. 'Raw human flesh, freshly cut off and still warm, and human blood, O lotus-eyed monarch, is the food and drink of Yakshas, O you who are strict in keeping your engagements.'

After which, they reassumed their own disfigured and frightful features, exhibiting their mouths rendered ferocious by large teeth, their eyes fierce and red, flaming and squinting, their flat noses, wide-opened and misshapen. Their hair and beard had the tawny colour of flames, and their complexion was as dark as clouds big with rain. Looking at them, the king knew them to be goblins[1], not men, and understood that for that reason they did not like the food and drink served by his orders.

17. And according to his compassionate nature and his pure-heartedness, the pity of the monarch towards them increased by this reflection.

Absorbed with commiseration and pitying those Yakshas, he entered surely upon this thought:

18, 19. 'For a merciful man such food and drink is not only hard to be found, but it were also to be searched for day after day. Oh, the immense grief it would cause him! A cruel man may be either able to get it for them, or not. If not able, his effort would have no other effect than that of mere destruction; if able, what can be more miserable than such a one constantly exercising that evil practice?

20. 'These Yakshas, on the other hand, who live on food of that kind, with hearts wicked and pitiless, are destroying their own happiness every day. When will their sufferings ever end?

'This being so, how is it possible for me to procure

---

[1] Lit. 'to be Pisâkas,' apparently a general term. The different classes of goblins, Yakshas, Râkshasas, Pisâkas, are often confounded; in stanza 27 the general appellation is Râkshasas. In Story IX, verse 66, yaksha and pisâka are used promiscuously in the sense of 'ogre.' In the sixth story of the Pâli Gâtaka (translated by Rhys Davids in his Birth Stories, p. 180) the water-sprite is sometimes called rakkhaso, sometimes yakkho.

such food for them? Not even for one single day could I injure others and destroy life.

21. 'Indeed, I do not remember having ever saddened the faces of those who came to me as supplicants, and bereaved them of splendour by the disappointment of their hopes, so as to make them appear like lotuses withered by the winter-wind.

'But, why muse any longer? I have found what I will do.

22, 23. 'I will give them lumps of solid and fat flesh and draughts of blood taken from my own body. What way, if not this, can be more suitable for me to supply the wants of those beggars seeking their relief from my side? For the flesh of animals who have died a natural death is cold and bloodless, and of course does not please them; and their hunger is great and attested by their afflicted figures.

'On the one hand, how may I take flesh out of the body of any other living being? On the other, how may I suffer them who have resorted to me, to draw off in this manner, with countenances languishing and eyes sunken in consequence of their hunger and thirst, and still more sick with grief because of the fruitlessness of their request on which they had founded their hopes? It is, therefore, the right time to act in this way.

24. 'Like a malignant ulcer, this body is always sick and an abode of pain. Now I will return it that grief by availing myself of it for the accomplishment of an extraordinary performance of surpassing loveliness.'

Having so resolved, the Great-minded One, whose eyes and face received increase of splendour by the outburst of his gladness, spoke thus to the Yakshas, pointing out his body to them:

25. 'If this flesh and blood, which I bear only for the good of the creatures, were now to be disposed of with the object of entertaining guests, I would deem this a good fortune for myself and of great consequence.'

The Yakshas, though knowing the determination of the king, could not believe it; so marvellous did it appear to them. And they said to him:

26. 'After the mendicant has unveiled his suffering by wretched asking, from that very moment it is the giver alone who ought to know what should be done in the case.'

The king, understanding that they assented, was much rejoiced, and ordered his physicians to be sent for, to have his veins opened. Now the royal ministers, understanding his determination to offer his own flesh and blood, became agitated, irritated, and perplexed by it, and prompted by their affection, spoke emphatically to this purport: 'We pray Your Majesty not to give way to your excessive love of charity in such a degree as to disregard the consequences of your actions, whether they are to be good or evil to your loyal and devoted subjects. Your Majesty cannot be ignorant of the nature of the evil spirits.

27. 'Goblins, you know, rejoice in whatsoever may tend to the mishap of your subjects, most illustrious lord. They get satisfied by a livelihood necessitating injury to others. Such is the nature of that class of beings, benevolent master.

28. 'You, Your Majesty, not minding your own pleasures, sustain the toilsome burden of royalty exclusively for the happiness of your people. Cease, therefore, from this determination of offering your flesh and blood; it is a wrong action.

29. 'These goblins have no power over your people, Your Majesty, no doubt, as long as your strength protects your subjects. So being obstructed in their cleverness in bringing about mischief, they seek the calamity of the inhabitants of this country by means of an adroit scheme.

30. 'In fact, the Celestials are pleased with fat, suet, and the like, offered to them in the fire at sacrifices, and these goblins should not like Your Majesty's food, that is excellent and pure, being carefully prepared!

'Surely, Your Royal Majesty is not obliged to

communicate your designs to such as we. Notwithstanding this, the attachment to our duty forbids us to show in this matter our usual obedience. Can it be called a righteous action of Your Majesty to throw your whole people into calamity for the sake of those five? Moreover, for what reason do you make us feel to this degree your want of affection? How else could it happen that our flesh and blood, which we are employing in the service of our master, have remained unnoticed by you, but you form the desire of offering your own, while our bodies are entire and available?'

Then the king spoke to those ministers:

31. 'Being requested in distinct terms, how may anybody like me say "I have not," when having, or "I will not give," speaking falsely?

32. 'Since I pass for your leader in matters of righteousness, if I myself should walk in the wrong path, what would be the condition of my subjects, who are ready to follow the example of my behaviour?

33. 'Therefore, it is with regard to my very subjects that I will have the strength of my body taken out of it. Besides, if I were to be faint-hearted, subdued by self-love, what power should I have to promote the welfare of my people?

'As to the words of love and respect which you have spoken, words full of affection and cordial sympathy, when you asked why I showed such want of affection, wishing to offer my own limbs even now, while your flesh and blood are intact and available, I will convince you by argument. Surely, do not think that by want of trust I mean to close up the path in which you could show your affection towards me, or that suspicion has created an impenetrable thicket across it. Yet,

34. 'The proper time for friends to conceive the desire of succouring their friend is this, when his wealth has either diminished gradually, or has been destroyed by the disfavour of his destiny; but it would not befit the poor acting thus towards a wealthy man.

35. 'Now, my limbs are available. They are big,

VIII. THE STORY OF MAITRĪBALA.

solid, fleshy. Them I do sustain for the sake of supplicants. This being so, it would be unfit even for you to conceive such a desire.

36. 'I am not capable of bearing the pain of strangers, how then can you suppose I should bear your suffering? Therefore, I wish to offer my own flesh. It is I, whom they ask, not you.

'Well, then, though attachment to my person gave you the courage to put obstacles in the way of my righteous behaviour, do not oppose my determination any longer. Verily, Your Lordships are not in the habit of dealing in the proper manner with my mendicants. Besides, you should also consider this.

37. 'He who prohibits any one wishing for his own sake to give in charity food or the like, say, by what appellation is he to be called, a pious man or an impious one? How much less can there be any doubt about this in the case of a gift of this character?

'Why then insist any longer? Do but examine the matter duly, and you will keep your thoughts from the wrong path, as befits those who occupy a ministership in my service. In fact, sympathetic words of approval would now become Your Lordships more than these anxious looks. Why do I say so?

38, 39. 'Beggars, wanting money and goods, objects of various employment, are to be found every day, are they not? but mendicants like these cannot be obtained even by propitiating deities. Now considering the frailness of my body and that it is an abode of woe, it would be meanness of mind, I think, even to hesitate at the time of the appearance of such uncommon mendicants; but miserable self-love would be here the deepest darkness.

'Pray, do not withhold me, then, My Lords.'

Having so persuaded his council, he sent for the physicians, and after having five veins in his body opened by them, he spoke to the Yakshas:

40. 'Deign to assist me in this pious performance and to procure for me the highest gladness by accepting this bounty.'

F

They assented and began to drink, intercepting with the hollow of their joint hands the king's blood, the dark colour of which resembled fragrant red sandal.

41. While allowing the nocturnal monsters to drink the blood from his wounds, the monarch shone as if his body were of gold, and he had the appearance of Mount Meru covered with rain-clouds hanging down by their weight, and tinged with the hue of the twilight.

42. In consequence of the high degree of his gladness, of his magnanimous forbearance, and also of his corporeal strength, his body did not fade, nor did his mind faint, and the flowing blood did not lessen.

The Yakshas, having quenched their intense thirst, said to the king that it was enough.

43. Considering that he had now disposed of his body, that always ungrateful object and abode of many pains, so as to turn it into a means of honouring mendicants, his satisfaction grew no less when they ceased.

Then the king, the serenity of whose countenance was enhanced by his expanding joy, took a sharp sword. It had a spotless bluish blade, not unlike a petal of the blue lotus, and a beautiful hilt shining with brilliancy by the lustre of the jewels which adorned it. With it he cut pieces of flesh out of his body and presented the Yakshas with them.

44. And the joy he experienced by giving did not leave room for the sense of pain caused by cutting, and prevented his mind again and again from being immersed in sorrow.

45. So the pain, pushing on at each stroke of the sharp sword, but driven far back again by his gladness, was slow in penetrating his mind, as if it were tired by the trouble of being urged to and fro.

46. And he was feeling a sense of gladness alone, whilst he satisfied the nocturnal goblins with pieces of his flesh, to such an extent that the cruel hearts of those very beings unclosed themselves to softness.

47. He who, moved by love of the Law or by compassion, abandons his own dear body for the benefit of others, such a man may be able to regenerate the hearts

of men burnt by the fire of hatred, changing it into the gold of tenderness and faith[1].

The Yakshas, beholding the monarch, who, though intent on cutting out his own flesh, was yet as calm as ever, and exhibited an unshaken serenity of countenance and dauntless intrepidity against the pain caused by the work of his sword, became affected with the utmost tenderness and admiration.

48. 'Oh, it is a wonder! oh, it is a miracle! Can it be true, or is it perhaps a phantasm?' Such thoughts arose in their ecstatic minds; and the wrath they had fostered against the king was crushed, and they began to proclaim their faith by veneration and praise of his deed.

'No more, no more, Your Majesty,' they exclaimed; 'cease injuring your own body! This marvellous performance of yours, by which you win the hearts of all mendicants, has satisfied us.' So with great agitation, and respectfully bowing their heads, they bade the king stop; after which, they looked up to him with great regard, uplifting their faces moistened with tears of faithful contrition, and continued

49. 'Justly people are prompted by devoutness to proclaim everywhere your glory. Justly Srî, disdaining the lotus-pond, loves to reside with you. Verily, if Heaven, though protected by Sakra's sovereignty, does not feel something like jealousy, when it looks down on this earth, guarded by your heroism—Heaven, forsooth, is deceived.

'Why use many words? Mankind is happy, indeed, being under the protection of such a person as you; but we, we are utterly distressed at having approved of your suffering. Yet, we hope that applying to such a being as you are, may prove a means of salvation for us, be we ever so wicked as we are. Thus hoping, we put this question to you.

---

[1] 'Tender-heartedness' or 'softness of mind' and 'faith in the Buddha' are expressed by the one word prasâda. I have as a rule translated it according to the conception prevailing, but there is equivalence here.

50. 'What is that exceedingly marvellous rank for which you long, acting in this way without regard to your royal happiness, that beloved state which you possess at your ease?

51. 'Is it the sovereignty of the whole earth you covet by means of this penance, or is it the rank of Kubera or that of Indra, or entire deliverance and absorption into the Brahma?

52. 'Be it what it may, the goal you are striving after cannot be very far from this strong determination. If we are allowed to hear it, you would please us by telling it, sir.'

The king spoke: 'Hear then, for what I am exerting myself.

53–55. 'An illustrious high rank depends on existence, it is to be obtained by effort, and may be easily lost. It cannot give the pleasure of satisfaction, much less tend to serenity of mind. For this reason, I do not desire even the brilliancy of the Lord of the Devas, how much less, that of a king of the earth. Nor would my heart become content, if I were to succeed in destroying the suffering of myself alone[1]. I rather regard those helpless creatures, distressed by toil and sufferings because of the violent calamities and vices to which they are liable. For their sakes, may I by means of this my meritorious action attain All-knowingness, and vanquishing the evil passions, my enemies, may I save the creatures from the Ocean of Existence, that rough sea with its billows of old age, sickness and death!'

On hearing this, the Yakshas, the hairs on whose bodies bristled in consequence of the intense joy of faith, bowed to the king, and said: 'This performance of yours is consistent with your extraordinary determination. Accordingly we venture to express our conviction concerning it: the designs of such persons as you will be accomplished after a short time.

---

[1] This is said in answer to the question whether he aimed at absorption into Brahma [or 'into the Brahma,' the Sanskrit word being brahmabhûya].

VIII. THE STORY OF MAITRĪBALA.

56, 57. 'No doubt, all your exertions tend to the salvation of all creatures; yet deign to take a special care of us, pray do not forget us at that time[1]. And now forgive us what we have done from ignorance, causing you to be thus tortured: we did not understand even our own interest.

58. 'Further, we beg you to show us your favour by giving us some injunction which we may follow. Do it with the same confidence, as you would to your own officials.'

Upon which the king, knowing them to be converted and to have lost their hard-heartedness, spoke in this manner: 'Do not be in trouble without reason. It is no torment, in fact it is a benefit you have conferred on me. Moreover,

59. 'The path of righteousness (dharma) being thus (difficult), how should I ever forget my companions on that road, when once I shall have attained Supreme Wisdom (bodhi)? My first teaching of the Lore of Liberation shall be to you; to you I shall impart of that ambrosia first.

60. 'And if you now intend to do what may be agreeable to me, you must avoid like poison these sins: doing harm to others, coveting the goods or wives of others, speaking evil, and drinking intoxicating liquors.'

The Yakshas promised to do so, and having bowed to him and circumambulated him from left to right, disappeared on the spot.

But when the Great Being had made up his mind to give away his own flesh and blood, at that very time

61, 62. Earth trembled in many places and caused the Golden Mountain to waver, in consequence of which concussion the drums on that mountain began to sound and the trees to cast off their flowers. These spread about in the sky, and moved by the wind appeared like a cloud; at one place, like a flight of birds, they

---

[1] Viz. 'at the time of your All-knowingness, when you will have reached Buddhahood.'

resembled a canopy; at another they bore the appearance of a well-arranged garland. They fell down together on all sides of the place where the king was.

63. The great Ocean, as if he intended to prevent the monarch, showed his excitement and agitation by the increased commotion and noise of his waves, and his figure expressed great vigour as if he were ready to march [1].

64, 65. Then the Chief of the Devas became agitated by those phenomena; and discovering by reflection the cause of them, and being filled with apprehension at the sufferings to which the king exposed himself, hastily came to the royal residence, where he found every one perplexed with sorrow and fear, except the king. On beholding the calmness of his countenance, though he was in so miserable a condition, Sakra was affected with the utmost amazement. He approached the monarch, and impelled by gladness and joy, he eulogised his performance in his lovely voice.

66. 'Oh, thou hast reached the summit of pious behaviour! oh, the loftiness of thy treasure which is the practice of virtue! oh, how charmingly clever is thy mind in showing thy favour to others! Verily, being given to thee, Earth has obtained a protector!'

After so praising him, Sakra, the Lord of the Devas, applied excellent herbs, fit to heal wounds immediately, which herbs were partly divine, partly such as are used by men. So he put a stop to his pains, and made his body as it was before. In return for which the king honoured him by kind attendance in a courteous and reverent manner. Then Sakra went back to his own abode.

In this way, then, the intensely compassionate do not mind their own pleasure, being afflicted by the

---

[1] Viz. to relieve the king. In this simile the Ocean is represented as an auxiliary prince who raises his army to the succour of his ally.

sufferings of others; [who, then, ought not to set aside the attachment to anything so mean as wealth? Thus ought to be said when stimulating the zeal of charitable people. Likewise, when explaining the virtue of compassion; when glorifying the Tathâgata; also on the subject of listening with attention to the preaching of the Law. Moreover, the words said by the Lord: 'Monks, these Five have done much, indeed,' will be explained by their being connected with this story. For they were the five Yakshas of that time. To them the Lord imparted the first of the ambrosia of the Law, just as he had promised.]

The story of Maitribala is not met with in the *K*ariyâpi*t*aka nor in the five volumes of the Pâli *G*âtaka, which have appeared up to date; it will probably be found in the part not yet published. Something like it is told in the ninety-first pallava of Kshemendra's Avadânakalpalatâ. There a king of the *S*ibis gives up his flesh and blood in order to obtain a sûkta or well-said sentence[1]. This tale, however, is not yet printed, nor may we expect it soon to be so. But in another part of that poem, already published, I have met with the story of king Ma*n*ikû*d*a, which bears in many respects a striking resemblance to ours. See 3, 56 foll.

IX. THE STORY OF VISVANTARA.

The mean-spirited are not even capable of approving the behaviour of the Bodhisattva, how much less can they act after it. This will be taught by the following.

Once the *S*ibis were ruled by a king named Sa*m*g*aya, who performed his royal duties in the right manner. Having entirely subdued his organs of sense, and possessing in a high degree the virtues of valour, discretion, and modesty, he was victorious and mighty. Thanks to the constant and strict observance he paid to the elders, he had mastered the essential contents of the three Vedas (trayî) and of metaphysics. His good administration of justice was praised by his

---

[1] Somendra in his introductory *s*lokas describes the ninety-first story thus: svamâ*m*sâs*r*ikpradânena ya*h* *S*ibi*h* sûktam agrahît (*s*l. 36).

affectionate subjects, who loved the exercise of their different trades and duties, and enjoyed the benefits of security and peace.

1. By the progress of his virtues he had gained the affection of Royal Felicity, who, like an honest woman, was faithful to him, not to be thought of by the other monarchs; just as a den kept by a lion is inaccessible to other animals.

2. All such men as spent their labours in any kind of penance, science or art, used to come up to him, and if they proved their merit, they obtained distinguished honour from him.

Next to him in dignity, but not his inferior by a famous set of virtues, his son Visvantara held the rank of heir-apparent.

3. Though a youth, he possessed the lovely placidity of mind proper to old age; though he was full of ardour, his natural disposition was inclined to forbearance; though learned, he was free from the conceit of knowledge; though mighty and illustrious, he was void of pride.

4. As the extent[1] of his virtue was conspicuous in all regions and his fame penetrated the three worlds, there was no room for the feeble and trifling reputations of others; it seemed as if they did not venture to show themselves.

5. He could not endure the proud prevalence of calamities and other causes of sufferings among mankind. It was against these foes that he waged war and fought in battle, shooting from his large bow of compassion numberless arrows which had the form of gifts of charity.

So he was wont to fill day after day the mendicants who happened to come to him with the utmost gladness by his bounties, given without difficulty, surpassing the objects asked for, and the more lovely, as they were bestowed with deference and kind words. But on the

---

[1] I suppose the reading of the MSS. d*rish*/aprayâmâsu to be right.

knotdays[1], as he was distinguished by his strict observance of the restrictions and the quiet of the sabbath, after bathing his head and putting on a white linen dress, he mounted his excellent, well-trained, swift, and vigorous elephant, who (by his colour and size) might be compared to a peak of the Snow-mountain, whose face was adorned with the tracks of the juice flowing in rutting-time, and on whose body auspicious marks were found. Sitting, then, on the back of that far-famed scent-elephant[2] and royal vehicle, he was in the habit of making the round of his alms-halls, which he had established in all parts of the town to be like refreshing wells for the mendicants. So going about, he experienced an excessive gladness.

6. No opulence, in truth, within doors procures to a charitable man such rejoicing, as it produces when transferred to the mendicants.

Now his very great practice of charity being proclaimed everywhere by the rejoiced mendicants, some neighbouring king who had heard of it, considering that it would be possible to deceive the young prince by means of his passion for almsgiving, directed some Brâhmans, his emissaries, to rob him of that excellent elephant. Accordingly one day, when Viśvantara was inspecting his alms-halls, manifesting his gladness of mind by the enhanced beauty of his countenance, the said Brâhmans placed themselves in his way, uttering benedictions with their uplifted and outstretched right hands. He stopped his excellent elephant, and asked them respectfully the reason of their coming; they had but to express their want, he said. The Brâhmans spoke:

7, 8. 'Both the excellent qualities of this elephant of thine, who has so graceful a gait, and thy heroic love of charity make us like beggars. Present us with this (white) elephant, who is like a peak of the Kailâsa

---

[1] Viz. the sabbath-days.
[2] Cp. stanza 6 of Story II.

mountain, and thou wilt fill the world with astonishment.'

The Bodhisattva being thus addressed, was filled with sincere joy and entered upon this reflection: 'Truly, after a long time I now see mendicants requesting a grand boon. But, after all, what may be the want of such a lord of elephants to these Brâhmans? No doubt, this must be a miserable trick of some king, whose mind is troubled with covetousness, jealousy, and hatred.

9. 'Yet that prince, who, not minding either his reputation or the precepts of righteousness, is eager, as it were, to promote my good[1], must not be saddened by disappointment.'

Having thus considered, the Great-minded One alighted from the back of that excellent elephant and stood before them with uplifted golden pitcher; then he pronounced (the solemn formula) 'Accept.'

10. After which, though knowing that the science of politics follows the path of Righteousness (dharma) only as far as it may agree with material interest (artha), he gave away his foremost elephant. His attachment to Righteousness did not allow him to be frightened by the lie of political wisdom.

11. Having given away that lord of elephants, who, adorned with the lovely golden lattice-seat on his back, resembled a massy cloud of autumn, radiant with a flash of lightning[2], the royal prince obtained the utmost delight—but the citizens were stricken with consternation, for they were adherents of political wisdom.

In fact, when the Sibis heard of the gift of that lord of elephants, anger and wrath penetrated them, and the eldest of the Brâhmans, the ministers, the warriors,

---

[1] Inasmuch as his covetousness affords to the Bodhisattva an occasion of performing an extraordinary deed of charity. Compare a similar argument in Story XXXIII, stanza 15.

[2] In the Pâli redaction which is the source of Spence Hardy's narration of our tale, it is said that this white elephant had the power of causing rain.

and the chiefs of the townsmen, making hubbub went into the presence of king Sa*m*gaya. Owing to their agitation, resentment, and anger, they neglected the restraint imposed on them by the respect due to their monarch, and spoke: 'Why do you overlook in this manner, Your Majesty, the fortune of your kingdom being carried off? Your Majesty ought not to overlook that in this way you are fostering the misfortune of your realm.' When the king, alarmed, asked them what they meant by this, they replied: 'Why, are you not aware of what has happened, Your Majesty?

12, 13. 'That splendid animal, whose face, being fragrant with the scent of the flowing juice, intoxicates crowds of humming bees hovering about, and likewise impregnates the cherishing wind with its perfume, so as to induce him to wipe off gladly and easily the smell caught from the fluid of other haughty elephants; that war-elephant, whose brilliant vigour subdued the strength and the power of your enemies, and abated their pride even unto the motionlessness of sleep—see, that embodied victory has been given away by Visvantara and is now being carried off abroad.

14. 'Kine, gold, clothes, eatables, such are the goods fit to give to Brâhmans, but parting with our foremost elephant, the pledge of glorious victory, is an excess of charity, and goes too far.

15. 'How should success and might ever join this prince who acts up to this point contrary to the maxims of policy? In this matter forbearance from your side is out of place, Your Majesty, lest he should before long afford matter of rejoicing to your enemies.'

On hearing this, the king, who loved his son, was not very kindly disposed towards them; but submitting to necessity, he told them hastily, they were right; after which he tried to appease the Sibis. 'I know,' he said, 'that Visvantara indulges in his disproportionate passion for charity so as to neglect for it the rules of political wisdom, which behaviour is not suitable for a person appointed to the royal charge. But as he has resigned his own elephant, as if it were phlegm, who will bring back that animal? Nevertheless, I shall take such measures that Visvantara will know a limit in his almsgiving. This may suffice to appease your anger.'

The Sibis answered: 'No, Your Majesty, this will not do. Visvantara is no person to be brought to reason in this matter by a simple censure.'

Samgaya spoke: 'But what else can I do?

16. 'He is averse to sinful actions, only his attachment to virtuous practices is turning into a kind of passion. Why, should you then deem imprisonment or death inflicted on my own son to be the due requital for that elephant?

'Therefore, desist from your wrath! Henceforward I will prevent Visvantara from such actions.'

Notwithstanding this, the Sibis persisted in their anger and said:

17, 18. 'Who would be pleased, O king, with the pain of death, or prison, or flogging pronounced upon your son? But being devoted to his religious duties, Visvantara is not fit to be a bearer of the troublesome burden of royalty, because of his tenderness of heart and his compassion. Let the throne be occupied by such princes, as have obtained renown for their martial qualities and are skilled in the art of giving its due to each of the three members of the trivarga; but your son, who in consequence of his love of Righteousness (dharma), does not heed Policy (naya), is a proper person to dwell in a penance-grove.

19. 'Surely, if princes commit faults of bad policy, the results of those faults fall on their subjects[1]. They are however bearable for them, after all, as is taught by experience; not so for the kings themselves, the very roots of whose power they undermine.

20. 'Why, then, here say much? Not capable of conniving at a state of things which must lead to your

---

[1] This Indian parallel to the Horatian verse quidquid delirant reges, plectuntur Achivi, runs thus in the original: phalanti kâma*m* vasudhâdipânâ*m* durnîtidoshâs tadupâsriteshu.

ruin, the Sibis have taken this resolution. The royal prince must withdraw to Mount Vaṅkā, the residence of the Siddhas; there he may exert his penance.'

Being so addressed for his good in very harsh terms by those dignitaries, who moved by affection and love spoke frankly, foreseeing the calamities to be expected from bad policy, the king was ashamed of the wrath of the chiefs of his people, and with downcast eyes, overwhelmed by the sorrowful thought of a separation from his son, he heaved a deep, woeful sigh, and said to the Sibis : 'If this is your peremptory decision, allow him, at least, the delay of one day and night. To-morrow at day-break Viśvantara shall accomplish your desire.' This answer satisfied the Sibis. Then the king said to his chamberlain : 'Go and tell Viśvantara what has happened.' The chamberlain said he would do so, and, his face bathed in tears, went to Viśvantara, who was at that moment in his own palace. Overwhelmed by his sorrow, he threw himself at the feet of the prince, weeping aloud. Then Viśvantara anxiously inquired after the health of the royal family ; the other said in a voice rather indistinct by affliction: 'O, the royal family is well.' ' But why are you thus excited, then ?' Viśvantara replied. Being so asked once more, the chamberlain whose throat was choked with tears, uttered slowly and in a faltering tone these words, interrupting and disturbing them by his sobs :

21. ' Brusquely disregarding the royal command, though it was declared to them in gentle terms, the Sibis, moved by anger, order you to be banished from the kingdom, my prince.'

Viśvantara said : 'Me .... the Sibis .... order to be banished, moved by anger ! What you say is out of all reason.

22. ' Never did I take delight in leaving the path of discipline, and I detest carelessness about my duties. What evil action of mine, unknown to me, makes the Sibis angry with me ?'

The chamberlain said : ' They are offended at your exceeding loftiness of mind.

23, 24. 'Your satisfaction was pure by the disinterested feeling you experienced, but that of those mendicants was troubled by cupidity. When you gave away that foremost of elephants, O most noble prince, wrath put the *S*ibis out of patience and caused them to transgress the limits of their duty. They are furious against you. You must go, indeed, the way of those who live as ascetics.'

At this moment the Bodhisattva displayed both his deeply-rooted affection for the mendicants which his continuous practice of compassion had firmly established, and his grand, immense patience. He said: 'The nature of the *S*ibis is fickle, and they cannot understand mine, it seems.

25. 'The objects of sense being outside of ourselves, it is superfluous to say that I would give away my eyes or my head[1]. For the benefit of the creatures I support this body, how much more the possession of clothes and vehicles.

26. 'Me, wanting to honour the requests of the mendicants, if need be, with my own limbs, the *S*ibis believe to restrain from charity by fear! So considering, they do but unfold their foolish fickleness of mind.

27. 'Let all *S*ibis kill me or banish me, I shall not desist from charity for that reason. With this mind I am ready to set out for the penance-grove.'

After this, the Bodhisattva said to his wife, who had turned pale while hearing the sad news: 'Your Highness has heard the resolution of the *S*ibis.' Madrî[2] replied: 'I have.' Vi*s*vantara said:

28. 'Now make a deposit, fair-eyed one, of all your

---

[1] The Bodhisattva is said to have given away his eyes in one of his existences (Story II). The gift of his head is related in some *g*âtaka, not found in this selection of Ârya *S*ûra. It occurs in Kshemendra's Avadânakalpalatâ, pallava the fifth.

[2] It is plain that *S*ûra supposes the story of Vi*s*vantara to be known to his readers. Neither the name of Vi*s*vantara's wife nor even the fact of his being married has been told before.

property, taking what you have got from my part as well as from your father's side[1].'

Madrî answered: 'Where shall I lay the deposit, my prince?' Viśvantara spoke:

29, 30. 'You must always give in charity to people of good conduct, embellishing your bounty by kind observance. Goods deposited in this manner are imperishable and follow us after death. Be a loving daughter to your parents-in-law, a careful mother to our children. Continue in pious conduct, beware of inadvertence; but do not mourn for my absence, will you?'

Upon this, Madrî, avoiding what might impair the firmness of mind of her husband, suppressed the deep sorrow that put her heart to anguish, and said with feigned calmness:

31, 32. 'It is not right, Your Majesty, that you should go to the forest alone. I too will go with you where you must go, my lord. When attending on you, even death will be a festival to me; but living without you I deem worse than death.

'Nor do I think the forest-life to be unpleasant at all. Do but consider it well.

33. 'Removed from wicked people, haunted by deer, resounding with the warbling of manifold birds, the penance-groves with their rivulets and trees, both intact, with their grass-plots which have the loveliness of inlaid lapis lazuli floors, are by far more pleasing than our artificial gardens.

'Indeed, my prince,

34. 'When beholding these children neatly dressed and adorned with garlands, playing in the wild shrubs, you will not think of your royalty.

35. 'The water-carrying brooks, overhung by natural bowers of perpetually renewed beauty, varying according to the succession of the seasons, will delight you in the forest.

---

[1] On this strîdhana, or 'wife's property,' see the paper of Jolly in the Sitzungsber. der bair. Akad. der Wiss., 1876.

36, 37. 'The melodious music of the songs of birds longing for the pleasure of love, the dances of the peacocks whom Lasciviousness has taught that art, the sweet and praised buzzing of the honey-seeking bees: they make together a forest-concert that will rejoice your mind.

38, 39. 'Further, the rocks overspread at night with the silk garment of moonlight; the soft-stroking forest wind impregnated with the scent of flowering trees; the murmuring noise of the rivulets, pushing their waters over moving gravel so as to imitate the sound of a number of rattling female ornaments—all this will gladden your mind in the forest.'

This entreaty of his well-beloved wife filled him with a great desire to set out for the forest. Therefore he prepared to bestow great largesses on the mendicant people.

But in the king's palace the news of the banishment pronounced upon Visvantara caused great alarm and violent lamentations. Likewise the mendicants, agitated by sorrow and grief, became almost beside themselves, or behaved as if they were intoxicated or mad, and uttered many and various lamentations of this kind:

40. 'How is it that Earth does not feel ashamed, permitting the hatchets to hew down that shady tree, her foster-child, the giver of such sweet fruits? It is now plain she has been deprived of consciousness.'

41. 'If no one will prevent those who are about to destroy that well of cold, pure, and sweet water, then in truth the guardians of the world-quarters are falsely named so, or they are absent, or they are nothing ,but a mere sound.'

42. 'Oh! Indeed Injustice is awake and Righteousness either asleep or dead, since prince Visvantara is banished from his reign.'

43. 'Who possesses such a refined skill in occasioning distress, as to have the cruelty to aim at starving us, the guiltless, who obtain a scanty livelihood by begging?'

The Bodhisattva then gave away his wealth. He bestowed on the mendicants the contents of his treasury, filled to the very top with precious stones, gold, and silver, of the value of many hundred thousands; his magazines and granaries, containing stores of manifold goods and grains; all his other property, consisting of slaves of both sexes, beasts of draught, carriages, garments and the like. The whole of this he distributed according to the merit of the recipients. This being done, he paid his respectful homage to his father and mother, taking leave of them, who were overwhelmed with sadness and grief. Then he mounted his royal chariot with his wife and children. He left the capital, while a great body of people uttered lamentations, the streets being as noisy as on a holiday; nor did he succeed without difficulty in making the crowd turn back, who followed him out of affection, shedding tears of sorrow. Then himself taking the reins, he drove in the direction of Mount Vaṅka. And without the least agitation of mind he passed along the environs of the capital, crowned with charming gardens and groves, and approached the forest, betokened by the gradually increasing rareness of shady trees and of human beings, the sight of flocks of antelopes running at a far distance, and the chirping of crickets. Now by chance some Brâhmans came to meet him, who begged from him the horses that were drawing his chariot.

44. And he, though on a journey of many yoganas without attendants, and burdened with his wife, gave away to these Brâhmans his four horses, being rejoiced at this opportunity of giving, and not caring for the future.

Now, when the Bodhisattva was about to put himself under the yoke, and was fastening the girth tightly round his waist, there appeared four young Yakshas, under the form of red deer. Like well-trained excellent horses they put their shoulders under the yoke themselves. On seeing them, the Bodhisattva said to Madri, who stared at them with joy and surprise:

45. 'Behold the extraordinary might of the penance-groves honoured by the residence of ascetics. Their kindness towards guests has in this degree taken root in the breast of the foremost of deer.'
Madrî replied:
46. 'This is rather your superhuman power, I suppose. The practice of virtue by the pious, however deeply rooted, is not the same with respect to everybody.
47. 'When the beautiful reflection of the stars in the water is surpassed by the laughing lustre of the night-waterlilies, the cause thereof is to be found in the beams which the Moon-god sends down as if out of curiosity[1].'

While they were going on, so speaking to each other kind words of affection, see, another Brâhman came near, and asked the Bodhisattva for his royal chariot.

48. And the Bodhisattva, as he was indifferent to his own comfort, but to the beggars a loving kinsman, fulfilled the wish of that Brâhman.

He gladly caused his family to alight from the chariot, presented the Brâhman with it, and taking Gâlin, his boy, in his arms, he continued his way on foot. Madrî, she too free from sadness, took the girl, Krishnâginâ, in her arms and marched after him.

49. The trees, stretching out to him their branches adorned at their ends with charming fruits, invited him, as it were, to enjoy their hospitality, and paying homage to his merit-obtained dignity, bowed to him like obedient disciples, when they got sight of him.

50. And, where he longed for water, in those very places lotus-ponds appeared to his eyes, covered on their surface with the white and reddish-brown pollen fallen down from the anthers of the lotuses shaken by the wing-movements of the swans.

51. The clouds overspread him with a beautiful

---

[1] The white waterlilies (kumuda) are said to open at moonrise. The connection between these flowers and the moon is a commonplace in Indian poetry.

canopy; there blew an agreeable and odoriferous wind; and his path was shortened by Yakshas not enduring his labour and fatigue.

In this manner the Bodhisattva with his wife and children experienced the pleasure and the delight of a walk, without feeling the sensation of weariness, just as if he were in some park, and at last he perceived Mount Vaṅka. Being showed the way by some foresters, he went up to the penance-forest which was on that mountain. This forest was beset with manifold charming and smooth-barked, excellent trees, with their ornaments of twigs, flowers, and fruits; birds exulting with lust made it resound with their various notes; groups of dancing peacocks enhanced its beauty; many kinds of deer lived in it. It was encircled as with a girdle by a river of pure, blue water, and the wind was agreeable there, carrying red flower-dust. In this grove stood a desert hut of leaves, lovely to behold, and pleasing in every season. Visvakarman himself had built it by the orders of Sakra. There the Bodhisattva took up his residence.

52. Attended by his beloved wife, enjoying the artless and sweet talk of his children, not thinking of the cares of royalty, like one who is staying in his gardens, he practised in that grove strong penance for half a year.

One day, when the princess had gone to seek roots and fruits, and the prince watching the children kept himself within the borders of the hermitage, there arrived a Brâhman, whose feet and ankles were stiff with the dust of the journey, and whose eyes and cheeks were sunken by toil; he was bearing over his shoulder a wooden club, from which his waterpot hung down. His wife had despatched him with the pressing errand, to go and search after some attendance. When the Bodhisattva saw a mendicant coming up to him after a long time, his heart rejoiced, and his countenance began to beam. He went to meet him, and welcomed him with kind words. After the usual complimentary conversation he told him to enter the hermitage, where he entertained him with the honour due to a guest. Then he asked him the object of his coming. And the Brâhman, who through fondness for his wife had banished virtue and shame and was but eager to receive his boon, said in truth something like this:

53. 'Where a light is and an even road, there it is easy for men to go. But in this world the darkness of selfishness prevails to such a degree that no other men would support my words of request.

54. 'Thy brilliant renown of heroic almsgiving has penetrated everywhere. For this reason I have undertaken this labour of begging from thee. Give me both thy children to be my attendants.'

Being so addressed, the Bodhisattva, that Great Being,

55. As he was in the habit of cheerfully giving to mendicants and had never learnt to say no, bravely said that he would give even both his darlings.

'Bless thee! But what art thou still waiting for?' Thus speaking the Brâhman urged the Great Being. Now the children, having heard their father saying he would give them away, became afflicted, and their eyes filled with tears. His affection for them agitated him, and made his heart sink. So the Bodhisattva spoke:

56, 57. 'They are thine, being given by me to thee. But their mother is not at home. She went out to the forest in search of roots and fruits; she will come back at evening-time. Let their mother see them, neatly dressed as they are now and bearing wreaths, and kiss[1] them (farewell). Rest this night here; to-morrow thou shalt carry them away.'

The Brâhman said: 'Thy Reverence ought not to urge me.

58. 'A metaphorical name of womankind is "beau-

---

[1] The literal translation is 'to smell at.' This old and traditional manner of caressing is prescribed in the ritual-books, see for instance, Âsvalâyanagrihyasûtra I, 15, 9; Pâraskara I, 18; Gobhila II, 8, 22 and 25.

tiful charmers¹," thou knowest. She might prove a hindrance to the fulfilment of thy promise. Therefore I do not like staying here.'

The Bodhisattva said: 'Do not think of that. My wife will not obstruct the fulfilment of my promise. She is in fact the companion of my pious practice². But do as pleases Thy Reverence. Yet, great Brâhman, thou shouldst consider this:

59-61. 'How should these children satisfy thy wants by slavework? They are very young and weak and have never been accustomed to such kind of occupation. But the king of Sibi, their grandfather, seeing them fallen into this state of bondage, will doubtlessly give thee as much money as thou desirest to redeem them. Well, for this reason I pray thee, take them to his realm. When acting thus, thou wilt get the possession of great wealth and at the same time of righteousness.'

'No' (said the Brâhman), 'I do not venture to come to this king with an offer which would excite his anger; he would be unapproachable like a snake.

62. 'He would have the children torn from me by force, perhaps he would also inflict punishment on me. I shall bring them rather to my Brâhma*n*î that they may attend on her.'

Upon this the Bodhisattva said nothing but: 'Then as thou likest,' without finishing the sentence. He instructed the little ones with persuasive words how they had to act in accordance with their new condition of servants; after which he took the waterpot, bending

---

¹ I have tried to render approximately the ambiguousness of the original. Women are designated, says the Brâhman, by the appellation of vâmâ*h*. Now vâmâ means 'beautiful,' but pronounced with a different accent vâma, it is a word signifying 'left, contrary, opposite.'

² Visvantara uses here the solemn appellation of sahadharmakâri*n*î (='housewife') with its full meaning. The formula sahobhau ka*-*rata*m* dharmam is uttered in the fourth or Prâ*g*âpatya form of marriage. Manu III, 30.

it over the outstretched hand of the Brâhman, greedy to accept the ratification of the gift.

63. Yielding to his effort, the water poured down from the pot, and at the same time tears fell without effort from his eyes resembling dark red lotus-petals.

Overjoyed with his success, agitated by his excitement, and hastening to carry off the children of the Bodhisattva, the Brâhman uttered a short phrase of benediction, and telling the children with a harsh voice of command to go out, he prepared to make them leave the hermitage. They, however, could not bear the too intense grief of separation, their hearts shrunk together and they embraced the feet of their father. Bathed in tears, they exclaimed:

64. 'Mother is out of doors, while you are about to give us away. Do not give us away before we have bidden adieu to mother too.'

Now the Brâhman reflected: 'The mother will return erelong, or it is likely that his paternal love will make him repent.' Thus considering, he tied their hands like a bundle of lotuses with a creeper, and as they were reluctant and looked back at their father, he began to drag those young and delicate children along with him, threatening them. At this moment K*rish*nâgínâ the girl, having never before experienced a sudden calamity, cried out with tears to her father:

65, 66. 'This cruel Brâhman, father, hurts me with a creeper. No, it is no Brâhman, to be sure. Brâhmans are righteous, they say. It is an ogre under the guise of a Brâhman. Certainly he carries us off to eat us. Why do you suffer us, father, to be led away by this ogre?'

And *G*âlin the boy lamented on account of his mother, saying:

67. 'I do not suffer so much by the violence of this Brâhman, as by the absence of mother. It is as if my heart is pierced by grief that I did not see her.

68. 'Oh! certainly, mother will weep for us for a

long time in the empty hermitage, like the bird *k*âtaka[1] whose little ones have been killed.

69. 'How will mother behave, when coming back with the many roots and fruits she has gathered in the forest for us, she will find the hermitage empty?

70. 'Here, father, are our toy horses, elephants, and chariots. Half of them you must give to mother, that she may assuage her grief therewith.

71. 'You must also present to her our respectful salutations and withhold her at any rate from afflicting herself; for it will be difficult for us, father, to see you and her again.

72. 'Come, K*r*ish*n*â, let us die. Of what use is life to us? We have been delivered by the prince to a Brâhman who is in want of money.'

After so speaking they parted. But the Bodhisattva, though his mind was shaken by these most piteous laments of his children, did not move from the place where he was sitting. While representing to himself that it is not right to repent having given, his heart was burnt by the fire of irremediable grief, and his mind became troubled, as though it were paralysed by torpor occasioned by poison. The fanning of the cool wind made him soon recover his senses, and seeing the hermitage noiseless and silent, as it were, being devoid of his children, he said to himself in a voice choked with tears:

73. 'How is it possible that this man did not scruple to strike my very heart before my very eyes in my children?[2] O, fie on that shameless Brâhman!

74. 'How may they be capable of making the journey, going bare-footed, unable to bear fatigue by reason of their tender age, and become servants to that man?

---

[1] This bird, the cuculus melanoleucus, is a favourite with Indian poets and rhetoricians. It is said to feed on raindrops.

[2] Lit.: 'On my very heart, whose name is offspring.' This identification of the heart of the father with his children depends on an old formula, forming part of the prayers and sacred mantras of the g*ri*hya-books. Cp. also Kaushîtakibrâhma*n*opanishad II, 11.

75. 'Who will afford rest to them, when they are way-worn and exhausted? Whom may they go and ask, if vexed by the suffering of hunger and thirst?

76. 'If this sorrow strikes even me, the earnest striver after firmness of mind, what then will be the condition of those little ones, brought up in ease?

77. 'Oh! the separation from my children is to my mind like a burning fire.... Nevertheless, who, holding on to the righteous conduct of the virtuous, would give way to repentance?'

In the meanwhile Madrî was disquieted by ill omens and prognostics, the foretokens of some accident. Desiring therefore to get back with her roots and fruits as soon as possible, she was obstructed on the way by ferocious animals, and was obliged to return to the hermitage by a long circuitous way. And when she did not see her children neither on the way, where they were used to come to meet her, nor in the playground, her uneasiness greatly increased.

78. Apprehending evil because of these dreadful sensations of danger, she was agitated and anxious, and looked round about if she might get sight of the children; then she called them. Receiving no answer, she began to lament, being sore with grief.

79. 'Formerly the hermitage, resounding with the shouts of my children, appeared to me a much-frequented region; now not perceiving them, I feel myself helpless in the very same place as in a wilderness.

80. 'But perhaps they have fallen asleep and are slumbering, tired with playing. Or should they have gone astray in the thicket? Or should they have hidden themselves out of childishness, being displeased that I was so long in coming home?

81. 'But why do not yonder birds warble? Are they perhaps bewildered, having witnessed mischief done to the children? Can it be that my darlings have been carried away by that very rapid stream, which is eagerly pushing forth its dashing waves?

'Oh! that my suspicions may prove to be groundless

and false even now, and the prince and the children be well! Oh! may the evil-boding prognostics find their fulfilment on my body! But why then is my heart big with sadness because of them? Why is it enwrapt in the night of sorrow and as if it would sink away? Why is it that my limbs seem to slacken, that I am no more able to discern the objects around me, that this grove, deprived of its lustre, seems to turn round?'

Having entered the hermitage-ground and put aside her roots and fruits, she went to her husband. After performing the usual salutation, she asked him for the children. Now the Bodhisattva, knowing the tenderness of a mother's love and also considering that bad news is hard to be told, was not able to make any answer.

82. It is a very difficult matter for a pitiful man, indeed, to torment with evil tidings the mind of one who has come to him and deserves to hear pleasant words.

Then Madrî thought: 'Surely, some ill has befallen the children; his silence must be the effect of his being overwhelmed by grief and sadness,' and almost stricken with stupor she stared about the hermitage, but saw no children. And again she said in a voice rather indistinct by smothered tears:

83. 'I do not see the children, and you do not speak anything to me! Alas! I am wretched, I am forlorn. This silence speaks of some great evil.'

No sooner had she said these words, than overpowered by the sorrow that tortured her heart, she sank down like a creeper violently cut off. The Bodhisattva prevented her from falling to the ground, clasping his arms round her, and brought her to a grass couch, on which lying and being sprinkled with cold water she recovered her senses. Then he endeavoured to comfort her, saying:

84. 'I have not told the sad news straightway to you, Madrî, for firmness is not to be expected of a mind rendered weak by affection.

85. 'See, a Bráhman suffering from old age and poverty has come to me. To him I have given both children. Be appeased and do not mourn.

86. 'Look at me, Madri, do not look for the children, nor indulge in lamentations. Do not strike anew my heart, still pierced by the dart of sorrow on account of the children.

87. 'When asked for my life, should I be able to withhold it? Take this in account, my love, and approve the gift I have made of the children.'

Madri, whom the suspicion of the death of her children had put to anguish, now hearing by these words that they were alive, began to recover from her fright and affliction. She wiped away her tears with the object of comforting and strengthening her husband; then looking up, she beheld (something) that made her speak with amazement to her husband: 'A wonder! A wonder! To say it in a few words,

88. 'Surely, even the Celestials are wrapt in admiration at your heart being up to this point inaccessible to selfish feelings.

89. 'This is evident from the sounds of the divine drums, echoing in all directions. It is in order to celebrate your glory, that Heaven has composed the hymn which it thus pronounces in distinct language from afar.

90. 'Earth shakes, trembling, I suppose, from exultation, as is indicated by the heaving of her breasts, the huge mountains. Golden flowers, falling down from heaven, make the sky appear as if it were illuminated by lightnings.

91. 'Leave, then, grief and sadness. That you have given away in charity must rather tend to brighten up your mind. Become again the well that affords benefit to the creatures, and a giver as before!'

Now the surface of Earth being shaken, Sumeru, the lord of mountains, radiant with the lustre of its manifold gems, began to waver. Sakra, the Lord of the Devas, inquiring into the cause of the earthquake, was informed of it by the regents of the world-quarters, who, with eyes expanding with amazement, told him that it had been caused by Viśvantara giving away his children. Excited with joy and surprise, next day at day-break he went into the presence of Viśvantara, feigning to be a Brâhman come to him as a mendicant. The Bodhisattva showed him the hospitality due to a guest, after which he asked him to bring forth his request. Then Sakra begged him for his wife.

92. 'The practice of almsgiving in virtuous persons,' he said, ' comes as little to its end as the water in great lakes dries up. For this reason I ask thee for that woman there who is looking like a deity. Her, thy wife, give to me, I pray thee.'

The Bodhisattva did not lose his firmness of mind, however, and made the promise of giving her.

93. Then taking Madrî with his left hand and the waterpot with his right, he poured down water on the hand of the Brâhman, but fire of grief on the mind of the Love-god [1].

94. No anger arose in Madrî's breast, nor did she weep, for she knew her husband's nature. Only keeping her eyes fixed on him, she stood like an image, stupefied by the excessive heaviness of that fresh burden of suffering.

On beholding this, Sakra, the Lord of the Devas, affected with the utmost admiration, magnified the Great Being.

95. 'Oh! the wide distance which is between the conduct of the righteous and that of the impious! How will those who have not purified their hearts be even capable of believing this great performance?

96. 'To cherish an affectionate wife and much-beloved children, and yet to give them up, obeying the self-imposed vow of detachment—is it possible to conceive any loftiness like this?

97. 'When thy glory will be spread throughout the

---

[1] This means not so much that the Indian Amor was afflicted on account of the offence against conjugal love, as the defeat of Mâra, the Indian Satan. To conquer the senses and sensuality is to vanquish Mâra, who is the same as Kâma.

world by the tales of those who are enthusiastic about thy virtues, the brilliant reputations of others will disappear in thine, beyond doubt, just as the other luminaries dissolve in the splendour of the sunlight.

98. 'Even now this superhuman fact of thine is praisingly approved by the Yakshas, the Gandharvas, the snakes, and by the Devas, Vâsava[1] included.'

After so speaking, *S*akra reassumed his own brilliant figure and made himself known to the Bodhisattva. Which being done, he said:

99. 'To thee I now give back Madrî, thy wife.
 Where else should moonshine stay but with the moon?

100. 'Nor shouldst thou be anxious about the separation from thy son and daughter, nor grieve for the loss of thy royal dignity. Before long thy father will come to thee, accompanied by both thy children, and provide his kingdom with a protector, re-establishing thee in thy high rank.'

Having said these words, *S*akra disappeared on the spot.

And that Brâhman, in consequence of *S*akra's power, brought the children of the Bodhisattva to the very land of *S*ibi. And when the *S*ibis and Sa*m*gaya, their king, heard of the Bodhisattva's performance of the greatest compassion, hard to be done by others, their hearts became soft with tenderness. They redeemed the children from the hand of the Brâhman, and having obtained the pardon of Vi*s*vantara, led him back and reinstated him in his royal dignity.

[In this way, then, the behaviour of a Bodhisattva is exceedingly marvellous. For this reason such distinguished beings as strive for that state, must not be despised or hindered. This story is also to be adduced, when discoursing on the Tathâgata and when treating of listening with attention to the preaching of the Law.]

---

[1] Vâsava is another name of *S*akra.

Visvantara's birth being the last but one of the Lord, the person of that charitable king is held very high among Buddhists. His largesses are also considered to constitute the highest degree of practising the pâramitâ of charity. In the memorable night which preceded his attainment of the Buddhahood, the Sâkya prince had but to refer to his actions in the Visvantara-existence to demonstrate his having fulfilled that pâramitâ. In the Pâli Gâtaka that existence forms the subject-matter of the longest and last tale of the collection, but since it is the last, it is still unpublished; its contents, however, have been communicated by Spence Hardy in his 'Manual of Budhism' (pp. 118–127 of the second edition). From hence Prof. Kern borrowed his exposition of the tale in his Geschiedenis van het Buddhisme, I, pp. 303–317, to which he added copious notes with the object of exploring and expounding the mythological substratum which underlies it. It is curious to compare the redaction of the Pâli Gâtaka with that of Sûra. The latter omitted purposely, it seems, some particulars, for instance, the name of the old Brâhman, that of the mother of Visvantara, and the etymology of his name; his narration is different in some slight details. But the main features are the same, likewise in the redaction of the Kariyâpi/aka, where Visvantara's story is No. 9 of the dânaparamitâ and is told in 58 slokas. From this version it appears that the earthquake, caused by the great liberality of the prince, is something most essential; or rather the earthquakes, for this miracle occurred seven times, once, when he took the determination [not mentioned by Sûra] of giving his heart, eyes, flesh or blood, if requested; secondly, after the gift of the white elephant; thirdly, when he had made his great largesses preceding his withdrawal to Mount Vaṅka; fourthly and fifthly, after giving his children and his wife; the sixth time was when he met again with his father and mother in the forest; the seventh at his entrance in his capital. The sevenfold earthquake is also discussed in the Milinda Pañha, 119 foll. Cp. also the parallel performance told of the Bodhisattva, who afterwards was Maṅgala Buddha (Fausb. Gât. I, p. 31, translated by Rhys Davids, Birth-Stories, I, p. 33).

In Kshemendra's Avadânakalpalatâ the story of Visvantara is No. 23, not yet published.

X. THE STORY OF THE SACRIFICE.

Those whose hearts are pure do not act up to the enticement of the wicked. Knowing this, pure-heartedness is to be striven after. This will be taught by the following.

Long ago the Bodhisattva, it is said, was a king who had obtained his kingdom in the order of hereditary succession. He had reached this state as the effect of his merit, and ruled his realm in peace, not disturbed by any rival, his sovereignty being universally acknowledged. His country was free from any kind of annoyance, vexation or disaster, both his home relations and those with foreign countries being quiet in every respect; and all his vassals obeyed his commands.

1. This monarch having subdued the passions, his enemies, felt no inclination for such profits as are to be blamed when enjoyed, but was with his whole heart intent on promoting the happiness of his subjects. Holding virtuous practice (dharma) the only purpose of his actions, he behaved like a Muni.

2. For he knew the nature of mankind, that people set a high value on imitating the behaviour of the highest. For this reason, being desirous of bringing about salvation for his subjects, he was particularly attached to the due performance of his religious duties.

3. He practised almsgiving, kept strictly the precepts of moral conduct (sîla), cultivated forbearance, strove for the benefit of the creatures. His mild countenance being in accordance with his thoughts devoted to the happiness of his subjects, he appeared like the embodied Dharma.

Now it once happened that, though protected by his arm, his realm, both in consequence of the faulty actions of its inhabitants and inadvertence on the part of the angels charged with the care of rain, was afflicted in several districts by drought and the troublesome effects of such a disaster. Upon this the king, fully convinced that this plague had been brought about by the violation of righteousness by himself or his subjects, and taking much to heart the distress of his people, whose welfare was the constant object of his thoughts and cares, took the advice of men of acknowledged competence, who were reputed for their knowledge in matters of religion. So keeping counsel with the elders among the Brâhmans, headed by his family priest (purohita) and his ministers, he asked them for some means of putting an end to that calamity. Now they, believing a solemn sacrifice as is enjoined by the Veda to be a cause of abundant rain, explained to him that he must perform such a sacrifice of a frightful character, inasmuch as it requires the massacre of many hundreds of living beings. But after being informed of everything concerning such a slaughter as is prescribed for the sacrifice, his innate compassionateness forbade him to approve of their advice in his heart; yet out of civility, unwilling to offend them by harsh words of refusal, he slipped over this point, turning the conversation upon other topics. They, on the other hand, no sooner caught the opportunity of conversing with the king on matters of religion, than they once more admonished him to accomplish the sacrifice, for they did not understand his deeply hidden mind.

4. 'You constantly take care not to neglect the proper time of performing your different royal duties, established for the sake of obtaining the possession of land and ruling it. The due order of these actions of yours is in agreement with the precepts of Righteousness (dharma).

5. 'How then is this that you who (in all other respects) are so clever in the observance of the triad (of dharma, artha, and kâma), bearing your bow to defend the good of your people, are so careless and almost sluggish as to that bridge to the world of the Devas, the name of which is 'sacrifice'?

6. 'Like servants, the kings (your vassals) revere your commands, thinking them to be the surest gage of success. Now the time is come, O destroyer of your foes, to gather by means of sacrifice superior blessings, which are to procure for you a shining glory.

7, 8. 'Certainly, that holiness which is the requisite for a dikshita[1] is already yours, by reason of your

---

[1] Before undertaking the performance of a great sacrifice, its performer has to be purified by the initiatory ceremony of dikshâ. From that time till the final bath or avabhrîtha at the close of the sacrifice he is called a dikshita, and bound to the observance of many detailed prescriptions about his food, dress, residence, and his whole mode of living.

habitual practice of charity and your strictness in observing the restraint (of good conduct). Nevertheless, it would be fit for you to discharge your debt to the Devas[1] by such sacrifices as are the subject-matter of the Veda. The deities being satisfied by duly and faultlessly performed sacrifice, honour the creatures in return by (sending) rain. Thus considering, take to mind the welfare of your subjects and your own, and consent to the performance of a regular sacrifice, which will enhance your glory.'

Thereupon he entered upon this thought: 'Very badly guarded is my poor person indeed, being given in trust to such leaders. While faithfully believing and loving the Law, I should uproot my virtue of tenderheartedness by reliance upon the words of others. For, truly,

9. 'Those who are reputed among men to be the best refuge, are the very persons who intend to do harm, borrowing their arguments from the Law. Alas! such a man who follows the wrong path shown by them, will soon find himself driven to straits, for he will be surrounded by evils.

10. 'What connection may there be, forsooth, between righteousness and injuring animals? How may residence in the world of the Devas or propitiation of the deities have anything to do with the murder of victims?

11, 12. 'The animal slaughtered according to the rites with the prescribed prayers, as if those sacred formulae were so many darts to wound it, goes to heaven, they say, and with this object it is killed. In this way that action is interpreted to be done according to the Law. Yet it is a lie. For how is it possible that in the next world one should reap the fruits of what has been done by others? And by what reason

---

[1] By sacrifice, is the saying of the Hindus, man pays his debts to the Devas, by the Srâddha and by offspring to his ancestors, by study and penance to the rishis or old sages, by benevolence and kindness to men. See, for instance, Mhbh. I, 120, 17 foll.; Buddhakarita IX, 55.

X. THE STORY OF THE SACRIFICE. 97

will the sacrificial animal mount to heaven? though he has not abstained from wicked actions, though he has not devoted himself to the practice of good ones, simply because he has been killed in sacrifice, and not on the ground of his own actions?

13. 'And should the victim killed in sacrifice really go to heaven, should we not expect the Brâhmans to offer themselves to be immolated in sacrifice? A similar practice, however, is nowhere seen among them. Who, then, may take to heart the advice proffered by these counsellors?

14. 'As to the Celestials, should we believe that they who are wont to enjoy the fair ambrosia of incomparable scent, flavour, magnificence, and effective power, served to them by the beautiful Apsarasas, would abandon it to delight in the slaughter of a pitiable victim, that they might feast on the omentum and such other parts of his body as are offered to them in sacrifice?

'Therefore, it is the proper time to act so and so.' Having thus made up his mind, the king feigned to be eager to undertake the sacrifice; and in approval of their words he spoke to them in this manner: 'Verily, well protected am I, well gratified, having such counsellors as Your Lordships are, thus bent on securing my happiness! Therefore I will have a human sacrifice (purushamedha) of a thousand victims performed. Let my officials, each in his sphere of business, be ordered to bring together the requisites necessary for that purpose. Let also an inquiry be made of the most fitting ground whereon to raise the tents and other buildings for the sattra[1]. Further, the proper time for the sacrifice must be fixed (by the astrologers) examining the auspicious lunar days, karanas, muhûrtas, and constellations.' The purohita answered: 'In order to succeed in your enterprise, Your Majesty ought to take the avabhrïtha (final

---

[1] This is the appellation of great Soma-sacrifices lasting for many days, sometimes even for years.

bath) at the end of one sacrifice; after which you may successively undertake the others. For if the thousand human victims were to be seized at once, your subjects, to be sure, would blame you and be stirred up to great agitation on their account.' These words of the purohita having been approved by the (other) Brâhmans, the king replied: 'Do not apprehend the wrath of the people, Reverends. I shall take such measures as to prevent any agitation among my subjects.'

After this the king convoked an assembly of the townsmen and the landsmen, and said: 'I intend to perform a human sacrifice of a thousand victims. But nobody behaving honestly is fit to be designated for immolation on my part. With this in mind, I give you this advice: Whomsoever of you I shall henceforward perceive transgressing the boundaries of moral conduct, despising my royal will, him will I order to be caught to be a victim at my sacrifice, thinking such a one the stain of his family and a danger to my country. With the object of carrying this resolution into effect, I shall cause you to be observed by faultless and sharp-sighted emissaries, who have shaken off sleepy carelessness and will report to me concerning your conduct.'

Then the foremost of the assembly, folding their hands and bringing them to their foreheads, spoke:

15, 16. 'Your Majesty, all your actions tend to the happiness of your subjects, what reason can there be to despise you on that account? Even (god) Brahmâ cannot but sanction your behaviour. Your Majesty, who is the authority of the virtuous, be our highest authority. For this reason anything which pleases Your Majesty must please us, too. Indeed, you are pleased with nothing else but our enjoyment and our good.'

After the notables both of the town and the country had accepted his command in this manner, the king dispersed about his towns and all over his country officers, notified as such by their outward appearance to the people, with the charge of laying hold of the evildoers, and everywhere he ordered proclamations to be made by beat of drum day after day, of this kind:

17. 'The king, a granter of security as he is, warrants safety to every one who constantly cultivates honesty and good conduct, in short, to the virtuous. Yet, intending to perform a human sacrifice for the benefit of his subjects, he wants human victims by thousands to be taken out of those who delight in misconduct.

18. 'Therefore, whosoever henceforward, licentiously indulging in misbehaviour, shall disregard the command of our monarch, which is even observed by the kings, his vassals, shall be brought to the state of a sacrificial victim by the very force of his own actions; and people shall witness his miserable suffering, when he shall pine with pain, his body being fastened to the sacrificial post.'

When the inhabitants of that realm became aware of their king's careful search after evil-doers with the aim of destining them to be victims at his sacrifice—for they heard the most frightful royal proclamation day after day and saw the king's servants, who were appointed to look out for wicked people and to seize them, appearing every now and then everywhere—they abandoned their attachment to bad conduct, and grew intent on strictly observing the moral precepts and self-control. They avoided every occasion of hatred and enmity, and settling their quarrels and differences, cherished mutual love and mutual esteem. Obedience to the words of parents and teachers, a general spirit of liberality and sharing with others, hospitality, good manners, modesty, prevailed among them. In short, they lived as it were in the K*ri*ta Yuga.

19. The fear of death had awakened in them thoughts of the next world; the risk of tarnishing the honour of their families had stirred their care of guarding their reputation; the great purity of their hearts had strengthened their sense of shame. These factors being at work, people were soon distinguished by their spotless behaviour.

20. Even though every one became more than ever intent on keeping a righteous conduct, still the king's servants did not diminish their watchfulness in the pursuit of the evildoers. This also contributed to prevent people from falling short of righteousness.

21. The king, learning from his emissaries this state of things in his realm, felt extremely rejoiced. He bestowed rich presents on those messengers as a reward for the good news they told him, and enjoined his ministers, speaking something like this:

22-24. 'The protection of my subjects is my highest desire, you know. Now, they have become worthy to be recipients of sacrificial gifts[1], and it is for the purpose of my sacrifice that I have provided this wealth. Well, I intend to accomplish my sacrifice in the manner which I have considered to be the proper one. Let every one who wishes for money, that it may be fuel for his happiness, come and accept it from my hand to his heart's content. In this way the distress and poverty, which is vexing our country, may be soon driven out. Indeed, whenever I consider my own strong determination to protect my subjects and the great assistance I derive from you, my excellent companions in that task, it often seems to me as though those sufferings of my people, by exciting my anger, were burning in my mind like a blazing fire.'

The ministers accepted the royal command and anon went to execute it. They ordered alms-halls to be established in all villages, towns, and markets, likewise at all stations on the roads. This being done, they caused all who begged in order to satisfy their wants, to be provided day after day with a gift of those objects, just as had been ordered by the king.

25. So poverty disappeared, and the people, having received wealth from the part of the king, dressed and adorned with manifold and fine garments and ornaments, exhibited the splendour of festival days.

---

[1] Viz. by the purity of their life and the holiness of their conduct.

26. The glory of the king, magnified by the eulogies of the rejoiced recipients of his gifts, spread about in all directions in the same way, as the flowerdust of the lotuses carried forth by the small waves of a lake, extends itself over a larger and larger surface.

27[1]. And after the whole people, in consequence of the wise measures taken by their ruler, had become intent on virtuous behaviour, the plagues and calamities, overpowered by the growth of all such qualities as conduce to prosperity, faded away, having lost their hold.

28. The seasons succeeded each other in due course, rejoicing everybody by their regularity, and like kings newly established, complying with the lawful order of things. Consequently the earth produced the various kinds of corn in abundance, and there was fulness of pure and blue water and lotuses in all waterbasins.

29. No epidemics afflicted mankind; the medicinal herbs possessed their efficacious virtues more than ever; the monsoons blew in due time and regularly; the planets moved along in auspicious paths.

30. Nowhere there existed any danger to be feared, either from abroad, or from within, or such as might be caused by derangements of the elements. Continuing in righteousness and self-control, cultivating good behaviour and modesty, the people of that country enjoyed as it were the prerogatives of the Krita Yuga.

By the power, then, of the king performing his sacrifice in this manner in accordance with (the precepts of) the Law, the sufferings of the indigent were put to an end together with the plagues and calamities, and the country abounded in a prosperous and thriving population offering the pleasing aspect of felicity. Accordingly people never wearied of repeating benedictions on their king and extending his renown in all directions.

---

[1] In the printed text the first line of this stanza is deficient, two syllables at the end being wanting. I think this second pâda should be restored by the insertion of *gane* after *nikhile*.

One day one of the highest royal officials, whose heart had been inclined to the (True) Belief, spoke thus to the king: 'This is a true saying, in truth.

31. 'Monarchs, because they always deal with all kinds of business, the highest, the lowest, and the intermediate, by far surpass in their wisdom any wise men.

'For, Your Majesty, you have obtained the happiness of your subjects both in this world and in the next, as the effect of your sacrifice being performed in righteousness, free from the blameable sin of animal-slaughter. The hard times are all over and the sufferings of poverty have ceased, since men have been established in the precepts of good conduct. Why use many words? Your subjects are happy.

32 [1]. 'The black antelope's skin which covers your limbs has the resemblance of the spot on the bright moon's surface, nor can the natural loveliness of your demeanour be hindered by the restraint imposed on you by your being a dikshita [2]. Your head, adorned with such hair-dress as is in compliance with the rites of the dikshâ, possesses no less lustre than when it was embellished with the splendour of the royal umbrella [3]. And, last not least, by your largesses you

---

[1] The corruptions of this stanza in the MSS. have been corrected in the edition. In some points, however, I venture to propose some alterations.

To gâtre*n*a of the MSS., gâtre na of the ed., I should prefer gâtreshu.

For mandodyamâ*h* of the MSS., mandodyama*h* of the ed., I substitute mandodyamâ, and in pâda 3, I think ke*s*ara*k*ana*s*obhâ is one word.

[2] See note on p. 95 supra. The sattra and the dikshâ continue as long as the sacrifice is being performed. The king, therefore, is still wearing the skin of the black antelope, which he put on at the time of his consecration for the sake of performing the sacrifice, since he is obliged to observe this and many other restrictions of the dikshâ. The minister says that to the pious monarch these obligations are no restraint with respect to his behaviour, which already before has been in accordance with the strictest precepts of the Law.

[3] The white umbrella has been put aside for the time of the dikshâ.

have surpassed the renown and abated the pride of the famous performer of a hundred sacrifices [1].

33. 'As a rule, O you wise ruler, the sacrifice of those who long for the attainment of some good, is a vile act, accompanied as it is by injury done to living beings. Your sacrifice, on the contrary, this monument of your glory, is in complete accordance with your lovely behaviour and your aversion to vices.

34. 'Oh! Happy are the subjects who have their protector in you! It is certain that no father could be a better guardian to his children.'

Another said:

35. 'If the wealthy practise charity, they are commonly impelled to do so by the hopes they put in the cultivation of that virtue; good conduct, too, may be accounted for by the wish to obtain high regard among men or the desire of reaching heaven after death. But such a practice of both, as is seen in your skill in securing the benefit of others, cannot be found but in those who are accomplished both in learning and in virtuous exertions.'

In such a way, then, those whose hearts are pure do not act up to the enticement of the wicked. Knowing this, pure-heartedness is to be striven after.

[In the spiritual lessons for princes, also, this is to be said:

'Who to his subjects wishing good, himself exerts,
Thus brings about salvation, glory, happiness.
No other should be of a king the business.'

And it may be added as follows: '(The prince) who strives after material prosperity, ought to act in accordance with the precepts of religion, thinking a religious conduct of his subjects to be the source of prosperity.'

---

[1] Viz. Sakra, the Lord of the Devas. Here he is called *satayagvan*, which is well-nigh synonymous with his common epithet of *sata-kratu*.

Further this is here to be said: 'Injuring animals never tends to bliss, but charity, self-restraint, continence and the like have this power; for this reason he who longs for bliss must devote himself to these virtues.' And also when discoursing on the Tathâgata: 'In this manner the Lord showed his inclination to care for the interests of the world, when he was still in his previous existences.']

This story is not met with elsewhere, it seems, at least in this shape. No. 50 of the Pâli Gâtaka is told with the same intention but in a different manner. The resolve of the Bodhisattva and his stopping bloody sacrifices is better accounted for in our text.

XI. THE STORY OF SAKRA.

(Comp. Fausb., *Gât.* I, p. 202, translated by Rhys Davids, *Buddhist Birth Stories,* pp. 284–287.)

Neither adversity nor the brilliancy of sovereign power can relax in the high-minded the virtue of compassion towards living beings. This will be taught now.

In the time when the Bodhisattva, having well practised meritorious actions for a long time, and having come into possession of the virtues of charity, self-restraint, continence and compassion, was directing his extraordinary performances for the benefit of others, once, it is said, he became Sakra, the Lord of the Devas.

1. The magnificence of the Chief of the Celestials shone in a higher degree and displayed a greater majesty, since that rank had fallen to his share. Something analogous may be seen, when a palace adorned by a covering of fresh stucco is 'made resplendent by the moonbeams.

2. The rich lustre of that mighty state, to conquer which the sons of Diti dared push forward against the impetuous advance of the world-elephants and expose their breasts to their pestle-like tusks, that brilliancy was his. But though he easily enjoyed that happiness

at his command, nevertheless, that bliss did not stain his heart with pride.

Ruling heaven and earth in the proper manner, he acquired splendid glory, which pervaded the whole universe. Now the Demons[1] could not bear the renown nor the very wonderful bliss which he enjoyed, and waged war against him. They marched to his encounter to fight him with an enormous army of elephants, chariots, horsemen and footmen, being the more terrible, as they were drawn up in the proud array of battle and made a noise as awful as that of the wild Ocean. Through the glittering blaze of their various kinds of offensive and defensive weapons they hardly suffered themselves to be looked at.

3. He for his part, though attached to the precepts of righteousness, felt however within his heart the disposition to indulge in the frenzy of fighting. He was prompted to do so by the pride of his enemies, by the danger of his own men, unpleasantly interrupted in their peaceful sport, also by the regard of his majesty and of the traditional line of conduct along the path of political wisdom.

So he mounted his excellent golden chariot, to which a thousand excellent horses were put. This chariot was decorated in front with a beautiful, high-floating banner which bore a figure in the attire of an Arhat[2] for its emblem. Its outer appearance was exceedingly brilliant, owing to the lustre reflected by the manifold precious stones and jewels that adorned it, and to the brightness which irradiated its flanks and which proceeded from the different flaming weapons, sharp-pointed and well-disposed to be ready for use, on both sides of the chariot. On the inside it was covered with a fine

---

[1] The spirits of darkness, called Daityas (sons of Diti) or Dânavas (sons of Danu) or Asuras.

[2] It is curious to see this Sakra of the Buddhists making profession in this manner of his Buddhistical faith. If this trait is an old one, Sakra is here represented as a digambara, as he in fact is. The Sabdaratnâvalî gives Arha as a name of Indra; see Petr. Dict. s. v. arha 2).

white blanket. Standing on it and surrounded by his great divine host of different arms, elephants, chariots, horse and foot, the Great Being met the forces of the Demons just on the border-line of the Ocean.

4. Then a great battle took place, destructive of the firmness of the timid as well as of the shields and mail-coats pierced by the strokes of the weapons with which they fought each other.

5, 6. Various cries were heard in the tumult of that struggle. Stay! Not in this manner! Here! Look out! Where are you now? You will not escape me! Strike! You are a dead man! So challenging one another they fought. And this noise mixing with the clashing and crashing of the arms all over the battle-field and the sound of the drums, made Heaven shake and almost burst.

7. The elephants on both sides, rushing on each other with great fury increased by the smell of the flowing juice, offered the frightful spectacle of mountains swept along by the wind of a world-destroying period.

8. Like portentous clouds, the chariots swept over the field, their floating standards resembling the lightning, and the rattling noise they made being as the roaring of the thunder.

9. Sharp arrows were flying over both armies, and fell down amidst the warriors of both the Devas and the Demons, hitting banners and royal umbrellas, bows and spears, shields and cuirasses, and the heads of men.

10. At the end the army of Sakra took to flight, frightened by the fiery swords and arrows of the Demons. The Lord of the Celestials alone held still the field, barring with his chariot the host of his enemies.

When Mâtali, the charioteer of the Lord of the Devas, perceived that the army of the Demons, high-spirited and overjoyed, was coming over them with a tremendous noise of loud warcries and shouts of victory, whereas the army of the Devas was almost intent on flight, he thought it was now the proper time to retreat, and so he turned the chariot of the Ruler of the Devas. While they were making the ascent[1], Sakra, the Lord of the Devas, caught sight of some eagle-nests which were placed on a silk-cotton tree just in the line of direction of the chariot-pole, so that they must needs be crushed by it. No sooner had he seen them, than seized with compassion he said to Mâtali, his charioteer:

11. 'The birds' nests on this silk-cotton tree are filled with not yet winged young ones. Drive my chariot in such a manner that these nests will not fall down crushed by the chariot-pole.'

Mâtali answered: 'In the meanwhile the crowds of the Demons will overtake us, sir.'

Sakra said: 'Never mind. Do you but take the proper care in avoiding these eagle-nests.' Upon which Mâtali answered:

12. 'Nothing short of turning the chariot can save the birds, O Lotus-eyed One. But we have at our heels yon host of foes who after a long time are at last getting the better of the Devas.'

At this moment Sakra, the Lord of the Devas, moved by the utmost compassion, showed his extraordinary goodness of heart and firmness of intention.

13. 'Well then,' said he, 'turn the chariot. Better is it for me to die by the terrible club-strokes of the chiefs of the Demons than to live blameful and dishonoured, if I should have murdered those poor terror-stricken creatures.'

Mâtali promised to do so, and turned his car, drawn by a thousand horses.

14. Now the foes who had witnessed his heroism in battle, seeing that the chariot turned, were overtaken with fear, and got into confusion. Their ranks gave way like dark rain-clouds driven away by the wind.

---

[1] Returning from the battle-field on the border of the Ocean to his residence in Heaven, Sakra must needs drive upward.

15. In the case of a defeat one single man turning his face to the enemy and barring the way of the enemy's forces, will sometimes abate the pride and haughtiness of the victors by the unexpectedness of his heroic valour.

16. The sight of the broken ranks of the hostile army encouraging the host of the Devas, made them return. For the Demons, terror-stricken and fleeing, thought no more of rallying and resisting.

17. Then the Devas, whose joy was mingled with shame, paid homage to their Lord; after which, brilliant and beautiful by the radiance of victory, he quietly returned from the battle-field to his city, where his zenana impatiently longed for him.

In this way was the victory gained in that battle. It is for this reason that the saying goes:

18. The low-minded do wicked actions in consequence of their cruelty. Average men, though pitiful, will do so, when come into distress. But the virtuous, even when in danger of life, are as little capable of transgressing their proper line of conduct as the Ocean its boundary.

[In this way the Lord did long ago protect animal life even at the risk of his own and of the loss of the Celestial sway. Keeping then in mind that it does not at all befit a wise man to offend living beings, much less to sin against them, a pious man must be intent on practising compassion towards the creatures. And the saying that Dharma in truth watches him who walks in righteousness (dharma)[1], is to be propounded here too. Likewise this (story) may be adduced when discoursing on the Tathâgata, and when treating of listening with attention to the preaching of the Law.]

---

[1] We have here a remarkable quotation from the Holy Writ of Northern Buddhism. The wording of this sentence in the original: dharmo ha vai rakshati dharmakâri*n*am, is the exact Sanskrit counterpart of the first pâda of a well-known Pâli stanza uttered by

XII. THE STORY OF THE BRÂHMAN.

What forbids the virtuous to transgress the boundary of good behaviour is the very shame of the Self within their hearts. This will be taught by the following.

Once the Bodhisattva, it is told, came to life in an illustrious family of Brâhmans, well-reputed both on account of their ancestry and their conduct. They were highly esteemed and renowned, observing their traditional customs and setting a high value on good education and good manners. Having received in due order the different sacraments: garbhâdhâna, pum-savana, sîmantonnayana, gâtakarma, and the rest, he dwelt at his teacher's, who was a Brâhman distinguished by the superiority of his learning, by his birth, and by his practice of the customary conduct, with the object of studying the Veda.

1. His quickness in mastering and retaining the texts he was taught, his devoted obedience for which his family had always been reputed—a virtue his correctness of conduct embellished by tranquillity, a rare ornament in a youth, made him obtain the love and affection of his teacher.

2. For virtues practised without interruption are magic charms to win the affection even of such as are burnt by the fire of hatred, how much more of the sound-hearted.

Now his teacher, in the intervals of rest from sacred study, with the object of trying the morals of all his disciples, was used to tell them frequently of his own sufferings, the effect of his poverty.

3. 'To him no help his family affords,
   No joy is his, not e'en on holidays,
   And wretched alms-requesting makes him sick.
   A pauper's wish, how may it be fulfill'd?

---

the Lord (see Fausböll, Gâtaka I, p. 31; IV, p. 54, and the other passages quoted there):

    Dhammo have rakkhati dhammakârim
    Dhammo sukinno sukham âvahâti
    Esânisamso dhamme sukinne
    Na duggatim gakkhati dhammakâri.

4. 'The state of a moneyless man is the home of disregard, the abode of toil. And a very hard condition it is, devoid of pleasure, abounding in scantiness, and incessantly afflicting like a calamity.'

Like excellent horses, pricked with spurs, his disciples, very much moved by their attachment to their spiritual teacher, did their utmost to deliver to him ever more and better prepared food from their daily begging round. But he said to them: 'Good sirs, do not exert yourselves in this way. No offerings of food obtained by daily begging will diminish the distress of poverty to anybody. If you cannot bear my hardship, you ought rather to apply these your efforts to gaining wealth. Doing thus, you would act in the proper manner. Why do I say so?

5. 'Hunger is driven away by food, and thirst by water. The spell-uttering voice together with medicine expels illnesses. But poverty's pain is destroyed by wealth, that cause of being honoured by one's kinsmen.'

The pupils answered: 'What can we do for you? Unhappy we, that the extent of our power is so small. Moreover,

6, 7. 'If wealth, like food, were obtained by begging, we would not allow you to suffer by poverty in this degree, master. But the case is this. The proper, though weak, means for Brâhmans of gaining wealth is receiving gifts: and people here are not charitable. So we are powerless, and by this impotency we are smitten with grief.'

The teacher replied: 'But there are still other expedients for earning money, and they are explained in the law-books. Yet, my strength being exhausted by old age, I am not fit to put them into effect.'

The disciples said: 'But our strength is not impaired by old age, master. If, then, you think us capable of acting upon those precepts of the law-books, inform us of them, that we may requite you for your labour of teaching us.'

The teacher said: 'No, such means of earning money are hardly available, indeed, for young men, whose mind is too loose to carry out a strong resolution. Nevertheless, if Your Honours urge me, well[1], you may learn from me what one of the said expedients is.

8. 'In the law-precepts for the time of distress[2] theft is an approved livelihood for Brâhmans; and poverty, I suppose, is the extreme distress in this world. Consequently, it is no sin for us to enjoy the wealth of others, and the whole of these goods belongs, of a truth, to the Brâhmans.

9. 'Men such as you, would doubtlessly be able to seize on wealth even by violence. You should, however, not practise that mode of taking, minding your reputation. Therefore, you must show your energy in lonely places and times.'

By such language he loosened the bridle from his disciples. Accordingly they exclaimed 'Very well,' approving his bad words, as if they were good, and all of them engaged themselves to do so, all—save the Bodhisattva.

10. Him his innate goodness forbade to comply with the teacher's advice, and compelled him on the contrary to oppose it without delay, though it had been accepted as a duty by the other pupils.

Ashamed and with downcast looks he heaved a soft sigh and remained silent. The teacher perceived that the Bodhisattva did not approve of that fashion of making money, without, however, crying it down; and as he had a high regard for the virtue of that Great Being, he entered upon this reflection: 'For what reason does he disapprove of theft? Is it want of

---

[1] Instead of sâdhuh we must read sâdhu.
[2] Read âpaddharme steyam, &c. The âpaddharma substitutes for the precepts of right conduct and right livelihood some others to be followed in times of distress, if the primary ones cannot be observed. The permission to Brâhmans to make money by theft is of course not lawful; it is inferred from the well-known pretension of the Brâhmanical caste to be owners of the whole earth. Even Sarvilaka, the thief in the Mrikkhakatikâ, does not venture to defend his deeds by arguments borrowed from the law-books; he avows that theft is blameable, 'I blame it,' says he, 'and yet I do it.'

courage or disaffection towards me? Or does he really know it to be a wicked action?' Then in order to prompt him to open his true disposition of mind, he spoke in this way to the Bodhisattva: 'Say, noble Brâhman,

11. 'Those twice-born men, incapable of bearing my misfortune, are willing to resort to the course of life followed by the energetic and the heroes; but in you I find nothing but indolence and dullness. Surely, it is not you who are affected by our distress.

12. 'My suffering is evident. Its whole extent lies open to your eyes. I have made it plain by speech. Notwithstanding this, you are keeping quiet! How is it that your mind is undisturbed and untouched by sorrow?'

Upon this the Bodhisattva, after making his respectful salute to the teacher, said quite alarmed: 'Heaven forbid such feelings! Verily, it is not want of affection or hard-heartedness which causes me to keep apart, nor am I unmoved by the sufferings of my teacher, but I think the mode of acting which my master has shown us, cannot be put into practice. It is impossible, indeed, to commit a wicked action without being seen. Why? Because there does not exist anything like loneliness.

13, 14. 'No, loneliness is not to be found anywhere in the world for the evildoer. Are not the invisible Beings and the purified Munis, whose eye is endowed with divine power, lookers-on of men's actions? Not seeing them, the fool thinks himself alone and commits sin [1].

15. 'But I know no lonely place at all. Wheresoever I do not see anybody else, is such a place for that reason empty of my own Self?

16, 17. 'And of a bad action my Self is a witness far more sharp-sighted than any other person. Another may perchance perceive me, or he may not, his mind being occupied with his own business, but

---

[1] Cp. Manu VIII, 85; Mahâbhârata (ed. Bombay) I, 74, 39.

my Self, eagerly surrendering my whole mind to passion, knows with certainty that I am doing evil.

'For this reason, then, I keep aloof from the others.' And understanding that his teacher was fully appeased, the Bodhisattva continued :

18. 'Nor can I persuade myself into the belief that you would deceive us in this way for the sake of obtaining wealth. Who, indeed, knowing the difference between virtue and vice, would allow himself to be seduced by the pursuit of wealth to oppression of virtue ?

'As to my own determination, I will inform you of it.

19. 'Better is it to take the almsbowl and vile garments, beholding the opulence of the mansions of one's enemies, than to bend one's mind shamelessly to the murder of Righteousness, be it even with the goal of attaining the Sovereignty of the Devas!'

At these words his teacher rapt with joy and admiration, rising from his seat, embraced him, and said to him : 'Very well, very well, my son! well-said, well-said, noble Brâhman! This is becoming to your keen intellect adorned by tranquillity.

20. 'Fools leave the path of duty, stirred by any motive whatever, but the virtuous do not allow themselves to be led astray even in the greatest distress; penance, learning, and wisdom being their wealth.

21. 'As the moon rising in autumn adorns the firmament, so you are the ornament of your entirely spotless family. For you the sacred texts you have been taught have their full import; that you have well understood them is made plain by your good behaviour; and my labour is crowned with success, it has not been fruitless.'

So, then, it is the very shame of the Self within their hearts that prevents the virtuous from transgressing the boundary of good behaviour. [For this reason the pious man (ârya) ought to have a powerful shelter in shame. (This story) is to be adduced on account

I

of such texts[1] as this: 'In this way the faithful votary of our creed (āryaśrâvaka), being well-guarded by the trench of his shame, avoids what is noxious and fosters what is wholesome.' Likewise in texts dealing with the feeling of shame and the regard of public opinion.]

The story of the Brâhman has the appearance of being the clumsy invention of some monk engaged in giving lessons of morality and in want of some story to illustrate the sinfulness of theft. I can scarcely believe it forms part of the old stock of traditional tales and folklore, as little as the story of the sacrifice (X). In its parallel in the Pâli *G*âtaka, No. 305, sîlavîma*m*sanagâtaka (Fausb. III, pp. 18, 19), the old teacher's trial of his disciples is better accounted for.

XIII. THE STORY OF UNMÂDAYANTÎ.

(Cp. Pâli *G*âtaka, No. 529; Fausb. V, 210–227.)

Even when sick with heavy sorrow, the virtuous are disinclined to follow the road of the low-minded, being prevented from such actions by the firmness of their constancy[2]. This will be taught as follows.

In the time when the Bodhisattva by the practice of his surpassing virtues, veracity, liberality, tranquillity of mind, wisdom &c., was exerting himself for the benefit of the creatures, he was, it is said, a king of the Sibis, behaving like the embodied Righteousness and Discipline, and being intent on promoting the welfare of his subjects like a father.

1. Being withheld from sinful actions and put in the possession of virtues by their king, (who was solicitous of their true happiness) as a father is of his son's, his people rejoiced both in this world and in the next.

2. For his administration of justice followed the path of righteousness, and made no difference between kinsmen and the rest of his subjects. It obstructed

---

[1] sûtreshu. The same term is used at the conclusion of Story XXI.
[2] Compare the note on p. 44.

XIII. THE STORY OF UNMÂDAYANTÎ.

for his people the road of wickedness, and accordingly became, so to speak, a flowery ladder to Heaven.

3. Perceiving the welfare of the creatures to be the effect of righteousness, this ruler of men knew no other purpose than this. With all his heart he delighted in the path of righteousness, and did not allow others to violate its precepts.

Now in the capital of that king one of the principal townsmen had a daughter of surpassing beauty, the acknowledged pearl of womanhood. The ravishing loveliness of her figure and charms made her appear like the embodied goddess Srî or Rati or one of the Apsarasas.

4. No one—except only the passionless—having got the sight of her, was able to withdraw his looks from her figure, as she fascinated by her beauty the eyes of all who beheld her.

And for this reason her relations called her Unmâdayantî ('she who makes mad').

Now her father apprised the king of the fact of his having such a daughter: 'Your Majesty, the very pearl of womanhood has appeared in your realm. May Your Majesty therefore deign to decide whether you will accept her as a wife or renounce her.' Then the king ordered some Brâhmans knowing the auspicious marks of women, to go and see the maiden, whether she would be a suitable wife for him or not. The father of Unmâdayantî led them to his house, and ordered his daughter to attend upon his guests herself. She said she would do so, and commenced to attend upon them at table in the proper manner. But no sooner did those Brâhmans

5. Behold her, than their eyes were compelled to remain closely fixed on her face. The god of Love had subdued their firmness. They had no power over their looks and minds, and they got rid of their consciousness as if drunkenness had befallen them.

Now, as they were not able to keep their grave and modest countenance nor their imperturbability, still less to take their meal, the householder removed his daughter out of the reach of their looks and attended himself on the Brâhmans. Afterwards they took their leave and went off. And they considered thus: 'The lovely beauty of that maiden is, in truth, of an exceedingly enchanting nature, it acts like a very magic spell. For this reason it is not suitable for the king to see her, much less to make her his queen. Having grown mad by her splendid beauty, as he doubtless would, he would abate his zeal for performing his religious and political duties, and his neglect of duly observing his royal occupations would prove of evil consequence to his subjects, inasmuch as it would obstruct the sources of their profit and welfare.

6. 'The sight of her would be sufficient to put an obstacle in the way even of Munis striving after perfect wisdom, how much more may it obstruct the success of a young prince, who lives in pleasure, and is in the habit of directing his looks to the objects of sense.

'Therefore it is now suitable to act so and so.' Having thus made up their mind, they went to the king's presence at a convenient time and reported this to him: 'We have seen that maiden, great king. She is a beauty and possesses lovely charms, but no more; she has inauspicious marks, the foretokens of ruin and ill luck. For this reason Your Majesty ought not even to see her, how can there be question about wedding her?

7. 'A reprehensible wife veils both the glory and the opulence of two families; just as a cloudy, moon-concealing night hides the beauty and the arrangement of all things upon earth and in heaven.'

Thus informed, the monarch imagining her to have inauspicious marks and not to suit his family, no more desired to possess her; and the householder, her father, knowing the king's disaffection, married his daughter to one Abhipâraga, officer of that very king.

Now once, on the occasion of the Kaumudî-festival, it happened that the king desired to contemplate the splendour of that festivity in his capital. He mounted his royal chariot and took a drive through the town, which exhibited a pleasant aspect. Its streets and squares had been sprinkled and cleansed; their white ground was strewed with many-coloured flowers; gay flags and banners were floating aloft; everywhere there was dancing and singing, representations of burlesques, ballets and music; the mingled scents of flowers, incense, odoriferous powders, perfumes, garlands, strong liquors, also of the perfumed water and the ointments used in ablutions, filled the air with fragrance; lovely articles were being exposed for sale; the principal streets were thronged by a merry crowd of townsmen and landsmen in their best dress. While making this tour, the king came near the house of Abhipâraga. Now Unmâdayantî, who was angry with the king because he had spurned her—had she not inauspicious marks?—feigning curiosity to see him, placed herself in his way, illuminating by her brilliant figure the flat roof of her house, as a flash of lightning does the top of a cloud; he at least, she thought within her heart, must be able to keep the firmness of his mind and the power over his senses unshaken by the sight of an inauspicious person such as I am. Accordingly, while the king, curious to behold the splendour of his capital, was looking around, his eye suddenly fell upon her, when she was facing him. On beholding her, the monarch,

8, 9. Though his eyes were accustomed to the attraction of the wanton graces of the beauties in his zenana; though, owing to his attachment to the path of virtue, his disposition was a modest one, and he had exercised himself in subduing his organs of sense; though he possessed in a high degree the virtue of constancy; though he had a strong feeling of shame and his looks were afraid of the looks of young women belonging to others—notwithstanding this, he could not prevent the Love-god's triumph, and gazed a long gaze at that woman, powerless to turn his eyes from her face.

10. 'Is she perhaps the embodied Kaumudî or the Deity of that house? is she an Apsaras or a Demoness? For it is no human figure she has.'

Thus the king considered and could not look enough at her; and the chariot passing away did not comply with his heart's desire. He went back to his palace, like one absent-minded, thinking of nothing but her; his firmness of mind had been confounded by Manmatha. So he asked his charioteer Sunanda secretly:

11. 'Do you know, whose is the house that was surrounded by a white wall, and who is she whose beauty did shine there like lightning in a white cloud?'

The charioteer answered: 'Your Majesty has a high official named Abhipâraga. His is that house, and she is his wife, a daughter to Kiri/avatsa, of herself she is called Unmâdayantî.' After hearing this, the thought that she was the wife of another caused his heart to faint, and sorrowful meditation made his eyes rigid. Often he heaved long and deep sighs, and thinking of nothing but her, said in a low voice to himself:

12. 'Alas! She bears her soft and lovely-sounding name rightly, indeed. This sweet-smiling Unmâdayantî has made me almost mad.

13. 'I would forget her, yet I see her always in my mind. For my thoughts are with her, or rather it is she who is the ruler of my mind.

14. 'And this weakness of mind is mine concerning the wife of another! No doubt, I am mad; shame, it seems, has left me, just as sleep has.

15. 'While absorbed in representing to myself with rapture the grace of her features, her smiles, her looks, O that sudden sound of the metal plate[1], reminding me by its bold tone of the regular order of my royal business, rouses my wrath.'

In such a way the king's firmness was shaken by the power of passionate love. And although he endeavoured to compose his mind, his languishing appearance and emaciating body, his frequent absorption

---

[1] Strokes on a metal plate, sounding every half-hour, are to announce the time to the king.

in thoughts together with his sighs indicated very clearly his state of being in love.

16. However great his firmness was in disguising his heart's disease, it manifested itself in his countenance, his eyes rigid from thoughtfulness, and his emaciated limbs.

Now Abhipâraga, the king's officer, was skilled in the interpretation of the expression of the face and of such gestures as betray internal feelings. When he had observed the behaviour of his master and discovered its cause, he apprehended evil consequences from it, for he loved the king and knew the excessive power of the God of Love. So he asked the king for a secret audience; which having been granted to him, he went up to his master, and having obtained permission, thus addressed him:

17, 18. 'While engaged in worshipping the Devas to-day, O lotus-eyed ruler of men, see, a Yaksha, presenting himself before my eyes, said to me: " How is it that you ignore the king having fallen in love with Unmâdayantî?" After speaking so, he disappeared immediately, and I, solicitous on this account, approached you. If this is true, why, Your Majesty, do you show in this manner your disaffection to me by your silence?

'Therefore, may Your Majesty do me the favour of accepting her from my hand.'

The king was confounded, and dared not lift up his eyes for shame. Nevertheless, even though he was in the power of Love, he did not suffer his firmness to falter, thanks to his being conversant with the Law by long and good practice, and refused that offer in plain terms. 'No, that may not be. For what reason? Hear.

19. 'I would lose my merit and I know myself not to be immortal. Further, my wicked deed would be known also to the public. Moreover, if the fire of sorrow should burn your heart because of that separation, it would erelong consume you, as fire consumes dry grass.

20. 'And such a deed, which would cause that distress in both this world and the next and would be committed for this reason by the unwise, the wise never will do, for this very reason.'

Abhipâraga answered: 'Do not fear, Your Majesty, that you will transgress the Law herein.

21. 'By assisting in the performance of a gift you will act in accordance with the Law, whereas by not receiving her from my hand you would do wrong, since you obstruct the practice of giving.

'Nor do I see in this matter any occasion of damage to the reputation of Your Majesty. Why?

22. 'This is an arrangement between us; nobody else need know of it? Do not, therefore, put in your mind the fear of blame by public opinion.

'Further, to me this will be a favour, not a source of grief. Why so?

23. 'What harm can be procured to a faithful heart by the satisfaction obtained by serving the interest of his master? For this reason you may quietly indulge in your love; do not apprehend any grief on my side.'

The king replied: 'Stop, stop! no more of that wicked reasoning.

24. 'Surely, your very great attachment to my person prevents you from understanding that the righteous action which consists in the assistance to a deed of giving does not exist in the case of every gift.

25. 'Who by exceeding attachment to my person does not heed even his own life, is my friend, dearer to me than my kinsmen. His wife I am bound to respect as a friend's.

'You do not well, therefore, enticing me to a sinful action. And what you assert, "nobody else will know of it," will it be less sinful for this reason?

26. 'How can happiness be expected for him who commits a wicked action, though unwitnessed? As little as for him who has taken poison unseen. Both the pure-sighted Celestials and the holy ascetics among men cannot fail to witness him.

'Moreover, I tell you this:

27. 'Who may in earnest believe that you do not love her, or that you will not get into harm, as soon as you have abandoned her?'

Abhipâraga said:

28. 'I am your slave, I with my wife and children. You are my master and my deity. What infringement of Law, Your Majesty, can there be, then, if you act as pleases you with respect to this your female slave? 'As to your asserting that I love her, what matters it?

29. 'Yea, my liege, she is my beloved wife, and it is for this very reason that I desire her to be given to you. He who has given in this world something dear to him, receives in the next dear objects of exceeding loveliness.

'Therefore, Your Majesty may take her.'

The king spoke: 'Oh, do not say so! It is impossible for me to do so. Why?

30. 'I should dare throw myself on a sharp sword or into a fire with blazing flames, but I shall not be able to offend against Righteousness, which I have always observed, and to which I owe my royal bliss.'

Abhipâraga said: 'If Your Majesty will not take her, because she is my wife, then myself will command her to lead the life of a harlot, whom no one is forbidden to woo. Then Your Majesty may take her.'

The king answered: 'Are you mad?

31. 'If you were to abandon your guiltless wife, you would not only incur punishment from my part, but having become an object of reproach, likewise unavoidable grief in this world and hereafter.

'Desist then; do not enforce a bad action. Rather direct your mind to justice and honesty.'

Abhipâraga said:

32. 'And if by persisting, I really were to do an action which might be in any respect a violation of Righteousness and the source of censure among men and of the loss of my happiness—be these consequences whatever they may—I fain shall front them with my breast, owing to the gladness of mind I shall feel for having promoted your happiness.

33. 'No one I know in the world is more worthy than you to be worshipped by a sacrificial offering, O most mighty ruler of the earth. Well then, with the object of increasing my merit, deign to accept, like an officiating priest, Unmâdayantî as your sacrificial fee¹.'

The king said: 'No doubt it is your great affection for me that prompts you to the effort to promote my interest without considering what is right and wrong on your side. But this very consideration induces me the more to prevent you. Verily, indifference as to the censure of men cannot at any rate be approved. Look here!

34. 'Who, neglecting Righteousness, does not mind either the censure of men or the evil consequences in the next world, will attain but this: in this world people will distrust him; and surely, after death he will be destitute of bliss.

'And therefore I press this upon your mind.

35. 'Never delight in injuring Righteousness for the sake of life². The sin you would incur would be great and unquestionable, the advantage trifling and doubtful.

'Moreover, you should consider also this.

36. 'The virtuous do not like for themselves a pleasure, procured at the expense of others, whom they have distressed by bringing them into disrepute and the like. For this reason, standing on the ground of Righteousness, I shall bear the charge of my private interests alone without causing pain to others.'

Abhipâraga replied: 'But how could there be any room for injustice here, after all, either on my side, if moved by attachment I should take care of the interest of my master, or on the side of Your Majesty receiving

---

¹ Properly speaking, giving the woman into marriage to the officiating priest at the end of a *srauta*-sacrifice as his fee (dakshi*n*â) is the second of the eight classical forms of wedding, the so-called daivo vivâha*h*.

² The meaning of this seems to be something like this: 'Do not seek after temporal pleasure here at the risk of long-lasting suffering after death.'

XIII. THE STORY OF UNMÂDAYANTÎ.

her as a present from my hand? All *S*ibis, townsmen and landsmen, would ask: what is the injustice of this deed? Therefore, be pleased to take her, Your Majesty.'

The king replied: 'Verily, you have the intense desire of assisting me. But reflect well upon this: Which of us knows the Law best, the whole of the *S*ibis, you, or I?'

Then Abhipâraga hastily answered:

37. 'Owing to your assiduous and respectful watching of the wise, and your great regard for sacred lore, and the sagacity of your mind, Your Majesty ranks with B*ri*haspati as the most competent judge in all matters taught in the sciences concerning the Triad of objects (trivarga).'

The king said: 'This being so, you ought not to mislead me in this matter. Why do I say so?

38. 'The evil and the good of the people depend on the behaviour of their rulers. For this reason, and taking into account the attachment of my subjects, I shall continue to love the Path of the Pious above all, in conformity with my reputation.

39. 'As cows go after the bull in any direction, whether the right or the wrong one, following his steps, in the very same manner the subjects imitate the behaviour of their ruler without any scruple and undauntedly.

'You must take also this into consideration.

40. 'If I should lack the power of ruling my own self, say, into what condition would I bring this people who long for protection from my side?

41. 'Thus considering and regardful of the good of my subjects, my own righteousness, and my spotless fame, I do not allow myself to submit to my passion. I am the leader of my subjects, the bull of my herd.'

Then Abhipâraga, the king's official, appeased by this constancy of the king, bowed his head and reverentially folding his hands, spoke:

42. 'Oh! excessively favoured by Destiny are these subjects, having such a ruler as you are, Illustrious King. Love of Righteousness utterly disregardful of

pleasures is to be searched for even among those who dwell in penance-groves.

43. 'In you the appellation of "great," O Mahârâga, is a brilliant ornament. For the name of a virtue, conferred upon persons devoid of virtue, has a rather harsh sound, as if used in contempt.

44. 'Nor is there any reason for me to be astonished or agitated by this grand deed of yours, who are a mine of virtues, as the sea is of jewels [1].'

In this manner, then, the virtuous, even when sick with heavy sorrow, are disinclined to follow the road of the low-minded, being prevented from such actions by the firmness of their constancy [and their being conversant with the Law by long and good practice. Thus considering, one ought to exert one's self in practising constancy and the precepts of the Law].

The tale of the maiden making mad all who see her, and the love-smitten monarch who prefers walking on the right path and even death to indulging in passion, is found also outside Buddhism. In the preface of his edition, Prof. Kern points out its being told thrice in the Kathâsaritsâgara; in the fifteenth, the thirty-third, and the ninety-first taranga. The last version, being a Vetâla-tale, is found also in the prose-work Vetâlapañkaviṃsati (Kathâ 14). Of the non-Buddhistic redactions all agree in this point, that the king at last dies from love, and that the faithful officer then kills himself. No doubt, this must be the original conclusion.

XIV. The Story of Supâraga.

(Cp. the Pâli Gâtaka, No. 463; Fausb. IV, 137-143.)

Even speaking the truth on the ground of Righteousness is sufficient to dispel calamity, what can be said more to assert the good results of observing the Law? Considering thus, one must observe the Law. This will be taught now.

In one of his Bodhisattva-existences, the Great Being was, it is said, an extremely clever steersman.

---

[1] This epithet of the sea is very common in Indian rhetorical style.

For this is the invariable nature of the Bodhisattvas, that owing to the innate acuteness of their mind, whatever branch of science or species of art they desire to know, they will in it surpass the wisest in the world. Accordingly the High-minded One possessed every quality required in such a one. Knowing the course of the celestial luminaries, he was never at a loss with respect to the regions of the sky; being perfectly acquainted with the different prognostics, the permanent, the occasional, and the miraculous ones, he was skilled in the establishment of a given time as proper or improper; by means of manifold marks, observing the fishes, the colour of the water, the species of the ground, birds, rocks, &c., he knew how to ascertain rightly the part of the sea; further he was vigilant, not subject to drowsiness and sleep, capable of enduring the fatigue of cold, heat, rain, and the like, careful and patient. So being skilled in the art of taking a ship out and bringing her home[1], he exercised the profession of one who conducts the merchants by sea to their destination. And as his navigation was very successful, he was named Supâraga[2]. The seaport where he lived bore the same name of Supâraga, which place is now known as Sûpâraga. Even in his old age, the sea-traders, longing for a prosperous voyage, applied to him, who was well-known to be an auspicious person, and entreating him in the most respectful terms, put him on their ships.

So it once happened that merchants who trafficked with Goldland, coming from Bharuka*kkh*a, longing for a prosperous voyage, touched at the town of Supâraga and requested that Great Being to embark with them. He answered them:

---

[1] The exact meaning of the Sanskrit terms âhara*n*a and apaha-ra*n*a is doubtful, but must be something like this.

[2] In the Pâli redaction he is called Suppâraka, and the seaport where he lives and from whence he undertakes his last voyage is Bharuka*kkh*a. The form Supâraga is Sanskritised wrongly, in order to fit the author's etymological fancy. See Prof. Kern's note on this passage in the various readings of his edition.

1. 'What kind of assistance do you think to find in me? Old age, having got power over me, makes my eyesight diminish[1]; in consequence of the many toils I have endured, my attentiveness has grown weak, and even in my bodily occupations I feel my strength almost gone.'

The merchants said: 'We are well acquainted with the bodily state of Your Honour. But this being so, and taking into account your inability for labour, we will not cause hardship to you nor give any task into your charge, but we want you for some other reason.

2. 'The dust touched and hallowed by your lotus-like feet will be auspicious to our ship and procure her a happy course over yonder sea, even if assailed by great danger. With this in mind we have applied to you.'

The Great Being, though subject to the infirmity of old age, went on board their vessel out of compassion. His embarkment was a cause of rejoicing for all those merchants, for they thought: 'Now we are assured of a very successful voyage.' And so they (set off, and) in course of their voyage reached that Abode of the Snakes who constitute the host of the Demons, that Pâtâla into which it is difficult to penetrate, that immense receptacle of water, the Great Ocean, which is haunted by different kinds of fishes and resounds with the murmuring of its never-quiet waves, whereas, when impelled by the power of the wind, it hurries on its billows after the whims of that element; on its bottom different sorts of ground extend, concealing manifold precious stones, and its surface is embellished by the various flower-garlands of its foam.

3. A dark-blue hue, like that of a heap of sapphires, was lying over the surface of the water, as if it were

---

[1] In the Pâli redaction Suppâraka is wholly blind. This must be the better tradition on account of his never perceiving himself, but always hearing from the traders the miraculous objects which will present themselves in this voyage.

sky melted by the glowing heat of the sunbeams, when they lost sight of the coast-line and were running over the profound ocean which surrounded them on all sides.

After they were in the open sea, it happened in the afternoon, at the time when the sun-rays begin to lose their strength, that a great and very fearful, portentous event appeared to them.

4. On a sudden the sea took a terrible aspect. A violent gale arose, causing a fearful noise of the waters, lashing their surface so that they were covered with foam scattered by the breaking billows. The whole sea was brought in commotion up from its very bottom.

5. Shaken by the hurricane, the immense masses of water were stirred up and rolled with formidable rapidity. The Ocean assumed a dreadful appearance, like that of Earth quivering with her mountains at the time of a world-destruction.

6. Like many-headed hissing serpents, clouds of a bluish-black colour with their flame-tongues of lightnings obstructed the path of the sun, and without interruption produced the terrible noise of their thunder.

7. The sun, whose network of rays was hidden by thick clouds, gradually reached the point where it set. Then darkness availing itself of the opportunity of evening-time and growing, as it were, more concrete, enveloped all around.

8, 9. Smitten on its wave-surface by the rain-darts of the showers, the sea rose up, as if in rage, and the poor ship trembled very much, as if afraid, saddening the hearts of the occupants, who manifested their different natures according to their inherent qualities. Some were overcome by affliction and stood speechless with terror, some behaved courageously and were busily working to avert the danger, and some were absorbed in prayers to their tutelar deities.

Now, the strong wind making the sea run high, the vessel drove along with the current. The merchants did not discover land for many days, nor did they observe favourable signs of the sea. The signs they saw, being new to them, made their sadness increase, and they grew perplexed by fear and dejection. But Supâraga, the Bodhisattva, comforted them, thus speaking: 'You must not wonder at the sea tossing about in a portentous state of commotion; are we not crossing the Great Ocean? There is no reasonable ground for Your Honours to indulge in affliction. Why so?

10, 11. 'It is not by dejection that mischief is warded off; therefore do not remain in low spirits. But it is by courage that those who are clever to do what is to be done surmount difficulties without difficulty. Well then, shake off that sadness and dejection, set rather to work, availing yourselves of the opportunity of working. The energy of a wise man, kindled by firmness of mind, is the hand by which success is grasped in any matter.

'Let each of you then be intent on performing his special duty.' And the merchants, in this way invigorated by the Great Being, longing for the sight of land and looking down into the sea, beheld beings who had the figure of men and looked as if they wore silver armour; they saw them diving up and down the water-surface. When they had well considered their figures and marks, they informed Supâraga of that phenomenon, expressing their amazement. 'Verily, here we meet in the great ocean with a phenomenon unheard of before. These, in truth, are

12. 'Some beings not unlike warriors of the Demons, wearing silver armour, with fierce looks and ugly noses that resemble a quadruped's hoof; it seems as if they are sporting in the ocean-water, incessantly shooting and diving up and down its surface.'

Supâraga said: 'These are no men nor demons, but fishes, to be sure. Do not be afraid of them. Still,

13. 'We are driven far off both seaports. This is the sea called Khuramâlin [= wearing hoof-garlands]. Therefore, you must try to turn back.'

But they could not veer on account of the vehemence of the high-running sea and of the strong wind, which continued to blow after them and drive the ship in the same direction. And as they advanced farther into the ocean, they perceived another sea shining with the lustre of silver and looking bright with the mass of white foam on its waves. On beholding this astonishing spectacle, they said to Supâraga:

14. 'What great sea is this, which is clothed, as it were, in fine white linen and veils its waters with its foam? It seems to bear on its surface fluid moonbeams, as it were, and to show all around a laughing face.'

Supâraga said: 'Alas! we are penetrating too far.

15. 'That is the sea Dadhimâlin [= wearing garlands of coagulated milk], called the "milk-ocean." It is not wise to go farther on, at least if it is possible to turn back.'

The merchants said: 'It is impossible, indeed, to reduce the speed of the ship, much less to change her course. She is being driven too swiftly by the current, and the wind blows contrary.'

Now, having crossed also that sea, the merchants perceived another sea, whose rolling waves were tinged with the splendour of gold resembling the red-brown colour of flames, and filled with amazement and curiosity they spoke about it to Supâraga.

16. 'It looks now as if the high, bright waves had been tinged with the brilliant hue of the rising sun. They appear to us like a great, blazing fire. Say, what sea is this and how is it named for this reason?'

Supâraga answered:

17. 'Agnimâlin [= wearing fire-garlands] is the celebrated name of this sea. It would be very prudent, indeed, if we were to turn back now.'

Thus saying the Great Being, far-seeing as he was, told them only the name of that sea, but concealed the cause of the change of colour of the water. After crossing also that sea, the merchants saw that the colour of the sea changed again; now its hue bore a resemblance to a grove of ripe kusa-grass, and its waters were illuminated with the lustre of topazes

K

and sapphires; and prompted by curiosity they asked Supâraga:

18. 'Which of the seas now appears to us? Its waters have the colour of the blades of ripe ku*s*a-grass. The breaking of its wind-stirred billows crowns it with a many-coloured foam-ornament, and makes it look as if it were overspread with flowers.'

Supâraga said: 'Say, merchants, you should now make efforts to turn back. Surely it is not advisable to go farther.

19. 'This is the sea named Ku*s*amâlin [= wearing ku*s*a-garlands]. Like an elephant not heeding the goad, it drags forcibly along with its irresistible waves, and will take away our enjoyment.'

And the merchants, not being able to turn the ship, however bravely they exerted themselves, crossed also that sea. Then perceiving another sea, the water of which had a greenish colour like that proceeding from the united brilliancy of emeralds and beryls, they asked Supâraga:

20. 'The sea we now behold has yet another appearance. Its waters have the green shine of emeralds and resemble a splendid meadow; they are adorned with foam as lovely as waterlilies. Which sea is this again?'

Upon this the Great Being, whose heart ached as he foresaw the calamity which was about to befall the merchants, heaved a long and deep sigh, and said in a low tone:

21. 'You have gone too far. It will be hard to return from hence. This sea, the Nalamâlin [= wearing reed-garlands[1]], is wellnigh at the end of the world.'

When they heard that answer, the poor merchants were utterly afflicted. Their minds lost their energy, their limbs became powerless, and sitting down in

---

[1] In the Pâli redaction this sea has the appearance of an immense reed-bed or bamboo-grove (nalavana*m* viya *k*a ve*l*uvana*m* viya *k*a), and the commentator argues that those names of grasses convey also the acceptation of some precious stones. But the stones there are of a red colour.

dull sadness, they did nothing but sigh. And after crossing that sea too, in the afternoon, when the Sun with his slackening circle of rays seemed to be about to enter the Ocean, a confused and tremendous noise, piercing both the ears and the hearts of the merchants, became audible. This noise rising from the sea may be compared to that of a sea swelling in rage, or of many thunderclaps together, or of bamboo-groves having caught fire and crackling. On hearing it, they suddenly jumped from their seats, trembling with fear and highly agitated, and examining the ocean all around, perceived that immense mass of water falling down as if over some precipice or chasm. That alarming sight filled them with the utmost fear, sadness, and dejection. They went to Supâraga, saying:

22. 'We hear a tremendous noise from afar, almost piercing our ears and crushing our minds, as if the Lord of the Rivers were angry, and this whole mass of ocean-water falls down, it seems, into an awful abyss. Say, then, what sea is that, and what do you think is best to be done now?'

Then the Great Being, agitated, said: 'Alas! alas!' and looking down over the sea, he spoke:

23. 'You have come to that dreadful place, from which no one returns, that mouth-like entrance of Death, the famous Mare-mouth[1].'

On hearing this the poor merchants, understanding that having reached the Mare-mouth, they must give up all hope of life, were distressed by the fear of death.

24-26. Some of them wept aloud or lamented and cried out. Others did nothing at all, being torpid from anxiety. Some with sorrow-stricken minds worshipped the deities, especially the Lord of the Devas, others resorted to the Âdityas, the Rudras, the Maruts, the Vasus, and to Sâgara himself [the Ocean]. Others again muttered various prayers, and there were those who paid in due form homage to Devî. Some again

---

[1] This va*d*avâmukha is the place where, according to Hindu mythology, the submarine fire resides.

went to Supâraga, and in various modes and ways lamented piteously.

27-29. 'Practised in the virtue of compassionateness for others, you are in the habit of relieving from fear those who are in distress. Now the time has arrived for employing that excessive power of yours. Resolve, then, O wise man, upon rescuing us, the distressed, the helpless, who have taken our refuge in you. The Ocean in his wrath is now about to swallow us with his Mare-mouth, like a mouthful of food. It does not become you to neglect this poor crew perishing in the rolling waves. The great Ocean obeys your orders. Therefore, put a stop to his rage.'

But the Great Being felt his heart oppressed with great compassion and spoke thus, comforting the poor merchants: 'There is still an expedient to rescue us even now. It occurs to my mind. Why, I will make use of it. But you must show courage for a moment.' Now, when the merchants heard this, the hope that there was still some remedy, after all, revived their courage, and fixing their whole attention upon him, they became silent. But Supâraga, the Bodhisattva, after throwing his upper-garment on one shoulder and bending his right knee on the ship's deck[1], made his veneration to the Tathâgatas, having his whole heart absorbed by that deed of devotion; after which he thus addressed the company: 'Be you, honourable sea-traders, and you, different gods, who have your dwelling in the sky, my witnesses.

30. 'Since I have remembrance of my Self, since the time when I have become conscious of my deeds, I do not recollect, however much I ponder, having injured in any respect any living being.

31. 'By the power of this Act of Truth and by the strength of my store of meritorious actions may the ship turn safely without reaching the Mare-mouth!'

---

[1] In the Pâli redaction the Bodhisatta orders the merchants to bathe his body with fragrant water and to clothe him with unwashed, i.e. new, garments, and to prepare a vessel filled with water, to pour out while performing his sakkakiriyâ.

And so great was the power of the veracity of the Great Being, so great also the splendour of his merit [1], that the current and the wind changed to the opposite direction and made the vessel go back. The merchants beholding the ship go back, exulted with the highest admiration and joy, and expressing their veneration to Supâraga by reverential bows, told him that the ship went back. Then the Great Being instructed them to be calm and to hoist the sails quickly. And being thus ordered, they who had the charge of that work, having regained by their gladness their ability and energy, did as he had said.

32. Then, resplendent with the lovely outspread wings of her white sails, and filled with the sound of her merry and laughing crew, the ship flew over the sea, like a flamingo in the pure and cloudless sky.

Now while the ship, favoured by both current and wind, returned with as much ease as the heavenly cars move through the air, and was flying, so to speak, at her will, at that time of the day, when the gathering darkness extends far and wide, and the sky, no more adorned by the dimming glow of the twilight, begins to make the ornaments of its constellations appear on the firmament, where still a faint remnant of light is left, in that moment, then, of the commencement of the rule of Night, Supâraga addressed the merchants in these terms: 'Well, traders, while crossing the Nalamâlin sea and the others, you must draw up sand and stones from the bottom of the seas and charge your ship with as much as she can contain. By this practice she will keep her sides firm, if assailed by a violent hurricane; besides, that sand and gravel being pronounced to be auspicious, will doubtless tend to your profit and gain.' And the merchants, being shown the fit places all along by the deities, who did so out of affection and veneration for Supâraga, drew up from thence what they meant to be sand and stones, and loaded their ship with that

---

[1] In the Pâli version it is the power of the Great Being's veracity alone that causes the winds to change.

burden. But, in fact, that sand and those stones were beryls and other jewels. And in that one night's course they reached Bharuka*kkh*a¹.

33. At day-break they beheld with gladness their ship filled with treasures: silver, gold, sapphires, beryls, and at the same time they saw that they had arrived in their country; and exulting with joy they praised their saviour.

In this manner even speaking the truth on the ground of Righteousness is sufficient to dispel calamity, what can be said more to assert the good results of observing the Law? Thus considering, one must observe the Law. [Likewise, when discoursing on the assistance of a virtuous friend, it is to be said: 'In this way those who rest on a virtuous friend attain happiness.']

XV. THE STORY OF THE FISH.

(Cp. Pâli *G*âtaka, No. 75, Fau*s*b. I, 331–32; *K*ariyâp*i/a*ka III, 10.)

The designs of those who practise good conduct will be successful and thrive even in this world, how much more in the next. For this reason perfect pureness of conduct ought to be striven after, as will be taught by the following.

The Bodhisattva, it is said, was once a chief of fishes, living in a certain small lake, the lovely water of which was embellished with various lotuses and water-lilies, white, red, and blue, adorned with couples of swans, ducks, and geese, and covered with the blossoms of the trees growing on its borders. Yet, owing to his constant practice of (the virtue of) helping others in many previous births, he was wholly given up to the business of procuring for others what would be good and agreeable to them, even in this fish-existence.

1. By the power of a long practice, actions good or

---

¹ According to the Pâli story, they had spent a four months' voyage before they reached the Mare-mouth.

wicked become inherent in mankind to such an extent that they will perform them in a new existence without any effort and, as it were, while sleeping[1].

The Great Being, then, had set his heart on those fishes, as if they were his own dear offspring, and showed them his favour in various ways: by gifts, kind words, attending to their interests, and the like.

2. He restrained them from desiring to injure each other and made their mutual affection grow. Owing to this, and his efforts, and his knowledge of every expedient, he made them forget their habit of feeding in the (cruel) manner of fishes.

3. Duly protected by him, that shoal of fishes came to great prosperity, just as a town, when ruled by a king that acts in the proper manner, enjoys freedom from every kind of mishap.

One time, because of the deficiency of good fortune in the creatures and the neglect of the angels who have the charge of rain, the (rain)god did not rain his due amount. In consequence of this scantiness of rain, the lake was not filled up as before with new water yellow-coloured by the expanding flowers of the kadamba-trees. Afterwards, when the hot season arrived, the rays of the sun, burning more ardently and being, as it were, exhausted with fatigue, drank from that lake day after day; so did Earth heated by those rays; likewise Wind, who being, as it were, accompanied by flames, would long for refreshment. All three assuaging their thirst in the lake, so to speak, made it at last turn into a pool.

4. In the hot season the flaming Sun, the pungent Wind who seems to send forth flames, and heat-wearied Earth sick with fever, dry up the waters, as if they would allay their wrath.

That shoal of fishes, then, had come into a miserable condition. Not only the crowds of birds haunting the borders of the lake, but even troops of crows com-

---

[1] The technical name for that imbibing of good qualities is sâtmibhâva.

menced to look upon them as their prey, for they could do nothing but lie and gasp. The Bodhisattva perceived the affliction and grief of his tribe, and moved with compassion entered upon this reflection: 'Oh! these wretched fishes, what a calamity has befallen them!

5. 'The water is decreasing every day, as if it vied with the life of mortals, and as yet clouds are not to be expected to come at all for a long time.

6, 7. 'There is no opportunity of withdrawing; and if there were, who should lead us elsewhere? Besides, our enemies, invited by our calamity, throng together against us. No doubt, they do but wait for the remainder of the water to dry up to devour these prostrate fishes under my very eyes.

'Now, what may be the proper act to be done here?' Thus considering, the Great Being saw but one means for relief, if he should avail himself of his veracity. Accordingly, while grieved by compassion in his mind and heaving a long and deep sigh, he looked upwards to the sky and spoke:

8. 'As truly as I do not recollect, however pondering, that I ever did harm to any living being, not even in the highest distress, by the power of this truth may the King of the Devas fill the water-basins with the water of his rains.'

When the Great Being had pronounced these words, there happened a miracle, occasioned by the power of his veracity joined to the store of his merit and to the favour shown to him by Devas, Snakes and Yakshas, who put into effect their might. In all parts of the sky there appeared rain-clouds, though out of season yet in the proper time[1]. They were hanging low, being loaded with rain; the deep and soft sound of approaching thunder was heard out of them; while flashes of lightning adorned their big and dark-blue tops, they were spreading over the sky, as if they embraced each other with their heads and arms gradually approaching.

---

[1] Or 'rain-clouds, out of season and black.' The pun is in the word kâlamegha.

9. Like the shadows of mountains projected in the mirror of the sky, the black clouds appeared, diminishing like those the circumference of the horizon and occasioning darkness with their tops.

10. The rumbling noise of the thunderclaps now resounded around, inducing the peacocks to utter cries of gladness and to perform various dancing movements, as if they praised the clouds. These accessories together with the incessant illumination by lightning gave the effect of great merriness and laughter irradiating those cloud-masses.

11. Then the clouds let loose streams of rain, which fell down like pearls loosened from their shells. The dust subsided, and a strong smell extended itself, carried about by means of the wind which accompanied the thunder-shower.

12. The sun-rays, though their power had reached its highest degree because of the hot season, were now hidden, and currents of water ran down from the mountains, troubling their banks with the rows of foam which they deposited.

13. And it was as if the slender figure of Lightning, illuminating the firmament again and again with her gold-yellow light-appearances, performed her dances, rejoiced at the music of the cloud-instruments.

Now, while the currents of palish water flowing to the lake from all sides were filling it, the crows and other birds had flown away at the very outset of the thunderstorm. The crowds of fishes recovering the hope of life, were much rejoiced. Yet the Bodhisattva, though his heart was pervaded with gladness, fearing lest the rain should cease, thus spoke to Parganya again and again:

14. 'Roar, Parganya, roar a roaring, loud and deep; dispel the joy of the crows, pouring out thy waters like jewels endowed with the flaming brilliancy of lightning, their companion [1].'

---

[1] The corresponding gâthâ in the Pâli *Gâtaka* (Fausb. I, p. 332) is also found in the *Kariyâpitaka* (III, 10, 7) with some preferable

When *Sakra*, the Lord of the Devas, heard this, he became highly astonished and went in person to him. And eulogizing him, he spoke :

15. 'Surely, it is thy power, the effect of thy transcendent veracity, O mighty lord of fishes, that makes these rain-clouds pour out their waters with the lovely noise of thunder, as if they were waterpots bent down.

16. ' But I should incur the blame of great inattention if I neglected to approve of the exertions of such beings as thou, intent on performing such deeds for the benefit of the world.

17. 'Therefore, thou must be henceforth no more anxious. I am bound to assist the virtuous in carrying out their designs. Never shall this region, since it is the abode of thy virtues, be visited another time by a similar plague.'

After thus praising him in kind terms, he disappeared on the spot. And that lake obtained a very large increase of water.

In this manner the designs of those who practise good conduct will be successful and thrive even in this world, how much more in the next. For this reason entire pureness of conduct ought to be striven after.

XVI. THE STORY OF THE QUAIL'S YOUNG.

(Cp. the Páli *Gátaka*, No. 35, Fausb. I, 213-14; *K*ariyápi*t*aka III, 9.)

Not even fire is able to surpass speech purified by truth. Having this in mind, one must addict one's self to speaking the truth. This will be taught as follows.

Once the Bodhisattva, it is said, lived in some part

---

various readings. In both redactions the birds have already begun to kill and devour the fishes, when the Bodhisatta performs his sa*kk*a-kiriyá and addresses Pa*gg*unna, commanding him, says the *G*átaka prose-writer, ' as a man would do his attendant slave.' This exhortation is uttered before the appearance of the clouds, which I suppose to be the older version of our story.

of the forest as a young quail. He had come out of the egg some nights before, and could not fly, his tender wings having still to grow both in height and in width; in his very small and weak body the different limbs, principal and minor, were hardly discernible. So he dwelt with his numerous brothers in the nest which his parents had built with great care and made impervious by a strong covering of grass. This nest was placed on a creeper within a thicket. Yet, still in this existence, he had not lost his consciousness of the Law, and would not feed on such living beings as his father and mother offered to them, but exclusively sustained himself by (the vegetable food) which was brought by his parents: grass-seeds, figs of the banian tree, &c. In consequence of this coarse and insufficient nourishment, his body did not thrive nor would his wings develop. The other young quails, on the contrary, who fed on everything offered to them, became strong and got full-grown wings. For this, indeed, is an invariable rule:

1. He who, not anxious about the precepts of the Law, eats everything, will thrive at his ease, but such a one as seeks for his livelihood in accordance with the precepts, and is careful about the choice of his food, will endure pain in this world [1].

Now, while they were living in this manner, a great forest-conflagration took place not far from them. It

---

[1] Here follows an interpolation, which the editor of the original has placed within brackets. It is a quotation, which was originally no doubt a marginal note. Here is its translation:

'This is also declared by our Lord in the two gâthâs: "Easy is the livelihood &c."

2. 'Easy is the livelihood of the shameless crow, that bold and impetuous animal, who practises impure actions, but it is a very sinful life.

3. 'But the modest one who always strives after purity has a hard livelihood, the bashful one who is scrupulous and sustains himself only by pure modes of living.

'This couple of gâthâs is found in the Âryasthâviriyanikâya.'

The gâthâs quoted are substantially and partly verbally the same as two stanzas of the Dhammapada (244 and 245) that are their Pâli counterpart.

was characterised by an incessant tremendous noise, by the appearance of clouds of rising smoke, then by flying sparks of fire scattered about from the line of flames. This fire caused much terror to such animals as haunted the forest, and was a ruin to its groves and thickets.

4. The fire excited by the whirling of the wind, that seemed to induce it to perform manifold and different figures of dance, agitated its wide-outstretched flame-arms, leaped shaking its dishevelled smoke-hair, and crackled, taking away the courage and strength of those (animals and plants).

5. It jumped, as if in wrath, on the grasses, which trembling under the violent touch of the fierce wind, seemed to take to flight; and covering them with its glittering sparks, burnt them.

6. Yea, it seemed as if the forest itself, with its crowds of birds flying about terror-stricken and alarmed, with its terrified quadrupeds roaming on all sides, with the thick smoke which enveloped it, and with the sharp noise of the fire's crackling, uttered strong roars of pain.

So that conflagration, pushed forward as if pressed on by the violent wind, and following the grasses and shrubs, reached at last the vicinity of that nest. In this moment the young quails, uttering confused and discordant shrieks of fear, each caring for himself, none for the rest, suddenly flew up all together. Only the Bodhisattva, because of the great weakness of his body and because he had as yet no wings, made no such effort. Yet the Great Being knew his power and was not at all disturbed. When the fire with impetuosity approached, and was about to seize upon the nest, he addressed it with these persuasive words:

7. 'My feet are not strong enough to deserve that name, nor are my wings able to fly, and the disturbance caused by thee put to flight also my parents. Nothing worth offering to a guest like thee, is to be found here. For this reason it becomes thee to turn back from hence, Agni.'

When the Great Being had spoken these words, hallowed by the power of Truth,

8. That fire, though stirred by the wind, though raging in dry underwood mixed with very arid grasses, abated suddenly, as if it had reached a swollen river, having come near to his utterance of speech.

9. Still up to this day any forest-conflagration, reaching that famous place in the Himâlaya, however high its flames may rise by the power of the wind, will lessen its fire and slacken its rage, in the same way as a many-headed serpent is charmed by a spell.

For what reason, then, has this (tale) been adduced? It will be said.

10. As little as the sea with its rolling billows will transgress the shore, or he who loves Truth the discipline ordained by the Lord of Munis, so little even fire is able to transgress the command of the veracious. For this reason one must never leave Truth.

In this manner, then, not even fire is able to surpass speech purified by truth. Having this in view, one must addict one's self to speaking the truth. [This story is also to be told, when discoursing on the Tathâgata.]

XVII. THE STORY OF THE JAR.

(Cp. Pâli *Gâtaka*, No. 512, Fausb. V, pp. 11–20)

Drinking intoxicating liquors is an exceedingly bad action, attended by many evils. Having this in mind, the virtuous will keep back their neighbour from that sin, how much more their own selves. This will be taught as follows.

One time the Bodhisattva, having by his excessive compassion purified his mind, always intent on bringing about the good and the happiness of others, manifesting his holy practice of good conduct by his deeds of charity, modesty, self-restraint, and the like, held the dignity of

Sakra, the Lord of the Devas. In this existence, though he enjoyed to his heart's content such paramount sensual pleasures as are proper to the Celestials, yet Compassionateness ruled his mind so as not to allow him to relax his exertions for the benefit of the world.

1. As a rule the creatures, drinking from the wine [1] of prosperity, are not watchful, not even with respect to their own interests. He, on the contrary, was not only free from the drunkenness originating from the transcendent enjoyments which attend the sovereign rank among the Devas, but his watchfulness for the interests of others was as great as ever.

2. Being full of affection towards the creatures, as if they were his kinsmen, those poor creatures harassed by many violent calamities, he never forgot to take care of the interests of others, persisting in his strong determination and being well aware of his own (extraordinary) nature.

Now, one day the Great Being was casting His eyes over the world of men. His eye, great as His nature and mildly looking according to His friendliness, while bending down to mankind with compassion, perceived a certain king, whose name was Sarvamitra [= every one's friend], who by the sin of his intercourse with wicked friends was inclined to the habit of drinking strong liquors, himself with his people, townsmen and landsmen. Now, having understood that the king saw no sin in this habit, and knowing that drinking constitutes a great sin, the Great Being, affected with great compassion, entered upon this reflection: 'It is a pity, indeed, how great a misery has befallen this people!

3. 'Drinking, like a lovely but wrong path—for it is a sweet thing at the outset—leads away from salvation such people as fail to recognise the evils which it causes.

---

[1] The juice of grapes not being among the national intoxicating liquors of India, Sanskrit has no proper word for 'wine.' For rhetorical purposes, however, it will meet no objection to use this term in a translation. Moreover, nowadays 'wine' is signified in Sanskrit by words meaning 'strong liquor.'

'What, then, may be the proper way to act here? ... Why, I have found it.

4. 'People like to imitate the behaviour of him who is the foremost among them; this is their constant nature. Accordingly, here the king alone is the person to be cured, for it is from him that originates the good as well as the evil of his people.'

Having thus made up his mind, the Great Being took on himself the majestic figure of a Brâhman. His colour shone like pure gold; he wore his hair matted and twisted up, which gave him a rather stern appearance; he had his body covered with the bark-garment and the deer-skin [1]. A jar of moderate size, filled with surâ, was hanging down from his left side. In this shape, standing in the air he showed himself to king Sarvamitra, while he was sitting with his company in his audience-hall, and their conversation had turned to be such as attends drinking surâ, âsava, maireya[2], rum, and honeyed liquor. On seeing him, the assembly, moved by surprise and veneration, rose from their seats, and reverentially folded their hands to him. After which, he began to speak in a loud voice, resembling the deep noise of a cloud big with rain:

5.   'See, 'tis fill'd up to its neck,
    Flowers laugh around its neck;
    Well 'tis dress'd, a splendid jar;
    Who will buy from me this jar?

6. 'I have here a jar adorned with this bracelet-like wide wreath of flowers, fluttering in the wind. See how proud it looks, decorated as it is by tender foliage. Which of you desires to possess it by purchase?'

Upon which, that king, whose curiosity was excited by astonishment, reverentially fixing his eyes on him and raising his folded hands, spoke these words:

7. 'Like the morning-sun thou appearest to us by

---

[1] The matted hair, the bark-garment, and the deer-skin are the attributes of an anchorite or muni. Cp. Dhammapada, verses 393, 394.

[2] All of them names of different kinds of spirituous liquor.

thy lustre, like the moon by thy gracefulness, and by thy figure like some Muni. Deign to tell us, then, by what name thou art known in the world. Thy different illustrious qualities make us uncertain about thee.'

Sakra said:

8. 'Afterwards you will know me, who I am, but now be intent on purchasing this jar from me—at least if you are not afraid of the sufferings in the next world or heavy calamities to be expected still in this.'

The king replied: 'Verily, such an introduction to a bargain as is made by Thy Reverence, I never saw before.

9, 10. 'The ordinary mode of offering objects for sale among men is to extol their good qualities and conceal their faults. Surely, that manner practised by thee is becoming such men as thou, who abhor falsehood. For the virtuous will never forsake veracity, even when in distress!

11. 'Tell us then, Eminent One, with what this jar is filled. And what is it, that such a mighty being as thou may desire from our side by the barter?'

Sakra said: 'Hear, mighty sovereign.

12. 'It is not filled with water, either the largess of the clouds or drawn from a holy stream; nor with fragrant honey gathered out of the filaments of flowers; nor with excellent butter; nor with milk, whose hue equals that of the moonbeams awaking the waterlilies in a cloudless night. No, this jar is filled up with mischievous liquor. Now, learn the virtue of this liquor.

13. 'He who drinks it will lose the control of himself, in consequence of mind-perplexing intoxication; as his mindfulness will slacken, he will stumble even on plain ground; he will not make a difference between food allowed and forbidden, and will make his meals of whatever he may get. Of such a nature is the fluid within this jar. Buy it, it is for sale, that worst of jars!

14. 'This liquor has the power of taking away your consciousness, so as to make you lose the control of

XVII. THE STORY OF THE JAR. 145

your thoughts and behave like a brute beast, giving your enemies the trouble of laughing at you. Thanks to it, you may also dance in the midst of an assembly, accompanying yourself with the music of your mouth. Being of such a nature, it is worth purchasing by you, that liquor within the jar, devoid as it is of any good!

15. 'Even the bashful lose shame by drinking it, and will have done with the trouble and restraint of dress; unclothed like Nirgranthas[1] they will walk boldly on the highways crowded with people. Of such a nature is the liquor contained in this jar and now offered for sale[2].

16. 'Drinking it may cause men even to lie senseless asleep on the king's roads, having their figures soiled with food ejected by their vomitings and licked from their face by bold dogs. Such is the beverage, lovely to purchase, which has been poured into this jar!

17. 'Even a woman enjoying it may be brought by the power of intoxication into such a state, that she would be able to fasten her parents to a tree and to disregard her husband, may he be as wealthy as Kubera[3]. Of this kind is the merchandise which is contained within this jar!

18. 'That liquor, by drinking which the V*ri*sh*n*ayas and the Andhakâs were put out of their senses to this degree, that without minding[4] their relationship they crushed down each other with their clubs, that very beverage of maddening effect is enclosed within this jar!

19. 'Addicted to which whole families of the highest rank and dignity, the abodes of splendour, perished,

---

[1] The Nirgranthas are a class of monks, especially Gain monks, who wander about naked.
[2] Instead of the reading of the printed text, the fourth pâda, I suppose, should be read thus: sâ pa*n*yatâm upagatâ nihitâtra ku*m*bhe.
[3] The strange examples for illustration are occasioned by the exigencies of a metrical tour de force, very skilfully executed.
[4] It is evident that vismitabandhubhâvâ*h* is a misprint for vism*ri*tabandhubhâvâ*h*.

I.

that liquor which has caused likewise the ruin of wealthy families, here in this jar it is exposed for sale.

20. 'Here in this jar is that which makes the tongue and the feet unrestrained, and puts off every check in weeping and laughing; that by which the eyes look heavy and dull as of one possessed of a demon; that which impairing a man's mind, of necessity reduces him to an object of contempt.

21. 'In this jar is ready for sale that which, disturbing the senses of even aged people and making them timid to continue the road which leads to their good, induces them to talk much without purpose and rashly.

22. 'It is the fault of this beverage, that the old gods, having become careless, were bereaved of their splendour by the King of the Devas, and seeking for relief were drowned in the Ocean. With that drink this jar is filled. Well, take it!

23. 'Like an Incarnation of Curse she[1] lies within this jar, she by whose power falsehood is spoken with confidence, as if it were truth, and forbidden actions are committed with joy, as if they were prescribed. It is she who causes men to hold for good what is bad and for bad what is good.

24. 'Well, purchase then this madness-producing philtre, this abode of calamities, this embodied Disaster, this mother of sins, this sole and unparalleled road of sin[2], this dreadful darkness of mind.

25. 'Purchase from me, O king, that beverage which is able to take away a man's senses entirely, so that, without caring for his happiness or future state, he may strike his own innocent father or mother or a holy ascetic.

26. 'Such is this liquor, known among men by the name of surâ, O you lord of men, who by your splendour equal the celestials (surâs). Let him endeavour to buy it, who is no partisan of virtues.

---

[1] The word surâ is feminine.
[2] Kali is here used as an appellative with the general meaning it has in Pâli (see Childers' Dict. s. v.)

27. 'People, being addicted to this liquor, grow accustomed to ill-behaviour, and will consequently fall into the precipices of dreadful hells or come to the state of beasts or to the attenuated condition of pretâs. Who then, forsooth, should make up his mind even to look at this liquor?

28. 'And, be the result of drinking intoxicating liquors ever so trifling, still that vice destroys the good conduct and the good understanding of those who pass through human existence. Moreover it leads afterwards to the residence in the tremendous hell Avî*k*i, burning with flaming fire, or in the world of spectres[1], or in the bodies of vile beasts.

29. 'In short, drinking this destroys every virtue. It deadens good conduct (*s*ila), forcibly kills good reputation, banishes shame, and defiles the mind. How should you allow yourself to drink intoxicating liquors henceforward, O king?'

By these persuasive words of *S*akra and his strong arguments the king became aware of the sinfulness of drinking intoxicating liquors. He cast off the desire of taking them, and addressing his interlocutor said:

30. 'As an affectionate father would deign to speak to his son, or a teacher to his pupil in reward for his discipline and attachment, or a Muni who knows the difference between the good and the evil modes of life, such an import is conveyed in the well-said words thou hast spoken to me out of benevolence. For this reason I will endeavour to honour thee, as is due, by a deed.

'In return for thy well-said sentences Thy Reverence will at least deign to accept from us this honour.

31. 'I give thee five excellent villages, a hundred female slaves, five hundred cows, and these ten chariots with the best horses harnessed to them. As a speaker of wholesome words thou art a Guru to me.

---

[1] '"The world of spectres"=pit*r*ilo ke. In Buddhist terminology the pitara*h* are a synonym of preta*h*, considered to be a class of spectres and ghosts. 'In appearance they are extremely attenuated, like a dry leaf.' Spence Hardy, Manual, p. 48.

'Or, wert thou to desire anything else to be done from my side, Thy Reverence would favour me once more by ordering so.'
Sakra replied:

32, 33. 'I do not want villages or other boons. Know me to be the Lord of the Celestials, O King. But the speaker of wholesome words is to be honoured by accepting his words and acting up to them. For this is the way which leads to glory and bliss, and after death to the many different forms of happiness. Therefore, throw off the habit of taking intoxicating drinks. Holding fast to Righteousness you shall partake of my heaven.'

After thus speaking, Sakra disappeared on the spot, and the king, with his townsmen and landsmen, desisted from the vice of drinking strong liquors.

In this manner, then, the virtuous, considering the use of intoxicating liquors an exceedingly bad action, attended by many evils, will keep back their neighbour from this sin, how much more their own selves. [And when discoursing about the Tathâgata, this is also to be propounded: 'In this manner the Lord was careful of the good of the world already in his previous existences.']

XVIII. THE STORY OF THE CHILDLESS ONE.

The state of a householder is beset with occupations inimical to religious conduct and tranquillity. For this reason it does not please those who long only for the Self[1]. This will be taught by the following.

One time the Bodhisattva was born in a wealthy family, noted for their virtuous mode of life and

---

[1] Though the Buddhist lore denies the existence of the individual soul, the Self (âtman), Buddhist Sanskrit, as well as Pâli, often employs that name, as it is used in pagan and profane writings, in such cases as where it may suit to signify that part of the individual being, to whose profit or damage the good or evil karma will tend.

good behaviour, so as to be much sought in alliance and highly esteemed by the people. That family was like a refreshing well to persons of good birth; they shared the stores of their treasuries and magazines with *S*rama*n*as and Brâhmans; their houses were open to friends and kinsmen; the poor and the mendicants lived by their gifts; the artisans found business and protection with them; and by their splendid riches they were permitted to bestow their favour and hospitality on the king. Being born in this family, he grew up in course of time, and studied such branches of science as are reputed of much value in the world, while he turned his mind with no less zeal to various arts, the knowledge of which is optional. Owing to his accomplished education, his beautiful figure pleasing the eyes of men, and the knowledge of the world he displayed without infringing the precepts of the Law, he won the hearts of his fellow-citizens, who considered him like their kinsman.

1, 2. For it is not on account of their relationship that we honour our relations, nor do we consider the rest of men as strangers because they are not related to us. No, men are considered relations or strangers, according as their virtues or vices make them meet with esteem or disregard.

But that Great Being had familiarised himself with world-renunciation.

3. He had had experience of the householder's life, and knew it to be a state not consistent with the practice of religious duties, since the pain of seeking after profit is necessarily implied by it. On the other hand, he understood the happiness of the penance-groves. So his mind became detached from the pleasures of the home-life.

So, when his father and mother had died, he was utterly alarmed in his heart, and forsaking his splendid house and estate, an amount of many hundred thousands, duly bestowed it upon his friends and kinsmen, the poor, the *S*rama*n*as, and the Brâhmans; after which he abandoned his home.

He passed successively through villages and towns and boroughs, through kingdoms and capitals of kingdoms, and took up his abode on a certain woody plateau in the vicinity of a town. There he soon became conspicuous by his tranquillity, his conversation, and his behaviour. The calmness of his senses, the result of a long practice of meditation, was natural and sincere. His language delighted both minds and ears, and while betraying his wisdom, still was full of modesty; and his discourses being entirely free from miserable and troublesome hope for gain, were distinguished by his solid learning, by his softness in addressing the audience to whom he paid due honour, and by the skill he displayed in tracing the boundary between actions allowed and forbidden by the Law. His behaviour, adorned with such practices as are proper to a homeless ascetic, was quite in accordance with that approved by the virtuous. And when the people who were curious about his person, became aware of how he had renounced a high rank in the world, they loved him the more for it.

4. Virtues obtain a more favourable reception, if found in persons distinguished by a high birth; in the same way as the beams shooting from the moon have more loveliness, when coming in contact with any object of excellent qualities.

Now some friend and companion of his father, having heard he had taken up his abode in that place, went up to him, moved by a great esteem for his virtues. After the usual friendly inquiries concerning his health, the visitor made himself known to the ascetic, and told him of the paternal relation. Then there ensued a conversation between them, in the course of which the said friend spoke these affectionate words: 'Your Reverence is likely to have acted inconsiderately, after all, renouncing the world in this age without further regard to your family and (the maintenance of) your lineage.

5. 'For what have you left your rich dwelling, setting your mind on the forest-life? Those who

practise a virtuous life may observe this Law in their homes as well as in the wilderness.

6, 7. 'How, then, is it that you give yourself up to a life of pain, embracing this state of incarnate Poverty, as it were? You are sustaining yourself by alms obtained from the charity of strangers, and you are not a bit more regarded than a vagabond. Covered with rags and devoid of relations and friends, you are hiding yourself in this abode in the midst of the forest. Even the eyes of your enemies would be filled with tears, if they were to see you in this condition.

8. 'Therefore, return to your paternal house. Certainly, the abundance of its estate must be known also to you. Living there, you might fulfil at the same time both your religious duties and your desire of possessing a virtuous son.

' For such is the saying, indeed, you know :

9. ' Even to a hired labourer his home is comforting, like a well of fresh water, how much more an easily obtained luxurious residence, resplendent with wealth!'

But the Bodhisattva's mind was purified by that delicious and comforting ambrosia, the name of which is detachment. His heart clung to it, for he knew well the difference between the life of a householder and the forest-life; and the invitation to enjoy worldly pleasures had the same effect of discomfort upon him, as talking of a meal would have upon one who is satiated. So he spoke:

10. 'What you said was spoken out of affection, of a truth, and on this account your words did not grieve me so much. Nevertheless, do not employ the term "comfort," when speaking of one who lives in the world.

11. 'The householder's state is a state of great uneasiness, whether he have money or not. The rich man is vexed by the toil of guarding his wealth, and the poor one by the labour of earning it.

12. 'Now, since there is no comfort to be found in that state either for the rich or for the poor, it is

mere folly to delight in it. It must have such consequences as are the result of wickedness.

'As to your statement that a householder, too, may be able to observe the precepts of the Law, certainly, this is true. But it is a very, very difficult thing, methinks. The life in the world is crowded with business quite adverse to the precepts of the Law, and implies a great amount of toil. Do but consider it well, sir.

13. 'The life of a householder is not suitable for one who desires nothing, nor for such a one as never speaks a falsehood, nor for him who never uses violence, nor for such a one as never injures others.

'And he whose heart is attached to the " comfort of home-life," cannot but strive to put into effect the means by which this is secured.

14. 'If you devote yourself to the Law, you must leave your house, and inversely, how can the Law exist for him who is attached to his house? It is tranquillity from which the road of the Law derives its flavour, but the success of a householder requires him to follow the way of courageous enterprise.

15, 16. ' Now, as the life of a householder is reprehensible for this reason, that it is in opposition to the Law, who, then, having got the true insight of his Self, will keep to it? He, indeed, whom the prospect of pleasure has once induced to neglect the Law, will feel himself not at all restrained as to the means of procuring those pleasures. Besides, they will certainly be followed by the loss of good reputation, by remorse and misfortune. For this reason the wise do not embrace that state, which procures pleasures to the detriment of the Law; they rather look on it as a calamity.

' Further I should think, the statement that living in the world procures happiness is only supported by belief (not by evidence).

17, 18. 'The pain caused by earning wealth or by guarding it never ceases for the householder. He is more than anybody else exposed to murder, captivity, and other calamities. Even if a king, he would not be satisfied with his riches, no more than the sea may be with showers of rain. Why can there be happiness in that state, or how, or when, if man does not attain by it the longing for self-perfection, but on the contrary in his infatuation fancies happiness is to be obtained by attachment to sensual objects? Such a person may be compared to one who tries to heal his wounds by rubbing.

'As a rule, in truth, I dare say.

19. 'As a rule, material prosperity makes the householder arrogant, nobility of extraction makes him proud, strength makes him insolent. His anger is roused by grief, and adversity puts him to dejection. At what time may that state offer an opportunity for tranquillity?

'And for this reason it is that I would persuade Your Honour not to oppose my determination.

20. 'The house is the home of many and heavy sufferings. It is haunted by the serpents named arrogance, pride, and infatuation. In it the lovely happiness of tranquillity comes to ruin. Who then should choose that abode that tends to dissolution?

21. 'In the forest, on the other hand, that home of the nothing-desirers, the mind is calm, enjoying the happiness of detachment. Can there exist so great a contentment in *S*akra's heaven?

22. 'Thus considering, I delight in the midst of the forests, although covered with rags and getting my livelihood through the kindheartedness of strangers. I do not long for such happiness as is tainted with unrighteousness. I abhor it like food besmeared with poison; I have got the insight of my Self.'

These persuasive words did not fail to make an impression on his paternal friend, who showed his high respect to the Great Being by entertaining him with a meal in the most distinguished manner.

In this manner, then, those who long only for the Self abandon the state of a householder, understanding that it is beset with occupations inimical to religious conduct and to tranquillity. [When treating of the virtue of detachment, this is to be propounded: 'Those who have once got the taste for detachment will not go back to worldly pleasures.']

<small>The Pâli version of this story is not found in the Pâli Gâtaka nor in the Kariyâpi/aka. The whole tale is nothing but a plea for the virtue of world-renunciation, the naishkrama, roughly dressed in the shape of a story, and may serve as a kind of introduction to the subsequent tales, where the state of an ascetic is glorified.</small>

XIX. THE STORY OF THE LOTUS-STALKS.

(Cp. the Pâli Gâtaka, No. 488, Fausb. IV, 305–314; Kariyâpi/aka III, 4.)

Those who have learnt to appreciate the happiness of detachment are hostile to worldly pleasures; they will oppose them, like one opposes a deception, an injury. This will be taught as follows.

One time the Bodhisattva was born in an illustrious family of Brâhmans, far-famed for their virtues and their freedom from reprehensible vices. In this existence he had six younger brothers endowed with virtues similar to his, and who out of affection and esteem for him always imitated him; he had also a sister, who was the seventh. Having studied the Vedas with their auxiliary sciences, likewise the Upavedas[1], he obtained great renown on account of his learning, and high respect from the side of the people. Attending on his father and mother with the utmost piety, yea, worshipping them like deities, and instructing his brothers in different branches of science like a spiritual teacher or a father, he dwelt in the world, being

---

<small>[1] The Upavedas are the four sciences of medicine (âyurveda), military sciences (dhanurveda), music (gândharvaveda), and mechanics (silpaṡâstra), which theory attaches to the Rig-, Yagur-, Sâma-, and Atharva-veda respectively.</small>

XIX. THE STORY OF THE LOTUS-STALKS. 155

skilled in the art of dealing with worldly affairs, and distinguished by his good manners. In course of time his parents died, which loss deeply moved his soul. Having performed the funeral ceremonies for them, after some days spent in mourning, he assembled his brothers and thus spoke to them :

1, 2. 'This is the necessary order of things in the world and a source of grief and excessive pain, that Death separates us at last from those with whom we have lived together for a time, however long. For this reason I desire to walk homeless on that laudable road to salvation, before Death, our foe, seizes me while attached to the householder's life.

'Having thus resolved, I have to advise you this, one and all. Our Brâhmanical family is in the lawful possession of some wealth obtained in an honest way. With it you are able to sustain yourselves. Well, then, you must dwell here as householders in a becoming manner. Let all of you be intent on loving and respecting each other, take care not to slacken your regard of the moral precepts and the practice of a righteous behaviour, keep up the assiduous study of the Veda, be prepared to meet the wishes of your friends, your guests, and your kinsmen. In short, above all things observe Righteousness.

3. 'Always continuing in good behaviour, observing your daily Veda-study, and delighting in almsgiving, you must keep the householder's state (so) as it ought to be kept.

4. 'In this way not only will your reputation increase, not only will you extend your virtue and your wealth, the substance of welfare, but you may expect your entrance in the other life to be happy. Do not commit, therefore, any inadvertence while living the householder's life.'

But his brothers, hearing him speak of the homeless life, felt their hearts grieved with the apprehension of separation. Their faces grew wet with tears of sorrow, and respectfully bowing they spoke to him :
'The wound caused by the sorrow-arrow of our father's

decease is not yet healed. Pray do not rub it open afresh with the salt of this new assault of grief.

5. 'Even now the wound is still open which was inflicted on our minds by the death of our father. Oh! you must retract your resolution, wise brother, you must not strew salt on our wound.

6. 'Or, if indeed you are convinced that attachment to the house is unfit, or that the happiness of the forest-life is the road to salvation, why is it that you desire to depart for the forest alone, leaving us in this house destitute of our protector?

'For this reason, the state of life which is yours, that will be ours, too. We too will renounce the world.'

The Bodhisattva answered:

7. 'People who have not familiarised themselves with Detachment cannot but follow after worldly desires. As a rule they look upon it as the same thing to give up the world or to fall over a precipice.

'Thus considering, I restrained myself and did not exhort you to adopt the homeless life, though knowing the difference between both states. But if my choice please you too, why, let us abandon our home!' And so all seven brothers, with their sister as the eighth, gave up their wealthy estate and precious goods, took leave of their weeping friends, kinsmen and relations, and resorted to the state of homeless ascetics. And with them, out of affection also one comrade, one male, and one female servant set out for the forest.

In a certain place in the forest there was a large lake of pure, blue water. It exhibited a resplendent fiery beauty, when its lotus-beds were expanded, and offered a gay aspect, when its groups of waterlilies disclosed their calyxes [1]; swarms of bees were always humming there. On the shore of that lake they built as many huts of leaves as they numbered, one for

---

[1] The former happened at daytime, the latter in the nights bright with moonshine.

each, placing them at some distance from one another, hidden in the shadow of the trees in the midst of a lovely solitude. There they lived, devoted to their self-imposed vows and observances, and having their minds bound to meditation. On each fifth day they were in the habit of going to the Bodhisattva in order to listen to his preaching of the Law. Then he delivered some or other edifying discourse to show them the way of tranquillity and placidity of mind. In those discourses he exhorted to meditation, asserted the sinfulness of worldly pleasures, expatiated on the sense of satisfaction which is the result of detachment, blamed hypocrisy, loquacity, idleness and other vices, and made a deep impression on his audience.

Now, their maid-servant, prompted by respect and affection, did not cease to attend upon them still in the forest. She was wont to draw eatable lotus-stalks out of the lake and to put equal shares of them upon large lotus-leaves in a clean place on the lake-shore; when she had thus prepared the meal, she would announce the time by taking two pieces of wood and clashing them against each other, after which she withdrew. Then those holy men, after performing the proper and usual prayers and libations, would come to the lake-side one after another according to their age, and each having taken successively his share of the stalks, return to his hut. There they would enjoy the meal in the prescribed manner and pass the rest of the time absorbed in meditation. By this practice they avoided seeing each other, except at preaching-time.

Such irreproachable morals, way of living, and behaviour, such love of detachment, and such proneness to meditation made them renowned everywhere. Sakra, the Lord of the Devas, having heard of their reputation, came to their abode for the purpose of trying them. Now, when he perceived their disposition to meditation, their purity from bad actions, their freedom from lusts and the constancy of their serene calmness, his high opinion of their virtues grew stronger, and he became the more anxious to try them.

8. He who lives in the depth of the forest without any desire, only intent on calmness of mind, such a man causes reverence for his virtues to arise in the hearts of the pious.

Sakra, then, the Lord of the Devas, watched the time when the maid-servant, after gathering her provision of eatable lotus-stalks, as white and tender as the teeth of a young elephant, washed them and arranged them in equal portions on lotus-leaves with the green hue of emeralds, taking care to adorn each share by adding to it some petals and filaments of the lotuses. After announcing the mealtime to the holy ascetics, as usual, by the noise of the clashing pieces of wood, she withdrew. At this moment Sakra, with the object of trying the Bodhisattva, made the very first share disappear (from the lotus-leaf).

9. When mishap arises and happiness disappears, then there is opportunity for measuring the constancy of the virtuous, as it cannot fail to start into view.

When the Bodhisattva, coming to the place of the first share of stalks, perceived that the eatable stalks were missing on his lotus-leaf, while the adornment of petals and filaments was disarranged, he thought: 'Somebody has taken my share of food.' Then, without feeling agitation or anger in his heart, he went back to his hut, where he entered upon his practices of meditation, as he was wont to do. Nor did he inform the other holy ascetics of the matter, to avoid grieving them. And those again, thinking it to be a matter of course that he had taken his share of the stalks, took their portions too, as usual, successively and in due order, and ate them severally, each in his hut; after which they became absorbed in meditation. In the same manner Sakra concealed the Bodhisattva's portion of the lotus-stalks on the second, the third, the fourth and the fifth day. But the effect was the same. The Great Being remained as calm in mind as ever, and was entirely free from trouble.

10. The virtuous consider the agitation of the mind, not the extinction of life, to be death. It is for this reason that the wise never become alarmed, not even when in danger of life.

In the afternoon of that (fifth) day those *Ri*shis went up to the leaf-hut of the Bodhisattva, as they were in the habit of doing, in order to listen to his preaching of the Law. On seeing him, they perceived the leanness of his body. His cheeks looked hollow, his eyes were sunken, the splendour of his face had faded, his sonorous voice had lost its full sound. Yet, however emaciated, he was lovely to behold like the crescent; for his virtues, wisdom, constancy, tranquillity had not diminished. Accordingly, after coming into his presence and paying him the usual homage, they asked him with anxious excitement the cause of that emaciation. And the Bodhisattva told them the matter as he had experienced it. The ascetics, who could not suppose any one among themselves to have done an action so unbecoming as this, and who felt quite alarmed at his pain, expressed their sorrow by exclamations, and kept their eyes fixed on the ground for shame. But *S*akra having by his power obstructed their free movement on the ways in which they could obtain knowledge, they were unable to come to a conclusion as to the cause of the disappearance. Then the brother of the Bodhisattva, who was born next to him, showing both his alarmed mind and his guiltlessness, made this extraordinary protestation[1]:

11. 'May he who took thy lotus-stalks, O Brâhman, obtain a house betokening by its rich decoration the wealth of its owner, a wife to his heart's desire, and may he be blessed with many children and grandchildren![2]'

---

[1] The following set of remarkable protestations are also found in the same order and in a substantially identical form in the Pâli redaction. They are very old, and not wholly free from corruptions and misunderstandings.

[2] The Pâli redaction adds, that the audience on hearing this

The second brother said:

12. 'May he who took thy lotus-stalks, O foremost Brâhman, be tainted with a strong attachment to worldliness, may he wear wreaths and garlands and sandal-powder and fine garments and ornaments, touched by his (playing) children!'

The third brother said:

13. 'May he who took thy lotus-stalks even once, be a husbandman who, having obtained wealth in consequence of his husbandry and delighting in the prattle of his children, enjoys the home-life without thinking of the time when he must retire from the world!'[1]

The fourth brother spoke:

14. 'May he who prompted by cupidity took thy lotus-stalks, rule the whole earth as a monarch, and be worshipped by kings attending on him in the humble attitude of slaves, lowering their trembling heads!'

The fifth brother spoke:

15. 'May he be a king's family-priest in the possession of evil-charming mantras and the like, may he also be treated with distinction by his king, whosoever he be who took thy lotus-stalks!'

The sixth brother said:

16. 'May he who has been eager to possess thy lotus-stalks rather than thy virtues, be a famous teacher well-versed in the Veda and largely enjoy the worship of an ascetic from the people crowding together to see him!'

The friend spoke:

17. 'May he who could not subdue his greediness for thy lotus-stalks obtain from the part of the king an excellent village endowed with the four plenties (abounding in population, corn, wood and water)[2], and may he die without having subdued his passions!'

---

protestation shut their ears, saying: 'Do not speak in this manner, friend! thy curse is too tremendous.'

[1] The Sanskrit text has vayo 'py apasyan = Pâli vayam appassan. I follow the explication of the Pâli commentary.

[2] The said four plenties are thus explained in the commentary on

The male-servant said :

18. 'May he be the head of a village, cheerfully living with his comrades, exhilarated by the dances and chants of women, and never meet with harm from the king's side, he who destroyed his own interest for the sake of those lotus-stalks!'

The sister said:

19. 'May that person[1] who ventured to take the lotus-stalks of such a being as you, be a woman of resplendent beauty and figure, may a king make her his wife and put her at the head of his zenana of a thousand females!'

The maid-servant said:

20. 'May she much delight in eating sweetmeats alone stealthily, disregarding the pious, and be greatly rejoiced when she gets a dainty dish, she who set her heart on thy lotus-stalks, not on thy righteousness!'

Now three inhabitants of the forest had also come to that place to hear the preaching of the Law, namely a Yaksha, an elephant, and a monkey. They had heard the conversation and were overcome with the utmost shame and confusion. Among them, the Yaksha attested his innocence, uttering in their presence this solemn protestation:

21. 'May he who failed against thee for the sake of the lotus-stalks, have his residence in the Great Monastery, entrusted with the charge of the reparations in (the town of) Ka/cangalâ, and make one window every day![2]'

---

the Pâli Gâtaka, which proves here of essential help, since /tatu/sa tam of the Sanskrit text is a wrong Sanskritisation of Pâli /atussada*m*. and does not suit the context.

[1] Both the Sanskrit and the Pâli redaction have here the masculine pron. demonstr. The fault must be a very ancient one. In the imprecation of the female servant the grammatical gender is respected by Sûra, not so in the Gâtaka.

[2] This imprecation alludes to the story of a certain devaputra, who in the time of the Buddha Kâsyapa dwelt in the said monastery and was obliged to do the labour imposed on him, whereby he suffered much. A brief account of that tale is given in the commentary on

The elephant spoke:

22. 'May he come into captivity from the lovely forest into the company of men, fettered with six hundred solid chains[1], and suffer pain from the sharp goads of his driver, he who took thy lotus-stalks, O most excellent of Munis!'

The monkey said:

23. 'May he who moved by greediness took thy lotus-stalks wear a flower-garland and a tin collar rubbing his neck, and beaten with a stick pass before the face of a serpent[2], and with a long wreath hanging from his shoulder, live in the houses (of men)!'

In reply, the Bodhisattva addressed all of them with words both persuasive and kind, indicating how deep-rooted was his dispassionateness.

24. 'May he who falsely said "they have disappeared," though he had them, obtain to his heart's desire worldly pleasures and die a householder. May the same be the fate of him who suspects you of a similar action!'

Those extraordinary protestations of them, indicative of their abhorrence of the enjoyment of worldly pleasures, roused the astonishment and respect of Sakra, the Lord of the Devas. He made himself visible in his own brilliant shape, and drawing near to those *Ri*shis, said as if with resentment: 'You ought not to speak so.

25. 'Those enjoyments—to obtain which everybody who longs for happiness strives after to such a degree as to banish sleep from his eyes and to undertake any form of penance and toil—you censure, calling them "worldly pleasures!" Why do you judge so?'

---

the Pâli *Gâ*taka, where the speaker of this stanza is called a Devatâ, not a Yaksha.

[1] I suppose the author of the Sanskrit original did not understand the meaning of the text he Sanskritised. The corresponding stanza of the Pâli redaction has so bag*gh*atû pâsasatehî *kh*ambhî, where *kh*ambhî is explained in the commentary as signifying the six parts of the elephant's body fastened by many chains (pâsasatehiti bahûhi pâsehi), viz. the four feet, the neck, and the loins.

[2] In other words, may he be the monkey of a serpent-charmer.

XIX. THE STORY OF THE LOTUS-STALKS.

The Bodhisattva spoke: 'Sensual enjoyments are accompanied by endless sins, sir. Why, hear then, I will tell thee concisely, what the Munis have in view that makes them blame sensual enjoyments.

26. 'On account of them, men incur captivity and death, grief, fatigue, danger, in short manifold sufferings. For the sake of them, kings are eager to oppress righteousness, and consequently fall into hell after death.

27. 'When the ties of friendship are suddenly loosened, when men enter the road of political wisdom, that unclean path of falseness, when they lose their good reputation and hereafter come to meet with sufferings —is it not sensual enjoyments that are the cause thereof?

28. 'Now, since worldly pleasures in this manner tend to the destruction of all conditions of men, the highest, the middle and the lowest, both in this world and in the next, the Munis, O *S*akra, who long only for the Self, keep aloof from them, as they would from angry serpents.'

Then *S*akra, the Lord of the Devas, approved his words, saying, 'Well spoken,' and as he was propitiated by the greatness of mind of those *R*ishis, he confessed that he himself had committed the theft.

29, 30. 'A high opinion of virtue may be tested by trial. Thus considering, I hid the lotus-stalks in order to try you. And now, how fortunate is the world in that it possesses such Munis as you, whose glory is tested by fact. And thou, here, take these lotus-stalks, as a proof of a constant holy behaviour.'

With these words he handed the stalks over to the Bodhisattva. But the Bodhisattva reproved his unbecoming and audacious way of proceeding in terms though modest, yet expressive of noble self-esteem.

31. 'We are no kinsfolk of thine, nor thy comrades, nor are we thy actors or buffoons. What, then, is the reason for thy coming here, Lord of the Devas, to play with *R*ishis in this manner?'

At these words *S*akra, the Lord of the Devas,

hastily divested himself of his divine appearance, brilliant with his ear-rings, his head-ornament, and his lightning, and respectfully bowing to the Bodhisattva, spoke thus in order to appease him:

32. 'O thou who art free from all selfishness, deign to forgive me the thoughtless deed I did with the aforesaid purpose; pardon it like a father, like a teacher!

33. 'It is proper, indeed, to those whose eyes are not yet opened to wisdom, to offend against others, be they even their equals. Likewise it is proper to (the wise) who know the Self, to pardon such offences. Also for this reason, pray do not feel anger in thy heart concerning that deed!'

Having thus appeased him, *S*akra disappeared on the spot.

In this manner, then, those who have learnt to appreciate the happiness of detachment are hostile to worldly pleasures; they will oppose them like one opposes a deception, an injury [1].

XX. The Story of the Treasurer.

(Cp. Pâli *G*âtaka, No. 171, Fausb. II, 64, 65.)

An unfounded opinion of their possession of some virtue acts upon the virtuous like a stirring spur.

---

[1] In the original some lines follow here, bracketed by the editor. No doubt, we have here an interpolation, as is also indicated by its very collocation after the ethical maxim which must be the final part of our tale. This is its translation:

'And this *g*âtaka has thus been explained by the Lord:

34-36. "I, the son of Sâradvatî [viz. *S*âriputra], Maudgalyâyana, Kâsyapa, Pûr*n*a, Aniruddha, and Ânanda, we were the brothers of that time. Utpalâvar*n*â was the sister and Kub*g*ottarâ was the maidservant. *K*itra the householder was then the male slave, Sâtâgiri the Yaksha, Pârileya the elephant, Madhudâtar the monkey, Kâlodâyin the *S*akra of that time. Retain well this *g*âtaka thus explained."'

Almost the same verses and names are found in the conclusion of this story in the Pâli *G*âtaka.

Considering thus, one ought to strive after the realisation of virtues; as will be taught in the following.

One time the Bodhisattva is said to have been a king's treasurer, illustrious for his learning, his noble family and his modest behaviour. He had lofty aspirations and a clever intellect, loved honest practices in business, and owing to his thorough study of many branches of science, attracted notice by his elegance of speech. Compassionate as he was and in the possession of a large estate, he made the bliss of his wealth flow in all directions by his great gifts of charity. So he was considered the jewel of householders.

1. As he was by his nature fond of righteousness, and was adorned by (acquired) qualities, sacred learning and the like, people were wont to look upon him as worthy of veneration above all others.

One day, when that Great Being had gone out for some business to the king's palace, his mother-in-law came to his house to see her daughter. After the usual welcome and inquiries as to health, there ensued a conversation, in the course of which, being alone with her daughter, the wife of the Bodhisattva, she turned to put questions to her such as these: ' Your husband does not disregard you, my dear, I hope? And does he know how to show you attention? He does not grieve you by misconduct, I hope?' And she answered with downcast looks bashfully in a soft tone : 'Virtuous conduct and behaviour such as his are hardly to be met with even in a mendicant who has renounced the world.' But her mother, whose hearing and understanding were impaired by old age, did not well catch the meaning of these words of her daughter, as they were spoken with shame in a rather low voice, and having heard the mention of a mendicant who had renounced the world, drew the inference that her son-in-law had become a religious mendicant. She burst into tears, and overpowered by the violence of her grief, indulged in lamenting and bewailing her daughter. 'What virtuous behaviour and conduct is shown by him who leaves the world in this manner, abandoning his affectionate family? And what has he to do with world-renunciation, after all?

2. 'What is the reason that such a person as he is, young, handsome, delicate, accustomed to a life of comfort, a favourite with the king, should feel a vocation for the forest-life?

3. 'How did it come to pass that without experiencing any wrong from the side of his family and before the deformity of old age had come, he left suddenly and without pain his home abounding in wealth?

4. 'He, adorned by a decent behaviour, by wisdom and love of righteousness, he, full of compassion for others—how is it that he could come to such a reckless deed without mercy for his own family?

5. 'As he was in the habit of honouring Sramaṇas and Brâhmans, friends and clients, his own family and (that larger family of) the distressed, and as he considered a spotless conduct his (highest) wealth, say, could he not attain in the world that which he seeks in the forest?

6. 'Abandoning his chaste and devoted wife, the companion of his religious duties, how is it that he does not perceive that by excessive love of the Law he is here transgressing the path of the Law?

7. 'Alas! It is a pity! Fie upon the bad management of Destiny, that men can leave their beloved relations without being withheld by Compassion, or that they can be successful even in the slightest part of the holiness they pursue!'

When the Bodhisattva's wife heard those piteous and sincere lamentations of her mother on account of her husband having renounced the world, she grew alarmed (being impressionable) after the nature of women. Her disturbed countenance expressed the dejection of her mind shaken by the sudden assault of sorrow and pain. She wholly forgot the subject and the connection of the conversation, and reflected: 'My husband has forsaken the world, and my mother on hearing the sad news has come here in order to comfort me.' Having thus made up her mind, the young, girlish woman began to lament and to weep, and with a loud cry swooned away. The other members of the family and the attendants, hearing the matter, became utterly distressed, and burst into lamentations. On hearing that noise, neighbours, friends, kinsmen, and other relations, clients, chiefs of Brâhmanical families, in short, the bulk of the citizens, as they were much attached to the treasurer, gathered round his house.

8. As a rule, he had always shared the good and the ill fortune of the people. In consequence thereof the people, as if they had learnt this behaviour from him, showed him the like sympathy in both fortunes.

Now, when the Bodhisattva on his return from the king's residence approached his dwelling-place, he heard the lamentations resounding from his house, and saw the large multitude there assembled. He ordered his attendant to go and learn what was the matter, who having got that information came back and reported it to him.

9. 'It has been rumoured, I do not know in what way, that Your Honour has given up her wealthy home to become a mendicant. This news has induced this large body of people to crowd here out of affection.'

Upon hearing these words, the Great Being felt something like shame. His heart of innate pureness was alarmed by what appeared to him like a reproof. And he entered upon this reflection : ' Oh ! how much am I honoured by this opinion of the people !

10. ' If after obtaining this high opinion of my virtues from the part of the citizens, I should cling to the home-life henceforward, should I not be a coward ?

11. ' I should make myself reputed as one attached to vice, ill-behaving and a despiser of virtues; and would consequently lose the esteem I now enjoy from the virtuous. So living, life would be insupportable to me.

12. ' For this reason, in return for the honour conferred upon me by public opinion, I will honour them

again by realising it, and affected with a pious love of the forest-groves, detach myself from my home with its vice-producing evil passions.'

Having thus considered, the Great Being forthwith turned back, and caused himself to be announced to the king: 'The treasurer wants to see Your Majesty once more.' After being admitted to the king's presence, and after the usual salutations, being asked by the king the reason of his return, he said: 'I desire to renounce the world, and beg you to grant me your permission, Your Majesty.'

On hearing this, the king was troubled and alarmed, and said these affectionate words:

13. 'What ails you that, while I am living who love you more than your friends and kinsmen, you should want to withdraw to the forest, as if I were unable to relieve you from that pain either by my wealth or my policy or my great power?

14. 'Are you in want of money: take it from my side. Is it some grief that makes you suffer: I will cure it. Or is it for any other purpose that you desire to withdraw to the forest, leaving your relations and me, who entreat you in this manner?'

To these affectionate and honorific words of the monarch he answered in a tone of friendly persuasiveness:

15. 'From whence can there arise grief to those whom your arm protects, or sadness caused by want of wealth? It is, therefore, not sorrow that induces me to withdraw to the forest, but another reason. Hear what it is.

16. 'The report is current, Your Majesty, that I have taken the vows of a religious mendicant. A crowd of people mourn for it, and weep for sorrow. It is for this reason that I want to live in the solitude of the forests, since I have been judged a person capable of conceiving this virtuous purpose.'

The king replied: 'Your Honour ought not to leave us on account of a mere rumour. The worth of persons like you does not depend on public opinion, nor do they acquire their illustrious virtues nor lose them conformably to idle gossip.

17. 'Rumour is the result of unrestrained imagination. Once abroad, it runs about free and unchecked. Ridiculous is he who in earnest minds such gossip, more ridiculous is he who acts up to it!'

The Bodhisattva said: 'No, no, Your Majesty, do not speak so! A high opinion of men must be acted up to. Will Your Majesty deign to consider this.

18. 'When a man becomes famous for holiness, Your Majesty, that person ought not to remain behind his reputation, if in fact he is pious, but, to say nothing more, his very shame must induce him to take upon himself the burden of that virtue.

19. 'For, if he is seen in any way acting in accordance with that high opinion of his virtue, the renown of his glory will shine the more, whereas he will be like a dried-up well in the opposite case.

20. 'By a false reputation of virtue, which will spread up to the time when subdued by further knowledge it will disappear, the good renown of men is utterly destroyed. Once destroyed, it is hardly able to shoot forth anew.

21. 'Thus considering, I am about to abandon my family and property, since those goods are the root of strife and trouble, and worth avoiding like black-hooded snakes with wrath-raised heads. It does not become you, Your Majesty, to oppose my determination.

22. '(Do not supply me with money.) You are accustomed to show your attachment and gratitude to your loyal servants, as becomes you, I know; yet what to a homeless mendicant would be the use of money, which of necessity involves worldly goods and passions?'

So speaking the Great Being persuaded the king to give him his permission. After which he immediately set out for the forest.

But his friends, relations, and clients met him, and shedding tears and embracing his feet, tried to prevent him. Some obstructed his way, placing themselves before him with respectfully folded hands. Some again endeavoured to lead him in the direction of his house (with soft violence), by embraces and similar persuasive practices. Others again were prompted by their affection to address him in somewhat harsh terms, expressing their blame in some way or other. Some also tried to persuade him that he ought to have regard to his friends and family, for whom he should feel compassion. Others, too, directed their efforts to convince him by argument, combining sacred texts with deductions of reasoning, to the effect that the state of a householder must be the holiest one. There were others again who exerted themselves in different ways to make him give up his design; partly dwelling on the hardships of the life in a penance-grove, partly urging him to fulfil his obligations and duties in the world to the end, partly expressing their doubt as to the existence of anything like reward in the other world. Now when he looked on his friends thus opposing his world-renunciation and earnestly endeavouring to hinder his departure for the forest with faces wet with tears, surely, this thought arose in his mind:

23. 'If a person acts inconsiderately, it is the duty of those who claim to be his friends to care for the good of their friend, be it even in a rough manner. Such, indeed, is acknowledged to be the righteous way of proceeding among the pious. How much the more, if the good they advise be at the same time something pleasant.

24. 'But as to them, how is it possible that preferring the home-life and boldly deterring me from the forest-life as from the contact of some evil, they should express the judgment of a sound mind?

25. 'A dead man or one in danger of death is a person to be wept for, likewise one fallen from righteousness. But what may be the meaning of this weeping for me who am alive but desirous of living in the forest?

26. 'Suppose the separation from me should be the cause of their sorrow, why will they not dwell in the

forest with me? If however they prefer their homes to me, why are they prodigal of their tears?

27. 'But granted that attachment to their family prevents them from adopting the state of an ascetic, how is it that the like consideration did not formerly present itself to them on so many battle-fields?

28. 'I have often experienced the heroism of their sincere friendship in adversity, and now behold that deep-rooted friendship, as it were, embodied in their tears. Yet, notwithstanding this, it will seem mere guile to me, since they do not follow my example.

29, 30. 'As surely as it is great regard for their friend deserving regard, that makes their eyes full of tears, their heads reverentially bent, their words interrupted with sobs, while they are exerting themselves to hinder my departure, so surely ought their love to have the effect of bringing them to the praiseworthy resolution to go and wander about with me, lest they should appear like actors in a theatrical performance, to the shame of the pious!

31. 'If anybody be in distress, be he ever so wicked a person, some two or three friends will keep with him, at least; but for a man, however excellent by virtue, it will be oh! so hard, to get one single comrade, when setting out for the forest!

32. 'Those who in battles, when danger was imminent from furious elephants, used to set an example (of fearlessness) to me, even they do not follow me now, when I lead them to the forest. Verily am I, are they, the same as we were before?

33. 'I do not recollect having done them any wrong that could cause the ruin of their attachment ... So this behaviour of my friends may, perhaps, issue from the care for what they consider my happiness.

34. 'Or is it rather my lack of virtues that hinders them from being my companions in the forest? For who may possess the power of loosening hearts that have been won by virtue?

35. 'But why indulge in idle reflections about these persons? Of a truth, since they are unable to

perceive the evils, however obvious, inherent in the home-life, nor the virtues to be found in the penance-groves, the eye of knowledge is shut to them!

36. 'They are not capable of parting with worldly pleasures, the cause of suffering both in this world and in the next, but forsake both the penance-grove which frees from those sufferings, and me! Fie upon their infatuation!

37. 'O, those very sins by the delusions of which these friends of mine and the whole of the creatures are prevented from tranquillity, I will crush down forcibly whenever I shall have obtained by residence in the penance-forest the excellent power of doing so!'

Of such a kind were his reflections. And after thus making up his mind, he put aside the manifold affectionate entreaties of his friends, made plain to them his firm resolution in kind and gentle terms, and set out for the penance-forest.

In this manner, then, an unfounded opinion of their possession of some virtue acts upon the virtuous in the same way as a stirring spur. Thus considering, one ought to strive after the realisation of virtues. [For this reason a pious man, being esteemed for his virtues as a monk or as a lay-devotee, must strive to be in fact adorned with the virtues fit for that state. Further, this story may be adduced with the object of showing the difficulty of finding companions for a religious life.]

XXI. THE STORY OF *K*UDDABODHI[1].

(Cp. the Pâli Gâtaka, No. 443, Fausb. IV, 22-27; *K*ariyâpi*t*aka II, 4.)

By keeping down his anger a man appeases his enemies, but doing otherwise he will inflame them. This will be taught as follows.

---

[1] Though *S*ûra does not mention the Bodhisattva's name which he bore in this existence, yet it appears from the Pâli redactions, that *K*ud*d*abodhi, literally = 'Little Bodhi,' is intended as his proper name.

XXI. THE STORY OF KUDDABODHI.

One time the Bodhisattva, that Great Being, was born in this world in a certain noble Brâhmanical family, it is said, who enjoyed great renown for their practise of virtues in a grand style, owned a large and well-secured estate, were honoured by the king and favoured by the gods. In course of time he grew up, and having duly received the sacraments, as he exerted himself to excel in the virtue of learning, within a short time he became renowned in the assemblies of the learned.

1. The fame of the learned unfolds itself in the assemblies of the learned, in the same way as jewels get their reputation with jewellers, as heroes are known on the battle-field.

Now when the Great-minded One, according to his constant observance of the Law in previous existences and to the enlightenment of his mind by wisdom, had familiarised himself with world-renunciation, his house no longer pleased him. He understood that worldly pleasures are the abode of many evils and sins, since they are attended by a great deal of discomfort in consequence of strife, quarrel, infatuation, and subject to (losses of wealth either from the side of) the king, or (because of) water, or fire, or thieves, or unfriendly kinsmen; so he was convinced that they can never yield satisfaction. Accordingly, shunning them like poisonous food and longing for the Self, he parted with his fair hair and beard, resigned the delusive brilliancy of a householder's dress, and putting on the vile orange-coloured robes, embraced that glorious state of the ascetic life disciplined by rules and restrained by vows. His wife, who loved him much, likewise cut off her hair, and forsook the care of apparelling her body and beautifying it with ornaments. Then, only adorned by the natural beauty of her form and virtues, she covered her limbs with the orange-coloured robes, and followed her husband.

Now, when the Bodhisattva understood her determination of going with him to the penance-forest, knowing that the delicate constitution of a woman is unfit for the ascetic life, he spoke to her: 'My dear, truly, you have now shown me your sincere affection. Yet this be sufficient. Do not persist in your determination of being my companion in the forest. It would rather be suitable for you to take up your abode in such a place, where other women dwell who have forsaken the world; with them you should live. It is a hard thing to pass the night in forest-dwellings. Look here.

2. 'Cemeteries, desert houses, mountains, forests infested by ferocious animals, are the resting-places of the homeless ascetics; they take their rest in whatsoever place they are when the sun sets.

3. 'Being intent on meditation, they always like to walk alone, and are averse even to the sight of a woman. Therefore, make up your mind to desist from your purpose. What profit may you have from that wandering life?'

But she who had firmly resolved upon accompanying him, answered him something like this, while her eyes grew dim with tears:

4, 5. 'If I should suppose my going with you a matter of weariness rather than of joy, do you think I should desire a thing which causes suffering to myself and displeasure to you? But it is because I cannot bear to live without you, that you must pardon this lack of obedience to your orders.'

And though he repeated his entreaties, she never would turn back. Then the Bodhisattva gave up his opposition, and silently suffered her companionship. As the female *k*akravâka goes after her mate, so she went along with him in his wanderings through villages and towns and markets.

One day after meal-time he performed the usual rite of profound meditation (dhyâna) in a lonely part of some forest. It was a splendid landscape, adorned with many groves of trees affording much shade, and waited on, as it were, by the sunbeams peeping here and there through the thick foliage with the softness of the moonlight; the dust of various flowers overspread the ground; in short, it was a fair spot. In the afternoon he rose from his profound meditation, and sewed rags together to make clothes [1]. And at no great distance from him, she, the companion of his homeless life, embellishing by the splendour of her beauty the trunk of a tree in whose shade she was seated like a deity, was meditating on such subject and in such manner as he had enjoined her. It was the season of spring, when gardens and groves are at their loveliest. On all sides young and tender shoots abounded; the soft humming of crowds of bees roaming about was heard, as well as the cries of joy uttered by the lascivious cuckoos; the lakes and ponds, adorned with laughing lotuses and water-lilies, were an attraction for the eyes; there blew soft winds scented with the odours and perfumes of manifold blossoms. To enjoy that magnificence of spring, the king of that country made a tour in the groves, and came to that very spot.

6, 7. It does, indeed, afford gladness to the mind to behold forest-regions at spring-time, when their various blossoms and flower-clusters make them bright, as if that season enveloped them with its pomp, when the he-cuckoo and the peacock sing, the drunken bees make their buzzing sound, when soft and fresh grass-plots cover the earth and lotuses fill up the water-basins. Then the groves are the play-grounds of the Love-god.

On seeing the Bodhisattva, the king respectfully drew near to him, and after the usual ceremonial greetings and complimentary words, sat down apart. Then, on perceiving the female ascetic, that very lovely appari-tion, the beauty of her figure perturbed his heart, and though understanding that she must certainly be the companion of his religious duties, owing to the lasciviousness of his nature, he reflected on some contrivance to carry her away.

8. But having heard of the transcendent power of

---

[1] Pâ*m*sukûlâni sîvyati sma.

the ascetics, that the fire of their wrath can shoot a curse as its flame, he refrained from a rash deed of contempt against him, even though the Love-god had destroyed the moral checks (that might have restrained him).

Then this thought entered his mind: 'Let me examine the extent of his penance-obtained power. Then I shall be able to act in a proper manner, not otherwise. If his mind is ruled by passionate affection for her, surely, he has no power gained by penance. But if he were to prove dispassionate or to show little interest in her, then he may be supposed to possess that sublime power.' Having thus considered, the king, desirous of proving that penance-power, spoke to the Bodhisattva, as if he wished his good. 'Say, ascetic, this world abounds in rogues and bold adventurers. Why, it is not fit for Your Reverence to have with you such a handsome person as this companion of your religious duties in remote forests, where you are destitute of protection. If she were to be injured by somebody, certainly people would censure me, too. Look here.

9, 10. 'Suppose, while living in these lonely regions, some man disregarding both you, a penance-exhausted ascetic, and Righteousness, were to carry her off by force, what else could you do in that case but wail on her account? Indulging in anger, forsooth, agitates the mind and destroys the glory of a religious life, since it tends to the detriment of it. It is, therefore, best to let her live in an inhabited place. Of what use, after all, is female company to ascetics?'

The Bodhisattva said: 'Your Majesty has spoken truth. Yet hear to what I would resort in such circumstances.

11. 'Who were to act in such a case against me,
   Should pride incite or thoughtless rashness
      move him,
   In truth, I would, while living, not release him,
   A rain-cloud like that never will endure dust.'

Then the king thought: 'He takes a great interest

in her, he does not possess penance-power,' and despising the Great Being, was no longer afraid of injuring him. Obeying his passion, he ordered his attendants who were in charge of his zenana: 'Go and fetch this female ascetic into my zenana.' On hearing this order, she, like a deer assailed by a ferocious animal, showed her fear, alarm, and dismay by her (changed) countenance, her eyes filled with tears, and overpowered by her grief, she lamented in a faltering voice somewhat in this manner:

12. 'To mankind, overcome by sufferings, the king is the best refuge, it is said, like a father. But whose help can be implored by him, to whom the king himself acts as an evildoer?

13. 'Alas! The guardians of the world-quarters (lokapâlâs) have been dismissed from their office, or they do not exist at all, or they are dead, since they make no effort to protect the oppressed. Dharma himself is but a mere sound, I suppose.

14. 'But why do I reproach the Celestials, while my lord himself is thus keeping silence, undisturbed by my fate? Are you not bound to protect even a stranger who is ill-treated by wicked people?

15. 'By the thunderbolt of his curse he might change a mountain into dust, if he were to pronounce the word "perish," and still, he does not break silence, whilst his wife is thus injured! And I must live to see this, wretched woman that I am!

16. 'Or am I a bad person, scarcely deserving pity after coming into this distress? But ascetics ought to behave with compassion towards any one in distress. Is not this their proper line of conduct?

17. 'I am afraid you bear in mind even now my refusal to leave you, when you ordered me to turn back. Alas! Is then this catastrophe the happiness I longed for through the fulfilment of my own wish though contrary to yours?'

While she thus lamented—and what else could she do, that female ascetic, but cry and wail and weep in piteous accents?—the royal attendants, obeying the orders of the king, placed her on a chariot, and before the very eyes of the Great Being carried her off to the zenana. The Bodhisattva, however, had repressed his powerful anger by the power of his tranquillity, and was sewing his rags just as before without the slightest perturbation, as calm and serene as ever. To him the king spoke:

18. 'Threatening words of indignation and anger you uttered in a loud and strength-betraying voice, but now, on seeing that beauty ravished before your eyes, you keep quiet and are cast down because you have no power.

19. 'Why, show your wrath, either by the strength of your arm or by the splendid power you have accumulated as the result of your penance. He who, not knowing the compass of his own faculties, takes an engagement he cannot keep, such a one loses his splendour, you know.'

The Bodhisattva replied: 'Know that I did keep my engagement, Your Majesty.

20. 'He who was ready in that case against me
   To act and struggled—I did not release him,
   But kept him down, made him by force be
      quiet,
   So you must own that I made true my promise.'

That excessive firmness of mind of the Bodhisattva, proved by his tranquillity, did not fail to inspire the king with respect for the virtues of the ascetic. And he began to reflect: 'This Brâhman must have hinted at something else, speaking thus, and I, not understanding his mind, committed a rash action.' This reflection arising within him, induced him to ask the Bodhisattva:

21. 'Who was that other who acted against you and was not released by you, however much he struggled, no more than rising dust is by a rain-cloud? Whom did you quiet then?'

The Bodhisattva answered: 'Hearken, great prince.

22. 'He, whose forthcoming robs the insight and without whose appearance a man sees clearly, rose

within me, but I repressed him; Anger is the name of that being, disastrous to his fosterer.

23. 'He, at whose appearance the foes of mankind rejoice, rose within me, but I repressed him, that Anger who would have caused gladness to my enemies.

24. 'Him who, when bursting forth, induces man to nothing good and blinds the eye of the mind, him I did subdue, O king; Anger is his name.

25. 'Yea, I have destroyed that hideous-looking ferocious monster rising up within me, that anger, which becomes to him whom it has subdued the cause of leaving his good and losing even the profit obtained before.

26. 'As fire, by the process of attrition, arises from a piece of wood to the destruction of that very log, in the same way wrath, breaking out by the false conceptions it produces in the mind of a man, tends to his ruin.

27. 'He who is not able to appease the heart-burning fever of anger, when fire-like it bursts forth with fierceness, such a man is little esteemed; his reputation fades away, just as moonshine, that friend of the waterlilies, fades in the blush of dawn.

28. 'But he who, not heeding insults from the side of other people, considers anger as his real enemy, the reputation of such a man shines with brightness, like the auspicious lustre which streams down the disc of the crescent.

'Further, anger is also attended by other noxious qualities of importance.

29. 'An angry man, though resplendent with ornaments, looks ugly; the fire of wrath has taken away the splendour of his beauty. And lying on a precious couch, he does not rest at his ease, his heart being wounded by the arrow of anger.

30. 'Bewildered by wrath, a man forgets to keep the side by which to reach the happiness suitable for himself, and runs off on the wrong road, so that he forfeits the happiness consisting in a good reputation,

as the moon is deprived of its lustre in the dark part of its menstrual course.

31. 'By wrath he throws himself headlong into his ruin, in spite of the efforts of his friends to restrain him. As a rule he gets into a stupid rage of hatred, and the power of his mind being impaired, he is unable to distinguish between what is good for him and what is bad.

32. 'Carried away by his anger, he will commit sinful actions to be repented of with many misfortunes for centuries. Can enemies, whose wrath has been provoked by severe injuries, do anything worse?

33. 'Anger is our adversary within us, this I know. Who may bear the free course of its insolence?

34. 'For this reason I did not release that anger, although it was struggling within me. Who, indeed, may suffer himself to overlook an enemy able to do such mischief?'

These heart-moving words and the marvellous forbearance he had proved by them to possess, softened and converted the mind of that king who spoke:

35. 'Worthy, indeed, of your tranquillity of mind are these words you have spoken! ... But, why use many words? I was deceived because I did not understand you.'

After thus praising the Bodhisattva, he went near to him and throwing himself at his feet, confessed his sin. And he dismissed also that female ascetic, after obtaining her pardon, and offered himself to the disposal of the Bodhisattva as his attendant.

In this manner a man by keeping down his anger appeases his enemies, but doing otherwise he will inflame them. Thus considering, one ought to strive after the suppression of anger. [This story is also to be told in connection with such sayings as praise the precept of forbearance, viz. 'in this manner unfriendly feelings are set at rest by friendliness, and by self-restraint hatred is not allowed to grow,' and 'in this manner he who banishes anger acts to the benefit of both.' Likewise when expounding the sinfulness of anger, and treating of the high-mindedness of the Tathâgata.]

XXII. THE STORY OF THE HOLY SWANS.

(Comp. Pâli Gâtaka, No. 533, Fausb. V, 337-354.)

The virtuous, even when in distress, behave in such a manner as cannot be imitated by the impious; how much less are the latter able to follow up the conduct of the virtuous, when favoured by fortune! This will be taught as follows.

One time, it is told, the Bodhisattva was a king of swans. He was the chief of a large tribe of swans, numbering many hundred thousands, who lived in Lake Mânasa. His name was Dhri̇tarâshtra. The commander of his army, who was called Sumukha[1], was skilled in the management of affairs, knowing the right and the wrong policy very well; his keen intellect encompassed the objects and events over a large extent of space and time; born of an illustrious family, he embellished the nobility of his extraction by his talent, his courtesy, his modesty; he was endowed with the virtues of constancy, honesty, courage, and distinguished by the purity of his conduct, mode of life, and behaviour; moreover he was capable of enduring fatigue, vigilant and clever in military marches as well as in battles, and bore a great affection to his master. In consequence of their mutual love the grandeur of their qualities shone the more; and as they were in the habit of instructing that flock of swans, as a teacher and his foremost disciple would instruct all his other pupils, or a father with his eldest son his other sons, inculcating upon their mind a peaceable behaviour towards others, and such other matters as lead to the benefit of the creatures, they offered a spectacle for the

---

[1] The original text has here this interpolation, 'who was the presbyter Ânanda at that time,' of course bracketed by the editor. Cp. the note on p. 164.

great admiration of the Devas, Snakes, Yakshas, Vidyâdharas, and holy ascetics who witnessed them.

1. As of a bird in the sky both wings are incessantly occupied in holding up his body, so these two knew no other business than that of supporting the body of Salvation for their flock of swans.

Now that tribe of swans, being thus favoured by them, attained a state of great plenty, in the same way as mankind by the extension of righteousness and material prosperity. Consequently that lake bore the utmost beauty.

2, 3. Adorned by that tribe of swans, who by their sound would call to mind the soft and lovely noise of the anklets of women, that lake was splendid. When in a mass, the swans resembled a moving grove of lotuses. When dispersed or divided into separate groups of unequal size, they made the lake surpass even the beauty of a sky embellished with scattered banks of clouds.

Enchanted with that exceeding splendour, which was the effect of the virtue of that lord of swans intent on the good of all creatures, and of Sumukha, his commander-in-chief, crowds of Siddhas, *R*ishis, Vidyâdharas, and deities often and in many places delighted in conversing on the glory of those two.

4. 'Their magnificent figures resemble pure gold, their voices utter articulate speech, righteousness is the rule of their modest behaviour and their policy. Whosoever they may be, they bear but the shape of swans.'

5. The fame of those two, spreading through the world by the report of those superhuman beings who, free from jealousy, celebrated their virtues, found a general belief to such an extent, that it became a topic of conversation in the councils of kings, where the account of their glory circulated like a present.

Now in that time one Brahmadatta[1] was king in

---

[1] Brahmadatta, the king of Benares, is the fabulous prince, during whose reign a great number of the stories of the Pâli *G*âtaka-book take place.

XXII. THE STORY OF THE HOLY SWANS.

Benares. Having often heard in his council his trustworthy officials and the foremost among the Brâhmans highly extol the extraordinary qualities of that lord of swans and of his commander-in-chief, he became more and more affected with curiosity to see them. So he said to his ministers, who were very clever, having studied many branches of science: 'Well, sirs, set to work the cleverness of your minds, and try to devise some means by which I might obtain at least the sight of those two excellent swans.' Then those wise ministers let their thoughts range over the road of political wisdom, and (having discovered by thinking the means wanted) said to the king:

6. 'The prospect of happiness allures the creatures to withdraw from any place, Your Majesty. For this reason the rumour of the existence of some extremely good qualities conducive to their happiness may bring them hither.

'Therefore, let Your Majesty deign to order a beautiful lake, of the same kind as that where those lovely-shaped swans are reported to live, but still surpassing it in brilliancy, to be constructed here in one of your forests; which being done, you must make known by proclamation, to be repeated every day, that you grant safety to all birds. Perhaps the rumour of the surpassing excellence of this lake, conducive to their happiness, may excite their curiosity and draw them hither. Do but consider, Your Majesty.

7. 'As a rule happiness once obtained loses its charm, and ceases to be taken into account; but such happiness as rests upon hearsay seems lovely, and fascinates the mind, because it is remote from the eyes.'

The king accepted their proposal, and had a great lake, which by the splendour of its magnificence rivalled with Lake Mânasa, constructed in a short time in a place not too near the park which skirted his capital. It was a most charming basin of pure water, and very rich in water-plants, embracing various kinds of lotuses and waterlilies: padma, utpala, kumuda, pu*nd*arika, saugandhika, tâmarasa, kahlâra.

8. Flowery trees, bright with their quivering twigs, surrounded its shore, as if they had taken possession of that place in order to contemplate that lake.

9. Swarms of bees, as if attracted by its laughing lotuses, which were rocking on its gently trembling waves, roamed hovering over its surface.

10, 11. Here its beauty was enhanced by its various waterlilies, sleepless through the gentle touch of the moonbeams, which made them resemble patches of moonshine piercing through the foliage. There the pollen of lotuses and waterlilies, conveyed by the finger-like waves, would ornament its shore as if with gold wires.

12. In many other places, where it was covered with the lovely petals and filaments of lotuses and waterlilies, it showed a widespread splendour, as if it bore a gift of homage.

13. Another beauty was due to the limpidity and calmness of its water, which was so transparent as to show the sharp contours and the fair hues of its crowds of fishes, no less conspicuous while swimming beneath its surface than they would have been, if moving in the sky.

14. Near such places, where the elephants, dipping their trunks in it, blew forth cascades of spray glittering like a string of loosened pearls, it seemed as if the lake carried waves ground to dust after being driven upon rocks and scattered in the air.

15. Here and there it was perfumed, so to speak, with the fragrances emanating from the ointments used by bathing Vidyâdhara women, from the streams of juice of elephants in rut and from the dust of its (own) flowers.

16. Being so brilliant, that lake was like a general mirror for the stars, the wives of the Moon-god. Gay birds abounded, and their warbling resounded in it.

Such, then, was the lake he had ordered to be constructed, and which he gave to the whole nation of birds to have the unobstructed use and enjoyment of it. Accordingly, in order to inspire all birds with confidence, he ordered a proclamation, by which he granted them security, to be repeated day after day. It ran in these terms :

17. 'The king is glad to give this lake, inclusive of the groups of lotuses and waterlilies covering its waters, to the birds, and grants safety to them.'

One time, when autumn having drawn away the dark curtain of clouds, dispensed its beautiful gifts, enlarging the horizon clear and pure, the lakes were lovely to behold, with their limpid water and with the full brilliancy of their clusters of lotuses disclosed. It was the season when the Moon, with increased power of rays, as it were, reaches the highest pitch of loveliness and youthfulness, when Earth, adorned with the harvest-bliss of manifold crops, offers a fair aspect, and when the younger among the swans begin to show themselves. Now, a couple of swans, who belonged to that very tribe of the Bodhisattva, flew up from Lake Mânasa, and passing over different regions overspread with autumn's mildness, at last came to the realm of that king. And there they saw that lake and the wonderful beauty caused by its flowers; for its lotuses, when expanded, made it glow as with flames, and its waterlilies, when unclosed, gave it a laughing aspect. They heard the echoes of the confused sounds of crowds of birds and the humming of the bees who were busily roaming over its flowers. They smelt the scent of the dust of its lotuses and waterlilies scattered about by the gentle, cool, and soft breezes, which seemed to have the task of gliding over the wreaths of its waves. Though accustomed to Lake Mânasa, those two swans were touched by the surpassing loveliness and splendour of that other lake; and this thought entered their mind: 'Oh! our whole tribe must come here!'

18. Generally people, obtaining some pleasure within the reach of everybody, will in the first place remember their friends, owing to the suggestion of their love.

That couple remained there, diverting themselves as they best liked, till the next rainy season. At the commencement of that period, when masses of clouds like hosts of the Daityas advance causing darkness, yet not too thick and interrupted by flashes of lightning glittering like brandished weapons; when the gay troops of peacocks perform their dances and display the beauty of their wide-opened feather-tails, while uttering their loud and continual cries, as if they exulted at the triumph of the clouds, and also the smaller birds have become loquacious; when brisk winds blow, fragrant with the flower-dust of forest trees: the sâl, the kadamba, the arguna, and the ketaka, and produce a welcome coolness, as if they were the breath of the forest; when flocks of young cranes, showing themselves in the sky, contrast with the dark background of the clouds, so as to resemble their rows of teeth, so to speak; when the tribes of swans are anxious to leave, and give vent to their longing by soft and gentle cries—on that opportunity our couple of swans returned to their Lake Mânasa. And paying their respects to their lord, they told him, first of the regions they had visited, then gave him an account of the surpassing advantages of that lake (whence they had just returned). 'Your Majesty, south of Mount Himavat,' they said, 'there lives at Benares a king of men, named Brahmadatta, who has delivered to the birds a large lake of marvellous beauty, possessing delights of indescribable loveliness. All birds may enjoy it at their free will and wish, and safety is warranted to them by a royal decree which is made known every day by proclamation. The birds divert themselves there as unrestrained and fearless as if they stayed in their homes. When the rains are over, Your Majesty ought to go there.' On hearing this, the whole tribe of swans were affected with a strong desire to see that lake. The Bodhisattva, then, fixing his eyes with an inquisitive expression upon the face of Sumukha, his commander-in-chief, said: 'What do you think about this?' Sumukha, after bowing his head, answered: 'I deem it unfit for Your Majesty to go there. Why? Those delights of charming loveliness are, after all, but a kind of allurement, and here we are in want of nothing. Generally speaking, the hearts of men are false, their tender compassion is deceitful, and under the guise of delusive sweet words and kind attentions they conceal a cruel and wicked nature. Will Your Highness deign to consider this.

19. 'Quadrupeds and birds are wont to express their true feelings by the import of their cries. But men are the only animals skilled in producing sound meaning the contrary of their intentions.

20. 'Their language, of course, is sweet, well-intentioned, and wholesome. Merchants also make expenses in the hope of obtaining gain.

21. 'Therefore, Your Majesty, it is unfit at any time to put confidence (in them) because of something as trifling (as their words). A line of conduct which is dangerous and wrong, cannot be but unsuccessful, even if followed in pursuit of some object.

'Should, however, the excursion to that lake be indispensable, it is not suitable for us to stay there for a long time, or to make up our minds to resolve to take up our residence there; we have only to go and, after enjoying its magnificent beauties, return shortly. Such is my advice.'

Now, as the tribe of swans, whose curiosity to see the Benares lake was ever increasing, did not cease to request the Bodhisattva again and again to set out for that place, once on a bright autumn night, adorned with the pure lustre of the moon, the asterisms, and the stars, he complied with their wishes. And, accompanied by Sumukha and a numerous crowd of swans, he set out in that direction, resembling the Moon-god with his attendant band of (white) autumn clouds.

22. As soon as they beheld the charming splendour of that lake, surprise mingled with gladness overwhelmed their minds. When they entered it, they added to it no less brilliancy by their gay shapes and the lovely groups they formed, taking possession of it.

23. Owing to the manifold varieties of its sites, by which it surpassed Lake Mânasa, they were delighted,

and in time their attachment to the new place of abode effaced Mânasa from their hearts.

They heard the proclamation of safety, perceived the freedom of movement of the birds residing there, and were gladdened by the display of the beauty of the lake. Their delight rose to the highest degree when they wandered over its waters, enjoying the pleasure of one who makes an excursion in a park.

Now the guardians of that lake reported the arrival of those swans to the king, saying: 'Your Majesty, two excellent swans, who bear the very same shape and are distinguished by the very same qualities as those famous ones are said to possess, have arrived at Your Majesty's lake, as if to enhance its beauty. Their beautiful wings shine like gold, their beaks and feet have a lustre which even surpasses that of gold, their size exceeds the average, and they have well-shaped bodies. A retinue of many hundred thousands of swans have come with them.' Having been thus informed, the king selected among his fowlers one who was renowned and recognised for his skill in the art of bird-catching, and committed to him the honourable charge of catching them. The fowler promised to do so, and having carefully watched the places which those two swans were in the habit of frequenting and haunting, laid down on different spots strong snares well concealed. Now, while the swans were wandering far and wide over the lake, with minds cheerful and rejoiced and without suspecting any mischief, trusting the grant of safety, their lord got one foot entangled in a snare.

24. Trustfulness, indeed, is pernicious. Aroused by the subtle contrivances of those who inspire confidence, it first obliterates the suspicion of danger, then displays carelessness and want of policy.

Then the Bodhisattva, lest a similar misfortune should befall also anybody else of his tribe, announced by a special cry the dangerousness of the lake. Upon which, the swans, alarmed at the capture of their lord, flew up to the sky, uttering confused and dissonant cries of fear, without regarding each other, like soldiers whose chief warrior has been killed. Yet Sumukha, the commander-in-chief, did not withdraw from the side of the lord of swans.

25. A heart bound by affection does not mind imminent peril. Worse than death to such a one is the sorrow which the miserable distress of a friend inflicts on it.

To him the Bodhisattva said:

26. 'Go, Sumukha, go; it is not wise to linger here. What opportunity couldst thou have of helping me who am in this state?'

Sumukha spoke:

27. 'No final death can I incur, if I stay here, nor shall I, if I go, be freed from old age and death. I always attended on thee in thy prosperity. How, master, should I be capable of leaving thee in thy calamity?

28. 'If I were to leave thee, prince of birds, on account of such a trifle as the thread of my own life, where could I find a shield against the rain-shower of blame?

29. 'It is not right, my liege, that I should leave thee in thy distress. Whatever fate may be thine, I am pleased with it, O lord of birds.'

The Bodhisattva spoke:

30. 'What other may be the fate of an insnared bird than the kitchen? How can that prospect please thee who art in the free possession of thy mind and thy limbs?

31, 32. 'Or what profit dost thou see for me or thyself or the whole of our kindred in the death of both of us? And what profit mayst thou explain to be in giving up thy life on an occurrence, when that profit is as little to be seen as level and unlevel in the dark?'

Sumukha spoke:

33, 34. 'How, most excellent of birds, dost thou not perceive the profit in following the path of Righteousness? Honouring the Law of Righteousness in the

right manner¹ produces the highest profit. For this reason I, knowing the precepts of Righteousness and the profit arising therefrom, also moved by attachment to thee, my liege, do not cling to life.'
The Bodhisattva spoke:
35, 36. 'Verily, this is the law for the virtuous, that a friend, minding his duty, shall not abandon his friend in distress, even at the cost of his life. Now, thou didst observe the Law of Righteousness, thou didst show me thy devoted affection. Grant me then, I pray thee, this last request. Fly away, I give thee leave.

37. 'Moreover, the affair having taken this turn, it is thy task, wise-minded one, to fill up the gap caused to our friends by the loss of me.'

38. While they were thus conversing, vying with each other in mutual affection, lo, the Nishâda² appeared, rushing upon them like the God of Death.

As soon as they became aware of his approach, the two excellent birds became silent. Now, the Nishâda seeing that the tribe of swans had flown away, was persuaded 'certainly, some one of them has been caught;' and going round the different places, where he had laid down his snares, discovered those two foremost swans. He was surprised at their beauty, and thinking both of them to be insnared, shook the snares placed in their neighbourhood. But when he perceived that one was caught and the other, loose and free, was keeping him company, his astonishment increased, and drawing near to Sumukha, he spoke to him:

39, 40. 'This bird, being caught in a strong snare, loses his freedom of movement. For this reason he cannot mount to the sky, although I approach. But thou who art not fastened, who art free and

---

¹ Instead of upakitaḥ in the Sanskrit text, the Pâli redaction has apakito, which no doubt is the true reading. I have translated accordingly, comparing also stanza 36 tadarkitas tvayâ dharmaḥ.
² The fowler belonged to that low class of people.

XXII. THE STORY OF THE HOLY SWANS.

strong and hast thy winged carriage at thy disposal, why dost thou not hastily fly up to the sky at my arrival?'

On hearing this, Sumukha addressed him with human language in a voice which distinctly articulated syllables and words, and by its sonorousness manifested the firmness of mind of the speaker, being employed to show his (virtuous) nature.

41, 42. 'How is it, thou askest me, that I, being able to go, do not go. Why, the cause thereof is this. This bird here suffers the misfortune of being insnared. Thou hast power over him, whose foot is entangled in this strong snare, but he has power over me by still stronger fetters, his virtues, by which he has fastened my heart.'

Upon this the Nishâda, affected with high admiration and almost in ecstasy [1], once more asked Sumukha.

43. 'Being afraid of me, the other swans left him and flew up to the sky. But thou dost not leave him. Say, what is this bird to thee?'

Sumukha spoke:

44. 'My king he is, my friend he is, whom I love no less than life, my benefactor he is, and he is in distress. On this account I may never desert him, not even in order to save my own life.'

And observing the feelings of growing tenderness and admiration which appeared in the Nishâda, he continued:

45. 'Oh! If this our conversation might lead to a happy end, my friend! If thou wert to obtain the glory of a virtuous action by setting us free now!'

The Nishâda spoke:

46. 'I do not wish thee harm, and it is not thee I have caught. Why then, go free and join thy relations who will be glad at the sight of thee!'

Sumukha spoke:

47, 48. 'If thou dost not wish my sorrow, then thou must grant my request. If thou art content with one,

---

[1] Literally: on whose body the hairs stood up.

well, leave him and take me. Our bodies have an equal size and compass, and our age is the same, I tell thee. So, taking me as a ransom for him, thou wilt not lose thy profit.

49, 50. 'Why, sir, do consider it well. O that thou mayst be greedy to possess me! Thou mayst tie me first, and afterwards release the king of birds. Thus doing, thou wouldst enjoy the same amount of gain, thou wouldst have granted my request, thou wouldst also cause gladness to the tribe of swans and obtain their friendship, too.

51. 'Now then, gladden the host of swans by setting their lord at liberty, that they may see him again in his resplendent beauty in the clear sky, resembling the Moon released from the Lord of Daityas (Râhu).'

The Nishâda, though accustomed to a cruel trade and hard-hearted by practice, was much touched by these words of the bird uttered in a firm yet soft tone and imposing by their import. For they magnified the attachment to one's master without minding one's own life, and were a strong manifestation of the virtue of gratitude. Overpowered by admiration and respect, he folded his hands, and lifting them up to Sumukha, said: 'Well said, well said, noble being.

52, 53. 'If met with among men or deities, such self-denial would pass for a miracle, as is practised by thee claiming it thy duty to give up thy life for the sake of thy master. I will pay thee my homage, therefore, and set free thy king. Who, indeed, may be capable of doing evil to him who is dearer to thee than life?'

With these words the Nishâda, without caring for the mandate of his king, listening to the voice of his compassion, paid honour to the king of swans, and released him from the snare. And Sumukha, the commander-in-chief, greatly rejoiced at the rescue of his king, fixed a glad and kind look on the Nishâda and spoke:

54. 'As thou hast rejoiced me now by the release of the king of swans, O thou source of gladness to

XXII. THE STORY OF THE HOLY SWANS.

thy friends, mayst thou in the same way be rejoiced with thy friends and kinsmen for many thousands of years!

55. 'Then, that thy labour may not be fruitless, well, take me and also this king of swans, and carrying us on thy shoulder-pole, free and unbound, show us to thy king in his zenana.

56. 'Beholding the king of swans with his minister, this ruler, no doubt, will show thee his gladness by a gift of riches larger than that thou didst dream of, a source to thee of great rejoicing.'

The Nishâda acceded to his request, thinking, the king must see at all events this marvellous couple of swans, and placing them (in baskets) on his pole unhurt and unbound, showed those excellent swans to the king.

57. 'Deign to see,' quoth he, 'the wonderful present I offer you, my lord. Here is that famous king of swans, together with his commander-in-chief!'

On beholding those two foremost of swans, who by the glittering splendour of their lovely figures resembled two solid pieces of gold, the king filled with amazement and exulting with gladness said to the Nishâda:

58. 'How didst thou obtain possession of those two who remain in thy hands, unhurt and unbound, though able to fly away from thee who art on foot? Tell it me at length.'

Being thus addressed, the Nishâda bowing to the king, answered:

59-62. 'I had laid down many snares, O so cruel causes of pain, in pools and ponds, the places of recreation of the birds. Then this foremost of swans, moving unsuspectingly, owing to his trustfulness, got his foot entangled in a hidden snare. The other, though free, was keeping him company, and entreated me to take him in redemption for the life of his king, uttering in a human voice articulate and sweet-sounding language. His ardent request derived its power from his readiness to sacrifice his own life.

O

63. 'So great was the effect of his soft words and his strong deeds in behalf of his master, that I was converted to tenderness, and dismissed his lord together with my own cruel temper.

64. 'After which, rejoiced at the release of the king of birds, he returned many thanks and blessings to me, and instructed me to go up in this manner to you, that my labour, so he said, should not have been a burden by lack of reward.

65. 'And so it is out of gratitude for the deliverance of his king and in my behalf, that this most righteous being, whosoever he may be, who under the outward appearance of a bird roused in one moment tenderness of mind in the heart of a person like me, has arrived of his own accord together with his master at your zenana.'

The king was filled by these words with great joy and amazement. He assigned to the king of swans a golden throne with a footstool, a seat well becoming a king; for it had brilliant feet glittering with the lustre of various jewels, was spread with a most costly and lovely cover, and provided with a soft cushion on its back. To Sumukha he offered a bamboo seat fit for a chief minister to sit upon. Then the Bodhisattva, considering that it was now the proper time to make a complimentary address, spoke to the king in a voice as soft as the sound of anklets.

66. 'Thy body, adorned with lustre and loveliness, is in good health, I hope, O health-deserving prince. And so, I hope, is also that other body of thine which is made up of thy righteousness. Does it frequently emit, so to speak, its breath of pious discourses and gifts?

67. 'Thou hast dedicated thyself, hast thou not? to the task of protecting thy subjects, distributing reward or punishment in due time, so as to make both thy illustrious glory and the people's affection, together with their welfare, always increase?

68. 'Hast thou not the assistance of affectionate and honest ministers, averse to fraud and skilled in

the management of affairs, with whom to consider the interest of thy subjects? Thy mind is not indifferent to this important matter, I hope?

69. 'When the kings, thy vassals, after incurring abatement of their splendour by thy policy and vigour, entreat thee to show them mercy, thou wilt generously follow the impulse of pity, I hope, without, however, indulging in trustfulness, which is nothing but the sleep of carelessness?

70. 'Are thy actions, tending to secure the unobstructed pursuit of dharma, artha, and kâma, not applauded by the virtuous, O hero among men, and widespread in the world, so to say, by the effect of thy renown? And thy enemies have but sighs to hurt them, I hope?'

In reply to these questions the king, manifesting by his gladness the placidity of his senses[1], spoke to him:

71. 'Now my welfare is assured in every respect, O swan, for I have obtained the long wished-for happiness of meeting with your holy persons.

72, 73. 'This man, having captured thee in the snare, did not hurt thee, I hope, in the exuberance of his joy with his pain-inflicting stick? So it happens, in fact, when there arises calamity to birds, that the mind of those knaves, soiled by exulting joy, impels them to sinful actions.'

The Bodhisattva spoke:

74-77. 'I did not suffer, great king, while in that most distressing condition, nor did this man behave towards me at all like an enemy. When he perceived Sumukha staying there, though uncaught, out of love for me, as if he, too, had been caught, he addressed him with great kindness, prompted by curiosity and astonishment. Afterwards, having been propitiated

---

[1] The placidity of his senses is indicative of his having subdued his evil passions, so that he could give a satisfactory account of his royal occupations. In the Pâli redactions of our story, each question is immediately followed by its answer, which is affirmative, of course, and the wording of which exactly corresponds to the question.

by the gentle words of Sumukha, he released me from the snare, and setting me free, showed respect and honour to me. It is for this reason that Sumukha, wishing this man's good, told him to bring us hither. May then our arrival cause happiness also to him!'

The king said:

78, 79. 'Having eagerly longed for your arrival, I bid welcome here to both of you. The sight of you is a feast to my eyes and causes me extreme gladness. As to that Nishâda, I will bestow a rich gift upon him presently. Having shown kindness to both of you, he deserves a high reward.'

Then the king honoured the Nishâda by a munificent gift of great wealth. After which, he again addressed the king of swans :

80. 'Ye have come here to this residence, which is yours, indeed. Pray, set aside, then, cramping reserve with respect to me, and make known in what way and how I may serve your wants. For my riches are at your service.

81. 'A friend expressing his wants in frank speech, causes a greater satisfaction to a wealthy man, than he could obtain from his riches. For this reason, unreservedness among friends is a great benefit.'

Then, being also very curious to converse with Sumukha, the king casting his admiring looks on him, addressed him thus :

82. 'Surely, new acquaintances are not bold enough to speak frankly to the newly acquired friend, in whose mind they have not yet got footing. Still, they will use at least kind language, adorned by courteous terms.

83. 'It is for this reason that I beg also Thy Honour to favour me with thy conversation. So thou wouldst realise my desire of acquiring thy friendship and increase the gladness of my heart.'

On these words, Sumukha, the commander-in-chief of swans, bowing respectfully to the king, spoke :

84. 'A conversation with thee who art great Indra's equal, is a kind of festival. Who, therefore, would not

feel that this token of thy friendly disposition surpassed his wishes?

85, 86. 'But would it not have been an unbecoming act of insolence for an attendant to join in the conversation of the two monarchs, of men and of birds, while they were exchanging lovely words of friendship? No, a well-educated person does not act in that way. How, then, could I, knowing this, follow that way? On this account, great prince, I was silent, and if I need thy pardon, I deserve it.'

In reply to these words the king, expressing by his countenance his gladness and admiration, eulogised Sumukha.

87. 'Justly the world takes delight in hearing the fame of thy virtues. Justly the king of swans made thee his friend. Such modesty and accomplished demeanour is displayed by none but those who have subdued their inner self.

88. 'Therefore I sincerely trust that these friendly relations, now commenced between us, will never be broken off. The meeting of pious persons, indeed, produces friendship.'

Then the Bodhisattva, understanding that the king was eagerly desirous of their friendship and inclined to show them his affection, addressed him in terms of praise:

89. 'Following the impulse of thy generous nature, thou hast acted towards us as one should act to one's best friend, although our acquaintance has only been made just now.

90. 'Whose heart, then, would not be won, illustrious prince, by such honourable treatment as thou hast shown us?

91. 'Whatever profit thou expectest from relations with me, O lord, or however important thou mayst deem them, it is a matter of fact that thou hast displayed thy hospitable disposition by practising hospitality, O thou lover of virtues!

92. 'But this is no wonder in a self-subdued prince such as thou, who bearest thy royal duties for the

interest of thy subjects, intent on penance and profound contemplation, like a Muni. Thou, in truth, hadst but to follow the inclination of thy excellent nature to become a storehouse of virtues.

93. 'It is virtues that procure to their possessor the satisfaction of such praise, as I did celebrate of thee. They afford happiness, but in the strongholds of vice there dwells no bliss. What conscious being, then, knowing this to be the constant law as to virtue and vice, would resort to the wrong way which diverges from his good?

94. 'Not by military prowess nor by the strength of his treasury nor by a successful policy will a prince reach that high rank, which he may obtain even without exertion and expense, if he but follow the right path which consists in the cultivation of virtues.

95. 'Virtues are visited even by such bliss, as attends the Lord of the Devas; the virtuous alone attain humility; virtues alone are the sources of glory; it is on them that the magnificence of sovereignty rests.

96. 'Virtues alone, possessing greater loveliness than moonshine, are able to appease enemies, be their mind never so ferocious by indulgence in jealous anger and pride, be their selfishness never so deep-rooted by a long continuance of hatred.

97. 'For this reason, O sovereign, whose rule earth obeys with its proud kings who bow to thy lustre, foster the love of virtues in thy people, setting them an example by the undiminished splendour of thy modesty and the rest of thy virtues.

98. 'The good of his subjects is the first care of a king, and the way leading to it tends to his bliss both (in this world and in the next)[1]. And this end will be attained, if the king loves righteousness; for people like to follow the conduct of their ruler[2].

---

[1] Or perhaps: tends to the happiness of both (his subjects and himself).
[2] Cp. Story XIII, stanzas 38, 39.

99. 'Mayst thou, then, rule thy land with righteousness, and may the Lord of the Celestials have thee in his guard! But though thy presence purifies those who rest on thee, yet must I leave thee now. The sorrow of my fellow-swans draws me to them, so to speak.'

The king and all those present approved of the words spoken by the Bodhisattva. Then he dismissed both excellent swans in the most honourable and kind terms.

The Bodhisattva mounted upward to the sky, which, adorned by the serene beauty of autumn, was as dark-blue as a spotless sword-blade, and followed by Sumukha, his commander-in-chief, as by his reflected image, joined his tribe of swans. And those, by the very sight of him, were filled with the utmost gladness.

100. And after some time that swan, a passionate lover as he was of compassion for his neighbour, came back to the king with his swans, and discoursed to him on the Law of Righteousness. And the king with respectfully bowed head in return honoured him.

In this way, then, the virtuous, even when in distress, behave in such manner as cannot be imitated by the impious; how much less are the latter able to follow up the conduct of the virtuous, when favoured by fortune! [This story is also to be adduced, when praising pious language: 'In this manner a pious language conduces to the good of both[1].' Likewise, when treating of pious friends: 'In this manner they who possess a pious friend will be successful even in dangerous circumstances.' Also to exemplify the fact of the presbyter Ânanda having been a companion (to the Lord) still in previous births: 'So this presbyter sharing the vicissitudes of the Bodhisattva, cherished affection and veneration (for the Lord) for a long, long time.']

---

[1] Viz. the speaker and the listener.

This much-renowned tale of the two fabulous swans is thrice told in the collection of Pâli *G*âtakas, edited by Fausböll: No. 502 Ha*m*sa-gâtakam, No. 533 *K*ullaha*m*sagât., and No. 534 Mahâha*m*sagât. Of them No. 502 is almost an abridgement of No. 534. These two show another redaction of the tale than that which is contained in No. 533. Our author used some recension closely related to the redaction of No. 533; some of his stanzas are almost identical with the Pâli gâthâs.

From a note in Tawney's translation of the Kathâsaritsâgara (II, p. 506) I learn that Râgendralâla Mitra found the story of the golden swans in the Bodhisattva Avadâna, one of the Hodgson MSS. It is probable that the work quoted is the Bodhisattvâvadânakalpalatâ, which is being edited by Sara*k Kandra Dâs, in the Bibliotheca Indica. But as the story in question has not yet been published and the list of contents in the preface of that work is here of no help, I could not find out in which pallava it is told.

Moreover compare Kathâsaritsâgara 3, 26–35 and 114, 17 foll. The self-denial of the commander-in-chief has its counterpart in the behaviour of the sârasa bird in the main story of the third book of the Hitopadesa.

XXIII. THE STORY OF MAHÂBODHI.

(Cp. the Pâli *G*âtaka, No. 528, Fausb. V, 227–246.)

The compassion of the virtuous for those who once were their benefactors, does not diminish even by injuries done to them. Such is their gratitude, and to this extent have they imbibed the virtue of forbearance. This will be taught as follows.

In the time when the Lord was a Bodhisattva, he was a wandering ascetic, it is said, named Mahâbodhi[1]. When still a householder, he had made a regular and thorough study of such branches of learning as are esteemed in the world, and being curious of fine arts, had also acquainted himself with them. Afterwards, having renounced the world, as he was exerting himself for the benefit of the world, he directed his mind more earnestly to the study of the law-books, and obtained the mastership in that science. Thanks to his possession of a store of merit, the loftiness of his

---

[1] This name means ' (possessing) great wisdom.'

wisdom, his knowledge of the world, and his superior skill in the art of conversing with men, it happened that to whatever country he went, his company was sought for, and his person cherished by the learned as well as by such princes as patronized the learned, by Brâhmans living in the world as well as by other ascetics.

1. Virtues acquire splendour by their appearing on the ground of meritorious actions[1], but it is by the gracefulness of their practice, that they will gain the affection of men and partake of the most distinguished worship even from the side of one's enemies, obliged to do so by regard for their own reputation.

Now that Great-minded One, wandering about with the object of doing good to men, in villages, towns, markets, countries, kingdoms, royal residences, reached the realm of a king who, having heard of the splendour of his many virtues, was rejoiced at the report of his arrival. Having been informed of it long before, he had a dwelling-place built for him in a lovely spot in his own pleasure-gardens. At his arrival, he made him enter his kingdom in the most honourable manner, going to meet him and showing him other tokens of esteem. He attended on him and listened to his teaching, as a pupil observes his spiritual teacher.

2. To a lover of virtues, the arrival of a virtuous guest, coming confidingly to his wealth-abounding home, is a kind of feast[2].

And the Bodhisattva for his part favoured him with daily discourses on religious subjects, delightful to both the ears and the heart, by which he gradually prepared him to walk on the road to salvation.

3. Those who love the Law desire to give religious instruction even to such people as have not shown them their attachment, they will do so out of com-

---

[1] Our author never forgets to point out the importance of the possession of much pu*n*ya, cp. Story XIV, p. 133, and Story XV, p. 136.
[2] Cp. Story VI, stanza 30.

passion for their neighbour. How should they not teach him who, like a pure vessel, is eager to accept their instruction and to manifest his love?

But the ministers of that king, though receiving the honour due to their learning, and his counsellors, though also treated with respect, could not bear the constantly increasing honour paid to the magnificence of the Bodhisattva's virtues. Jealousy had tainted their minds.

4. The glory and renown of a man who shows his ability to fascinate mankind by the superiority of his virtues, suffices to kindle the fire of envious feeling in those who are honoured only on account of their professional skill.

They were unable to vanquish him in open contest in disputes on topics of the law-books, and at the same time were sorry to see the king's constant attachment to the Law of Righteousness. Then, in order to rouse his disaffection towards the Bodhisattva, they proceeded almost in this manner. 'Your Majesty,' so would they say, ' should not put his confidence in that wandering monk Bodhi. It is evident that he must be a kind of spy of some rival king, who having learnt Your Majesty's love of virtues and inclination towards Righteousness, avails himself of this clever fellow with his soft, smooth, and deceitful tongue, to entice you into baleful habits and to be informed of your actions. For this devotee of Righteousness, as he pretends to be, instructing Your Majesty exclusively to practise compassionateness and to foster the miserable feeling of shame, induces you to take upon yourself such vows of a religious life as are incompatible with your royal and military duties, prejudicial to the promotion of material interests (artha) and pleasures (kâma), and subject to the dangers attending a bad policy. Indeed, it is out of pure charity that, in the way of exhorting you, he suggests the line of conduct you should follow; nevertheless, he likes to converse with the messengers of other kings, and is far from being a stranger to the contents of the manuals of political wisdom which treat of the duties of kings. Accordingly this matter fills our hearts with apprehension.' Such language spoken with the intention of causing estrangement, being often repeated and by many who feigned to have in view the good of the king, could not fail to have its effect. His attachment and veneration for the Bodhisattva shrunk under the influence of his distrust, and his disposition towards him became changed.

5. Whether a succession of loud-roaring tremendous thunderbolts or of those other thunderbolts, whose name is calumny, pierce the ears of men, does there exist anybody who can remain unshaken by them, trustful and firm in the confidence of his own power?

Now, as the absence of trust lessened the king's affection and veneration for the Great Being, the king was no more, as before, careful to pay him due honour. But the Bodhisattva, owing to his pure-heartedness, did not mind it; 'kings are distracted by many occupations,' so he thought. Still, when he perceived the coolness and lack of attention from the side of the courtiers, he understood that he had incurred the king's displeasure, and taking his triple staff, his waterpot and the other utensils of a wandering ascetic, made preparations for his departure. The king, hearing his resolution, as he was partly moved by a remnant of his old affection, partly would not neglect an act of politeness and civility, went up to him, and in order to show his trouble and pretended desire to retain him, said:

6. 'For what reason are you determined to go away, leaving us all of a sudden? Have you perhaps to complain of some lack of attention on our part, which has roused your fears? If this is the case, you suspect us without reason, it must have been an omission.'

The Bodhisattva replied:

7. 'My departure has a good reason. Not that so trifling a matter as ill-treatment has irritated me, but because you have ceased to be a vessel of

righteousness in consequence of your deceitful behaviour, for this reason I set out from hence.'

At this moment the king's favourite dog came running to the Bodhisattva in a hostile manner and barked at him with wide-opened mouth. Pointing at this dog, he said again: 'Why, let this animal bear witness to the case, Your Majesty.

8, 9. 'Formerly this dog was accustomed to fondle me; then he was imitating your example. But now he betrays your feelings by his barks, for he does not know how to feign. Surely, he must have heard from you harsh words on my account, as will happen when former affection has been destroyed; and now, forsooth, he is acting up to them, that he may please you; for such is the behaviour of servants who eat the bread of their lord.'

This reproof filled the king with shame, and made him cast down his eyes. The acuteness of mind of the Bodhisattva touched him and moved his heart. He thought it was not proper to continue his false protestations of love, and bowing reverentially to him, spoke:

10. 'You were indeed the subject of such conversation as you said. Audacious people used that language in my council, and I, absorbed in business, overlooked the matter. You must forgive me, then, and stay here. Pray, do not go.'

The Bodhisattva said: 'Surely, it is not on account of ill-treatment that I want to go, Your Majesty, nor am I driven out by resentment. But considering, it is now no proper time to stay here, Your Majesty, for this reason I go. Do but take this in view.

11. 'If, either by attachment or from apathy, I should not go of my own accord now, as I needs must, after the honourable hospitality shown to me has lost its beauty, having become an ordinary one, verily, would it not hereafter come to the point that I should be seized by the neck and turned out?

12. 'Not with a heart sore with hatred am I about to leave you, but considering this the proper course to

follow now. Former benefits are not effaced from the heart of the pious by the stroke of one affront.

13. 'But an ill-disposed man is not fit to be had for a patron, no more than a dried-up pond will serve him who is in want of water. If profit may be gained from the side of such a one, it requires much care to acquire it, and the result will be meagre and not unmixed.

14. 'He, however, who desires ease and dislikes trouble, must attend only on such a patron who has composed his mind and by his placidity resembles a great lake of pure water in autumn. So is the well-known line of conduct approved of men.

15. 'Further, he who is averse to one intent on showing his attachment; likewise he who, attending on somebody who dislikes him, afflicts himself; thirdly, he who is slow in remembering former benefits—such persons bear only the shape of a man and raise doubts as to their real nature.

16. 'Friendship is destroyed both by lack of intercourse and profusion of attentions, also by frequent requests. Therefore, desiring to protect this remnant of our affection from the dangers of my residing here, I now take my leave.'

The king said : 'If Your Reverence has a strong determination to go, thinking your departure to be indispensable, pray, deign to favour us by coming back here again, will you ? Friendship ought to be kept safe also from the fault of lack of intercourse, did you not say so ?' The Bodhisattva replied : 'Your Majesty, sojourning in the world is something subject to many hindrances, for a great many adversaries in the shape of various calamities attend it. Thus considering, I cannot make the positive promise, that I shall come again. I can only express my wish to see you another time, when there may be some indispensable reason for coming.' Having in this way appeased the king, who dismissed him in the most honourable manner, he set off from his realm, and feeling his mind troubled by intercourse with people living in the world, took up his abode in some forest-place. Staying there,

he directed his mind to the exercise of meditation and
before long came to the possession of the four ecstatic
trances (dhyâna) and the five kinds of transcendent
knowledge (abhigñâ).

Now, while he was enjoying the exquisite happiness
of tranquillity, the remembrance of the king, accompanied by a feeling of compassion, appeared to his
mind. And, as he was concerned about the present
state of that prince, he directed his thoughts towards
him, and saw[1] that his ministers were each enticing
him to the tenets of the (false) doctrine which he
professed. One among them endeavoured to win
him for the doctrine according to which there should
be no causality, taking for examples such instances,
where it is difficult to demonstrate causality.

17. 'What,' said he, 'is the cause of the shape, the
colour, the arrangement, the softness and so on of the
stalks, the petals, the filaments and the pericarps of
the lotuses? Who diversifies the feathers of the birds
in this world? In just the same manner this whole
universe is the product of the work of essential and
inherent properties, to be sure.'

Another, who held a Supreme Being (Îsvara) for the
first cause, expounded him the tenets of his lore.

18. 'It is not probable that this universe should exist
without a cause. There is some being who rules it,
Eternal and One. It is He who in consequence of
the fixation of His mind on His transcendental volition,
creates the world and again dissolves it.'

Another, on the contrary, deceived him by this
doctrine: This universe is the result of former actions,
which are the cause of fortune, good and ill; personal
energy has no effect at all to modify it.

19. 'How, indeed, may one being create at the
same time the manifold and boundless variety of the
different substances and properties? No, this universe
is the product of former actions. For even he who

---

[1] Viz. as the effect of his divine eye (divya*m* *k*akshu*h*), one of the
five abhigñâs.

is skilled in striving for his happiness comes into mishap.'

Another again enticed him to be solely attached to the enjoyment of sensual pleasures, by means of such reasoning as is heard from the adherents of the doctrine of annihilation.

20. 'Pieces of wood, differing in colour, properties, and shape, cannot be said to exist as the result of actions, and yet they exist, and once perished they do not grow up again. Something similar is to be said of this world. For this reason one must consider pleasures the main object of life.'

Another, pretending to instruct him in his royal duties, recommended to him such practices as are taught in the science of the Kshatriyas, and which, following the winding paths of political wisdom (nîti), are soiled by cruelty and contrary to righteousness (dharma).

21. 'You must avail yourself of men, as of shady trees, considering them fit objects to resort to. Accordingly, endeavour to extend your glory by showing them gratitude, only as long, until your policy ceases to want their use. They are to be appointed to their task in the manner of victims destined for the sacrifice.'

So those ministers desired to lead the king astray, each on the path of his own false doctrines.

The Bodhisattva, then, perceiving that the king, owing to his intercourse with wicked people and his readiness to allow himself to be guided by others whom he trusted, was about to fall into the precipice of false doctrines, was affected with compassion and pondered on some means of rescuing him.

22. The pious, in consequence of their constant practice of virtues, retain in their mind the good done to them, whereas the evil they experienced drops from their mind, like water from a lotus-petal.

Having taken his resolution as to the proper thing to be done in the case, he created in his own hermitage, by dint of magic, a large monkey, whose skin he stripped off, making the rest of his body disappear. Wearing that skin, created by himself, he presented himself at the entrance-gate of the king's palace. After being ushered in by the doorkeepers, he was admitted to the royal presence. He passed successively the guards who were posted outside, and the different courts filled with officers, Brâhmans, military men, messengers, and notable townsmen, and entered the audience-hall, the doors of which were kept outside by doorkeepers with swords and staves; the king was sitting on his throne surrounded by his assembly of learned and wise men, magnificently dressed and orderly arranged. The monarch went to meet him, and showed him every honour and respect due to a guest. After the usual exchange of compliments and kind reception, when the Bodhisattva had taken the seat offered to him, the king, who was curious about that monkey-skin, asked him how he got it, saying: 'Who bestowed this monkey-skin on the Reverend, procuring by that deed a great favour to himself?'

The Bodhisattva answered: 'I got to it by myself, Your Majesty, I did not receive it from anybody else. While sitting or sleeping on the hard ground strewed only with thin straw, the body suffers, and the religious duties cannot be performed at ease. Now, I saw a large monkey in the hermitage and thought so within myself: "Oh! here is the right instrument I want to perform my religion, if I had but the skin of this monkey! sitting or sleeping on it, I shall be able to accomplish the rules of my religion, without caring even for royal couches spread with the most precious clothes." In consequence of this reflection, after subduing the animal I took his skin.' On hearing that account, the king who was polite and well-educated replied nothing to the Bodhisattva, but feeling something like shame, cast down his eyes. His ministers, however, who before that already bore a grudge to the Great Being, seized this opportunity of declaring their opinion, and looking with beaming faces at the king and pointing at the Bodhisattva, exclaimed: 'How entirely the Reverend is devoted to the love of his religion which is his only delight!

What a constancy is his! What ability to put into effect the best means for the realisation of his aims! It is a wonder that being alone and emaciated by penance, he was able to subdue so large a monkey, who had just entered his hermitage! At all events, may his penance be successful[1]!' In reply to them, the Bodhisattva, without losing his placidity of mind, said: 'Your honours, blaming me, should not disregard the fair tenets of your doctrines. This is not the way by which to make the glory of learning shine. Your honours must consider this.

23. 'He who despises his adversaries with such words as are destructive to his own doctrine, such a one, so to speak, wishes the dishonour of his enemy at the cost of his own life.'

After thus reproaching those ministers collectively, the Great Being, wishing to revile them once more individually, addressed that minister who denied causality in these terms:

24. 'You profess that this universe is the product of essential and inherent properties. Now, if this be true, why do you blame me? What fault is mine, if this ape died in consequence of his nature? Therefore, I have rightly killed him.

25. 'If, however, I committed a sin by killing him, it is evident that his death is produced by an (external) cause. This being so, you must either renounce your doctrine of non-causality or use here such reasoning as does not befit you.

26. 'Further, if the arrangement, colour &c. of the stalks, petals &c. of lotuses were not the effect of some cause, would they not be found always and everywhere? But this is not so, they are produced from seeds being in water &c.; where this condition is found, they appear, not where it is not found.

'This, too, I would propound to Your Worship, to consider it well.

---

[1] The last words are the usual complimentary blessing said to ascetics. When asking after their health, it is similarly said: 'is your penance successful?'

27. 'He who denies the agency of cause by means of reasoning with arguments, does not such a one desert his own tenets[1]? On the other hand, if he is averse to the use of argument, say, what will he do with his sole tenet (not supported by argument)?

28. 'And he who, not perceiving the cause in some particular case, proclaims for this very reason, that there does not exist causality at all, will not such a one, when he learns the manifest power of causality in that case, grow angry at it and oppose it with invectives?

29. 'And if somewhere the cause is latent, why do you say with assurance, it does not exist? Though it is, it is not perceived for some other cause, as for instance the white colour of the sun's disc is not seen at sunset.

'Moreover, sir,

30. 'For the sake of happiness you pursue the objects you desire, and will not follow such things as are opposed to it. And it is for the same purpose that you attend on the king. And notwithstanding this, you dare deny causality!

31. 'And, if nevertheless you should persist in your doctrine of non-causality, then it follows that the death of the monkey is not to be ascribed to any cause. Why do you blame me?'

So with clear arguments the High-minded One confounded that advocate of the doctrine of non-causality. Then addressing himself to the believer in a Supreme Being, he said: 'You, too, never ought to blame me, noble sir. According to your doctrine, the Lord is the cause of everything. Look here.

32, 33. 'If the Lord does everything, He alone is the killer of that ape, is He not? How can you bear such unfriendliness in your heart as to throw blame on me on account of the fault of another? If, however, you do not ascribe the murder of that valiant monkey to

---

[1] As far as using argument by means of reasoning implies adherence to causality. Moreover, the word hetu the Bodhisattva employs here means both 'cause' and 'reason.'

Him because of His compassionateness, how is it that you loudly proclaim, the Lord is the cause of this Universe?

'Moreover, friend, believing, as you do, that everything is done by the Lord[1],

34. 'What hope have you of propitiating the Lord by praise, supplication, and the like? For the Self-born Being works those actions of yours himself.

35. 'If, however, you say, the sacrifice is performed by yourself, still you cannot disavow that He is the author of it. He who is self-acting out of the fulness of His power, is the author of a deed, no other.

36, 37. 'Again, if the Lord is the performer of all sins, however many there are committed, what virtue of His have you in view that you should foster devotion to Him? On the other hand, if it is not He who commits them, since He abhors wickedness, it is not right to say that everything is created by the Lord.

38, 39. 'Further, the sovereignty of the Lord must rest either on the lawful order of things (Dharma) or on something else. If on the former, then the Lord cannot have existed before the Dharma. If effected by some external cause, it should rather be called "bondage;" for if a state of dependency should not bear that name, what state may not be called "sovereignty?"

'Nevertheless, if in spite of this reasoning, attached to the doctrine of Devotion[2] and without having well reflected on its probability or improbability,

40. 'You persist in holding the Supreme Being and Lord for the sole cause of the whole universe, does it, then, become you to impute to me the murder of that chief of monkeys, which has been decided by the Supreme Being?'

---

[1] The Bodhisattva is much helped here by the double sense implied by the words sarvam îsvarakritam, meaning 'all is created by the Lord' as well as 'everything is done by the Lord.'

[2] The belief in a Supreme Being, Lord (Îsvara), is in itself of course also a belief in the strong effectiveness of devotion (bhakti).

So reasoning with a well-connected series of conclusive arguments, the High-minded One struck dumb, so to speak, the minister who was an adherent of the Lord (Îsvara)-supreme cause. And turning to that minister who was a partisan of the doctrine of former actions, he addressed him in a very skilful manner, saying: 'No more does it become you, too, to censure me. According to your opinion, everything is the consequence of former actions. For this reason, I tell you,

41. 'If everything ought to be imputed exclusively to the power of former actions, then this monkey has been rightly killed by me. He has been burnt by the wild fire of his former actions. What fault of mine is to be found here that you should blame me?

42. 'On the other hand, suppose I did a bad action in killing the ape, I must be the cause of his death, not his former actions. Further, if you state, that karma (always) produces (fresh) karma, nobody will reach final emancipation[1] in your system.

43. 'Verily, if something like this should be seen: happiness enjoyed by him who lives in circumstances productive of suffering, or sufferings visiting such a one whose circumstances are instruments of happiness, then we should have the right to infer, it is beyond question, that good and evil fortune depend exclusively on former actions.

44. 'But, in fact, this rule as to the appearance of happiness and sufferings is nowhere seen. Consequently, former actions are not the sole and entire cause of them. Further, it is possible that there ceases to be new karma. And this lacking, whence should you get the "old karma" (indispensable for the maintenance of the Universe)?

45. 'If, nevertheless, you persist in your doctrine of the former actions, for what reason do you judge me to have caused the death of that ape?'

---

[1] Final emancipation necessarily implies cessation of actions, for it is the same thing as total extinction.

In this manner the High-minded One, expounding irrefutable arguments, put him to silence so that it seemed as if he had made him take the vow of silence. Next he said smilingly to that minister who was an adherent of the doctrine of annihilation: 'How extremely eager your honour is to blame me, if at least you really are a partisan of the doctrine of annihilation.

46. 'If there does not exist anything like a future existence after death, why should we avoid evil actions, and what have we to do with the folly of holding good actions in esteem? He alone would be wise who behaves according to impulse, as he likes best. If this doctrine be true, it is right indeed, that I killed that ape.

47, 48. 'If, however, it is fear of public opinion which causes such a one to eschew bad actions by following the path of virtue, he will, nevertheless, not escape the criticism of public opinion, because of the contradiction between his words and his deeds: nor will he obtain the happiness presenting itself on the road of his destiny, owing to the same awe of public opinion. Is, then, such a one, allowing himself to be misled by a fruitless and delusive doctrine, not the meanest of simpletons?

'As to your statement, when you said:

49. '" Pieces of wood, differing in colour, properties and shape, cannot be said to exist as the result of actions, and yet they exist, and once perished they do not grow up again. Something similar is to be said of this world," pray, tell me, what reason have you for believing so, after all?

50. 'If, notwithstanding this, you persist in your attachment to the doctrine of annihilation, what reason is it that you should censure the murderer of a monkey or a man?'

So the Great Being silenced that adherent of annihilation by means of a refutation of conspicuous elegance. Then he addressed that minister who was so skilled in the science of princes. 'For what reason,' he said, 'do you also censure me, if you really consider the line of conduct as taught in the love of political science to be the right one?

51. 'According to that doctrine, in truth, deeds good or evil are to be performed for the sake of material profit; having once risen, a man shall bestow his wealth, indeed, for his benefit on actions of righteousness (dharma[1]).
'On this account I tell you.

52. 'If for the sake of personal interest honest proceedings may be neglected even with respect to affectionate relations[2], what reason have you to censure me about that ape whom I killed for the sake of his skin, putting into effect the policy taught also in your books?

53[3]. 'On the other hand, if such a deed is to be blamed for its cruelty, and is certain to have evil consequences, by what means do you resort to a lore which does not acknowledge this?

54. 'Now, if such is the manifestation of what is called "policy" in your system, say, of what kind may be the error, called "want of policy"? Oh! the audacious who, despising mankind, propound injustice by the way of authoritative law-books!

55. 'Nevertheless, if you maintain that false doctrine—is it not prescribed in the books of your sect in plain terms?—well, it is not I who should be blamed on account of the death of that ape, since I followed the path of that policy which is taught in your books.'

In this manner, then, the High-minded One vanquished by a strong assault those ministers in spite of their influence on the bystanders, in spite also of their habitual boldness. And when he understood he

---

[1] Cp. Story V, stanzas 18-22.
[2] The Pâli recension expresses this by the drastic utterance: 'the would-be wise advocates of the khattavi*gg*â say: you may kill your father or mother or eldest brother, yea your children and wife, if such be your interest.'
[3] I follow the emendation of the editor mukhena, not the senseless reading of the MSS. sukhena.

had won over the assembly with the king, wishing to expel from their hearts the grief he had caused them by killing the monkey, he addressed the king, saying: 'In fact, Your Majesty, I never killed any living creature [1]. I did but put into effect my power of creation. This skin I stripped off a monkey whom I had created, with the object of using it as the topic of this very conversation. Do not therefore judge me falsely.' So speaking, he dissolved the illusion (of the ape-skin) he had produced by magic. Then, seeing that the king and his assembly were now in apt state of mind to be converted, he said:

56. 'What person, who perceives that all things produced emanate from causes; who feels himself acting by his free will; who believes in another world after this; who maintains right tenets; who cherishes compassionateness—may kill any living being?

'Do but consider this, great prince.

57. 'How should the believer in the true and rational doctrine commit a deed which, to be sure, neither the denier of causality, nor the believer in absolute dependence, nor the materialist, nor the follower of the lore of political wisdom would perform for the sake of a little glory?

58. 'A man's creed, O best of men, be it the true or a false one, is the motive which induces him to actions corresponding with it. For people show the tenets of their belief by their words and actions, since their purposes comply with the line of conduct, prescribed by their creed.

59. 'And for this reason the excellent lore is to be cherished, but a bad lore must be abandoned, for it is a source of calamity. One must take this course in this way: keeping with the virtuous, but keeping afar from wicked people.

60. 'Indeed, there are such monks—goblins they should rather be called—who wander about in the dress of the self-restrained, but have not subdued their

---

[1] Vânara*m* is a gloss, I suppose.

senses. It is they who ruin simple people by their false views, not unlike such serpents as cause harm by the venom of their looks.

61. 'The discordant voices of the adherents of the doctrine of non-causality and the rest, disclose their special natures, in the same manner as jackals are betrayed by their howling. For this reason a wise man ought not to cherish such persons but should (rather) care for their good, if he have the power to do so.

62. 'But no one, however illustrious his glory may be in the world, should make friends with an unfit person, not even for interest's sake. Even the moon suffers loss of loveliness, when soiled by its conjunction with a gloomy winter-day.

63. 'Therefore, avoiding the company of those who are avoiders of virtues and frequenting those who know how to foster virtues, make your glory shine by rousing in your subjects the love of virtue and dissolving their attachment to vice.

64. 'Observing the Law of Righteousness, you might cause your subjects, for the greater part indeed, to be intent on good behaviour and to keep to the path which leads to Heaven. Now you have to protect your people and you are willing to exert yourself with this object. Well, then, betake yourself to the Dharma; its rules of discipline (vinaya) make its road a lovely one.

65. 'Purify your moral conduct (*sila*), earn the glory of a charitable giver, direct your mind to friendliness towards strangers, just as if they were your relations, and may you rule your land for a long time with righteousness and an uninterrupted observance of your duties! In this way you will gain happiness, glory, and Heaven.

66. 'If he fail to protect the peasants, his tax-payers, both the husbandmen and the cattle-breeders, who are like trees abounding in flowers and fruits, a king gets into difficulties concerning such wealth as consists in fruits of the earth.

67. 'If he fail to protect those who live by buying and selling different merchandises, traders, and townsmen, who gratify him by paying the customs, he raises difficulties for himself with respect to his treasury.

68. 'Likewise a prince who, having no reason to complain of his army, fails to honour it, and disregards his military men who have shown their valour on the battle-field and are renowned for their skill in the science of arms, surely such a king will be deserted by victory in battle.

69. 'In the very same way a king who stains his behaviour by disregard of the religious men, excellent by morals or learning or supernatural power (yoga) and illustrious by such virtues as attend on high-mindedness, will be destitute of the rejoicings of Heaven.

70. 'As one who plucks an unripe fruit kills the seed without finding juice, so a king raising unlawful tributes, ruins his country without obtaining profit from them.

71. 'On the other hand, as a tree abounding in excellent properties, grants the enjoyment of its fruits at the time of their ripeness, in the very same manner a country, well protected by its ruler, provides him with the triad of religious and material prosperity and enjoyment.

72. 'Keep attached to yourself faithful ministers, clever and wise in promoting your interests, likewise honest friends, and your family, attaching their hearts by words agreeable to them, and by gifts offered to them in a flattering manner.

73. 'For this reason, then, let Righteousness be always the guide of your actions, having your mind bent on securing the salvation of your subjects. May you, while saving your people by administering justice free from partiality and hatred, secure the worlds for yourself [1]!'

---

[1] This term 'worlds' lokâh is a common appellation of the happy state or states after death.

Thus the High-minded One led that king away from the wrong road of false doctrines and put him and his attendants on the Excellent Path. After which he directly mounted to the sky, worshipped by the assembly with heads reverentially bowed and hands folded, and returned to his residence in the forest.

In this manner, then, the compassion of the virtuous for those who were once their benefactors does not diminish even by injuries done to them; such is their gratitude, and to this extent have they imbibed the virtue of forbearance. [Considering thus, one must not forget a former benefit because of such a trifle as an injury. Also, when discoursing on the Buddha, it may be said: 'In this manner the Lord, even before he reached Supreme Wisdom, defeated the doctrines of other teachers and taught the Truth.' Further, when censuring erroneous doctrines or inversely when praising the true faith, this story is to be adduced, saying: 'In this manner a false doctrine cannot bear strong arguments, because it has no support, and is to be avoided.']

XXIV. THE STORY OF THE GREAT APE.

(Cp. the Pâli *Gâtaka*, No. 516, Fausb. V, 68-74.)

The virtuous grieve not so much for their own pain as for the loss of happiness incurred by their injurers. This will be taught now.

There is a blessed region on one side of the Himavat. Its soil, pervaded with different metallic ores, might be called its body perfumed with lovely and various ointments; and its magnificent woods and forests constituted its upper garment, as it were, consisting in a mantle of dark silk. The slopes and declivities of that landscape were adorned by their picturesque scenery, which harmonized the inequality of colours and shapes and combinations, so that they seemed to have been arranged purposely and with

XXIV. THE STORY OF THE GREAT APE. 219

care. In this recreation-ground of the Vidyâdharas, moistened by the waters of many mountain-streams passing through it, abounding in deep holes, chasms, and precipices, resounding with the dull and shrill noise of humming bees and caressed by lovely winds fanning its various trees with their beautiful flowers, fruits, and stems, the Bodhisattva was once, it is said, an ape of great size who lived alone. But even in that state he had not lost his consciousness of the Dharma, he was grateful, noble-natured, and endowed with great patience; and Compassion, as if retained by attachment, would never leave him.

1. The earth with its forests, its great mountains and its oceans perished many hundred times at the end of the yuga, either by water or fire or wind, but the great compassion of the Bodhisattva never perishes.

Subsisting, then, like an ascetic, exclusively on the simple fare of leaves and fruits of the forest-trees, and showing pity in various circumstances and ways to such creatures as he met within the sphere of his power, the High-minded One lived in the said forest-region.

Now, one time a certain man wandering about in all directions in search of a stray cow, lost his way, and being utterly unable to find out the regions of the sky, roamed at random, and reached that place. There, being exhausted by hunger, thirst, heat, and toil, and suffering from the fire of sorrow which blazed within his heart, he sat down at the foot of a tree, as if pressed down by the exceeding weight of his sadness. Looking around, he saw a number of very tawny tinduka-fruits[1], which being ripe had fallen off. After enjoying them, as the hunger which tortured him much made them seem very sweet to him, he felt a very strong desire to find out their origin; and

---

[1] The tinduka or tindukî is the diospcros embryopteris, a common tree, not tall, evergreen with long, glimmering leaves. See Watt, Dictionary of the Economic Products of India, III, pp. 141-145. 'The fruit is eatable, but excessively sour;' it is a food of the poor.

looking sharply around on all sides, he discovered the tree from whence they came. This tree had its roots on the border of the sloping bank of a waterfall, and hung down its branches, loaded with very ripe fruits which gave them a tawny hue at their ends. Craving for those fruits, the man mounted to that slope, and climbing up the tinduka-tree, reached a branch with fruit overhanging the precipice. And his eagerness to get the fruit induced him to go along it to its very end.

2. Then on a sudden, that branch, hanging down, unable to bear its too heavy burden, broke off with a noise and fell down, as if hewn with a hatchet.

And with that branch he fell headlong in a large precipice surrounded on all sides by steep rock-walls, like a pit; but as he was protected by the leaves and plunged into deep water, he came off without breaking any of his bones. After getting out of the water, he went about on all sides, looking out for some way by which he might escape, but saw none. As he found no outlet and realised that he must starve there very soon, he despaired of his life, and tortured by the heart-piercing dart of heavy sorrow burst into tears, that moistened his sad face. Overwhelmed by discouragement and painful thoughts, he lamented somewhat in this manner.

3. 'Down I fell into this precipice in the midst of this forest remote from human approach. Who, however carefully seeking, may discover me, except Death?

4. 'Who will rescue me out of this place, into which I was precipitated, like a wild beast caught in a pit-fall? No relations, no friends have I near, only swarms of mosquitoes drinking my blood.

5. 'Alas, the night within this pit conceals from me the aspect of the universe. I shall no more see the manifold loveliness of gardens, groves, arbours, and streams. No more the sky resplendent with its jewel ornament of wide-scattered stars. Thick darkness, like a night in the dark half of the month, surrounds me.'

Thus lamenting, that man passed there some days,

feeding on the water and the tinduka-fruits which had come down together with himself.

Now, that great ape wandering through that part of the forest with the purpose of taking his food, came to that place, beckoned as it were by the wind-agitated branches of that tinduka-tree. Climbing on it and looking over the waterfall, he perceived that man lying there and in want of relief, and saw also his eyes and cheeks sunken, and his limbs emaciated, pale, and suffering from hunger. The wretched situation of the man roused the compassion of the great monkey, who setting aside the care for his meal, fixed his eyes intently on the man and in a human voice uttered this:

6. 'Thou art in this precipice inaccessible to men. Well, tell me then, please, who thou art and by what cause thou hast come there.'

Then the man, casting up his eyes to the great ape, bowing his head and folding his hands as a supplicant, spoke:

7, 8. 'I am a man, illustrious being. Having lost my way and roaming in the forest, I came into this distress, while seeking to get fruits from this tree. Befallen by this heavy calamity, while away from my friends and kindred, I beseech thee, protector of troops of monkeys, be also my protector.'

These words succeeded in stirring the boundless pity of the Great Being.

9. A person in distress, without friends or family to help him, imploring help with anxious looks and folded hands, would rouse compassion in the heart even of his enemies; to the compassionate he is a great attraction.

Then the Bodhisattva, pitying him, comforted him with kind words, such as he could hardly expect in that time.

10. 'Be not afflicted, thinking thou hast lost thy strength by the fall into this precipice or that thou hast no relations to help thee. What those would do for thee, I will do it all. Do not fear.'

And after these comforting words the Great Being provided the man with tindukas and other fruits. Then with the object of rescuing him, he went away to some other place, and exercised himself in climbing having on his back a stone of a man's weight. Having learnt the measure of his strength and convinced himself that he was able to bring up the man out of the waterfall, he descended to the bottom of it, and moved by compassion, said these words to the man:

11. 'Come, climb upon my back and cling fast to me, while I shall bring out both thee and the usefulness of my body.

12. 'For the pious pronounce this to be the usefulness of the body, otherwise a worthless thing, that it may be employed by the wise as an instrument for benefiting our neighbour.'

The other agreed, and after reverentially bowing to the ape, mounted on his back.

13. So with that man on his back, stooping under the pain of the exceeding heaviness of his burden, yet, owing to the intensity of his goodness, with unshaken firmness of mind, he succeeded in rescuing him, though with great difficulty.

14. And having delivered him, he enjoyed the highest gladness, but was so exhausted, that he walked with an unstable and tottering step, and chose some cloud-black slab of stone to lie upon, that he might take his rest.

Pure-hearted as he was and being his benefactor, the Bodhisattva did not suspect danger from the part of that man, and trustingly said to him:

15, 16. 'This part of the forest being easily accessible, is exposed to the free course of ferocious animals. Therefore, that nobody may kill me and his own future happiness by a sudden attack, while I am taking my rest from fatigue, thou must carefully look out in all directions and keep guard over me and thyself. My body is utterly tired, and I want to sleep a little while.'

The man promised to do so. Assuming the frank language of honesty, he said: 'Sleep, sir, as long as you like, and may your awaking be glad! I stay here, keeping guard over you.' But when the Great Being, in consequence of his fatigue, had fallen asleep, he conceived wicked thoughts within his mind.

17. 'Roots to be obtained with hard effort or forest-fruits offered by chance are my livelihood here. How can my emaciated body sustain life by them? how much less, recover its strength?

18. 'And how shall I succeed in traversing this wilderness hard to pass, if I am infirm? Yet, in the body of this ape I should have food amply sufficient to get out of this troublesome wilderness.

19. 'Although he has done good to me, I may feed on him, I may, for he has been created such a being. I may, for here the rules given for times of distress[1] are applicable, to be sure. For this reason I have to get my provisions from his body.

20. 'But I am only able to kill him while he is sleeping the profound and quiet sleep of trustfulness. For if he were to be attacked in open fight, even a lion would not be assured of victory.

'Therefore, there is no time to lose now.' Having thus made up his mind, that scoundrel, troubled in his thoughts by sinful lust which had destroyed within him his gratitude, his consciousness of the moral precepts, and even his tender innate feeling of compassion, not minding his great weakness of body, and listening only to his extreme desire to perform that vile action, took a stone, and made it fall straight down on the head of the great ape.

21, 22. But, being sent by a hand trembling with weakness and hastily, because of his great cupidity, that stone, flung with the desire of sending the monkey to the complete sleep (of death), destroyed his sleep. It did not strike him with its whole weight, so that it did not dash his head to pieces; it only bruised it with one of its edges, and fell down on the earth with a thundering noise.

---

[1] The so-called âpaddharma, cp. stanza 8 of Story XII.

23, 24. The Bodhisattva, whose head had been injured by the stone, jumped up hastily; and looking around him that he might discover his injurer, saw nobody else but that very man who stood before him in the attitude of shame, confounded, timid, perplexed, and dejected, betraying his confusion by the ashy-pale colour of his face, which had lost its brightness-; sudden fright had dried up his throat, drops of sweat covered his body, and he did not venture to lift up his eyes.

As soon as the great ape realised that the man himself was the evildoer, without minding the pain of his wound any longer, he felt himself utterly moved. He did not become angry, nor was he subdued by the sinful feeling of wrath. He was rather affected with compassion for him who, disregarding his own happiness, had committed that exceedingly vile deed. Looking at him with eyes wet with tears, he lamented over the man, saying:

25, 26. 'Friend, how hast thou, a man, been capable of doing an action like this? How couldst thou conceive it? how undertake it? Thou, who wast bound to oppose with heroic valour any foe whosoever eager to hurt me would have assailed me!

27. 'If I felt something like pride, thinking I performed a deed hard to be done, thou hast cast away from me that idea of haughtiness, having done something still more difficult to do.

28. 'After being brought back from the other world, from the mouth of Death, as it were, thou, scarcely saved from one precipice, hast fallen into another, in truth!

29. 'Fie upon ignorance, that vile and most cruel thing! for it is ignorance that throws the miserable creatures into distress, (deceiving them) with (false) hope of prosperity.

30, 31. 'Thou hast ruined thyself, kindled the fire of sorrow in me, obscured the splendour of thy reputation, obstructed thy former love of virtues, and destroyed thy trustworthiness, having become a mark for (the arrows of) reproach. What great profit, then, didst thou expect by acting in that manner?

32. 'The pain of this wound does not grieve me so much as this thought which makes my mind suffer, that it is on account of me that thou hast plunged into evil, but that I have not the power of wiping off that sin.

33, 34. 'Well then, go with me, keeping by my side, but mind to be always in my sight, for thou art much to be distrusted. I will conduct thee out of this forest, the abode of manifold dangers, again into the path which leads to the dwellings of men, lest roaming alone in this forest, emaciated and ignorant of the way, thou shouldst be assailed by somebody who, hurting thee, would make fruitless my labour spent in thy behalf.'

So commiserating that man, the High-minded One conducted him to the border of the inhabited region, and having put him on his way, said again:

35. 'Thou hast reached the habitations of men, friend; now thou mayst leave this forest-region with its fearful thickets and wildernesses. I bid thee a happy journey and wish that thou mayst endeavour to avoid evil actions. For the harvest of their evil results is an extremely painful time.'

So the great ape pitying the man, instructed him as if he were his disciple; after which he went back to his abode in the forest. But the man who had attempted that exceedingly vile and sinful deed, tortured by the blazing fire of remorse, was on a sudden struck with a dreadful attack of leprosy. His figure became changed, his skin was spotted with vesicles which, becoming ulcers and bursting, wetted his body with their matter, and made it putrid in a high degree. To whatever country he came, he was an object of horror to men; so hideous was his distorted form; neither by his appearance did he resemble a human being nor by his changed voice, indicative of his pain. And people, thinking him to be the embodied Devil, drove him away, threatening him with uplifted clods

and clubs and harsh words of menace. One time,
roaming about in some forest, he was seen by a certain
king who was hunting there. On perceiving his most
horrible appearance—for he looked like a Preta[1], the
dirty remains of his garments having at last dropped
off, so that he had hardly enough to cover his shame—
that king, affected with curiosity mingled with fear,
asked him thus:

36, 37. 'Thy body is disfigured by leprosy, thy skin
spotted with ulcers; thou art pale, emaciated, miserable; thy hair is dirty with dust. Who art thou?
Art thou a Preta, or a goblin, or the embodied Devil,
or a Pûtana[2]? Or if one out of the number of sicknesses, which art thou who displayest the assemblage
of many diseases?'

Upon which the other, bowing to the prince, answered in a faltering tone: 'I am a man, great king,
not a spirit.' And being asked again by the king, how
he had come into that state, he confessed to him his
wicked deed, and added these words:

38. 'This suffering here is only the blossom of the
tree sown by that treacherous deed against my friend.
O, surely, its fruit will be still more miserable than
this.

39. 'Therefore, you ought to consider a treacherous
deed against a friend as your foe. With kindheartedness you must look upon friends, who are kindhearted
towards you.

40. 'Those who adopt a hostile behaviour against
their friends, come into such a wretched state already
in this world. From hence you may infer what will
be in the other world the fate of those who, sullied in
their mind by covetousness and other vices, attempted
the life of their friends.

41. 'He, on the other hand, whose mind is pervaded

---

[1] See supra, note on p. 147.—As to the punishment of this
treacherous man (mitradhruk), cp. a similar punishment of the slanderer Kokâliya in Suttanipâta III, 10.

[2] A Pûtana is a kind of ghost looking terrible. They live in
cemeteries, and like to feed on human flesh.

with kindness and affection for his friends, obtains a good reputation, is trusted by his friends and enjoys their benefits. He will possess gladness of mind and the virtue of humility, his enemies will consider him a man hard to offend, and finally he will gain residence in Heaven.

42. 'Thus knowing the power and the consequences of good and evil behaviour with respect to friends, O king, hold fast to the road followed by the virtuous. He who goes along on this will attain happiness.'

In this manner, then, the virtuous grieve not so much for their own pain as for the loss of happiness incurred by their injurers. [So is to be said, when discoursing on the great-mindedness of the Tathâgata, and when treating of listening with attention to the preaching of the Law; likewise when dealing with the subjects of forbearance and faithfulness towards friends; also when demonstrating the sinfulness of evil deeds.]

XXV. THE STORY OF THE SARABHA.

(Cp. the Pâli Gâtaka, No. 483, Fausb. IV, 267-275.)

Even to him who attempts their life the intensely compassionate show pity in his distress; they will not disregard such a one. This will be taught in the following.

One time, it is said, the Bodhisattva was a sarabha[1], living in a remote part of a certain forest. That region, lying beyond the path and the noise of men, was a dwelling-place of manifold tribes of forest-animals. Its many roots, trees, and shrubs were immersed in the thick and high grass which covered its soil, untrodden by travellers and showing nowhere any trace of vehicles and carriages, the tracks of whose

---

[1] Not the common deer of that name seems to be meant, but the fabulous animal sarabha, said to be eight-legged, very strong, and a match for lions and elephants.

feet or wheels might have beaten something like a road or border-line; yet, it was intersected with channels and full of ant-hills and holes. That *s*arabha had a solid body, endowed with strength, vigour, and swiftness; he was distinguished by the beautiful colour of his skin. As he was addicted to practising compassion, he cherished friendly feelings towards all animals. Possessing the virtue of contentment, he subsisted only on grasses, leaves and water, and was pleased with his residence in the forest. So he adorned that part of the forest, longing, like a Yogin, for complete detachment.

1. Bearing the shape of a forest-animal, but possessing the intellectual faculties of a man, he lived in that solitary wilderness, showing, like an ascetic, mercy to all living beings, and contenting himself, like a Yogin, with blades of grass.

Now once upon a time it happened that the king who was the ruler of that country came near that place. Mounted on his excellent horse, holding his bent bow and arrow in his hand, and being eager to try his skill of arms on the game, he was pursuing the deer with speed, indulging in the excitement (of the chase). So he was carried away by his horse, an animal of extraordinary swiftness, and separated by no small distance from his retinue, a body of elephants, horse, chariots, and footmen. As soon as he saw the Great Being from afar, he was resolved on killing him, and keeping ready his bow strung with a sharp arrow, spurred his horse to chase the High-minded One. But the Bodhisattva had no sooner perceived the king on horseback assailing him, than he took to flight with the utmost swiftness; not because he would have been powerless to stand and fight his aggressor, but because he had desisted from acts of violence and anger. While being pursued by the king, meeting with a large hole on his way, he quickly jumped over it, as if it were a small puddle, and continued his flight. When the excellent horse, running after the *s*arabha in the same direction as swiftly as ever he could, arrived at that hole, he hesitated to risk the leap, and of a sudden stood still.

2. Then the king, as he was, his bow in his hands, tumbled down from horseback and fell headlong into the large hole, as a warrior of the Daityas sinks into the Ocean.

3. Keeping his eyes fixed on the *sarabha*, he had not noticed that chasm. So he fell by the fault of his want of circumspection, as he lost his balance by the sudden stopping of his horse from his great swiftness.

Now, the sound of the trampling of hoofs ceasing, the Bodhisattva began to think: 'has that king, perhaps, really turned back?' Then, turning his head and looking behind, he saw the horse without his rider standing on the brink of that chasm. On perceiving this, his thoughts turned to this reasoning: ' No doubt, the king must have fallen into this chasm. No tree is here spreading its thick foliage, the sheltering shade of which might invite to sit down and rest, nor is here any lake to be found fit for bathing in its water as blue and as pure as a petal of a blue lotus. Nor, since he entered this wild forest-region haunted by ferocious animals, is he likely to have dismounted and left his excellent horse in some place, that he might either take his rest or continue hunting alone. No more is there here any jungle in which he might be hidden. Surely, that king must have fallen into this hole.' After he had convinced himself of this, the High-minded One felt the utmost commiseration for him who sought his life.

4, 5. 'But lately this monarch possessed the enjoyments of royalty, being worshipped like the Lord of the Devas by crowds of people revering him with clasped hands. His army attended him, a mixed host of chariots, horsemen, footmen, and elephants, adorned with gay banners, glittering in their armour and weapons, and marching to the brisk tones of music. His head was sheltered by the lovely umbrella, and the chowries fanning him made a beautiful effect with the shine of their (jewelled) handles.

6. 'And now at this moment he is lying below in this large chasm. By the shock of his fall he must have broken his bones, he has swooned or pines with sorrow. Alas! To what a distress has he come!

7. 'Common people, whose mind has grown callous with suffering, so to speak, are not so much afflicted by their sorrows, as men of high rank, when calamities visiting them plunge them into grief, something new to such as are accustomed to great delicacy.

'He will never be able to escape from thence by himself. If there is still some remnant of life in him, then it is not right to abandon him to his fate.' So considering, the High-minded One, impelled by his compassion, went to the brink of the precipice and perceived him struggling there. His armour, covered with dust, had lost its splendour, his diadem and his garments were utterly disarranged, and the pain caused by the blows he had got in falling down afflicted his mind, and brought him to despondency.

8. Having seen the king in that wretched situation, he forgot that it was his enemy, and affected with pity felt an equal pain to his; tears welled up in his eyes.

9. And he addressed him with modest and kind language, manifesting his innate pious disposition and comforting him by the proper and respectful words he used in a distinct and lovely-sounding voice.

10. 'Thou hast received no hurt, Your Majesty, I hope, coming into this hell-resembling chasm? Thou hast broken no limb, I hope? Do thy pains grow less already?

11. 'I am no goblin, O most distinguished of men, I am a forest-animal living within thy realm, reared upon thy grass and water. So thou mayst put confidence in me.

12. 'Do not despond, then, because of thy fall into the precipice. I have the power to rescue thee from thence. If thou thinkest me trustworthy, then quickly command me and I come.'

This marvellous speech of the animal roused the

admiration of the king. Shame arose within his mind and he began, in truth, to reflect in this manner:

13. 'How is it possible that he shows pity towards me, his enemy, of whose prowess he perceived himself to be the goal? And how could I act so unbecomingly to this innocent one?

14. 'Oh! How he confounds me by the sharp reproach of his softness! It is I who am the animal, the brute, he is some being bearing only the shape of a *s*arabha.

'He deserves, therefore, to be honoured by my acceptance of his friendly offer.' Having thus made up his mind, he spoke:

15–17. 'My body being covered by my armour has not been too heavily injured, and the pain I feel from being crushed in this chasm is at least bearable. Yet, that grievance caused by my fall does not torment me so much as my offence against a being so purehearted and holy as thou. Do not mind it, I pray thee, that relying on thy outward shape I took thee for a forest-animal, not being aware of thy real nature.'

Then the *s*arabha, inferring from these friendly words of the king, that he agreed to his proposal, exercised himself with the object of rescuing him, bearing on his back a stone of a man's weight. Having learnt the extent of his strength, determined upon rescuing the king, he went down into the hole and drawing near to him, spoke in a respectful tone:

18. 'Pray, put up for a while with the necessity of touching this body of mine, that, with the object of obtaining my own happiness, I may make thy face resplendent with contentment and joy.

'Your Majesty, deign therefore to mount upon my back and cling fast to me.' And he, after declaring his approval, mounted his back, as if it were a horse's.

19. Then, with the king on his back, he climbed aloft with surpassing vigour and swiftness, and holding high the forepart of his body, resembled some (stone-)elephant rising in the air, as is represented on arches.

20. After carrying the king out of that inaccessible place and making him rejoin his horse, he was much rejoiced and told him the way to his capital, and himself prepared to retire to his forest.

But the king, moved with gratitude for his kind service, so modestly rendered, embraced the *sa*rabha affectionately, saying :

21. 'This life of mine is at thy disposal, O *sa*rabha. It is, therefore, unnecessary to add that thou must consider as thy property all that is within my power. Give me, then, the pleasure of visiting my capital, and if thou likest it, take up thy residence there.

22. 'Is it not unbecoming to me that I should set out for home alone, leaving thee in this dreadful forest haunted by hunters, where thou art exposed to suffering because of cold, heat, rain, and other calamities ?

'Well then, let us go together.'

Then the Bodhisattva eulogized him in modest, soft and respectful terms, answering thus :

23. 'In lovers of virtues, like thee, O most excellent of men, a behaviour like thine is the proper one. For virtues, constantly practised by pious persons, turn out to be an essential part of their very nature.

24. 'But since thou thinkest, that I who am accustomed to the forest might be favoured by taking up my residence at thy home, pray, no more of this. Of one kind is the pleasure of men, of another that of the forest-animals conformable to the habits of their kind.

25. 'If, however, thou wantest to do something pleasant to me, then desist from hunting, O hero, for ever! The poor beasts of the forest, being brute and dull of intellect, are worth pitying for this very reason.

26. 'With respect to the pursuit of happiness and the removal of mischief, the animals, thou shouldst know, are subject to the same feelings as men. Keeping this in mind, deem it improper to do to others what would be a cause of displeasure, if done to thyself.

27. 'Understanding that evil deeds entail loss of

reputation, censure by the virtuous, and moreover suffering, thou must extirpate the evil within thee, considering it thy adversary. It never becomes thee to overlook it, no more than illness.

28. 'It is by pursuing meritorious actions that thou obtainedst the royal dignity, a thing highly esteemed by men and the abode of bliss. That very store of merit thou must enlarge, thou shouldst not enfeeble the ranks of the benefactors.

29. 'Gather meritorious actions, the instruments of glory and happiness, by munificent gifts, (taking care) to enhance their charm by (distributing them at the right) time and in a respectful manner; by a moral conduct, the right laws of which thou mayst learn by intercourse with virtuous persons [1]; and by succeeding in making thy dispositions towards all creatures as well-wishing as to thyself.'

In this manner the High-minded One favoured the king, firmly establishing him in the matters relating to the future life. And the king accepted his words. After which he entered his dwelling-place in the forest, followed with respectful looks by the king.

In this manner the intensely compassionate show pity even to him who attempts their life, when he is in distress; they will not disregard such a one. [This story is to be told also when treating of commiseration, when discoursing on the high-mindedness of the Tathâgata and on the subject of listening with attention to the preaching of the Law. Likewise it is to be propounded when demonstrating that enmities are appeased by means of friendliness, also when treating of the virtue of forbearance. 'In this way it is seen that the High-minded, even when in the state of beasts, behave mercifully towards those who attempt their life. How, indeed, should it become

---

[1] In the original two short syllables are wanting in the second pâda of this stanza. I imagine it should be read thus, sîlena sâdhu(gana)-sa*m*gatanis*k*ayena.

a human being or one who has taken the vow of a homeless life to be wanting in mercy towards the animals? For this reason a pious man (ârya) must show mercy to living beings.']

XXVI. THE STORY OF THE RURU-DEER.

(Cp. the Pâli *G*âtaka, No. 482, Fausb. IV, 255-263; *K*ariyâ-pi*t*aka II, 6.)

To the virtuous no suffering exists but that of others. It is this they cannot bear, not their own suffering, as will be taught by the following.

One time the Bodhisattva, it is said, lived in the forest as a ruru-deer. He had his residence in a remote part of a large wilderness, far from the paths of men and overgrown with a rich, manifold vegetation. There were a great number of sâls, bakulas, piyâlas, hintâlas, tamâlas, naktamâlas, of vidula and ni*k*ula reeds and of shrubs; thickets of *s*im*s*apâs, tini*s*as, *s*ami*s*, palâ*s*as, *s*âkas, of ku*s*a-grass, bamboo and reeds encumbered it; kadambas, sar*g*as, ar*g*unas, dhavas, khadiras, and ku*t*a*g*as abounded in it; and the outstretched branches of many trees were covered as if by a veil with the tendrils of manifold creeping plants. It was the abode of a great many forest-animals: deer of the ruru, p*r*ishata and s*r*imara varieties, yaks, elephants, gavaya-oxen, buffaloes, antelopes of the hari*n*a and the nyanku kind, boars, panthers, hyenas, tigers, wolves, lions, bears, and others. Among them that ruru-deer was conspicuous by its hue brilliant like pure gold and the very soft hair of his body, which was moreover adorned and resplendent with spots of different lovely colours, shining like rubies, sapphires, emeralds, and beryls. With his large blue eyes of incomparable mildness and brightness, with his horns and hoofs endowed with a soft splendour, as if they were made of precious stones, that ruru-deer of surpassing beauty had the appearance of a moving treasury of jewels. Then, knowing his body to be a much desirable object and being aware of the pitiless nature of man, he liked to frequent such forest-tracks as were free from human intercourse, and in consequence of his keen intellect, was careful to avoid such places as were unsafe by the artifices of huntsmen, their traps, nets, snares, holes, lime-twigs, and the seeds and other food they strew down. Moreover, he warned also the animals who followed after him to avoid them. He exercised his rule over them like a teacher, like a father.

1. Where on earth will not people, longing for their happiness, honour the combination of paramount beauty and paramount intelligence, hallowed by accomplished good actions?

Now once upon a time it happened that the Highminded One, residing in that wild part of the forest, heard cries for help uttered by some man who was being carried away by the current of a rapid stream flowing near and lately swollen by the rains.

2. 'The rapid and swollen stream carries me away, and there is nobody to help, no vessel to take me. Come to me, pitiful people; come quickly to rescue a wretch.

3. 'My arms, exhausted from fatigue, are not able to keep my body on the water, and nowhere can I find a ford. Help me then and soon, there is no time to lose.'

These piteous cries of distress struck the Bodhisattva, and as if he were wounded by them in his heart, he rushed out of the thicket, exclaiming those comforting words he had been wont to use in hundreds of previous existences and by which he had banished fear, grief, sadness, and fatigue. So even now he succeeded in bringing forth the words 'do not fear! do not fear!' in plain human voice repeatedly and loudly. And coming out of the forest he saw from afar that man, like a precious present brought to him by the stream.

4. Then, resolved upon rescuing him and without minding the risk of his own life, he entered the river

that was running with tremendous rapidity, like a brave warrior disturbing a hostile army.

5. He placed himself across his way, then told him to cling fast to him. And the man, who was in the paroxysm of fear and had almost lost the power of his limbs, his strength being exhausted, climbed on his back.

6. Nevertheless, though he was mounted by the man and forced out of his way by the violence of the current, the paramount excellence of his nature enabled him to keep his great vigour intact, and he reached the riverbank according to the wish of that man.

7. Having brought the man to the riverside and dispelled his weariness and pain, obtaining by this a very great rejoicing himself, he warmed his cold limbs with the warmth of his own body, then dismissed him. 'Go,' he said, showing him the way.

This marvellous propensity for affording succour, such as is unparalleled in affectionate relations and friends, touched the man to the quick, and the beautiful shape of the ruru-deer roused his admiration and respect. Bowing his head to him, he addressed him with kind words like these :

8–10. 'No friend from childhood nor kinsman is capable of performing such a deed as thou hast done for me. This life of mine, therefore, is thine. If it were to be spent for some matter of thy interest, however small, I would esteem myself highly favoured. Why, procure me that favour by ordering me to do something for thee, in whatever respect Thy Honour thinks me fit for employment.'

In reply to this the Bodhisattva said approvingly :

11. 'Gratitude is not at all to be wondered at in a gentleman. For this quality proceeds from his very nature. But seeing the corruptness of the world, even gratitude is nowadays reckoned among the virtues.

'For this reason, I tell thee this. Let thy grateful disposition not induce thee to relate to anybody, that thou wast rescued by such an extraordinary animal. My beautiful figure makes me too desirable a prey. Lo, as a rule, the hearts of men, owing to their great covetousness, possess little mercy or self-restraint.

12. 'Therefore, take care to guard both thy own good properties and me. A treacherous behaviour towards a friend never tends to bliss.

'Do not either trouble thy mind by anger because I speak so to thee. I am but a deer, unskilled in the deceitful politeness of men. Moreover,

13. 'It is the fault of such people as are clever in fallacy and possess the talent of assuming a show of feigned honesty that even those whose honesty is sincere are looked at with suspicion.

'So then, thou wilt please me by doing as I said.' And the man promised to do so, and after bowing to the Great Being and circumambulating him, set out for his home.

Now at that time there lived in that country a queen of some king who saw true dreams. Whatever extraordinary dream she dreamt was realised. One time, being asleep she had this dream about day-break. She saw a ruru-deer of resplendent brilliancy, shining like a heap of jewels of every kind, standing on a throne and surrounded by the king and his assembly, preaching the Law in a human voice of an articulate and distinct sound. Affected with astonishment she awoke with the beating of drums which were to arouse her husband from sleep[1]. And she took the first opportunity to go and see the king, who kindly received her not only with the honour she deserved but also with solicitous affection.

14. Then she, whose bright eyes enlarged with astonishment and whose lovely cheeks were trembling from gladness, presented her lord with the account of that marvellous dream as with a gift of homage.

---

[1] It was the custom to awake the king by the sound of music and songs. See, for instance, Râmâyana II, sarga 65.

When she had told her wonderful dream to the king, she added this earnest request:

15. 'Therefore, my lord, pray endeavour to obtain that deer. Adorned with this jewel-deer, your zenana would be as resplendent as the sky with the Deer-asterism[1].'

The king, who trusted by experience the visions of her dreams, readily complied with her desire, partly that he might do something agreeable to her, partly because he himself was covetous of obtaining that jewel-deer. Accordingly he ordered all his huntsmen to search for that deer, and had this proclamation made public in his capital day after day:

16. 'There exists a deer gold-skinned and spotted with various colours shining like hundreds of jewels. It is celebrated in the holy texts, and some have got the sight of it. Whosoever will show that deer, to him the king gives a very rich village and full ten lovely women.'

Now the man (who had been rescued by the Bodhisattva) heard that proclamation again and again.

17. As he was poor, the reflection on the sufferings of poverty afflicted his heart, but on the other hand he kept in mind the great benefit he had received from the ruru-deer. Distracted by cupidity and gratitude, he was moved in both directions as in a swing by different considerations like these:

'What, then, have I to do now? Shall I have regard to Virtue or Wealth? Shall I keep the promise to my benefactor rather than the duty of sustaining my family? Which must I esteem most highly, the other world or this? Which must I follow, the conduct of the pious or rather that of the world? Shall I strive after riches or rather after such good as is cherished by the virtuous? Whether to mind the present time or the time hereafter?' At last his mind disturbed by covetousness came to this conclusion. 'If I have once obtained great wealth,' so he

---

[1] Viz. M*riga*siras, corresponding with the head of Orion.

thought, 'I shall be able by means of these riches to gain, while enjoying the pleasures of this world, also happiness in the other world, being intent on honouring my kinsmen and friends, guests and mendicants[1].' Having so resolved, putting out of his mind the benefit of the ruru-deer, he went up to the king and said: 'I, Your Majesty, know that excellent deer and his dwelling-place. Pray, tell me to whom I shall show him.' On hearing this, the king much rejoiced answered him, 'Well, friend, show him to myself,' and putting on his hunting-dress left his capital, accompanied by a large body of his army. Conducted by the man, he went to the aforesaid riverside. Then he encircled the forest adjoining it with the whole of his forces, but himself bearing his bow, wearing his finger-guard[2] and surrounded by a select number of resolute and faithful men, entered the thicket, being shown the way by that man. As they went onward, the man discovering the ruru-deer who quietly and unsuspectingly was staying in his forest, showed him to the king, exclaiming: 'Here, here is that precious deer, Your Majesty. May Your Majesty deign to look at him and be careful.'

18. So saying he raised his arm, eager as he was to point at the deer, and lo, his hand fell down off his arm, as if it had been cut off with a sword.

19. Indeed, when directed at such objects hallowed by their extraordinary performances, one's actions come immediately to ripeness, provided that they are of consequence and there is but little to counterbalance them[3].

Then the king, curious to get the sight of the ruru-deer, let his eyes pass along the way shown by the man.

---

[1] A similar reasoning is made by Sakra, when he tries the Bodhisattva in his Avishahya-existence, see Story V, stanzas 18-21.

[2] The finger-guard (aṅgulitrâna) is a contrivance used by archers to protect the thumb and fingers from being injured by the bow-string.

[3] In other words, in such cases the evil karma has so great a strength that a considerable amount of good works would be required in order to check the rapidity of the development of its fruit.

20. And in the midst of that wood, dark as clouds newly formed, he perceived a body shining with the lustre of a treasury of jewels, and saw that deer, dear by his illustrious properties. So does the fire of lightning appear out of the womb of the cloud.

21. Charmed by the beauty of his figure, the king, eagerly desirous of catching him, immediately curved his bow, made the arrow bite its string and went up to him that he might hit him.

But the Bodhisattva, on hearing the noise of people on every side, had thereby concluded that he must have been surrounded, to be sure. Afterwards perceiving the king coming up ready to shoot off his arrow at him, he understood there was no opportunity for running away. Then he uttered distinct articulate language, addressing the king in a human voice.

22, 23. 'Stop a moment, mighty prince, do not hit me, hero among men! Pray, first satisfy my curiosity, and tell me this. Who may have discovered my abode to thee, far as it is from the paths of men, saying that I, such a deer, dwell in this thicket?'

The king, touched by this wonderful address in a human voice and taking still more interest in him, showed him that man with the point of his arrow. 'This man,' he said, 'has disclosed thy extremely marvellous person to us.' But the Bodhisattva knowing again that man, spoke disapprovingly: 'Fie upon him!

24, 25. 'It is a true saying, in truth "better is it to take a log out of the water than to save an ungrateful person from it." In this manner he returns that exertion made in his behalf! How is it that he did not see that he destroyed his own happiness, too, at the same time?'

Now the king, being curious to know what he might thus reproach, vividly said to the ruru-deer:

26, 27. 'On hearing thee censure somebody without catching the meaning of thy obscure words or knowing with respect of whom thou spokest them, my mind is

XXVI. THE STORY OF THE RURU-DEER.

somewhat alarmed. Therefore, tell me, wonderful deer, who is he on whose account thou speakest so? Is it a man or a spirit, a bird or perhaps a forest-animal?'

The Bodhisattva spoke:

28. 'No desire of blaming prompted me, O king, to this utterance, but becoming aware of this blame-deserving action, I spoke sharp words in order to prevent him from attempting to do such a thing again.

29. 'For who would like to use harsh language to those who have committed a sin, strewing, so to speak, salt upon the wound of their fault? But even to his beloved son a physician is obliged to apply such medical treatment as is made necessary by his illness.

30. 'He whom I, moved by pity, rescued, when he was carried off by the current, is the man who made this danger arise for me, O best of men. Indeed, intercourse with wicked people does not tend to bliss.'

Then the king, casting on that man a stern look expressive of harsh reproach, asked him: 'Oh, in truth, wast thou rescued before from such a distress by this deer?' And the man, who was pale and perspired with fear, sorrow, and dejection, answered in a low tone of shame: 'Yes, I was.' Upon which the king revilingly exclaimed: 'Fie upon thee!' and placing the arrow on the bowstring he continued: 'Do not think it a trifle!

31. 'He whose heart was not even softened by an exertion like that employed in thy behalf, is a vile representative of his fellow-creatures and brings them into dishonour. Why should this lowest of men live any longer?'

With these words he grasped his bow in the middle and bent it in order to kill him. But the Bodhisattva, overpowered by his great compassion, placed himself between, saying to the king: 'Stop, Your Majesty, stop, do not strike one already stricken!

32. 'At the very moment that he listened to the culpable enticement of Cupidity, his enemy, at that

moment surely, he was ruined both in this world, because of the loss of his good name, and in the next too, his righteousness being destroyed.

33. 'Yea, in this way, when their soundness of mind has faded away in consequence of unbearable sufferings, men fall into calamities, being allured by the prospect of rich profit, like foolish moths attracted by the shining of a light.

34. 'Thou must, therefore, rather pity him and restrain thy wrath. And if he wanted to obtain something by so acting, let not his rash deed lack that reward. For lo, I am standing here with bent head awaiting thy orders.'

This merciful and sincere desire to reward even the man who had ill-treated him excited the highest surprise of the king. His heart became converted, and looking up with veneration to the ruru-deer, he exclaimed: 'Well said, well said, holy being.

35. 'Verily, showing such mercy to him whose cruel offence against thee is evident, thou art a human being by thy properties, we do bear but the shape of men.

36. 'Further, since thou deemest this knave worth commiseration, and since he has been the cause of my seeing a virtuous person, I give him the wealth he coveted and to thee the permission to go freely in this kingdom wherever it pleases thee.'

The ruru-deer said: 'I accept this royal boon, illustrious king, which is not given in vain. Therefore, deign to give me thy orders, that our meeting here may afford thee profit and that I may be of some use to thee.' Then the king made the ruru-deer mount his royal chariot, worshipping him like his teacher, and led him with great pomp to his capital. And having given him the reception due to a guest and invited him to place himself on the royal throne, he with his wives and the whole retinue of his officers exhorted him to preach the Law, and raising his eyes to him with a kind expression of gladness mixed with reverence, entreated him in this manner:

37. 'There is a great diversity of opinions among

men concerning the Law, but thou possessest the certainty about the Law. Deign, therefore, to preach it to us.'

Upon which the Bodhisattva raised his voice and preached the Law to the king and his royal assembly in words distinctly spoken in a soft tone and elegantly composed.

38. 'Of the Law with the manifold performances depending on it and with its subdivisions: abstaining from injuring others, from theft, &c., this, I believe, is the brief summary "Mercy to the creatures."

'Look here, illustrious prince.

39. 'If mercy to all creatures should make men hold them like themselves or their own family, whose heart would ever cherish the baleful desire for wickedness?

40. 'But the lack of mercy is to men the cause of the greatest disturbance, as it corrupts the action of their minds and words and bodies no less with respect to their family than to strangers.

41. 'For this reason he who strives for Righteousness ought to keep to mercy, which will yield rich profit. Mercy[1], indeed, engenders virtues, as a fructifying rain makes the crops grow.

42. 'Mercy, possessing a man's mind, destroys in it the passion for injuring one's neighbour; and his mind being pure, neither his speech nor his body will be perverted. So the love of one's neighbour's good always increases and becomes the source of many other virtues: charity, forbearance, and so on, which are followed by gladness of mind and are conducive to reputation.

43. 'The merciful one does not arouse apprehension in the mind of others because of his tranquillity. Owing to his mercy, everybody will hold him a person to be trusted, as if he were their kinsman. No agitation of passion will seize him whose heart has been made firm by mercy, nor does the fire of anger blaze within his mind which enjoys the coolness of water, thanks to mercy.

---

[1] In the fourth pâda of this stanza sa is a misprint for sâ.

44. 'Why use many words? For this reason the wise firmly believe that in Mercy the whole of Righteousness is contained. What virtue, indeed, cherished by the pious does there exist which is not the consequence of Mercy? Having this in mind, be intent on ever fortifying thy mercy to all people, holding them like thy son, like thyself; and winning by thy pious conduct the hearts of thy people, mayst thou glorify thy royalty!'

Then the king praised these words of the ruru-deer, and with his townsmen and landsmen became intent on acting up to the Law of Righteousness. And he granted security to all quadrupeds and birds.

In this manner, then, for the virtuous no suffering exists but that of others. It is this they cannot bear, not their own suffering. [This story is also to be told when discoursing on compassion, and may be adduced when treating of the high-mindedness of the virtuous, also when censuring the mischievous.]

XXVII. THE STORY OF THE GREAT MONKEY.

(Cp. the Pâli *G*âtaka, No. 407, Fausb. III, 370-375.)

Those who follow the behaviour of the virtuous win over even the hearts of their enemies. This will be taught as follows.

In the heart of the Himavat there is a blessed region, whose soil is covered with many kinds of herbs of different efficacious properties, and abounds in hundreds of forest-trees with their great variety and manifold arrangement of boughs, twigs, flowers, and fruits. It is irrigated by mountain-currents whose water possesses the limpidity of crystals, and resounds with the music of manifold crowds of birds. In that forest the Bodhisattva lived, it is said, a chief of a troop of monkeys. But even in that state—in consequence of his constant practice of charity and compassion—jealousy, selfishness, and cruelty, as if they were at war with him because he attended on their enemies (the virtues), would not enter his mind. There he had his residence on a large banian tree, which by its height, standing out superior against the sky like the top of a mountain, might pass for the lord of that forest, and by the thickness of its branches beset with dark foliage, resembled a mass of clouds. Those branches were somewhat curved, being loaded with excellent fruits of a size surpassing that of palmyra-nuts, and distinguished by an exceedingly sweet flavour and a lovely colour and smell.

1. The virtuous, even when they are in the state of animals, have still some remainder of good fortune[1] which tends to the happiness of their friends, for whose sake they employ it, in the same manner as the remainder of the wealth of people abroad may serve the wants of their friends.

Now one branch of that tree hung over a river which passed by that place[2]. Now the Bodhisattva, far-sighted as he was, had instructed his flock of monkeys in this manner: 'Unless ye prevent this banian-branch from having fruit, none of you will ever be able to eat any fruit from the other branches[3].' Now it once happened that the monkeys overlooked one young and for this reason not very big fruit, hidden as it was in the cavity of some leaf crooked by ants. So that fruit grew on, and in time developed its fine colour, smell, flavour, and softness; when it had ripened and its stalk became loose, it dropped into the river. Being carried down the stream, it stuck at last

---

[1] In other words it is said, that though their store of merit, producing good fortune, must have been exhausted according to their being born beasts, yet there is left some remainder, the effect of which may assuage them in that low state. Cp. Story XXXIII, stanza 2.

[2] In the Pâli redaction that river is the Ganges and the king Brahmadatta of Benares.

[3] Considering the abruptness of the narration, it seems there is something wanting in the text. In the Pâli redaction it is told that the Bodhisattva, having warned the monkeys that a fruit of that tree would fall in the water and bring them mischief, causes them to destroy all germs of fruit on that branch in blossom-time.

in the net-work of a fence (let down in the river by the orders) of a certain king, who, with his harem, was sporting at that time in the water of that river.

2. Spreading about its delicious smell of great excellency and delightful to the nose, that fruit made the different other odours disappear, that exhaled there from the garlands, the rum, and the perfumes of the bathing women, however those scents were intensified by the union of the women interlacing each other.

3. This smell soon enchanted the women; they enjoyed it with prolonged inhalations and half-shut eyes. And being curious to know its origin, they cast their eyes in all directions.

And while casting their eyes, stirred by curiosity, all around, the women perceived that banian fig, surpassing by its size a ripe palmyra-nut, as it stuck to the net-work of the fence, and having once discovered it, they could not keep their eyes from it. Nor was the king less curious to know the nature of that fruit. He had it brought to him, and after examination by reliable physicians tasted it himself.

4. Its marvellous flavour (rasa) raised the king's amazement, as (in a dramatic composition) the marvellous sentiment (rasa), ravishing (the mind of the spectators) by a good representation, rouses their admiration.

5. Had its extraordinary colour and smell stirred his surprise before, now its flavour filled him with the highest admiration, and agitated him with lust.

Though accustomed to dainties, the king became so eager to enjoy that relish that this thought came to him:

6. 'If one does not eat those fruits, in truth, what fruit does one enjoy from his royalty? But he who gets them is really a king, and this without the toil of exercising royal power.'

Accordingly, having made up his mind to find out its origin, he reasoned in this way to himself. 'Surely, the excellent tree, whence came this fruit, cannot be far from here and it must stand on the riverside. For it cannot have been in contact with the water for a long time, since it has kept its colour, smell, and flavour intact, and is moreover undamaged and shows no trace of decomposition. For this reason, it is possible to pursue its origin.' Having so resolved, as he was possessed by a strong desire for that delicious flavour, he ceased that water-sport, and, after taking such measures as were suitable for the maintenance of order in his capital (during his absence), set out, accompanied by a great body of armed people equipped for expedition. With them he marched up the river and enjoyed the different and various sensations proper to journeying in a forest-region, clearing his way through thickets haunted by ferocious animals, beholding woodlands of great natural beauty, and frightening elephants and deer by the noise of his drums. At last he reached the neighbourhood of that tree, a place difficult for men to approach.

7. Like a mass of clouds hanging down by the burden of their water, this lord of trees appeared from afar to the eyes of the king, dominating the other trees which seemed to look up to it as to their sovereign, and, though it stood near a steep mountain, resembling a mountain itself.

The exceedingly lovely smell, more fragrant than that of ripe mango fruits, which was spreading from it and met the army as if it went to receive it, made the king sure that this was the tree he sought for. Coming near, he saw many hundreds of apes filling its boughs and branches and occupied in eating its fruits. The king became angry with those monkeys who robbed him of the objects so ardently longed for, and with harsh words as 'Hit them! hit them! drive them away, destroy them all, these scoundrels of monkeys!' he ordered his men to assail them. And those warriors made themselves ready to shoot off the arrows from their bows (strung), and uttered cries to frighten away the monkeys; others lifted up clods and sticks and spears to throw at them. They invaded the tree, as if they were to attack a hostile fortress.

But the Bodhisattva had perceived the approach of that noisy royal army moving with loud tumult and uproar, like the billows of a sea roused by the violence of the wind; he had seen the assault made on all sides of his excellent tree with a shower of arrows, spears, clods, sticks, which resembled a shower of thunderbolts; and he beheld his monkeys unable to do anything but utter discordant cries of fear, while they looked up to him with faces pale with dejection. His mind was affected with the utmost compassion. Being himself free from affliction, sadness, and anxiety, he comforted his tribe of monkeys, and having resolved upon their rescue, climbed to the top of the tree, desirous to jump over to the mountain-peak near it. And although that place could be reached only by many successive leaps, the Great Being, by dint of his surpassing heroism, passed across like a bird and held the spot.

8. Other monkeys would not be able to traverse that space even in two successive leaps, but he, the courageous one, swiftly crossed it with one single bound, as if it were a small distance.

9. His compassion had fostered his strong determination, but it was his heroism which brought it to its perfection. So he made his utmost effort to carry it out, and by the earnestness of his exertion he found the way to it in his mind.

Having mounted, then, on some elevated place of the mountain-slope, he found a cane, tall and strong, deep-rooted and strong-rooted, the size of which surpassed the distance (between the mountain and the tree). This he fastened to his feet, after which he jumped back to the tree. But as the distance was great and he was embarrassed by his feet being tied, the Great Being hardly succeeded in seizing with his hands the nearest branch of the tree.

10. Then holding fast that branch and keeping the cane stretched by his effort, he ordered his tribe, making them the signal proper to his race, to come quickly off the tree.

And the monkeys, as they were bewildered by fear, having found that way of retreat, hastened to make use of it, wildly rushing over his body without regard to him, and safely escaped along that cane.

11. While being incessantly trodden by the feet of those fear-bewildered monkeys, his body lost the solidity of its flesh, but his mind did not lose its extraordinary firmness.

On beholding this, the king and his men were overcome with the utmost astonishment.

12. Such a splendid display of strength and wisdom, combined with such great self-denial and mercy to others, must rouse wonder in the minds of those who hear of it; how much more did it affect the bystanders who witnessed it?

Then the king commanded his men in this manner: 'This chief of apes,' he said, 'having his limbs shaken and bruised by the feet of the multitude of monkeys who, agitated by fear, ran over his body, and remaining in that same position for a long time, must be excessively tired. Surely, he will be unable to retire from this difficult posture by himself. Therefore, quickly dress a canopy underneath the place where he is, which being done, the cane and the banian branch must be shot off simultaneously, with one arrow each.' And they did so. Then the king ordered the monkey to be gently lifted off the canopy and placed on a soft couch. There he lay without consciousness, for in consequence of the pain of his wounds and his exhaustion he had swooned. After his wounds had been salved with clarified butter and other ointments suitable for the relief of fresh bruises, his faintness grew less. When he had recovered his senses, he was visited by the king, who, affected with curiosity, admiration, and respect, after asking him about his health, continued thus:

13. 'Thou madest thy body a bridge for those monkeys, and feeling no mercy for thy own life, rescuedst them. What art thou to them or what are they to thee?

14. 'If thou deemest me a person worth hearing this matter, pray, tell it me, foremost of monkeys. No small fetters of friendship, methinks, should fasten one's mind to enable it to do the like performances.'

In reply to these words the Bodhisattva, in return for the king's wish to relieve him, made himself known in a proper manner. He said:

15. 'Those, always prompt to act up to my orders, charged me with the burden of being their ruler. And I, for my part, bound to them with the affection of a father for his children, engaged myself to bear it; so I did.

16. 'This, mighty sovereign, is the kind of relation existing between them and me. It is rooted by time and has increased the friendly feelings existing between animals of the same species. Our dwelling together has strengthened it to the mutual affection of kinsmen.'

On hearing this, the king affected with great admiration replied:

17. 'The ministers and the rest of his officials are to serve the interest of their lord, not the king to serve theirs. For what, then, did Your Honour sacrifice yourself in behalf of your attendants?'

The Bodhisattva spoke: 'Verily, such is the lore of Political Wisdom (râganîti), Your Majesty, but to me it seems something difficult to follow.

18. 'It is excessively painful to overlook heavy and unbearable pain, even if the sufferer be somebody unacquainted with us. How much more, if those suffer who, having their minds intent on worshipping us, are like dear relations to us!

19. 'So, on seeing distress and despair overwhelming the monkeys in consequence of their sudden danger, a great sorrow overcame me, which did not leave me room to think of my personal interest.

20. 'Perceiving the bows bent and the glittering arrows fly upward on all sides, and hearing the dreadful noise of the strings, hastily and without further consideration I jumped over from the tree to the mountain.

21. 'Then—for the distress of my poor comrades,

overcome with the highest degree of terror, drew me back to them—I tied a cane fast to my feet, a well-rooted reed, suitable for the effort at which I aimed.

22. 'So I jumped once more, leaping from the mountain-side to the tree, in order to rescue my comrades, and with my hands I attained its nearest branch stretched out like a hand to meet me.

23. 'And while I was hanging there with extended body between that cane and that outstretched branch of the tree, those comrades of mine happily made their escape, running without hesitation over my body.'

The king, perceiving the ecstasy of gladness, which even in that miserable condition pervaded the Great Being, and much wondering at it, again spoke to him:

24. 'What good has Your Honour obtained, thus despising your own welfare and taking upon yourself the disaster which threatened others?'

The Bodhisattva spoke:

25. 'Verily, my body is broken, O king, but my mind is come to a state of the greatest soundness, since I removed the distress of those, over whom I exercised royal power for a long time.

26. 'As heroes who have vanquished their proud enemies in battle wear on their limbs the beautiful marks of their prowess like ornaments, so I gladly bear these pains.

27. 'Now I have requited them that long succession of prosperity which I got by the chieftaincy over my tribe, that showed me not only their reverence and other marks of worship, but also their affectionate attachment.

28. 'For this reason, this bodily pain does not grieve me, nor the separation from my friends, nor the destruction of my pleasure, nor my approaching death which I have incurred by thus acting. It seems to me rather the approach of a high festival.

29, 30. 'Self-satisfaction gained by requital of former benefits, appeasement of the solicitude (caused thereby), a spotless fame, honour on the part of a king, fearlessness of death, and the approbation which my grateful behaviour will meet with from the virtuous:

these good qualities, O thou who, like a tree[1], art the residence of excellent virtues!—have I obtained by falling in with this wretched state. But the vices opposite to these virtues will be met by such a king as is without mercy for his dependents.

31. 'For, if a king be devoid of virtues, if he have destroyed his good renown and vices have taken up their abode in him, say, what else may he expect than to go to the fierce-flaming fires of hell?

32. 'For this reason I have explained to thee, powerful prince, the power of virtues and vices. Rule, therefore, thy realm with righteousness. For Fortune shows in her affections the fickle nature of a woman.

33. 'His army, not only the military men but also the animals of war; his officials; his people, both townsmen and landsmen; those who have no protector; and both (classes of religious people) Srama*n*as and Brâhmans; all of them must a king endeavour to endow with such happiness as is conducive to their good, as if he were their father.

34. 'In this manner increasing in merit, wealth, and glory, thou mayst enjoy prosperity both in this world and in the next. With this kind of felicity proper to the holy kings of old (râ*g*arshis) and attainable by practising commiseration towards thy subjects, mayst thou be illustrious, O king of men!'

35. After thus instructing the king who, like a pupil, listened to him with devout attention and set a high value on his words, he left his body paralysed in its functions by the excess of his pains, and mounted to Heaven.

In this manner, then, those who imitate the behaviour of the virtuous win over even the hearts of their enemies. Thus considering, he who is desirous of gaining the affection of men ought to imitate the behaviour of the virtuous. [This story is also to be propounded, when discoursing on the Tathâgata. 'The

---

[1] This simile is not improper, the speaker being a monkey.

creatures are not as able to bring about their own profit, as the Lord was to bring about the profit of others.' Likewise, when treating of listening with attention to the preaching of the Law, when discoursing on compassion, and also when instructing princes, in which case this is to be said: 'In this manner a king must be merciful towards his subjects.' It may be adduced also, when treating of gratitude. 'In this manner the virtuous show their gratitude.']

XXVIII. THE STORY OF KSHÂNTIVÂDIN[1].

(Cp. the Pâli *Gâ*taka, No. 313, Fausb. III, 39-43.)

Truly, to those who have wholly imbibed the virtue of forbearance and are great in keeping their tranquillity there is nothing unbearable. This will be taught as follows.

One time the Bodhisattva, it is said, was an ascetic who had forsaken the world. He had become convinced that the life in a home, since it is beset with bad occupations, leaves but little room for righteousness; for it is visited by many sins and evils and unfit for quiet, inasmuch as it implies the prevalence of material interest (artha) and sensual pleasures (kâma); it is exposed to the inroad of defiling passions: love, hatred, infatuation, jealousy, anger, lasciviousness, pride, selfishness, and the rest; it involves the loss of the possession of shame and religion, and is the abode of covetousness and wicked lust. On the other hand he understood the homeless state, as it avoids material property and sensual objects, to be an agreeable one, being wholly free from those evils. Thus knowing, he became an ascetic, eminent by his conduct, his learning, his placidity of mind, his modesty, and his self-restraint. As he was in the habit of

---

[1] In the original K*s*hântig*â*takam. Kshânti must here be an abbreviation of the name Kshântivâdin; in the Pâli redaction the corresponding story bears the title of Khantivâdig*â*taka.

always preaching forbearance and teaching the Law from that point of view, in strict conformity with the vow he had taken to do so, people neglecting his proper name and that of his family, made him a name of their own invention, calling him Kshântivâdin (forbearance-preacher).

1. Illustrious domination or knowledge or penance, also an extreme passion for arts, likewise anomaly of body, language or behaviour are the causes of giving new names to men.

2. So was the case with him. His true name vanished for the appellation of Kshântivâdin, because knowing the power of forbearance and desiring to adorn mankind, like himself, with that virtue he constantly used to discourse on that topic.

3. The great endurance, which was a part of his very nature and the firmness of which he showed by his unaltered calm, when injured by others, as well as his excellent sermons on that subject, gave him the renown of a Muni.

The residence of the High-minded One was a place in the forest, lovely by its utter solitude and exhibiting the charming beauty of a garden; it bore flowers and fruits at all seasons, and encompassed a pond of pure water embellished by white and blue lotuses. By his dwelling there he procured for that place the holiness of a hermitage.

4. For where pious persons adorned with excellent virtues, have their residence, such a place is a very auspicious and lovely one, a sacred place of pilgrimage (tîrtha), a hermitage.

There he was venerated by the different deities, who were living there, and often visited by such people as were lovers of virtues and desirous of their salvation. To that multitude of visitors he showed the high favour of entertaining them with his sermons on the subject of forbearance, rejoicing both their ears and hearts.

Now one time in the season of summer it happened that the king of that country, in consequence of the hot weather, was seized with a great longing to play in the water, a very desirable thing at that time. So he went with his harem to that place in the forest, as it was distinguished by the different delights proper to gardens.

5. While he was rambling in the wood with the beauties of his zenana spreading about on all sides, he embellished its Nandana-like splendour, so to speak, by the rich display of the graceful sport of himself and his wanton retinue.

6. In the arbours and bowers, under the forest-trees with their laughing dress of flowers, and in the water with its expanding lotuses the king delighted in the unrestrained expansion of the natural dalliance of the females.

7. Smilingly he beheld the graceful movements of fear and its beautiful expression on the faces of some molested by bees, that were allured by the perfumes of the implements for bathing and anointing mixed with the fragrance of garlands and the odour of the rum.

8. Though they had adorned their ears with the most beautiful flowers, and their hair wore plenty of garlands, the women could not have enough of flowers. In the same way the king could not look enough at their wanton playing.

9. He beheld those chaplet-like clusters of females, now clinging to the arbours, now tarrying at the lotus-groups, sometimes hovering like bees about the flowery trees.

10. Even the bold lascivious cries of the cuckoos, the dances of the peacocks, and the humming of the bees were outdone by the tattle, the dances, and the songs of those women.

11. The sound of the royal drums, as strong as the rattling of thunder, induced the peacocks to utter their peculiar cries and make a wide-spread circle of their tails, as if they were actors worshipping the monarch by the virtue of their art.

Then, having enjoyed, with his harem, to his heart's

content the pleasure of walking about in that garden-like wood, as he was tired with incessant playing and drunkenness overcame his mind, the king laid himself down on his very precious royal couch in a beautiful arbour, and fell asleep.

Now, when the women perceived that their lord was no longer occupied with them, as they were not satiated with the manifold loveliness of the forest which kept them enchanted, they moved from that place, and rambled about in groups formed according to their liking, mixing the confused sounds of their rattling ornaments with the tinkling noise of their chatter.

12. Followed by the badges of sovereign power, the royal umbrella, the royal tail-fan, the royal seat &c., which were decorated with golden ornaments and borne by female slaves, the women walked about, indulging unrestrainedly in their natural wantonness.

13. Disregarding the entreaties of the female servants, they greedily laid hands upon the lovely flowers and twigs of the trees within their reach, prompted by their petulance.

14. Though they had plenty of flowers, both as ornaments and arranged as wreaths, they left on their way no shrub lovely by its flowers, nor tree with its waving twigs without stripping them, out of cupidity.

Now in the course of their rambling through the forest, the loveliness of which had captured their minds, the king's harem approached the hermitage of Kshântivâdin. But those who were in charge of the royal wives, although they knew the penance-power and high-mindedness of that Muni, did not venture to prevent them from entering, on account of the king's attachment to his darlings, lest he might resent their intervention. So the royal wives, as if they were attracted by the splendour of that hermitage, the loveliness of which was enhanced by (the) supernatural power (of its occupant), entered the hermitage and saw the eminent Muni sitting there with crossed legs under a tree, a view auspicious and purifying to behold. His tranquillity gave a soft expression to his countenance; the exceeding profundity of his mind inspired awe; his face radiated, as it were, from the splendour of his penance and, owing to his diligent exercise of dhyâna, bore the beautiful expression of calm, as is proper to undisturbed senses, even though the loftiest subjects of meditation were present to his thoughts. In short, he was like the embodied Dharma. The lustre of his penance subdued the minds of those royal wives, and the very sight of him was sufficient to make them abandon their dalliance, frivolity, and haughtiness. Accordingly they went to him in a humble attitude, and sat down respectfully in a circle around him. He, for his part, performed to them the usual salutation, welcoming them and saying to them kind and courteous things which are agreeable to guests; then availing himself of the opportunity which their questions procured him, he showed them his hospitality by a religious discourse, preaching in such terms as were easily understood by women, and illustrating his exposition of the Law with examples.

15. 'He who, having obtained the blameless human state, and being born in the full possession of organs and senses sound and vigorous, without any defect [1], neglects to do good actions every day from lack of attention—such a one is much deceived; is he not subject to the necessity of death?

16. 'A man may be ever so excellent by his birth, his figure, his age, his superior power, or the wealth of his estate, never will he enjoy happiness in the other world, unless he be purified by charity, good conduct (sîla), and the rest of the virtues.

17. 'For surely, he who though devoid of a noble birth and the rest, abhorring wickedness, resorts to the virtues of charity, good conduct &c., such a one is hereafter visited by every kind of bliss, as the sea in the rainy season by the water of the rivers.

---

[1] Bodily infirmities are the effect of former actions. They are with the Buddhists an impediment to proceeding on the way to salvation for the same reason, as they entail impurity and incompetence to assist at sacrificial performances in Brâhmanism.

S

18. 'To him who excels by his extraction, his figure, his age, his superior power, or the wealth of his estate, attachment to virtues is the most proper ornament already in this world; his golden garlands are only indicative of his riches.

19. 'Blossoms are the ornaments of trees, it is flashes of lightning that adorn the big rain-clouds, the lakes are adorned by lotuses and waterlilies with their drunken bees; but virtues brought to perfection are the proper ornament of living beings.

20. 'The various differences of men with respect to their health, duration of life, beauty of figure, wealth, birth may be classed under the heads of low, middle and high. This triad is not the effect of natural properties nor caused by external influences, indeed. No, it is the result of a man's actions (karma).

21. 'Knowing this to be the fixed law of human existence, and keeping in mind the fickleness and frailness of life, a man must avoid wickedness, directing his heart to pious behaviour. For this is the way leading to good reputation and to happiness.

22. 'But a defiled mind acts like a fire, it burns away the good of one's self and one's neighbour. He who is afraid of wickedness, therefore, ought carefully to keep off such defilement by cultivating what tends to the contrary.

23. 'As a fire, however fiercely burning, if it meet a great river, filled up to its borders with water, becomes extinguished, so does the fire which blazes within the mind of a man, if he relies on forbearance that will serve him both in this world and in the next.

24. 'So forbearance is of great benefit. He who practises this virtue avoids wickedness, for he has vanquished the causes of it. In consequence thereof he will not rouse enmity, owing to his cherishing friendliness. For this reason, he will be a person beloved and honoured, and accordingly enjoy a happy life. At the end he comes to Heaven (as easily) as if he entered his home, thanks to his attachment to a meritorious behaviour.

'Moreover, ladies, this virtue of forbearance, I say,

25. 'Is celebrated as the superior degree of a pious nature; as the highest development obtainable by merit and good repute; as that purification which is attained without touching water; as the highest wealth afforded by many affluents of virtuous properties.

26. 'It is praised also as the lovely firmness of mind of the virtuous which is always indifferent to injuries done to them by others; as having obtained by its properties its lovely name of kshamâ[1]; as benefiting mankind; as well acquainted with pity.

27. 'Forbearance is the ornament of the powerful; it is the highest pitch of the strength of ascetics; and since it has the effect of a shower of rain on the conflagration of evils, it may be called the extinguisher of misfortune both in this world and after death.

28. 'To the virtuous forbearance is a coat of mail, blunting the arrows which the tongue of the wicked shoots off against them. Mostly it changes those weapons into flowers of praise, which may be inserted in the garland of their glory.

29. 'It is stated to be the killer of Delusion, that adversary of the Dharma, and an easy contrivance by which to reach salvation. Who, then, ought not to do his utmost to obtain forbearance, that virtue invariably conducive to happiness?'

In this manner the High-minded One entertained those female guests with an edifying sermon.

Meanwhile the king, having satisfied his want of sleep, awoke; his lassitude was gone, but his eyes were still heavy with the dimness of inebriation, which had not entirely passed away. Desirous of continuing his amorous sport, he frowningly asked the female servants who were guarding his couch, where his wives were. 'Your Majesty,' they answered, 'Their Highnesses are now embellishing other parts of the forest, to admire the splendour of which they walked on.' Having been thus informed by them, the king, as he

---

[1] Kshamâ is a synonym of kshânti.

eagerly desired to witness the sportive sayings and doings of the royal wives, how they were laughing and jesting free and unrestrained, rose from his couch, and accompanied by his female warriors bearing his umbrella, his chowrie, his upper garment, and his sword, and followed by the eunuchs of his zenana, wearing their armour and having reed-staves in their hands, he marched through the forest after them. It was easy to follow the way they had taken; for they had traced it out with juvenile wantonness by means of a multitude of various blossoms, flower-clusters, and twigs, which they had strewed about, moreover by the red sap of the areca-nut and betel chewed by them. So then, going after them he went to the hermitage. But no sooner had the king seen that most excellent *R*ishi Kshântivâdin surrounded by the circle of the royal wives, than he was seized with a fit of wrath. This frenzy overtook him, partly because he was long since his enemy and bore him a grudge[1], partly in consequence of his intellect being still troubled by drunkenness and his mind overcome with jealousy. And as his power of composing himself was small, he lost his countenance, disregarding the laws of decency and politeness, and submitted to sinful wrath. So his colour altered, drops of sweat appeared on his face, his limbs trembled, his brows frowned, and his eyes tinged reddish, squinted, rolled, stared. The loveliness, grace, and beauty of his figure had waned. He pressed his hands together, and rubbing them, squeezing thereby his finger-rings and shaking his golden armlets, scolded that excellent *R*ishi, uttering many invectives: ' Ha, he exclaimed,

30. 'Who is that knave who injures our majesty, casting his eyes on our wives? Under the disguise of a Muni this hypocrite acts like a fowler.'

These words alarmed and disturbed the eunuchs, who said to the king: 'Your Majesty ought not to

---

[1] This can be no wonder, for in the Pâli *G*âtaka, that wicked king is identified with Devadatta.

speak so. This is a Muni who has purified his Self by a long life of vows and restraints and penance; Kshântivâdin is his name.' Nevertheless the king, in the pervertedness of his mind, did not take to heart their words, and continued: 'Alas! Ah!

31. 'So it is then a long time already since this hypocrite, setting himself up as the foremost of holy ascetics, has deceived people by his forgery!

'Well, then, I will lay open the true nature of that hypocrite, though he keeps it veiled with his ascetic's dress and well conceals it by practising the art of delusion and false godliness.' After thus speaking, he took his sword from the hand of the female guard (who was bearing it) and rushed on the holy *R*ishi with the determination of striking him, as if he were his rival. The royal wives, who had been informed by their attendants of the king's approach, on seeing his fine features changed by anger, became much afflicted, and with anxious looks expressive of their trouble and consternation rose from the earth, and took leave of the holy *R*ishi. Then they went to meet the king, and as they stood near him with their folded hands lifted up to their face, they had the appearance of an assemblage of lotuses in autumn, when the brightness of the flowers begins to peep out of the enclosure of the buds.

32. Yet their graceful demeanour, their modesty and comeliness did not appease his mind incensed with the fire of wrath.

But the queens who commenced already to recover from their first terror, perceiving that the king in the fierce manner of one whose behaviour is altered by anger was marching with a weapon in the direction of the holy *R*ishi, on whom he kept fixed his adverse looks, placed themselves in his way, and surrounding him entreated him: 'Your Majesty, pray, do not commit a reckless act, do not, pray. This man is the Reverend Kshântivâdin.' The king, however, owing to his heart's wickedness, became the more angry, thinking: 'Surely, he has already gained their affection.' He reproved their temerity in requesting by clear signs (of his discontent), frowning and casting on them angry looks, fierce as the jealousy which had taken possession of his mind. After which, turning to his eunuchs and shaking his head so that his royal diadem and ear-rings trembled, he said with a glance at his wives :

33. 'This man speaks only of forbearance, but he does not practise it. For example, he was not impassible to the covetousness of the contact with females.

34. 'His tongue does not at all agree with his actions, still less with his ill-intentioned heart. What has this man with unrestrained senses to do in the penance-forest, that he should simulate religious vows and dress and sit down in the hypocritical posture of a saint ?'

Now, the king in his fit of wrath having thus rebuked his queens and shown his hard-heartedness, they were affected with sorrow and sadness, for they knew his ferocious nature and his contumacy which made him inaccessible to persuasion. The eunuchs, who were likewise alarmed, affected with anxiety, and afflicted, made signs to them with their hands that they should withdraw. So they went away, lowering their faces with shame and lamenting over that best of *R*ishis.

35. 'We are the cause of the king's wrath against that sinless and self-subdued holy ascetic, wide-famed for his virtues. Who knows what will be the end of it ? In one way or other will the king perform some unbecoming deed, when he will make his wrath fall down on him, however virtuous.

36. 'Yea, this king would be able to destroy his own royal behaviour and his glory obtained by it, hurting the body of that Muni, as well as the body of his penance, and grieving our guiltless minds at the same time !'

After the queens thus lamenting and sighing on his account—for what could they else do for him ?—were gone, the king in wrath came up to the holy *R*ishi, threatening him with drawn sword, in order to strike him himself. On seeing that the Great Being, though thus assailed, kept his calmness unchanged with imperturbable constancy, he became the more excited, and said to him :

37. 'How skilled he is in playing the holy one, that he looks even at me as if he were a Muni, persisting in his guileful arrogance!'

The Bodhisattva, however, owing to his constant practice of forbearance, was not at all disturbed, and as he at once understood from that hostile proceeding, though not without astonishment, that it was the eagerness of wrath which caused the king to act in such an unbecoming way that he had thrown off all restraint of politeness and good manners and lost the faculty of distinguishing between his good and evil, he pitied that monarch and, with the object of appeasing him, said, in truth, something like this :

38. 'Meeting with disrespect is nothing strange in this world ; for this reason, since it may also happen to be the effect of destiny and guilt, I do not mind it. But this grieves me that I cannot perform towards you, not even with my voice, the usual kind reception, due to those who come to me.

'Moreover hear this, O sovereign.

39. 'To such as you, who are bound to put evildoers on the right way and to act for the interest of the creatures, it never behoves to do any rash action. You should rather follow, therefore, the way of reflection.

40. 'Something good may be considered evil ; inversely, something evil may appear in a false light. The truth about anything to be done cannot be discerned at once before inquiring by reasoning into the differences in the several modes of action.

41. 'But such a king as gets a true insight of his proper line of conduct by reflection and, after that, carries out his design with righteousness by the way of his policy, will always effect the thrift of dharma,

artha and kâma in his people, nor will he be devoid of that threefold prosperity himself.

42. 'For this reason, you ought to purify your mind of rashness, and to be only intent on such actions as tend to good repute. In fact, transgressions of a decent behaviour are highly notorious, if they are committed by persons of a high rank in whom they were not seen before.

43. 'In a penance-forest protected by your mighty arm, you would not suffer anybody else, in truth, to do what is blamed by the pious and destructive to good behaviour. How is it that you should be decided to act in this way yourself, O king?

44. 'If your harem came perchance to my hermitage together with their male attendants, what fault of mine may be found there that you should allow yourself to be thus altered by wrath?

45. 'Suppose, however, there is here some fault of mine, forbearance would become you even then, my lord. Forbearance, indeed, is the chief ornament of a powerful one; for it betrays his cleverness in keeping (the treasury of) his virtues.

46. 'Kings cannot so much be adorned either by their dark-blue ear-rings with their reverberation of dancing shine on the cheeks, or by the several brilliant jewels of their head-ornament, as they are adorned by forbearance. Thus considering, pray, do not disregard that virtue.

47. 'Set aside irascibility which is never fit to be relied upon, but maintain forbearance (as carefully) as your dominions[1]. In truth, the lovely behaviour of princes showing their esteem to ascetics, is full of bliss.'

Notwithstanding this admonition by that excellent Muni, the king, troubled by the crookedness of his mind, persisted in his false suspicion. So he addressed him again:

48. 'If you are not a mock-ascetic, but really

---

[1] Literally: as if it were the earth. The comparison constitutes a pun in the original, for kshamâ may convey the meaning of 'earth' while it also signifies 'forbearance.'

engaged in keeping your vow of restraint, for what reason then do you, under the pretext of exhorting me to forbearance, beg safety from my side ¹?'

The Bodhisattva answered : ' Hear then, great prince, for what reason I urged you.

49. ' I spoke so that your good renown might not break down under the blame you would incur because of me, if it were to be said of you " the king has killed a guiltless ascetic, a Brâhman."

50. ' Death is an invariable necessity for all creatures. For this reason I am not afraid of it, nor have I anything to fear, when I recollect my own behaviour.

51. ' But it was for your sake, that you should not suffer by injuring Righteousness, the source of happiness, that I praised forbearance to you as the fit instrument for attaining salvation.

52. ' Since it is a mine of virtues and an armour against vices, I gladly praise Forbearance, for it is an excellent boon, I offer you.'

But the king disdained these gentle flowers of speech which the Muni offered him. Scornfully he said to that foremost of *Ri*shis : ' Let us now see your attachment to forbearance,' and so speaking, he directed his sharp sword to the right hand of the Muni, which was a little extended towards him, with a prohibitive gesture, having its very fine and long fingers upward, and severed it from his arm like a lotus from its stalk.

53. Yet the Bodhisattva did not feel so much pain, even after his hand had been cut off—so steadfast was he in keeping his vow of forbearance—as sorrow concerning the cutter, whose future misfortune he saw, which was to fall terrible and irremediable upon that person hitherto accustomed to pleasures.

And thinking within himself : ' Alas ! he has transgressed the boundary of his good, he has ceased to be a person worth admonishing²,' and commiserating him, as he would do a sick man given up by the

---

¹ Instead of asmâd I read asmân.
² Cp. Story VII, stanzas 20-26.

doctors, he kept silent. But the king continued to speak threatening words to him.

54. 'And in this manner your body shall be cut to pieces until death. Desist from your hypocritical penance, and leave that villainous forgery.'

The Bodhisattva made no answer. He understood him to be deaf to admonition and had learnt his obstinacy. Then the king successively and in the same way cut off the other hand of the High-minded One, both his arms, his ears and nose, and his feet.

55. Yet that foremost of Munis did not feel sorrow or anger, when the sharp sword fell down on his body. His knowledge that the machinery of his body must eventually come to an end, and his habitual practice of forbearance against everybody made him so strong.

56. In consequence of its habitual friendliness, the mind of that virtuous one was inaccessible to the sense of sorrow on account of himself. Even while he saw his limbs being cut off, his forbearance remained unshaken, but that he saw the king fallen from Righteousness, made him sore with grief.

57. Verily, the compassionate who are great in retaining their tranquillity throughout are not so much afflicted by pain arising in themselves, as they grieve on account of the suffering of others.

58. But the king, after performing that cruel deed, was anon caught by a fire-like fever, and when he went out of the gardens, earth on a sudden opened and swallowed him.

After swallowing the king, the earth continued to make a fearful noise, and fiery flames appeared in the opening. This caused great consternation all around, and perplexed and alarmed the royal attendants. The king's ministers, knowing the grandeur of the penance-power of that Muni and imputing to it the catastrophe of the king, were affected with anxiety, lest that holy *R*ishi should burn down the whole country on account of the king. Thus apprehending, they went up to the holy *R*ishi, and bowing to him entreated him with folded hands to be propitious.

59. 'May that king, who impelled by his infatuated mind has put thee into this state by an exceedingly rash action, be alone the fuel for the fire of thy curse. Pray, do not burn his town!

60. 'Pray, do not destroy for his fault innocent people, women and children, the old and the sick, the Brâhmans and the poor! Rather shouldst thou, being a lover of virtues, preserve both the realm of that king and thy own righteousness.'

In reply to this, the Bodhisattva comforted them: 'Do not fear,' he said, 'sirs.

61, 62. 'As to that king who just cut off with his sword my hands and feet, my ears and nose, maiming an innocent ascetic living in the forest, how should a person like me aim at his hurt or conceive even such a thought? May that king live long and no evil befall him!

63. 'A being subject to sorrow, death and sickness, subdued by cupidity and hatred, consumed by his evil actions is a person to be pitied. Who ought to get angry with such a one?

64. 'And should that line of conduct[1] be ever so preferable, O that his sin might ripen (its unavoidable result) in detriment of no other but me! For to people accustomed to pleasure meeting with suffering, even for a short time, is keen and unbearable.

65. 'But now, as I am unable to protect that king who annihilated in this manner his own happiness, for what reason should I give up that state of powerlessness of myself and indulge in hatred against him?

66. 'Even without a king's intervention, everybody born has to deal with sufferings, arising from death, &c. Therefore in this (series of evils), it is birth alone which one has to oppose[2]. For this not being, what suffering may there arise and from whence?

67. 'For many kalpas I have lost my worthless

---

[1] Viz. indulging in anger and cursing that king. The curse of a *Ri*shi, who has obtained supernatural power by his penance, is a dreadful weapon.

[2] In other words, one has to strive for final extinction.

body in manifold ways in numbers of existences. How is it that I should give up forbearance on account of the destruction of that frame? Would it not be as if I were to give up a jewel of the first water for a straw?

68. 'Dwelling in the forest, bound to my vow of world-renunciation, a preacher of forbearance and soon a prey to death, how should I feel the desire of revenge? Do not fear me any longer, then, peace be to you, go!'

69. After thus instructing and at the same time admitting them as disciples in the Lore of the pious, that foremost of Munis, who kept his constancy unshaken owing to his relying on forbearance, left his earthly residence and mounted to Heaven.

So then, indeed, to those who have wholly imbibed the virtue of forbearance and are great in keeping their tranquillity there is nothing unbearable. [Thus is to be said when discoursing on the virtue of forbearance, taking the Muni for example. On account of the vices of rashness and wrath, taking the king for example, this story is also to be told, and when expounding the miserable consequences of sensual pleasures, saying: 'In this manner sensual pleasures lead a man to become addicted to wicked behaviour which brings him into ruin.' It may also be told with the object of showing the inconstancy of material prosperity.]

This story is also extant in the Avadânakalpalatâ, in pallava 38, as appears from the Anukramanî, verse 15 (ya*h* kshântisîla*h* sântyâbhû*k kh*innângo 'py avikâravân), but this part of the work has as yet not been published nor is it found in the Cambridge MSS.

XXIX. THE STORY OF THE INHABITANT OF THE BRAHMALOKA.

Since the tenets of unbelief are blameable, those who are possessed by the vice of clinging to a false belief are especially worth commiserating by the virtuous. This will be taught as follows.

XXIX. STORY OF INHABITANT OF BRAHMALOKA. 269

One time the Bodhisattva, our Lord, having gathered by a constant practice of dhyâna a store of good karma, obtained, it is said, a birth in the Brahmaloka, in consequence of the ripening of that merit. Nevertheless, owing to his having always been conversant with commiseration in his former existences, that high happiness of the Brahmaloka, which he had obtained as the effect of the excellence of his dhyâna, did not destroy in him his longing for the task of benefiting others.

1. By indulging in sensual pleasures, however material, worldly people become utterly careless. But a frequent absorption in the delight of meditation, however ideal, does not hide the desire for benefiting others from (the mind of) the pious.

Now one time it happened that the High-minded One was passing his looks over the Region of Sensuality[1] below (his Brahma-world), where Compassion finds its proper sphere of action, since this is the region visited by hundreds of different forms of sufferings and calamities, and containing the elements for moral illnesses, disasters, injuries against living beings, and sensual pleasures. And he perceived the king of Videha, named Aṅgadinna, erring in the wilderness of a wrong belief, partly by the fault of his intercourse with bad friends, partly also in consequence of his being ardently attached to false thoughts. That king had got this persuasion: 'there is no other world after this; how could there be anything like result ripening out of good or evil actions?' and in conformity with this belief his longing for religious practices was extinguished, he was averse to performing the pious works of charity, good conduct

---

[1] The Brahmaloka or Brahma-world is in Buddhist cosmology the world superior to the region of sensuality, the kâmadhâtu (see Burnouf, Introduction, &c., p. 604) or kâmâvakara (see Hardy, Manual, pp. 3, 261). Cp. Kern, Geschiedenis van het Buddhisme, I, pp. 290, 291. Cp. Story XXX, stanza 21, where we have this series of happiness: 1. royalty on earth, 2. heavenly bliss, 3. Brahma's world, 4. final extinction (Nirvâṇa).

(*s*îla), &c., felt a deep-rooted contempt for such as led a religious life, and owing to his want of faith, bore ill-will to the religious law-books. Being inclined to laugh at tales concerning the other world, and showing but little respect and honour to *S*rama*n*as and Brâhmans, whom he held in little esteem, he was exclusively given up to sensual pleasures.

2. He who is firm in the belief 'surely, there is a world hereafter where good and evil karma produce their fruit of happiness and mishap,' such a one will avoid evil actions and exert himself to cultivate pious ones. But by absence of faith a man follows his desires.

Now that king, whose disastrous attachment to a false lore must have mischievous consequences and become a source of calamities to his people, roused the compassion of that High-minded Devarshi. One time, when that king, always directed by his indulgence in sensual pleasures, was staying in a beautiful and lonely arbour, he descended in his flaming brilliancy from the Brahma-world before his eyes. On beholding that luminous being who blazed like a mass of fire, shone like an agglomeration of lightnings, and spread about a great brilliancy of intense light like a collection of sun-rays, the king, overwhelmed by that lustre, was alarmed and rose from his seat to meet him reverently with folded hands. Respectfully he looked up to him (who stood in the air) and said:

3. 'The sky makes thee a resting-place for thy feet, as if it were the earth, O thou being with lotus-like feet; thou shinest far and wide, bearing the lustre of the sun, so to speak. Who art thou, whose form is a delight to the eyes?'

The Bodhisattva replied:

4. 'Know me, O king, one of those Devarshis who attained Brahma's world, having by the power of their mind's strong and assiduous attachment to religion vanquished love and hatred[1], those two proud foes, like two haughty chiefs of a hostile army in battle.'

---

[1] Love, viz. sensual love and covetousness, and hatred (with anger)

After these words the king offered him the hospitable reception due to a worthy guest, water to wash his feet and the arghya-water[1], accompanying this act (of homage) with kind words of welcome and the like. Then, casting admiring looks at his face, he said: 'Very wonderful, O Great R*i*shi, is thy figure. Indeed, thy power is supernatural.

5. 'Without clinging to the walls of a building, thou walkest in the sky as easily as on earth. Tell me, O thou whose brightness has the lustre of a flash of lightning, how didst thou obtain this supernatural power?'

The Bodhisattva spoke:

6. 'Such superhuman power is the result, O king, of meditation (dhyâna), spotless good conduct (*s*ila), and an excellent restraint of the senses, which I have so practised in other existences that they became essential elements of my nature.'

The king said: 'Does there exist in earnest anything like a world hereafter?' The Brahman[2] said: 'Verily, Your Majesty, there is a world hereafter.' The king said: 'But, my dear sir, how should I too be able to believe so?' The Bodhisattva said: 'This is a tangible truth, Your Majesty, which may be proved by reasoning with the ordinary modes of proof (pramâ*n*a): perception by the senses and the rest[3]. It is exemplified by the declarations of reliable persons, and may be tested by the method of accurate examination. Do but consider this:

7. 'The heaven, with its ornament of sun, moon and stars, and the many-shaped variety of animals, are the

---

are the two great divisions of vyasanâni (vices, evil habits), not only with Buddhists. See, for instance, Manu VII, 45 foll.

[1] The arghya is the name of a worshipful offering of water to a worthy guest, given with the other ceremonial marks of hospitality: vish*t*ara, padya, madhuparka.

[2] The inhabitants of Brahma's world are called Brahmans.

[3] The others are inference and analogy; for it is unlikely that the Brahman would think of persuading a disbeliever by means of the fourth mode of proof, revelation.

world hereafter in a concrete and visible form. Let not thy mind be benumbed by scepticism so as not to perceive this truth.

8. 'Further there are now and then persons who, owing to their practice of dhyâna and the vividness of their memory, remember their former existences. From this it must likewise be inferred, there exists a world after this. And myself, do I not give thee the evidence of a witness?

9. 'Moreover, thou must infer its existence also from this. The perfection of the intellect presupposes a previous existence of that intellect. The rudimentary intellect of the fetus is the uninterrupted continuation of the intellect in the preceding existence.

10. 'Further, it is the faculty for catching matter of knowledge that is called intellect (buddhi). Therefore there must be a sphere of employment for the intellect at the beginning of existence [1]. But it is not possible to find it in this world, because of the absence of the eyes and the other (organs of sense). By inference, the place where it is to be found, is the other world.

11. 'It is known by experience that children diverge from the nature of their fathers and show discrepancies of conduct and the like. Now, since this fact cannot arise without a cause, it follows that we have to do here with habits acquired in other existences.

12, 13. 'That the new-born child, though his mental powers are wholly rude and his organs of sense in a torpid state, makes an effort to take the breast without being instructed so and almost in a state of deep sleep, this proves his having in former existences exercised himself as to the fit ways of taking his food. For practice, perfecting the mind, sharpens its faculty for acquiring knowledge for different special performances.

'Perhaps, since thou art not accustomed to the idea of the existence of another world, thou mayst still be

---

[1] In other words, in the state of the fetus.

doubtful about the last statement. (Should this be the case and shouldst thou reason in this way:)

14. '"Then the lotuses shutting and opening themselves are also a proof, indeed, of their having already practised those movements in other existences. Otherwise, this not being admitted, why dost thou affirm that the suckling's effort of taking the breast is the effect of exertion made in previous births?"

'then thou art obliged to put aside that doubt by the consideration that in one case there is compulsion, in the other freedom, and exertion is not made there, but that it is made here.

15. 'In the case of the lotuses, their opening and shutting depend on time, but the effort to take the breast not so. Moreover, there is no exertion in the lotus, but in the case of the suckling it is evident there is. It is the power of the sun that is the cause of the lotuses expanding.

'In this manner, then, Your Majesty, by a close and careful examination it is possible to have faith in the world hereafter.'

But the king, as he was deeply attached to the false lore he professed, also because the extent of his sin was large, felt uneasy on hearing that account of the other world, and spoke: 'Why, great *Ri*shi,

16. 'If the next world is not that (well-known) bugbear for children, or if thou judgest it fit for me to believe in it, well, lend me five hundred nishkas[1] here, and I shall give thee back one thousand in the next existence.'

Now when the king, according to his habitual boldness, had uttered without scruple this unbecoming language, which was as it were the vomiting of the poison of his wrong belief, the Bodhisattva answered him in a very proper way.

17. 'Still in this world those who wish to employ their money, in order to augment it, do not make any loan at all to a wicked person or a glutton or a block-

---

[1] A nishka is a gold coin, whose value varied at different times.

T

head or a sluggard. For wealth going to such persons, tends to their ruin.

18. 'But if they see one bashful, with thoroughly subdued senses, and skilled in business, to such a one they offer a loan, even unwitnessed. Such a bestowal of money produces bliss.

19. 'The very same line of conduct must be followed, O king, with respect to a debt payable in the world hereafter. But it is not suitable to contract such a loan with thee who art a person of a wicked behaviour because of the evil doctrine thou professest.

20. 'For, at the time when, being precipitated into hell by thy own cruel actions originating in the sin of a wicked lore, thou wilt lie there, sore with pains and paralysed in thy mental powers, who would then call upon thee for a debt of one thousand nishkas?

21. 'There the regions of the sky do not shine in their full feminine beauty[1] by the beams of sun and moon, the destroyers of their veil of darkness. Nor is the firmament there seen with its ornament of crowds of stars, like a lake embellished by unclosed waterlilies.

22. 'The place where the unbelievers dwell in the next world, is encompassed with thick darkness, and an icy wind prevails there, penetrating to the very bones and extremely painful. Who, being wise, would enter that hell in order to obtain money?

23. 'Some wander for a long time on the bottom of the hell, which is wrapt in dense obscurity and dull with pungent smoke; they are afflicted there, drawing along their rags fastened with leather thongs, and crying with pain as often as they tumble over each other.

24. 'Likewise others are running with wounded feet again and again in all directions in the Hell Gvalatkukûla [= Flaming Chaff], longing for deliver-

---

[1] The di*s*a*h* belong grammatically, and for this reason also mythologically, to the females. Hence they are spoken of as women (digaṅganâ*h*).

ance from thence, but they do not attain the end of their sin nor of their life.

25. 'Terrible servants of Yama carve like carpenters the limbs of others, having them fastened in different manners, and delight in shaping them by cutting with sharp knives, as if they wrought in fresh timber.

26. 'Others again are entirely stripped off their skin, groaning with pain, or are even bereaved of their flesh, living skeletons, but they cannot die, kept alive by their own evil actions. Likewise others who are cut to pieces.

27. 'Others draw flaming chariots for a long time. They wear broad flaming bits in their mouth and submit to harnesses and goads of a tawny hue, being fiery. The grounds on which they draw are of iron, heated by an unceasing fire.

28. 'Some have their bodies crushed, when they meet mount Sa*m*ghâta[1], and ground to dust by its incursion; nevertheless, even in that great suffering of the most intense degree, they cannot die before their evil karma is annihilated.

29. 'Some others are being ground to dust with big and flaming brazen pestles in troughs incandescent by fire during a succession of full five hundred years, and yet they do not lose life.

30. 'Others again are hanging with their heads or even feet to trees made red-hot like corals and of a rough surface, being beset with flaming thorns of sharp iron. They are beaten by demons, attendants of Yama, who chide them with harsh cries.

31. 'Others enjoy the fruit of their conduct, lying on large heaps of burning coals, flaming and resembling molten gold. (Helpless) they are exposed to their fate, they can do nothing but lie and moan.

32. 'Some howl with their tongues hanging out of their mouths, while their bodies are overcome by heavy

---

[1] Sa*m*ghâta is the name of a kind of infernal Symplegades. Cp. Journal Asiatique, 8e S., tome XX, p. 184 foll.

pains caused by hundreds of sharp spears on a ground illuminated by garlands of flames rising out of it. In that time they are made to believe that there exists something like a world beyond this.

33. 'There are others whose heads are encircled with flaming diadems of brass; others are boiled out in pots of brass. Of others the bodies are wounded by sharp stings of showers of weapons, and devoured by crowds of ferocious animals, who gnaw them off to the bones.

34. 'Others again, exhausted by toil, enter the salt water of the Vaitara*n*i, but that water is painful to touch like fire, and their flesh wastes away from their limbs, when in it, but not their life, kept up by their evil actions.

35. 'And those who afflicted because of the intense torment caused by burning, have resorted to (the hell named) A*s*u*k*iku*n*apa [the hell of unclean corpses] as to a pond of fresh water, meet there with unparalleled pain. Their bones are brought to decomposition by hundreds of worms.

36. 'Elsewhere others undergo the pain of being burnt for a long time. Surrounded by fire, their bodies flame like iron staves surrounded by flames. Yet they do not burn to ashes, being kept alive by their actions.

37. 'There is sawing of others with fiery saws, cutting of others with sharp razors. Of others the heads are crushed with hammers quickly swung, so as to make them yell with anguish. There is roasting on a smokeless fire of others, fixed on broad iron-spits which pierce through their bodies. Others again are compelled to drink liquid brass looking like blazing fire, which makes them utter raw cries.

38. 'Some are assailed by spotted dogs of great strength who with their sharp-biting teeth tear off the flesh from their limbs; they fall on the ground with lacerated bodies, crying loudly with pain.

39. 'Of such a nature are the tremendous torments in the different hells. If thou, impelled by thy karma,

shalt once have reached that state [1], who then would think of calling upon thee for that debt at that time, while thou art sore with sorrow and thy mind is afflicted with exhaustion and sadness?

40. 'It may happen that thou art staying in the hell of brazen jars filled with the corpses of wicked people and hard to approach because of the fire-flames, which heat them and make thee move helplessly exposed to the suffering of being boiled. Who then would think of calling upon thee for that debt at that time?

41. 'Or thou mayst lie with tied limbs on flaming iron pins or on the earth made red-hot by a blazing fire. While thou wilt be weeping piteously, thy body burning away, who then would think of calling upon thee for that debt at that time?

42. 'Who would require that debt from thee, when thou wilt have reached that wretched state of humiliation, undergoing terrible sufferings and not even able to make any answer?

43. 'Or suppose thy bones to be pierced by the icy wind which destroys even the power of groaning, or thy voice uttering roaring cries of pain, when thou wilt be torn asunder, who would dare ask thee for that money in the other world?

44. 'Or, if rather thou wert to be exposed to the injuries of Yama's attendants, or to lie in the midst of fiery flames, or if dogs and crows were to feast on thy flesh and blood, who would urge thee with a call for money in the other world?

45. 'Besides, when thou wert to undergo an uninterrupted torture by striking or cutting or beating or cleaving, by burning or carving or grinding or splitting, in short, by the most different modes of tearing up (thy body), how shouldst thou be able to give back that debt to me at that time?'

This extremely fearful account of the hells missed

---

[1] The second pâda of this stanza is wanting an iambus in its middle part. I think it is thus to be supplied: prâpto bhavishyasi (yadâ) svakritapranunnah.

not its effect upon the king. Hearing it, he became alarmed and left his attachment to the false lore. And having obtained faith in the world hereafter, he bowed to that illustrious R*i*shi and spoke:

46. 'After being apprised of the tortures in the different hells, my mind almost dissolves from fear, on the other hand I feel a burning sense of anxiety, considering how I may take shelter from that terrible pain.

47. 'For, short-sighted as I was, I walked on the wrong road, my mind being perverted by a wicked doctrine. Now then, let Thy Reverence be my guide here. Thou knowest the right way. Thou art my authority and my refuge, O Muni.

48. 'As the rising sun dispels darkness, so thou hast dispelled the darkness of my false opinions. In the very same manner, O R*i*shi, thou must teach me the road, going on which I may not attain misery after death.'

Then the Bodhisattva, perceiving his emotion and understanding that he had changed his opinion for the better and had now become a vessel fit for accepting the Law, instructed him—for he pitied him, like a father his son or a teacher his pupil—in this way.

49. 'The glorious way leading to Heaven, is that by which the old kings went, who displayed their love of virtues, behaving like good pupils towards *S*rama*n*as and Brâhmans, and manifested their compassion for their subjects by their own behaviour[1].

50. 'Therefore, subdue injustice which is very difficult to subdue, and overcome vile covetousness which is very difficult to overcome! So thou mayst mount a luminous being to the city of the Lord of Heaven, that city with golden gates resplendent with the most excellent jewels.

51. 'May thy approval of the lore cherished by the

---

[1] The following stanzas are of a very ingenious composition. In stanzas 50–54 each pâda ends in two homonymous syllables put twice in different functions, and from 55 the simile of the chariot is elaborated with great skill.

virtuous, and which thou acceptedst in a mind accustomed to a wicked lore, be steadfast. Renounce the latter, which is a system of injustice proclaimed by people intent on gratifying the fools.

52. 'For thou hast taken the (right) road, O king, now, in that very moment, when desiring to walk on it with the pious behaviour prescribed by the True Lore, thou destroyedst within thy heart the harsh feeling against virtues.

53. 'Let, therefore, thy wealth be an instrument for obtaining virtues, and to thy people exercise mercy, which is an auspicious thing and will increase thine own happiness. Be also constant in keeping the excellent restraint of senses and good conduct. In this way thou mayst incur no calamity in the next world.

54. 'Let thy rule, O king, derive its entire brilliancy from the lustre of thy meritorious actions; let it be relied upon by those who practise good actions, and be lovely by its purity. So ruling thou wilt strive for thy true happiness together with thy material interest, and exterminate the anguish of the creatures, increasing thereby thy glory in a lovely manner.

55. 'Thou art here (on earth) standing on thy royal war-chariot. Let worship of the pious be thy charioteer. Let thy own body, engendering virtues, be thy chariot. Let friendliness be its axle, self-restraint and charity its wheels, and the earnest desire for gathering merit its axletree.

56. 'Control thy horses, the organs of sense, with that splendid bridle named attentiveness. Make prudence thy goad and take thy weapons from the store of sacred learning. Let shame be the furniture of thy chariot, humility its lovely pole, forbearance its yoke. (Standing on that chariot,) thou wilt drive it skilfully, if thou art firm in courageous self-command.

57. 'By keeping down bad words thou wilt make it go without rattling of the wheels; if thou usest lovely language, the sound of them will be grave and deep. Never breaking thy self-restraint will

preserve thy chariot from looseness of its constituent parts. Thou wilt keep the right direction, if thou avoidest going astray on the winding paths of wicked actions.

58. 'Using this vehicle (yâna), brilliant with the lustre of wisdom, adorned by the flag of good renown and the high-floating banner of tranquillity, and followed by mercy as its attendance, thou wilt move in the direction of the Highest Âtman (paramâtmâ) and never shalt thou descend to the infernal regions, O king.'

Having thus dispelled by the brilliant beams of his words that darkness of false lore that lay upon the mind of the king, and shown him clearly the road to happiness, the High-minded One disappeared on the spot. But the king, having got a thorough knowledge concerning the matters of the next world, embraced the True Lore with his whole heart, and himself as well as his officials, his townsmen, and landsmen became intent on exercising charity, self-command, and self-restraint.

In this manner, then, those who are possessed by the vice of clinging to a false belief are especially worth commiserating by the virtuous; for the tenets of unbelief are blameable. [This story may also be adduced with this conclusion: 'In this manner listening to the preaching of the Excellent Law (saddharma), fills up with overflowing faith.' Or with this: 'In this manner hearing the Law preached by another, rouses faith productive of right belief.' And when adducing it in a discourse on praise of the virtuous, likewise on the subject of forbearance, this is to be said: 'In this manner the virtuous will parry even a hostile attack by counselling their enemy for his good, and they will do so without harshness in consequence of their being accustomed to forbearance.' Also when treating of sa*m*vega¹, it is to be said: 'In

---

¹ Sa*m*vega is the emotional state which prepares the mind to accept spiritual instruction or to take the vow of a religious life.

this manner emotion of the mind makes a man inclined to care for his salvation.']

Of this *G*âtaka no Pâli recension has been edited as yet, nor am I aware of its occurring in other texts of the Northern Buddhists. Yet, at least stanza 16, which contains the pointe of the tale, must be founded on some old traditional verse, one of those sacred sayings, of which the *G*âtaka-class of the Holy Writ is made up.

XXX. The Story of the Elephant.

If they may cause by it the happiness of others, even pain is highly esteemed by the righteous, as if it were gain. This will be taught by the following.

Once the Bodhisattva, it is said, was a huge elephant. He had his residence in some forest suitable for elephants, which had for its ornament, so to speak, the young offshoots of its excellent trees, whose tops were conspicuous by their twigs, flowers, and fruits. Its bottom was hidden under manifold kinds of shrubs and trees and grasses. It was beset with mountain-ridges and plateaus that made the effect, as if they were detained there by the charming beauty of the forest and would not long for another place. That wood was the abode of forest-animals, and contained a lake of abundant and deep water. It was far remote from the habitations of men, being surrounded on all sides by a large desert, where there was no tree, no shrub, no water. There he lived a solitary elephant.

1. Like an ascetic he stayed there, pleased with leaves of the trees, lotus-stalks and water, and with the virtues of contentment and tranquillity.

Now one time, when the Great Being was wandering near the border of that forest, it happened that he heard a noise of people from the side of the wilderness. Then this thought entered his mind: 'What may this be? First of all, there is in this direction no road leading to any country; nor is it likely, a hunting-party should have crossed a wilderness so large as this. Still less can there be question of an attempt to catch my fellow-elephants, on account of the heavy toil with which it would be attended.

2, 3. 'Surely, this people are either astray, their guides having lost their way, or have been banished in consequence of a king's anger or of their own misconduct. Such is the nature of the noise I hear, which is not made up of the strong tones of joy, cheerfulness, and merriment, but rather low-spirited sounds, as of people weeping under the overwhelming power of a great grief.

'At all events, I will know what it really is.' Thus reflecting, the Great Being impelled by his compassion, hastened forward in the direction from whence the noise of that multitude came. When he heard more distinctly those sad and piteous accents of lamentation, unpleasant to the ears, the High-minded One, understanding that they were cries for help uttered by people in distress, ran with still greater swiftness, his mind being filled with the yearning of compassion. After leaving the thicket, owing to the naked desert destitute of vegetation, he saw already from afar that body of persons who cried for assistance, keeping their eyes in the direction of the forest. They numbered seven hundred men, and were exhausted with hunger, thirst, and fatigue. And those men, on the other hand, saw the Great Being coming up to them, resembling a moving peak of a snow-covered mountain, or a condensed mass of white fog, or an autumn-cloud driven towards them by a strong wind; and as they were overcome with sorrow and utterly dejected, this sight frightened them much. In their fear they thought: 'Alas! now we are certainly lost!' but they could make no effort to run away; hunger, thirst, and fatigue had destroyed their energy.

4. Powerless by hunger, thirst, and fatigue, and being in low spirits, they made no preparations for flight, though the peril seemed imminent.

The Bodhisattva perceiving their anxiety, exclaimed: 'Be not afraid! Be not afraid! You have nothing to fear from my part,' and so comforting them, drew nigh, uplifting his trunk and showing its tip broad, soft, and dark-red as copper. Moved by compassion he asked them: 'Who are you, sirs, and how are you come to this state?

5. 'Your pale faces betray the effect of dust and sun, meagre you are and suffering from sorrow and dejection of mind. Who are you and by what cause have you come here?'

On hearing him utter in a human voice these words not only indicative of a peaceful disposition, but of the desire to succour, the men recovered their confidence, and the whole assembly bowed to him. Then they spoke:

6. 'An outburst of the king's anger blew us away to this region from the very eyes of our kinsmen, who sorrowful must behold that banishment, O lord of elephants.

7. 'Yet, forsooth, there must be still some remnant of our good fortune and some favour of Fortune towards us that we have drawn the attention of Thee, who art better than friends and kinsmen.

8. 'By the auspicious sight of Thee we know we have crossed our calamity. Who, in truth, having seen even in his dreams such a being as Thee, would not be saved from distress?'

Then that eminent elephant spoke: 'Well, how many are you, sirs?' The men said:

9, 10. 'We numbered one thousand men, O fair-figured being, when the king left us here, but many of us, being unacquainted with adversity, have perished overcome by hunger, thirst, and sorrow. And now, O lord of elephants, we estimate the number of those still alive to be seven hundred, who being about to sink down in the mouth of Death, look up to Thee as the embodied Comfort come to us to help.'

By these words the Great Being, as he was in the habit of compassion, was moved to tears, and commiserating them said, to be sure, something like this: 'Alas! alas!

11. 'Oh! How averse to tenderness, how devoid of

shame, how little anxious about the next world the mind of that king is! Oh! How his senses, caught by his royal splendour, something as fickle as lightning, are blind to his good!

12. 'Oh! He does not understand that Death is near, I suppose, nor has he been taught the unhappy end of wickedness! Alas! Oh! Those poor and helpless kings who, owing to the weakness of their judgment, are impatient of listening to words (of counsel).

13. 'And, verily, this cruelty towards living beings is performed on account of one single body, a perishable substratum of illnesses[1]! Alas! Fie upon ignorance!'

Now, while letting his eyes full of pity and tenderness go over that people, this thought appeared to the chief of elephants: 'Being so tortured by hunger, thirst and fatigue, and their bodies having become so weak, how may they overcome that wilderness of an extent of many yoganas, where they find neither water nor shade, unless they have wholesome food? Nor does the forest of elephants contain proper food for them, not even for one day, without much trouble. Nevertheless, if they were to take their provisions from the flesh of my limbs and to use my bowels instead of bags, putting water in them, they would be able to cross this desert; not otherwise.

14. 'Let me, therefore, in their behalf employ my body, the abode of many hundreds of illnesses, that it may be for this multitude of men overwhelmed by suffering, like a raft to get across their misery.

15. 'Being born a man is the proper state for reaching happiness, either heavenly bliss or final extinction, and it is difficult to attain that state. May then this advantage not be dissolved to them!

16. 'Further, since they are come within the compass of my dominion, I rightly may call them my

---

[1] I surmise that pâda 2 of this line is to be read rogibhûtasya nâsinah.

guests. And they are in distress and destitute of relations; hence I have to show the more pity to them.

17. 'And this vessel of many infirmities, this substratum of manifold toil caused by everlasting illness, this assemblage of evils, whose name is "body," will now, after a long time, have at last its proper employment, serving to relieve others.'

Then some of them, who suffered intensely from the pain of hunger, thirst, fatigue, and heat, after bowing to him with folded hands and eyes wet with tears, in the manner of supplicants, asked him for water by means of signs with their hands. Others spoke to him piteous words:

18. 'To us who are destitute of kindred, Thou art a kinsman, Thou art our recourse and refuge. Deign to shelter us in such a way as Thou deemest best, Illustrious One!'

Others again who had more energy of mind, asked him to show them some place where to find water and the way to get out of that dreadful desert.

19, 20. 'If there is here some pond or river with cold water, or perhaps some waterfall, if a shady tree may be found here on a grass-plot, tell it us, O chief of elephants. And since thou thinkest it possible to get out of this desert, show us mercy and point out the direction to us.

'It is a good many days that we have been staying in this wilderness. For this reason, pray make us, O lord, get across it.'

Then the High-minded One who felt his heart growing still more wet with pity by their piteous requests, uplifting his trunk as big as the coils of a mighty serpent, showed them the mountain, beyond which they could make their escape from the wilderness, and spoke: 'Underneath this mountain there is a large lake adorned with lotuses, white and red, and containing pure water. Go, therefore, by this way. With the water of that lake ye may quench your thirst, and dispel your fatigue and (the vexation of) heat. Then, continuing your way, not far from that place ye will meet with the corpse of an elephant, fallen down the mountain-plateau. The flesh of its limbs ye must take to serve for provisions on the journey, and provide yourselves with water, putting it in its bowels instead of bags; after which ye have to go farther in the very same direction. So ye will overcome this wilderness without much hardship.' With such comforting language the High-minded One induced them to set out, but himself, running quickly by another way, ascended to the top of that mountain. Standing there, about to give up his own body for the purpose of rescuing that body of people, he strengthened his determination[1], truly, by representing to his mind something like this.

21. 'This performance does not tend to the attainment of a high state for myself, neither the magnificence of a king of men, the possessor of the royal umbrella, nor Heaven with the singular flavour of its surpassing enjoyments, nor the bliss of Brahma's world, nor even the happiness of release[2];

22. 'But if there be any merit of mine in thus striving to help those men lost in the wilderness, may I become by it the Saviour of the World, of those creatures erring in the wilderness of Samsâra!'

Having thus resolved, and not minding because of his gladness, the painful death he would suffer by being crushed down that deep descent, the Highminded One gave up his body according to his design by precipitating himself down that steep mountain.

23. While falling, he shone like an autumn-cloud or like the moon sinking with reversed disc behind the

---

[1] This 'strong determination' is the praṇidhi, also called praṇidhâna. By it he who performs some extraordinary meritorious action with the object of attaining some definite result in a future existence proclaims his design before carrying out his performance. Its counterpart in the ritual of Hinduism is the so-called saṃkalpa preceding the ceremony and contributory to its success. For other instances of it, though the name of praṇidhi is not used there, see Story I, stanzas 30–32; VIII, stanzas 53–55.
[2] Viz. 'final extinction' or nirvâṇa.

mountain of setting, or like the snow-cover of the peak of that mountain, cast down by the violent swiftness of the wind moved by the wings of Garu*d*a.

24. With the heavy noise of a whirlwind he precipitated himself, shaking not only the earth and the mountains, but the mind of Mâra possessed by the infatuation of sovereignty[1]. And in his fall, he bent both the forest-creepers and the forest-deities.

25. No doubt, on that occasion the Celestials, residing about that forest, were affected with the utmost astonishment. From the ecstasy of their gladness the hairs on their body bristled, and they swung their arms in the sky, their fine fingers turned upwards.

26. Some overspread him with a thick shower of flowers sweet-scented and tinged with sandal-powder. Others covered him with their upper garments, wrought of (celestial) unwoven stuff and resplendent with golden decorations; others with their ornaments.

27. Others again worshipped him with hymns they had devoutly composed, and with the reverence of the a*ñ*gali, their folded hands resembling opening lotus-buds. Or they honoured him with bent heads, lowering their beautiful head-diadems, and with prayers of veneration.

28. Some fanned him with an agreeable wind, such as arranges garlands (of foam) on the waves and is perfumed with the scents borrowed from the dust of flowers. Others held a canopy of dense clouds in the sky over his head.

29. Some were prompted by devotion to make Heaven echo his praise with the sounds of the celestial drums. And more, others enamelled the trees with an untimely outburst of new twigs, flowers, and fruits.

30. The sky assumed the lovely splendour of autumn, the sun's rays seemed to become longer, and the Ocean trembled and shook its wave-surface as from impatience to go and visit him out of gladness.

---

[1] In the original *k*a put twice in the second pâda of this stanza is hardly right. In the latter place, I suppose that it should be changed to sa.

Meanwhile those men, following the way pointed out to them, had reached the lake; and after refreshing themselves and recovering from heat, thirst, and fatigue, going on as the High-minded One had instructed them, they saw at no great distance from that place the body of an elephant that had died not long before. And they reflected: 'What a strong likeness this elephant has to that chief of elephants!

31. 'Is he perhaps a brother to that mighty being, or some kinsman of his, or one of his sons? In fact, it is the self-same beautiful figure equalling a snow-peak that we behold in this body, even though it be crushed.

32. 'It looks like a condensation of the lustre of many groups of waterlilies, like the concrete form of moonshine, or rather like His image, reflected in a mirror.'

But some among them who had a keener judgment of the matter began to reflect thus: 'As far as we see, this animal, whose surpassing beauty rivals the elephants of the world-quarters, is that very elephant, indeed, who has thrown himself from this plateau, in order that He might save us from distress who are without relations and friends.' (And having understood so, they said:)

33. 'That noise we heard, as of a whirlwind, as of an earthquake, was caused by His fall, to be sure.

34. 'This body, in truth, is His. It has the same yellowish-white hue of a lotus-root, and is covered with similar hairs as white as moonbeams and adorned with fine spots. These are the same tortoise-like feet with white nails. And this is the same backbone gracefully curved in the guise of a bow.

35. 'Also this is the same face long and full, embellished by the furrows of his wind-perfuming juice. And this is the same head, tall, auspicious, never touched by a driver's goad, standing on a strong neck.

36. 'This is the same couple of tusks of a honey-colour; they boastingly bear the token (of his glory), being covered with the red dust of the mountain-slope.

And this is that trunk with long, finger-like tip, wherewith He showed us this way.

'Oh! This is, in truth, a wonder of surpassing strangeness!

37. 'Ah! So great a friendship has He shown to us, without first inquiring into our family, our conduct and faith, to us broken by misfortunes and never heard of by Him before! How great must His goodness be for His friends and relations!

'In every way veneration be to Him, that Illustrious One!

38. 'Assisting the likes of us, distressed people, overcome with fear and sorrow and desponding, He, bearing the shape of an elephant, holds up, as it were, the sinking behaviour of the pious[1].

39. 'Where has He been taught this extraordinary propitiousness? At the feet of what teacher may He have sat in the forest? The popular saying: 'no beauty of figure pleases without virtues' is exemplified in Him.

40. 'Oh! How He has manifested by the splendid loftiness of His nature the auspiciousness to be expected of (his auspicious figure)! Verily, even in His dead body, His self-satisfaction appears in His complexion shining like the Snow-mountain, as though it laughed with joy!

'Who, therefore, will allow himself to feed on the body of this exceedingly virtuous being, who, surpassing by his goodness affectionate relations and friends, was thus inclined to help us, thus ready to sacrifice even his own life for our benefit? No, it becomes us rather to pay him our debt of gratitude by the cremation of his body with the proper rites and worship.' Thus considering, they were inclined to indulge in mourning, as if a family-disaster had befallen them; their eyes grew dim with tears and they lamented

---

[1] I have not adopted the ingenious conjecture of Professor Kern, sishatsatâm, as I now think the text of the MSS. gives a good sense, if but the complex of aksharas sîdatsatâm is divided into two words. Accordingly I read sîdat satâm udvahatîva vrittam.

in a faltering voice. But some of them who had a stronger frame of mind, perceiving their attitude and understanding the difference of the cases, spoke to them: 'Verily, by doing so this excellent elephant would be neither worshipped nor gratified. For aught we know, it is by the accomplishment of his design that we ought to honour him.

41. 'For it was with the object of rescuing us, that he, a stranger to us, yea, not even knowing us, abandoned in this manner his body dear to him, to his guests, still dearer to him.

42. 'For this reason it is proper to fulfil his design. Otherwise, would not the exertion of that being be made fruitless?

43. 'He has offered affectionately his whole property, indeed, to entertain his guests. Who, then, would render his hospitality fruitless by not accepting it?

44. 'We are therefore bound to honour him by accepting it like the word of a teacher, whereby we will secure also our own welfare.

45. 'After surmounting our adversity, it will be the fit time to worship him either conjointly or severally, and to perform for this excellent elephant the whole of the funeral rites due to a deceased kinsman.'

Accordingly those men, keeping in mind that that chief of elephants had taken his determination with the object of rescuing them from the wilderness, obeyed his words. They took their provisions from the body of the Great Being, and filled his bowels with water, using them as water-bags. Then following the direction he had pointed out to them, they safely crossed that wilderness.

In this manner the righteous highly esteem even pain, as if it were gain, if they may cause by it the happiness of others. [So is to be said when praising the righteous. Likewise, when discoursing on the Tathâgata or on the subject of listening with attention to the preaching of the Law. When treating of how to acquire an auspicious nature, this is to be said:

'In this manner an auspicious nature obtained by exercise (of virtues) comes back in new existences.' This story may also be told, when demonstrating the virtue consisting in habitual charity. 'So the habit of abandoning material objects makes it easy to give up even self-love.' And on the words spoken by the Lord at the time of His Complete Nirvâ*n*a, when He was attended with celestial flowers and celestial music: 'Something like this, in truth, is not the right manner, Ânanda, to gratify the Tathâgata,' this story may serve as the comment, by taking it for example: 'In this manner worship consists in fulfilling the design (of the person honoured), not in offerings of perfumes, garlands, and the like.']

In the Avadânakalpalatâ this tale occurs in pallava 96, 9–15, where the Lord tells it succinctly. The elephant is called Bhadra (friendly; 'auspicious') there. Cp. supra, stanzas 39, 40, where his atibhadratâ, respecting bhadratâ, is praised. Concerning the Bhadra-elephants cp. Kielhorn, Indian Antiquary, 1890, p. 60.

XXXI. THE STORY OF SUTASOMA.

(Cp. the Pâli *G*âtaka, No. 537, Fausb. V, 456–511, and *K*ariyâpi*t*aka III, 12[1].)

Meeting with a virtuous person, in whatever way it may have been occasioned, promotes salvation. Thus considering, he who longs for salvation must strive after intercourse with virtuous persons. This will be taught as follows.

In the time when our Lord was a Bodhisattva, he happened to be born, it is said, in the illustrious royal family of the Kauravas, that dynasty wide-famed for its glory, who owing to their intentness on possessing

---

[1] Compare Professor Kern's interesting paper on the Old-Javanese poem Sutasoma in the Verslagen en Mededeelingen der Kon. Akademie van Wetenschappen afd. Letterkunde, 3de Reeks, dl. V. pp. 8–43, especially note on p. 21. This Javanese poem, composed by Tantular, a manuscript of which belongs to the Leiden University Library, is based on some unknown work named Bauddhakâvya, not mentioned in Bunyiu Nanjio's Catalogue.

virtues, possessed the deep-rooted affection of their subjects, and the splendour of whose power had put their proud neighbours to vassalage. His father gave him the name of Sutasoma, for he looked as lovely as Soma (the Moon-god), his face being irradiated by the nimbus of his hundreds of virtues. Like the moon in the bright half of the month, his loveliness and grace increased every day. Having in course of time attained skill in the Vedas with their Aṅgas and in the Upavedas, and having been also initiated in the worldly arts and sciences (kalâs), including the additional ones (uttarakalâs), he became an object of esteem and love to his people and might be called a kinsman of virtues, so to speak. For he was inclined to be a decided helper of virtues [1], his regard for them was ever increasing, and he kept himself under restraint to preserve them carefully.

1, 2. Good conduct (sîla), learning, charity, mercy, self-control, splendour, forbearance, wisdom, patience, humility, modesty, shame, judgment, loveliness, renown, civility, retentiveness, strength, pureness of mind, these and such were the excellent properties which dwelt with him. Embellished by his youth, as it were, and deriving an additional charm from the holiness and loftiness of his person, they were like his constituent parts, as the (sixteen) kalâs of the moon [2].

And for this reason the king, his father, raised him to the illustrious rank of heir-apparent, judging him the proper person for ruling his subjects, for he knew his high aspirations and the holiness of his nature.

3. But as he was fond of learning, he was a great lover of religious sentences well-turned, and paid the most distinguished reward to those who attended him with well-said sentences.

Once it was the season of spring, and the power of

---

[1] So elsewhere the pious are called 'partisans of virtue' (guṇapa-kshapâtinaḥ). See, for instance, Story VII, stanza 31.

[2] The exactness of the comparison would appear more, if the number of virtues of young Sutasoma were also sixteen. But I count nineteen.

the month of flowers had decorated the suburban parks. The young offshoots of shrubs and trees overspread them with a soft brilliancy; the opening flowers gave them a charming and laughing aspect; fresh grass-plots, like smooth woollen carpets, extended all around over their grounds; their water-basins with unstained and blue water were covered with the petals of lotuses white and blue; the humming noise of numbers of roaming bees was heard in them; crowds of bold cuckoos and peacocks showed themselves; and breezes, agreeable by their mildness, fragrancy, and coolness, blew over them. The splendour of those gardens roused gladness in the minds of men. So the High-minded One, walking about escorted by a small body of guards, went out to one of those pleasure-grounds in order to divert himself.

4. Its groves resounded with the chants of the he-cuckoo; its various trees were bending under the weight of their flowers; and the grace of the gardens was enhanced by their charming arbours, artfully arranged. Rambling through his groves in the company of his wives, he resembled one enjoying the fruit of his merit in Nandana.

5. There he delighted in the songs of the females blending with the soft tones of musical instruments, in their dances charmingly executed with exciting coquetry and graceful[1] gesticulation, in their brilliant amorous play in consequence of their excitement by liquors, but no less in the loveliness of the forest.

Now, while he was staying there, a certain Brâhman who professed to be a speaker of well-said sentences, called on him. After being received with due respect, he sat down in that place, absorbed in the contemplation of the prince's beautiful figure. So the Great Being, though he was enjoying at that time the sport allowed to his age and fallen to his share as the effect of the power of his rich store of merit,

---

[1] Professor Kern writes to me, that lulita° in the printed text ought to be changed into lalita°, the reading of the MSS.

was nevertheless filled with great regard for that Brâhman. Before the Brâhman could reap the profit of his coming by reciting some well-turned sentences, there suddenly arose a confused noise, checking the sounds of song and music, destroying the merriment of the company engaged in playful occupation, and rousing fear and anxiety in the females. On hearing this uproar, he kindly bade the guardians of his harem inquire about the matter. Then his doorkeepers hastily went to him, alarmed and with saddened faces expressive of their fear and anxiety. They reported to him: 'Your Majesty, this is the man-eater Kalmâshapâda, the son of Sudâsa, the cruel disposition of whose mind exceeds even that of the Râkshasas. It is he, who, as if he were an incarnation of the God of Death, is in the habit of destroying hundreds of men. Looking terrible and dreadful like a Rakshas, that embodied Terror of the World, so to speak, of superhuman strength, vigour, and insolence is coming up to this very place. Our guards are dispersed. Terror has devoured the courage of the warriors, consternation has dissolved their ranks, and put also the chariots, horse, and elephants into disorder. Therefore Your Majesty must be on your guard for your defence, or reflect on the proper measures to be taken.' Then Sutasoma, though knowing it well, asked them: 'Who is that man whom you call the son of Sudâsa?' And they said to him: 'Is it then unknown to Your Majesty that there was a king of the name, who having gone out a hunting, carried away by his horse penetrated into the very heart of the forest? There he cohabited with a lioness, who having become pregnant, after some time was delivered of a male human child. Some foresters took up that boy, and brought him to Sudâsa, who being childless, brought him up as his son, and when he passed away to the city of the Celestials [1], left him as his successor. So he came to the possession of his legitimate royal dignity, but by the fault of his

---

[1] In other words, 'when he died.'

maternal origin he was fond of raw flesh. Once having tasted human flesh and liking its relish surpassing any other flesh, he commenced to kill and eat the very inhabitants of his capital. Then the townsmen prepared to put him to death. The son of Sudâsa, being afraid of them, made this promise to the goblins who are wont to enjoy offerings of human flesh and blood: "If I am saved from this peril, I will perform a sacrifice of one hundred royal princes to the goblins." So he was saved from that peril of his life. And now he carried off by force many, many royal princes, and he is also come here in order to carry away[1] Your Majesty, too. You have heard the matter; we await your orders, Your Majesty.'

Now the Bodhisattva, who was formerly aware of the aberration of mind of the son of Sudâsa and his wicked behaviour, felt compassion for him. So he set his mind on the design of curing him; and since he trusted himself to possess the qualities adapted to the extinction of the monstrous abnormity of his conduct, the information about Sudâsa's son drawing near, like welcome news, made him feel the sense of gladness. And, indeed, he spoke in this manner:

6. 'This man who, dispossessed from his royalty because of his fondness for human flesh, acts like a madman utterly unable to govern himself, having left his royal duties and destroyed his (former) good repute and merit, such a person, I suppose, is in a state deserving commiseration.

7. 'This being so, what opportunity is there for me to use force now, or what room for alarm and fear from the side of such a one? Rather will I utterly destroy his wickedness without employing effort, violence, and force.

8. 'And now this man who would deserve commiseration from my side, if even he went away from me, comes himself to the place, where I am staying. For this reason it befits me to show him hospitality.

---

[1] Upahartum is of course a misprint for apahartum.

For it is in this way that the virtuous act towards guests.

'Therefore, it suffices that each of you mind his ordinary duty.' So he instructed the guard of his harem. And turning to his female life-guards, who with eyes great and bewildered with anxiety and with throats almost choked by agitation, prepared to bar the way of the monster, he made them desist from that purpose, addressing them with comforting words, and went forward in the direction of that alarming noise. And he saw his royal army dispersed and in flight, pursued by the son of Sudâsa, whose appearance was dreadful. His soiled garments, loosely kept together with a girdle, hung around his body; his hair dressed with a diadem of bark and coarse with dust, was dishevelled and hanging down his face wholly covered with a thick, rugged beard which lay upon it like darkness; his eyes rolling with wrath and anger looked tremendous; he brandished his sword and shield. The prince fearless and free from anxiety, called out to him: 'Hallo, here I am, I, Sutasoma. Turn to me. Why are you troubling yourself to assail those poor people?' These words of challenge stirred the pride of the son of Sudâsa, and turning from thence like a lion, he perceived the Bodhisattva (waiting for him) alone, unarmed, and placidly looking according to his nature. On seeing him he exclaimed, 'You are the very man I am seeking,' and at once without delay went hastily and with impetuosity to him, and placing him on his shoulder ran off. And the Bodhisattva, considering with solicitude that his mind was still troubled with agitation, and his heart infatuated by wrath and arrogance kindled by the insolence of his rejoicing at the royal forces put to flight, thought it was no proper time now for admonition, and persisted in his attitude of unconcern. On the other hand, the son of Sudâsa having obtained his wish and thinking to have made a capture of importance, entered much rejoiced the stronghold where he had his residence.

9, 10. That unholy dwelling, when appearing from afar to the eyes of the travellers, caused them to be frozen with horror; for it offered an aspect as dreadful as the dancing-place of giants and spectres[1]. It was encumbered with corpses of slain men, and wet with blood horribly moistening its ground; it seemed to threaten every one (approaching) with the cries of jackals roaring there most inauspiciously; and the trees standing on its area, exposed to the discolouring smoke of many funeral piles, bore dark-red leaves, the ferocious abode of vultures and crows.

Having set down the Bodhisattva in that place, he took his rest for a while, his eyes intently fixed on the face of his victim, charmed as he was by his exceeding beauty. Meanwhile the Bodhisattva remembered that poor Brâhman who had come to him in order to get some present for his sentences, whom he had not yet paid the due honour, and who must still be waiting for his return to the gardens with hope in his heart. And this thought entered in his mind: 'Alas! ho!

11. 'That Brâhman came to me from afar, bringing to me the present of his sentences and filled with hope. What will he do now on hearing of my capture?

12. 'Afflicted with a burning sorrow on account of the destruction of his hope, and vexed with fatigue felt the keener because of his despair, he will either sigh, commiserating my fate, or chide his own destiny.'

While the Great Being was reflecting in this manner, and his mind accustomed to commiserate (the sufferings of others) was sore with grief on account of that Brâhman, tears welled up in his eyes. The son of Sudâsa, seeing those tears, began to laugh aloud, and said: 'Do leave off.

13. 'You are renowned for your wisdom proved by many different virtues. But having come into my power, you too shed tears!

'Verily, this is a true saying:

---

[1] In other words, 'as dreadful as a cemetery.'

14. 'In calamities constancy has no effect, and in sorrow learning is of no use. No being is to be found, indeed, who does not shake, when stricken.

'Therefore, tell me the truth.

15. 'Do you bewail your life dear to yourself, or your wealth, the instrument of pleasures, or your relations, or perhaps your royal rank? Or is it the recollection of your father who loves his son so much, or that of your own children who now weep for you, which makes these tears burst from your eyes?'

The Bodhisattva said:

16. 'It is not the thought either of my life or my parents, children, relatives, and wives, or the recollection of the pleasures of royalty, that moves me to tears; but some Brâhman who came to me hopeful, relying on the well-said sentences he brings with him. Forsooth, hearing that I have been carried off, he must grieve with despair. This I remembered, and hence my eyes are wet with tears.

17. 'For this reason you ought to let me go in order that I may refresh the heart of that Brâhman, now distressed with the grief of disappointment, pouring on it the water of honourable reward, and on the other hand, that I may take from him the honey of sentences he offers me.

18. 'After thus paying my debt to that Brâhman, I will come back to you again, that I may be also free from debt with respect to you, and afford gladness to your eyes beholding me returning here.

19. 'Do not, however, suspect me, troubling your mind with the thought this may be some contrivance of mine to go off. Men like me, O king, follow a way different from that on which other people are wont to walk.'

The son of Sudâsa spoke:

20. 'What you say, as if it were something worth regard, is a thing which utterly exceeds belief. Who, indeed, being released from the mouth of Death and having recovered his freedom of movement, would go to meet it once more?

21. 'If, having passed the danger of death hard to overcome, you are in safety in your brilliant palace, say, what reason does there exist that should induce you to come back here to me?'

The Bodhisattva spoke: 'How? Does Your Honour not understand the motive of my returning here, though it is a strong one, to be sure? Have I not promised to come back? For this reason, do not suspect me any longer, taking me for an equal of the villain. Am I not Sutasoma?

22. 'It is true that some, out of cupidity and fear of death, leave veracity, as if it were a straw. But to the virtuous veracity is their property and life; therefore they do not give it up even in distress.

23. 'Neither life nor the pleasures of this world will preserve from mishap him who has fallen from veracity. Who, then, would leave veracity for the sake of these objects? that virtue which is a rich mine of praise, glory, and happiness?

24. 'Nevertheless, in a person who is seen walking on the road of sin or in whom there does not appear any effort to lead a holy life, a pious behaviour becomes a matter of disbelief. Now, what of the kind did you perceive in my person that you should suspect even me?

25. 'If I had really been afraid of you, or if my mind had been attached to pleasures, or my heart were devoid of compassion, do you not think I should have met an adversary so famous for his ferocity as you, in full armour and prepared to fight, as becomes one proud of his valour?

26. 'But it may be that I did even desire that conversation with you. Why, after satisfying the labour of that Brâhman, I will come back to you of my own accord. Persons like me, in truth, do not utter an untruth.'

Now these words of the Bodhisattva irritated the son of Sudâsa, as if they spoke of something fanciful, and he entered upon this reflection: 'Verily, he does greatly boast of his veracity and righteous behaviour.

Well then, I will see them, both his attachment to truth and his love of righteousness. What matters his loss to me, after all ? I have already my full number of one hundred royal princes whom I subdued by the overwhelming strength of my arm ; with them I may perform my sacrifice to the goblins according to my desire.' After thus considering, he said to the Bodhisattva : ' Well then, go. We wish to see your faithfulness in keeping your promise and your righteousness.

27. ' Go, and having done for that Brâhman what he longs for, return soon ; meanwhile I will dress your funeral pile.'

And the Bodhisattva promised him he would do so. Then he set out for his palace, where he was welcomed by his household. Having sent for that Brâhman, he learnt from him a tetrad of gâthâs. The Great Being, to whom the hearing of those well-said sentences procured an intense gladness, praised the Brâhman with kind words and marks of honour, and valuing each gâthâ at the rate of one thousand (pieces of gold), rewarded him with the wealth so much desired for.

Now his father, intending to avert him from expenses out of place and extravagant, availed himself of this opportunity, and admonished his son in friendly terms. ' My dear,' he said, ' when you reward well-said sentences, you should know the limit, should you not ? You have to maintain a large retinue ; besides, the splendour of kings depends on the affluence of their treasury. For this reason I tell you this.

28. ' Rewarding a well-said sentence with one hundred is a very high estimation. It is not fit to exceed this limit. If a man, however wealthy, be too liberal, he will never retain the splendour of his riches for long.

29. ' Wealth is the chief instrument of success and an effective one ; for no pleasure is attainable in defiance of Wealth. Fortune, indeed, like a harlot, disregards a king who lacks an abundant treasury.'

The Bodhisattva spoke:

30. 'If it were at all possible to settle a limit to the value of well-said sentences, Your Majesty, I would not incur your reprehension, to be sure, if I were to give up even my royal rank to purchase them.

31. 'Verily, such sayings by hearing which a man gains placidity of mind, his love for salvation is strengthened, and the darkness (of ignorance) disappears (from his intellect) by the increase of his wisdom—ought they not to be bought even at the price of one's own flesh?

32, 33. 'Holy texts are a light which destroys the darkness of delusion (moha); they are the highest wealth, a wealth beyond the reach of thieves and the rest[1]; the weapon to hurt that enemy whose name is infatuation; the best counsellor and adviser as to a man's course of conduct; an unalterable friend even in time of distress; the painless medicine of the disease called sorrow; a mighty army strong enough to crush the army of vices; the highest treasure of glory and bliss.

34–37. 'Moreover, the splendid possession of holy texts (Sruti) is also the principal cause of eloquent speech. When meeting with virtuous persons, this possession affords the opportunity of making a present of great value; in the assemblies it conciliates the favour of the learned; in disputes and controversies it casts its light like the sun, and destroys the arrogance and fame of envious adversaries. Its superiority is exhibited by the expression of delight and the high colour in the eyes and on the faces of even common people, when they are enraptured with ecstasy and applaud by clapping of hands. Further it enables its possessor to demonstrate a matter with plain argument and in a graceful way, owing to his quotations from manifold treatises and sacred books. By its softness, its culture, and its loveliness, eloquence may be compared to a string of unfaded garlands or to the blazing

---

[1] Compare note to Story III, stanza 21.

lustre of a tempered lamp[1], and (finally) it forcibly gains glory for its owner. So making use of sacred texts is a pleasant way to success.

38. 'And those who have heard them will betake themselves to the road leading to the threefold prosperity, and free of obstructing vices; and conforming their behaviour to the precepts imported by those texts, and making it excellent, they will easily cross the dangerous passage through existences.

39. 'For so many excellent properties holy texts are famous. Now then, having got them like a present, how should I, being able to reward the giver of them, not honour him in return? Or, (on the other hand,) how should I transgress your order?

40. 'I will go, therefore, to the son of Sudâsa. I do not want either the toil of royalty or that other anxiety I should incur by following the way of wickedness, if I were to transgress my duty of keeping my engagement to come back.'

These words alarmed his father, who moved by his affection replied with earnest entreaty: 'Verily, it is but for your good, my dear, that I spoke so. You must not take offence at it, will you? May your enemies come into the power of the son of Sudâsa! In fact, you made him the promise to return to him, and for this reason you, being wont to keep your faith, wish to accomplish your promise. Nevertheless, I will not allow it. No sin is incurred, truly, by following the way of untruth, if one may thereby save one's own life and also for the sake of one's parents and other venerable persons. Why should you exert yourself to avoid this precept, which is prescribed by the Veda? Besides, those who are skilled in the science of politics proclaim the attachment to righteousness (dharma) in such cases as where it evidently causes damage to material interests (artha) and pleasures (kâma), to be mismanagement and an evil habit in kings. No more, then, of that determination, wherewith you grieve my

---

[1] I read vinîtadîpapratibhoggvalasya.

heart and disregard your own interest.—But you will object, my dear, that acting thus is dishonourable and in contradiction to righteousness, and that it is for this reason you cannot decide to break your promise, having never been accustomed to do anything like this. Yet, why should you break your promise? Here I have an army of footmen, chariots, horse, and elephants, prepared for war, and ready to march to your rescue. They make up an excellent body of warriors attached to your person, yea, a legion of heroes skilled in arms and having distinguished themselves in many battles. In short, these forces are dreadful, like a violent stream of water. Well, come to him, surrounded by that army, and bring him either to submission or to death. In this manner you will have fulfilled your promise and at the same time saved your life.'

The Bodhisattva replied : ' I am not able to promise one thing, Your Majesty, and perform another ; nor can I strike at such people as deserve pity, who being immersed in the mud of wicked habits and moving in the direction of Hell, and whom I reckon my friends after their relations have abandoned them and there is nobody to protect them. Moreover,

41. 'That man-eater performed for me something generous and difficult to be done (by others), since he dismissed me out of his power, relying on my faith.

42. 'So it is thanks to him that I got those holy stanzas, father. For this reason he is my benefactor, and is especially entitled to be an object of my commiseration.

' Cease also to be afraid of any misfortune threatening me, Your Majesty. How should he be capable of injuring me when I come back to him, as I went ?' So speaking the High-minded One persuaded his father to give him leave. Then declining the entreaties of his friends and his faithful army, who were eager to prevent his going away, he set out for the dwelling of the son of Sudâsa, alone and free from fear and sadness, for he was keeping his faith, and marched with the aim of softening his heart, to the happiness of men.

As soon as the son of Sudâsa saw the Great Being approaching from afar, he became exceedingly astonished, and his esteem and liking for him increased. Not even his cruelty, however long practised and deep-rooted in his defiled mind, could prevent him from entering, indeed, upon a thought like this: 'Ah! Ah!!!

43. 'This is the wonder of wonders, to be sure, the marvel of marvels! That prince's lofty veracity exceeds all that may be expected of men and deities!

44. 'To me, a person as cruel-natured as Death, he comes back of himself, subduing fear and anxiety! Ah! What a constancy! Bravo for his veracity!

45. 'Justly, indeed, the renown of his truth-speaking is wide-spread, as he now gave up his life and royal state to keep his faith!'

While he was thus affected with amazement and admiration, the Bodhisattva drew near, saying:

46. 'I have obtained that treasure of well-said sentences, I have rewarded the indigent man who presented me with it, and gladness has been procured to my mind, thanks to you. Now I am back here. Eat me, if such is your desire, or use me as a victim at your sacrifice.'

The son of Sudâsa spoke:

47. 'I am not in a hurry to eat you; moreover, this funeral pile is still smoky, and flesh gets its proper relish only when roasted on a smokeless fire. Let us hear meanwhile these well-said sentences.'

The Bodhisattva replied: 'Of what use is it to you, in such a state, to listen to holy sentences?

48. 'You adopted this mode of living merciless to your subjects for the sake of your belly. Now these stanzas praise righteousness. Righteousness does not go together with injustice.

49. 'Following the wicked manner of life of Râkshasas and having left the way of the pious [1], you do

---

[1] In other words, 'having transgressed the precepts of morality.' Instead of sa*m*tyaktârthapathasya, I read sa*m*tyaktâryapathasya.

not possess faith, still less righteousness. What will you do with holy texts?'

This contempt roused the impatience of the son of Sudâsa. He answered: 'Do not speak so, sir.

50. 'Where is that king, say, who does not kill with his bent bow in his park the mates of the hinds of the forest? If I in a similar way kill men for my livelihood, I am the unjust one, so it is said, not those killers of deer!'

The Bodhisattva spoke:

51. 'Neither do those stand on the ground of righteousness, whose bent bows are directed against the frightened and fleeing deer. But by far more reprehensible than those is a man-eater. Human beings, indeed, occupy by their birth the highest place (in the scale of creatures), and are not allowed to serve as food.'

Now, though the Bodhisattva had spoken very harsh words to the son of Sudâsa, the friendliness of his nature exercised such a power that it outweighed the ferocious nature of the man-eater. So he quietly heard this reproof, only he laughed aloud at it, then he spoke: 'Say, Sutasoma.

52. 'After being released by me and having reached your home and lovely residence resplendent with the lustre of royalty, you came back to me. For this reason you are not skilled in political wisdom, I suppose.'

The Bodhisattva said: 'You are wrong. On the contrary, I am skilled in political wisdom, and therefore I do not put it into effect.

53. 'What, in truth, is the worth of skill in an art, resorting to which brings about the certain fall from righteousness without bringing about happiness?

'Moreover, I tell you,

54. 'Those who are wise in directing their actions along the way of political wisdom, commonly get into calamities after death. Therefore I put aside the winding paths of artful politics and keeping my faith, came back.

55. 'Also by this I show it is I who am skilled in politics, that, leaving untruth, I delight in veracity. For no action is declared by competent judges in the science of politics to be well-managed which is not attended by good reputation, satisfaction, and interest.'

The son of Sudâsa spoke:

56. 'What is that interest you perceive to be attained by holding on veracity, that giving up your own dear life, your relations who shed tears at your departure, and the charming pleasures attendant on royalty, you returned to me, in order to keep your faith before all?'

The Bodhisattva spoke: 'Many kinds of virtues rest on veracity. Hear but the succinct account of them.

57. 'Veracity surpasses splendid garlands by its lovely grace and every sweet flavour by its sweetness; and inasmuch as it produces merit, that excellent good, without toil, it is superior to every kind of penance and the troublesome pilgrimages to tîrthas.

58. 'Affording to glory the opportunity of spreading among men, veracity is the way to its penetrating the three worlds. It is the entrance-door of the abode of the Celestials, the bridge to cross the swamps of Samsâra.'

Then the son of Sudâsa exclaimed: 'Excellent! right!' and bowing to him and casting an admiring look on him, said again:

59. 'The other men come into my power, are paralysed by affliction, and fear robs them of their courage. In you, on the contrary, I see a splendid imperturbation. I suppose, you are not afraid of death, my prince.'

The Bodhisattva spoke:

60. 'Of what use is cowardous fear, the most unfit means of prevention, against a thing which cannot be avoided even with great effort?

'Nevertheless, and though knowing the natural course of things in the world, people are poltroons against death.

61. 'It is the vexation of their mind in consequence

of their wickedness; it is because they were wanting in exerting themselves to perform good actions; it is their apprehension of sufferings in the other world. That conscience makes them torpid from anxiety that they must die.

62. 'But I do not remember having done anything that should torture my conscience, and consequently I have imbibed pure actions into my very nature. Who, clinging to Righteousness, should be in fear of death?

63. 'Nor do I remember having made gifts to the indigent, which did not tend to the gladness of both the mendicants and myself. Who, having in this manner obtained contentment by his gifts, clinging to Righteousness, should be in fear of death?

64. 'Even when reflecting for a long time, I never recollect having taken any step towards evil, not even in my thoughts. So the path to Heaven is cleared for me. Why should I conceive fear of death?

65. 'On Brâhmans, on my relations and friends, on my dependents, on the poor, on ascetics who are the ornaments of their hermitages, I bestowed much wealth, giving according to the worthiness of the recipients; what each of them was in want of, that was done for him.

66. 'I built hundreds of magnificent temples, hospitals, court-yards, hermitages, halls, and tanks, and by this I obtained satisfaction. Therefore I do not fear death. Why, dress me for your sacrifice or eat me.'

On hearing this language, the son of Sudâsa was moved to tears of tenderness, the hairs on his body bristled, the darkness of his wicked nature vanished, and looking with reverence up to the Bodhisattva, he exclaimed: 'Beware! May the evil be averted!

67. 'Verily, may he who should wish evil to such a being as you, O foremost of princes, take the poison Hâlahala knowingly, or eat a furious serpent or flaming iron, or may his head, also his heart, burst asunder into a hundred pieces!

'Therefore you may tell me also those holy sentences. Touched to tenderness as I am by the flower-shower of your words, my curiosity to hear them grows stronger. Attend also to this.

68. 'Having beholden the ugliness of my conduct in the mirror of Righteousness, and being touched by emotion may I not, perhaps, be a person whose mind craves for the Law?'

Now the Bodhisattva, considering the eagerness of his desire to hear the Law, knew him to have become a fit vessel. He spoke: 'Being then desirous of hearing the Law, it is right that you listen to its preaching in the proper attitude suitable for that act. Look here.

69, 70. 'Sitting on a lower seat, which betokens illustrious modesty; enjoying the honey of the (sacred) words with eyes expanding from gladness, so to speak; bending one's mind calm and pure to the most intense reverential attention—in this way one must listen devoutly to the preaching of the Law, as a sick man to the words of a doctor.'

Then the son of Sudâsa covered a slab of stone with his upper garment, and having offered this higher seat to the Bodhisattva, himself sat down on the naked earth before the visage of the Bodhisattva. After which, keeping his eyes fixed with attention on his face, he invited the Great Being: 'Speak now, sir[1].' Then the Bodhisattva opened his mouth and filling as it were the forest with his voice deep and sonorous, like the lovely sound of a new formed rain-cloud, spoke:

71. 'Meeting a virtuous person but once and by chance will suffice for
Friendship strong and for ever, not wanting repeated assurance.'

On hearing this gâthâ, the son of Sudâsa exclaimed,

---

[1] This formula (brûhîdânîm mârsha) and the whole of this ceremonial shows a striking likeness to the observances prescribed for the instruction in the Veda of a pupil by his spiritual teacher.

'Well said! well said!' and nodding his head and waving his fingers said to the Bodhisattva: 'Go on, go on.'
Then the Bodhisattva uttered the second gâthâ.
72. 'From virtuous persons thou shouldst never keep remote,
But follow those; to worship them thyself devote.
Their fragrance-spreading virtues uncompelled must
Attain him who stands near them, as does flower-dust.'
The son of Sudâsa spoke:
73. 'You employed your wealth in the right manner, indeed; rightly you did not mind trouble, that you did your utmost, O virtuous one, to reward well-said sentences!
'Go on, go on.'
The Bodhisattva spoke:
74. 'The cars of kings, with jewels shining and with gold,
With their possessors lose their beauty, growing old.
But not to pious conduct has old age access.
So strong a love of virtues pious men possess[1].'
(The other replied): 'This is as a shower of ambrosia, to be sure. O how great a satisfaction you give me! Go on, go on.'
The Bodhisattva spoke:
75. 'How distant Earth from Heaven is, the East
How far from Sunset, and both Ocean's shores
From one another. Greater distance keeps
Of virtue sever'd and of wrong the lores.'
Then the son of Sudâsa, who in consequence of his gladness and surprise was filled with affection and reverence for the Bodhisattva, said to him:
76. 'Lovely are the gâthâs I heard from you. The elegance of their words is still surpassed by the

---

[1] Cp. Dhammapada, verse 151.

brilliancy of their contents. By reciting them you have procured me gladness. Let me honour you in return by offering you four boons.

'Therefore, choose whatever you desire from my side.'

Then the Bodhisattva, astonished at this offering, and esteeming him for it, spoke: 'Who are you that you should bestow boons?

77. 'You have no power over yourself, being dominated by a passion for sinful actions. Say, what boon, then, will you give to another, you, whose heart is averse to pious conduct?

78. 'It might be that I were to declare the boon I would ask, but that your mind would be disinclined to give it. Who, being compassionate[1], would like to provoke such a calamity? Enough, enough have you done for me.'

On these words the son of Sudâsa was somewhat ashamed, and lowering his face, said to the Bodhisattva: 'I beg Your Honour not to have so mean an opinion of me.

79. 'I will give you your boons, even if it were to cost my life. Therefore, choose freely, prince, be it what it may be that you desire.'

The Bodhisattva spoke: 'Well then,

80. 'Give me these four precious boons. Take the vow of veracity; give up injuring living beings; release all your prisoners, nobody excepted; and never more eat human flesh, O you hero among men!'

The son of Sudâsa said:

81. 'I grant you the first three, but choose another fourth boon. Are you not aware that I am unable to desist from eating human flesh?'

The Bodhisattva spoke: 'Ah! Indeed! There you are! Did not I say "who are you that you should bestow boons?" Moreover,

---

[1] Inasmuch as by his naming the four boons he would bring about for the man-eater an opportunity of breaking his faith, he might become the involuntary cause of infernal punishment to his neighbour. Cp. Story XXIV, stanza 32.

82. 'How can you keep the vow of veracity and refrain from injuring others, O king, if you do not give up the habit of being an eater of human flesh?
'Fie upon you!
83. 'Did not you say before, you were willing to give these boons even at the risk of your life? But now you act quite otherwise.
84. 'And how should you abstain from injury, killing men in order to get their flesh? And this being so, what may be the value of the three boons you did grant me?'

The son of Sudâsa spoke:
85. 'How shall I be able to give up that very habit, because of which I renounced my kingdom, bore hardship in the wilderness, and suffered myself to kill my righteousness and destroy my good renown?'

The Bodhisattva replied: 'For this very reason you ought to give it up.
86. 'How should you not leave that state because of which you have lost your righteousness, your royal power, your pleasures, and your good renown? Why cling to such an abode of misfortune?
87. 'Besides, it is but the vilest among men who repent having given. How, then, should this meanness of mind subdue a person like you?
'Cease then, cease following after mere wickedness. You ought to stir up yourself now. Is not Your Honour the son of Sudâsa?
88. 'Meat examined by physicians and dressed by skilful (cooks) is at your disposal. You may take the flesh of domestic animals, of fishes living in waterbasins, and also venison. With such meat satisfy your heart, but pray, desist from the reprehensible habit of eating human flesh.
89. 'How do you like to stay in this solitary forest and prefer it to your relations and children and your attendants (once) beloved? how prefer it to enjoying the melodious songs at night, the grave sounds of drums reminding you of water-clouds, and the other various pleasures of royalty?

90. 'It is not right, O monarch, that you allow yourself to be dominated by your passion. Take rather that line of conduct which is compatible with righteousness (dharma) and interest (artha). Having, all alone, vanquished in battle kings with their whole armies, do not become a great coward now, when you have to wage war with your passion.

91. 'And have you not to mind also the next world, O lord of men? For this reason you must not cherish what is bad, because it pleases you. But rather pursue that which is favourable to your renown and the way to which is a lovely one, and accept what is for your good, even though you dislike it, taking it as medicine.'

Then the son of Sudâsa was moved to tenderness and tears, which barred his throat with emotion. He threw himself before the Bodhisattva, and embracing his feet exclaimed:

92. 'Justly your fame pervades the world in all directions, spreading about the flower-dust of your virtues and the scent of your merit. For example, who else but you alone, in truth, could have felt compassion for such an evildoer as I was, accustomed to a cruel livelihood, which made me resemble a messenger of Death?

93. 'You are my master, my teacher, yea, my deity. I honour your words, accepting them with (bowed) head. Never more will I feed on human flesh, Sutasoma. Everything you told me I will accomplish according to your words.

94. 'Well then, those princes whom I brought here to be victims at my sacrifice, and who vexed by the sufferings of imprisonment have lost their splendour and are overwhelmed by grief, let us release them together, none excepted.'

The Bodhisattva, having promised him his assistance, set out with him to the very place where those royal princes were kept in confinement. And no sooner had they seen Sutasoma, than understanding that they were set at liberty, they became filled with extreme gladness.

95. At the sight of Sutasoma the royal princes became radiant with joy, and the loveliness of laughter burst out on their faces, in the same way as in the beginning of autumn the groups of waterlilies burst open, invigorated by the moon-beams.

And the Bodhisattva, having come to them, spoke to them comforting and kind words, and after making them take an oath not to do harm to the son of Sudâsa, released them. Then together with the son of Sudâsa and followed by those royal princes, he set out for his kingdom, and having there made to the princes and the son of Sudâsa an honourable reception according to their rank, he re-established them each on his royal throne.

In this manner meeting with a virtuous person, in whatever way it may have been occasioned, promotes salvation. Thus considering he who longs for salvation must strive after intercourse with virtuous persons. [This story may also be told when praising the Tathâgata: 'So Buddha the Lord always intent on doing good was a friend even to strangers still in his previous existences.' Likewise it is to be told, when discoursing on listening with attention to the preaching of the excellent Law: 'In this manner hearing the excellent Law tends to diminish wickedness and to acquire virtues.' Also it is to be told when extolling sacred learning: 'In this manner sacred learning has many advantages.' Likewise when discoursing on veracity: 'In this manner speaking the truth is approved by the virtuous and procures a large extent of merit.' And also when glorifying veracity, this may be propounded: 'In this manner the virtuous keep their faith without regard for their life, pleasures, or domination.' Likewise, when praising commiseration.]

Dr. S. d'Oldenburg has pointed out in his paper, quoted in my Introduction, p. xxii, another redaction of the story of Sutasoma in chap. 34 of the Bhadrakalpâvadâna, the contents of which are given in the translation of that paper, Journ. Roy. As. Soc., pp. 331–334. In some parts the account in that text is fuller, but for the most part, according to Dr. S. d'Oldenburg, it closely follows our *Gâtakamâlâ*, the verses of which it 'mostly copies word for word¹.' Nevertheless the extract shows one difference, I think, in a capital point. In the tale, as it is told by *Sûra*, Kalmâshapâda has already got his hundred princes, when he comes to carry away Sutasoma, but in the said extract of the Bhadrakalpâvadâna Sutasoma is the very hundredth one.

In the Mahâbhârata the legend of Kalmâshapâda Saudâsa, the man-eater, is told, I, adhy. 176 and 177. It is very different from the Buddhistic fashion, yet both versions must be derived from one source.

XXXII. The Story of Ayogriha[2].

(Cp. the Pâli *Gâtaka*, No. 510, Fausb. IV, 491–499; *Kariyâpi*/aka III, 3.)

To those, whose mind has been seized by emotion[3], even the brilliancy of royalty does not obstruct the way to salvation. Thus considering, one must make one's self familiar with the emotional state (sa*m*vega), as will be taught in the following.

At that time, when our Lord was still a Bodhisattva, seeing the world exposed to the assaults of hundreds of calamities: diseases, old age, death, separation from beloved persons, and so on, and understanding that it was woe-begone, without protector, without help, without guidance, He was impelled by His compassion to take the determination of saving the creatures according to His exceedingly good nature, bringing about again and again the good and the highest happiness even to people averse to him and unknown to him. At that time, then, he once took his birth, it is said, in a certain royal family distinguished for their modest behaviour and their surpassing lustre, which, in consequence of their intentness on possessing the affection of their subjects, was manifested by their

---

[1] In 1894 Dr. S. d'Oldenburg more fully dealt with the Bhadrakalpâvadâna in a Russian book on Buddhistic Legends in Bhadrakalpâvadâna and *Gâ*takamâlâ. As to Sutasoma, cp. pp. 83–85 of that book.

[2] That ayog*ri*ha is the name of the prince, not an appellative, appears from the Pâli recensions. He was named so, since he was brought up in the 'iron house' (ayog*ri*ha).

[3] Sa*m*vignamânasâm; compare note on p. 280.

XXXII. THE STORY OF AYOGRIHA. 315

increasing prosperity and riches without hindrance, as well as by the submissiveness of their proud vassals. His very birth adorned both that court and that capital, always sympathising with their princes in weal and woe, with the brilliant show of a festival day.

1, 2. (At the court) a large distribution of gifts filled the hands and satisfied the minds of Brâhmans, and the attendants were proud of their very brilliant festival garments[1]. (Outside the palace) the streets resounded with the tones of many instruments and with the blending noise of singing, jesting, laughing, as the gladness of the hearts manifested itself by various merriment, dancing, and wantonness. Everywhere people meeting told each other with exultation and embraces the happy news, which gave them the same contentment as a present, and they magnified the felicity of their king.

3. The doors of the prisons were opened, and the prisoners set at liberty. Flags floating at the tops of the houses decorated the places, and the ground was covered with fragrant powders and flowers, and moistened with spirituous liquors. So adorned, the town bore the lovely and bright appearance of a festival.

4. From the splendid dwellings of the wealthy abundant showers of different goods: clothes, gold, jewels &c. poured down, so that it seemed as if Felicity, doing her best to pervade the world, with lovely sport imitated Gaṅgâ in madness[2].

Now at that time it happened as a rule that every prince born to the king soon died. Supposing that rule to be the effect of goblin-power[3], he ordered, with

---

[1] Apparently the attendants had received that new attire as a present.
[2] The presents strewed about are compared either with the cascade of the Ganges at Gaṅgâdvâra, where the river rushes into the valley, or with the mythological account of Gaṅgâ hurling down from heaven to earth at the instance of Bhagîratha.
[3] In the Pâli redaction the new-born children are in fact carried away by a goblin, a Yakkhinî.

the object of saving the life of that son, the building which was to serve for lying-in chamber to be wholly constructed of iron, (though) ornamented with magnificent figures wrought of jewels, gold, and silver. The preservative rites destructive of goblins were performed there according to the precepts expounded in the Science of Spirits and ordained by the Veda; and likewise the different customary auspicious ceremonies which have the effect of securing prosperity. As to his son, he had the *gâtakarma*[1] and the other sacraments performed to him in that iron-house, and let him grow up there. Owing to that most careful guard, but no less to the excellent goodness of his nature and to the power of his store of merit, no goblins overpowered the Great Being. In course of time, after the sacraments and initiatory rites had been performed, he was instructed by teachers illustrious for their knowledge of the sacred texts, their extraction, and behaviour, who were renowned and honoured as scholars, and attached to the virtues of tranquillity, modesty, and discretion. Having learnt from them many branches of science, and being favoured by the loveliness of youth, which made his figure grow fuller day by day[2], further displaying that attachment to modesty which was innate in him, he became an object of the greatest love both to his relations and the people at large.

5. People go after a virtuous person, though no relation nor acquaintance of theirs, with the like joy as if they honoured a friend. It is the brilliancy of his virtues which is the cause thereof.

6. In the season of autumn, when the moon freely shooting his beams all around is the laugh of Heaven, say what kind of relation does there exist for the people to Him?

---

[1] The king had those sacraments performed by his purohita, the king's constant and customary representative in sacrificial and ceremonial matters.

[2] It is plain that the image of the crescent moon is present to the author's mind.

So then the Great Being was enjoying the bliss that had fallen to his share as the effect of the power of his merit. He was petted with plenty of objects of celestial brilliancy standing at his disposal, and his father, who loved him much and bore him high esteem, was no more anxious about him, trusting he would be safe. Now once on the occasion of the Kaumudî-festival recurring in course of time, it happened that the Bodhisattva was desirous of contemplating the lovely beauty and the display of brilliancy in his capital. Having obtained the permission of his father, he mounted the royal chariot to take a drive. This chariot was embellished with fair ornaments of gold, jewels, and silver; gay flags and banners of various colours were floating aloft on it; its horses well-trained and swift, were adorned with golden trappings; it was driven by a charioteer distinguished for his dexterity, skill, comeliness, honesty, modesty, and firmness, and followed by a retinue adorned with a picturesque and brilliant attire and armour. Preceded by the delightful tones of musical instruments, the prince with his train passed through the capital in many directions, and let his eyes roam over the spectacle of the streets crowded with townsmen and landsmen in their lovely festival array, who with looks agitated by curiosity, were wholly intent on seeing him, and all along his way received him with praise and worship, folded hands and bent heads, and pronounced blessings over him. Nevertheless, though the contemplation of this beautiful spectacle was a proper occasion for conceiving a great rejoicing within his mind, he regained by it the remembrance of his former births. So familiar to his nature was the feeling of sa*m*vega.

7. 'Alas' (he thought), 'piteous is the state of the world and displeasing because of its unsteadiness. The brilliant splendour of this Kaumudî-day, how soon will it exist but in the memory!

8. 'And yet, such being the condition of all creatures, how heedless of danger men are, that they hurry after

rejoicings with untroubled minds, though every way around them is obstructed by death!

9. 'Disease, old age and death, three enemies of irresistible strength, stand near ready to strike, and there is no escape from the dreadful world hereafter. How then may there be opportunity for merriment to an intelligent being?

10. 'The clouds, that poured out streams of water with tremendous noise, almost in anger, imitating, as it were, the uproar of great seas, the clouds with their golden garlands of flashing lightnings, being born of agglomeration come again to dissolution.

11. 'The rivers, that flowing with increased rapidity carried away trees together with the river-banks, upon which they had their roots, afterwards and in course of time assume again a mean appearance, as if they were burnt away by sorrow.

12. 'The violence of the wind, too, blowing down peaks of mountains, dispersing masses of clouds, rolling and stirring up the waves of the ocean, becomes extinguished.

13. 'With high and blazing flame sparkling about, the fire destroys the grass, then it abates and ceases. By turns the different beauties of the groves and forests appear and disappear, as time goes on.

14. 'What union does there exist which has not its end in separation? what felicity which is not liable to mishap[1]? Since inconstancy, then, is proper to the course of worldly things, that mirth of the multitude is a very thoughtless one.'

In this manner the High-minded One reasoned within himself. Utterly touched with emotion, his heart became averse to that rejoicing and festival mirth; he paid no longer attention to the groups of people, however picturesque, flocking to embellish

---

[1] This sentence is expressed in a similar way in a *sloka*, recurring several times in Divyâvadâna (ed. Cowell, p. 27; 100; 486):
    sarve kshayântâ ni*k*ayâ*h* patanântâ*h* samu*kkh*rayâ*h*
    sa*m*yogâ viprayogântâ mara*n*ânta*m k*a *g*îvitam.
Cp. also supra, Story VI, stanza 7.

the capital. In this disposition of mind he perceived that he had already returned to his palace. His emotion increased still by this, and considering that there is no other refuge but Righteousness, since it is unconcerned with sensual pleasures, he made up his mind to embrace the state of a virtuous life. At the first opportunity he visited the king, his father, and with folded hands asked leave to set out for the penance-forest.

15. 'By taking the vow of world-renunciation I wish to bring about the good of my Self, and I want your leave which I shall hold for a favour and a guidance to this (goal).'

16. On hearing this request of his well-beloved son, the king, as if he were an elephant wounded by an empoisoned arrow or a deep sea shaken by the wind, was seized with shivering, for his heart was sore through grief.

17. And desiring to withhold him, he embraced him affectionately, and in a faltering voice obstructed by his tears spoke: 'My son, why have you made up your mind to leave us so suddenly?

18. 'Who is that man who, being a cause of displeasure to you, causes his own ruin, rousing in this manner Death (against himself)? Say, whose relations have to wet their faces with tears of sorrow?

19. 'Or do you perhaps apprehend, or have you heard of, any improper act of mine? Then, tell it, that I may put an end to it. But I myself do not perceive anything of the kind.'

The Bodhisattva spoke:

20. 'What improper act may be found in you, being thus intent to show me your affection? And who would be capable of assailing me with grief?'

'But why then do you want to leave us?' replied the king with tears. Then the Great Being answered: 'Because of the peril of death. Do but consider, Your Majesty.

21. 'From the very night when a man obtains his residence in the maternal womb, he moves towards

death, O hero among men, marching without interruption in that direction day after day.

22. 'May a man be ever so skilled in the management of his affairs, ever so strong, nobody escapes Death or Old Age, both of whom infest every place in this world. For this reason I will resort to the forest to lead a virtuous life.

23. 'Haughty princes vanquish by bold attack whole armies in splendid battle-array of footmen, horse, chariots, and elephants; but they are powerless to defeat that enemy named Death, though he is alone. Therefore I am resolved on taking my refuge in Righteousness.

24. 'Guarded by their forces made up of brisk horses and elephants and footmen and chariots, princes succeed in making their escape from their enemies; but all princes since Manu, together with their armies, succumbed helplessly to the superior power of that enemy whose name is Death.

25. 'Furious elephants crush in battle with their pestle-like tusks the gates of towns, the bodies of men, chariots, and other elephants. Yet the same tusks that were victorious even over town-walls will not push back Death, when that foe rushes on them.

26. 'Skilled archers pierce their enemies with their arrows in battle, though distant and sheltered by shield and armour strong and artfully wrought; but they never hit that enemy of old, named Death.

27. 'Lions may abate the martial lustre of elephants, plunging their cutting claws in their frontal globes, and with their roarings they may pierce the ears and frighten the hearts of their adversaries; but when they encounter Death, their insolence and strength are broken, and they fall asleep.

28. 'Kings inflict punishment on their enemies having sinned against them according to the measure of their guilt; but if that enemy whose name is Death has greatly sinned against them, they do not think of enforcing their law-sentences upon him.

29. 'Likewise kings may conquer a foe who has

offended them by means of the (well-known) expedients: conciliation and the rest; but Death, that ferocious enemy, whose insolence is strengthened by the long duration of his hatred, is not to be subdued with such craft.

30. 'Serpents in wrath bite men, and the poison of their pointed teeth has the burning effect of a fire blazing awfully, kindled as it is by their anger; but against Death, though always clever in doing harm and therefore deserving of punishment, their effort of biting is deficient.

31. 'If a man has been bitten by serpents, however furious, medical men will appease the poison by means of charms and medicines; but Death is a serpent with imperishable teeth and irresistible poison, his power cannot be put down by charms, medicines and the like.

32. 'Garu*d*as will stir up the abode of crowds of playing fishes, shaking with the flapping of their wings the water out of the seas with a thunderlike dreadful noise, then seize the serpents with their outstretched fangs; yet they are unable to destroy Death in that boisterous manner.

33. 'Tigers by their surpassing swiftness overtake the deer of the forest running away with fear, and easily crushing them upon the earth, as if playing, with the thunderbolt of their unequalled claws, drink their blood; but they have no skill to proceed in the same way with Death.

34. 'It may happen perchance that a deer having come within the reach of a tiger's mouth with its tremendous teeth, makes his escape even then. But who, having reached the mouth of Death with the big teeth named disease or old age or grief, can become sound again?

35. 'Demons (grahas), deformed and ferocious-looking, drink up the vital strength and absorb the lives of the men they hold with a strong grasp[1]; but

---

[1] In the Pâli redaction these demons are specified by the names of yakkhâ, pisâ*k*â, and petâ (= Sans. pretâ*h*), different classes of goblins.

when time has come for them likewise to wage war with Death, they will lose their insolence and ferocity.

36. 'Such as are masters in magic arts may subdue those demons, if they come up to do harm to godly persons, by the use of penance-power, evil-averting spells, and medicinal herbs; but against that demon, whose name is Death, there is no remedy at all.

37. 'Such as are skilled in the art of bringing about magical illusions, perplex the eyes of a great assembly[1]. Yet Death, too, must have still some power, that his eye is not bewildered even by those.

38. 'Both those who by their penance-powerful charms checked the virulence of poison, and the excellent physicians who extinguished the diseases of men, even Dhanvantari and such as he, have disappeared. Therefore my mind is bent on practising righteousness in the forest.

39. 'The Vidyâdharas, owing to their might made up of manifold spells and powers, make themselves visible and again invisible, go through the air or descend to the earth. Nevertheless, when they meet Death, they too have lost their might.

40. 'The lords of the Celestials (the Devas) drive back the Asuras in spite of their haughtiness, and themselves in turn in spite of their haughtiness are driven back by the Asuras. Yet, even both armies combined, a host that would march with just pride against any adversary, are not able to vanquish Death.

41. 'Understanding this ferocity of the nature of Death, our enemy, and his irresistibleness, I am no longer pleased with the life at home. It is not from anger that I leave nor in consequence of diminished affection, but I have resolved upon a life of righteousness in the forest.'

The king said: 'But what hope do you set upon the forest-life, the danger of death being thus irremediable? what hope on taking the vow of a holy life?

42. 'Shall not Death, our enemy, attain you also in

---

[1] Jugglers may effect illusions of the kind. The fourth act of the Ratnâvali affords an instance of that indragâla.

the forest? Did not the *R*ishis die who kept their vows of righteousness in the forest? In every place the course of life you wish to adopt is practicable, indeed. What profit, then, do you see in leaving your home and resorting to the forest?'

The Bodhisattva spoke:

43. 'No doubt, Death equally visits those at home and those in the forest, the righteous as well as the vicious. Yet the righteous have no reason for remorse, and righteousness is nowhere easier to be attained than in the forest, to be sure.

'Will Your Majesty deign to consider this?

44. 'The house is an abode of carelessness (about one's moral and religious duties), of infatuation, sensual love, concupiscence, hatred, of everything contrary to righteousness. What opportunity of applying one's self to it may be found at home?

45. 'A householder is distracted by many bad occupations; the care of earning and guarding his goods agitates his mind, which is also troubled by calamities arising or approaching. At what time may a householder take the way of tranquillity?

46. 'In the forest, on the other hand, after leaving that multitude of bad occupations and being freed from the troublesome care of worldly goods, a man is at his ease and may strive for tranquillity exclusively and with a satisfied mind. So he will come to happiness and righteousness and glory.

47. 'Not his wealth nor his power preserves a man, nothing but his righteousness. It is righteousness that procures him great happiness, not the possession of a large estate. And to a righteous man death cannot but procure gladness. For no fear of mishap exists for him who is devoted to a holy life.

48. 'And as good and evil are distinguished by their different characteristic marks and separated from each other by the discrepancy of the actions belonging to each, in the same way the result, too, of wickedness is mishap, but that of beautiful righteousness a happy state.'

In this manner the Great-minded One persuaded his father. He obtained his father's permission and renouncing his brilliant royal bliss, as if it were a straw, took up his abode in the penance-grove. Having acquired there dhyânas of immense extent and established mankind in them, he mounted to Brahma's world.

In this manner even the brilliancy of royalty does not obstruct the way of salvation to those, whose mind has been seized by emotion. Thus considering, one must make one's self familiar with the emotional state (sa*m*vega). [This is also to be told, when expounding the right conception of death: 'So the thought that one may die soon causes the sense of sa*m*vega.' Likewise, when expounding that death should always be present to our mind, and when teaching the temporariness of everything: 'So all phenomena[1] are perishable.' Also, when inculcating the tenet of taking no delight in the whole Universe: 'So nothing which has form (sa*m*skr*i*ta)[2] is reliable.' And also with this conclusion: 'So this world is helpless and succourless.' Also this may be propounded: 'In this manner it is easy to obtain righteousness in the forest, but not so for a householder.']

XXXIII. THE STORY OF THE BUFFALO.

(Cp. the Pâli *G*âtaka, No. 278, Fausb. II, 385–388; *K*ariyâpi*t*aka II, 5.)

Forbearance deserves this name only if there exists some opportunity for showing it, not otherwise. Thus

---

[1] Anityâ*h* sarvasa*m*skârâ*h*, one of the most popular sayings of the Lord.
[2] Properly speaking, the sa*m*skr*i*ta is the phenomenon, and the sa*m*skârâ*h* are the 'fashions' or 'forms' of the perceptible objects as well as of the perceiving mind. But the latter term is not rarely likewise indicative of the things or objects (see Childers, Dictionary, s. v. sa*m*khâro), and the former is here nearly a synonym of nâmarûpa.

considering, the virtuous appreciate even their injurer, deeming him a profit. This will be shown by the following.

The Bodhisattva, it is said, one time lived in some forest-region as a wild buffalo-bull of grim appearance, owing to his being dirty with mud, and so dark of complexion that he resembled a moving piece of a dark-blue cloud. Nevertheless, though in that animal-state, in which there prevails complete ignorance and it is difficult to come to the conception of righteousness, he in consequence of his keen understanding, was exerting himself to practise righteousness.

1. Compassion, as if it had a deep-rooted affection for him in return for his long service, never left him. But some power too, either of his karma or his nature, must be taken into account to explain the fact that he was so.

2. And it is for this reason, in truth, that the Lord[1] declared the mystery of the result of karma to be inscrutable, since He, though compassion was at the bottom of his nature, obtained the state of a beast, yet even in this condition retained his knowledge of righteousness.

3. Without karma the series of existences cannot be; it is also an impossibility that good actions should have evil as their result. But it must be the influence of small portions of (evil) karma that caused him now and then, notwithstanding his knowledge of righteousness, to be in such (low) states[2].

Now some wicked monkey, knowing his natural goodness which had manifested itself in course of time, and understanding from his habitual mercy that anger and wrath had no power over him, was in the

---

[1] In his Buddha-existence, of course.
[2] This apology is not superfluous, indeed. Though fables of animals have been adapted of old so as to form part of the stock of sacred lore of the Buddhists, the contradiction between the low existences of the most virtuous ones and the doctrines about the karma is as great as possible.

habit of vexing the Great Being very much by different injuries. 'From him I have nothing to fear,' so he thought.

4. A rascal is never more eager to insult and never displays greater insolence than towards people meek and merciful. Against those he performs his worst tricks, for he sees no danger from their side. But with respect to those from whence a suspicion of danger, however slight, strikes him, he will behave, oh! so modestly, like an honest man; his petulance is quieted there.

Sometimes, then, while the Great Being was calmly asleep or nodding from drowsiness, that monkey would of a sudden leap upon his back. Another time, having climbed on (his head), as if he were a tree, he swung repeatedly (between his horns). Sometimes again, when he was hungry, he would stand before his feet, obstructing his grazing. It happened also now and then that he rubbed his ears with a log. When he was longing to bathe, he would sometimes climb on his head and cover his eyes with his hands. Or having mounted on his back, he would ride him perforce, and holding a stick in his hand counterfeit Yama [1]. And the Bodhisattva, that Great Being, bore all that unbecoming behaviour of the monkey without irritation and anger, quite untroubled, for he considered it a benefit, as it were.

5. It is the very nature of the wicked, indeed, to walk aside from the way of decent behaviour, whereas forbearance is something like a benefit to the virtuous, owing to their habitual practice of going that way.

Now of a truth, some Yaksha who was scandalised at those insults of the Great Being, or perhaps wished to try his nature, one time when the wicked monkey was riding the buffalo-bull, placed himself in his way, saying: 'Be not so patient. Art thou the slave of

---

[1] The common representation of Yama is sitting on the back of a buffalo with a staff in his hand. See, for instance, Varâhamihira Br*i*hatsa*m*hitâ 58, 57 da*nd*î Yamo mahishaga*h*.

that wicked monkey by purchase or by loss at play, or dost thou suspect any danger from his part, or dost thou not know thine own strength, that thou sufferest thyself to be so abused by him as to become his riding animal? Verily, my friend,

6. 'The thunderbolt of thy pointed horns swung with swiftness could pierce a diamond, or like the thunderbolt, cleave huge trees. And these thy feet treading with furious anger, would sink in the mountain-rock as in mud.

7. 'And this body of thine is, like a rock, solid and compact, the splendid strength of its muscles makes its beauty perfect. So thy power is well-known to the vigorous by nature, and thou wouldst be hard to approach even for a lion.

8. 'Therefore, either crush him with thy hoof by an energetic effort, or destroy his insolence with the sharp edges of thy horns. Why dost thou suffer this rogue of a monkey to torment thee and to cause pain to thee, as if thou wert powerless?

9. 'Where is it ever seen that an evildoer is brought to reason by a cure consisting in a virtuous behaviour towards him, modesty, and kindness? This treatment being applied to such a one who is to be cured by pungent and burning and harsh remedies, his insolence will wax like a disease arising from the phlegm[1].'

Then the Bodhisattva looking at the Yaksha spoke to him mild words expressive of his adherence to the virtue of forbearance.

10. 'Surely, I know him a fickle-minded one and always fond of iniquity, but for this very reason it is right, in truth, that I put up with him.

11. 'What forbearance is that, practised towards somebody of greater strength, against whom it is impossible to retaliate? And with respect to virtuous

---

[1] Indian medicine divides the diseases into three classes, according to their origin from one of the three humours: phlegm (kapha), wind (vâta), and bile (pitta).

people standing firm in honesty and decent behaviour, what is there to be endured at all?

12. 'Therefore we ought to endure injuries by a feeble one, though having the power of revenge. Better to bear insults from such a one than to get rid of virtues.

13. 'Ill-treatment by a powerless one is the best opportunity, in truth, for showing virtues. With what purpose, then, should the lover of virtues make use of his strength in such cases so as to lose his firmness of mind?

14. 'Besides, the opportunity for forbearance, that virtue always of use, being difficult to obtain inasmuch as it depends on others, what reason could there be to resort to anger just then, when that opportunity has been afforded by another?

15. 'And if I did not use forbearance against him who disregarding the damage of his own righteousness (dharma), acts as if to cleanse my sins, say who else should be ungrateful, if not I?'

The Yaksha spoke: 'Then wilt thou never be delivered from his persecutions.

16. 'Who may be able to chastise the ill-behaviour of a rascal having no respect for virtues, unless he sets aside humble forbearance?'

The Bodhisattva spoke:

17. 'It is not suitable for him who longs for happiness to pursue comfort or prevention of discomfort by inflicting grief on another. The result of such actions will not tend to the production of happiness.

18. 'My persistence in patient endurance is, in fact, an admonition to awake his conscience. If he does not understand it, he will afterwards assail others of a hasty temper who will stop him in his pursuit of the wrong way.

19. 'And having been ill-treated by such a one, he will no more do these things to such as me. For having received punishment, he will not act in this (unbecoming) manner again. And so I will get rid of him.'

On these words the Yaksha, affected with faithful contentment, amazement, and respect, exclaimed: 'Well said! well said!' and moving his head and shaking his (extended) fingers, magnified the Great Being with kind words such as these:

20. 'How is it possible that beasts should possess a conduct like this? How didst thou come to this degree of regard for virtues? Having assumed with some purpose or other this animal-shape, thou must be somebody practising penance in the penance-forest!'

After thus eulogising him, he threw the wicked monkey off his back, and taught him a preservative charm; after which he disappeared on the spot.

In this manner, then, forbearance deserves this name only, if there exists some opportunity for showing it, not otherwise: thus considering the virtuous appreciate even their injurer, deeming him a profit. [So is to be said, when discoursing on forbearance. And this may also be said: 'In this manner is shown the imperturbable tranquillity of the Bodhisattvas, even when in the state of a beast; how, indeed, should it become a human being or one who has taken the vow of a homeless life to be deficient in it[1]?' This story is also to be told, when praising the Tathâgata and when discoursing on listening with attention to the preaching of the Law.]

XXXIV. THE STORY OF THE WOODPECKER.

(Cp. the Pâli *Gâtaka*, No. 308, Fausb. III, 25-27.)

Even though provoked, a virtuous person is incapable of betaking himself to wickedness, having never learnt to do so. This will be taught as follows.

The Bodhisattva, it is said, lived in some place of a forest as a woodpecker distinguished by his beautiful

---

[1] Cp. the conclusion of Story XXV.

and lovely feathers of manifold colours. But though in that state, owing to his habitual compassion, he did not follow the way of living of his kind, a sinful one since it involves injuries to living beings.

1. With the young shoots of the trees, with the sweet and delicious flavours of their flowers, and with their fruits of different hue, scent, and relish he kept such diet as was dictated by his contentment.

2. He manifested his care for the interests of others by preaching to others the precepts of righteousness on proper opportunities, by helping the distressed according to his power, and by preventing the baseminded from immodest actions.

The whole multitude of animals in that part of the forest, being thus protected by the Great Being, thrived and were happy; for in him they possessed a teacher, as it were, a kinsman, a physician, a king.

3. In the same degree as they, being well protected by the greatness of his mercy, increased in virtues, in the very same degree his protection endowed them, though making up a collection of substances, with increase of their qualities [1].

Now one time, when the Great Being, according to his pity for the creatures, was rambling through parts of the forest, it happened that he saw in some part of the wood a lion who overcome by an exceedingly heavy pain was lying on the earth, as if he were hit with a poisonous arrow, having his mane disarranged and dirty with dust. And drawing near to him, moved by compassion, he asked him: 'What is the matter, king of the quadrupeds? Thou art seriously ill, indeed, I see.

4. 'Is this illness caused by exhaustion after indulging too much in boldness against elephants? or

---

[1] The point of this stanza is lost in translation. The term sattvakâya admits of two acceptations, according to its being applied to the philosophical and to the ordinary use of the word sattva. So the same compound may signify 'a body of animals' and 'a collection of substances.' Similarly the term gu*n*a means 'virtue' as well as 'quality.'

in excessive running after deer? or art thou hit with an arrow by a hunter? or has some disease seized thee?

5. 'Say then, what ails thee, if at least it may be told to me. Likewise tell me what may be done for thee in this case. And if perhaps I possess some power for the benefit of my friends, thou must enjoy the profit I may bring about by it and recover thy health[1].'

The lion spoke: 'Thou, virtuous and best of birds, this illness is not the effect of exhaustion nor is it caused by disease nor occasioned by a hunter's arrow. But it is the fragment of a bone that sticks here in my throat and, like the point of an arrow, causes grievous pain to me. I can neither swallow it down nor throw it up. Therefore, it is now the time of assistance by friends. Now, if you know the way to make me sound, well, do it.' Then the Bodhisattva, owing to the keenness of his intellect, thought out some means of extracting the object which was the cause of his pain. Taking a piece of wood large enough to bar his mouth, he spoke to the lion: 'Open thy mouth as wide as ever thou canst.' After he had done so, the Bodhisattva having placed the log tightly between the two rows of his teeth, entered the bottom of his throat. With the top of his beak he seized that fragment of bone sticking athwart in it by one edge, and having loosened it, took it by another edge, and at last drew it out. And while retiring, he dropped the log which barred the lion's mouth.

6. No wound-healer, however skilled in his art and clever, would have succeeded even with great effort in extracting that extraneous substance, yet he pulled it out, thanks to his keen intellect, though not exercised by professional training[2], but proper to him through hundreds of existences.

---

[1] The last pâda of this sloka looks corrupt in the original, yet without encumbrance of the main sense which is evident.
[2] Cp. the beginning of Story XIV, p. 125.

7. After taking away together with the bone the pain and anguish caused by it, he felt no less gladness at having relieved his suffering fellow-creature, than the lion at being released from the pain-causing object.

This, indeed, is the essential property of a virtuous person.

8. A virtuous person having effected the happiness of another or stopped his mischief even with difficulty, will enjoy a greater amount of excessive gladness, than he would on account even of prosperity happening to himself and easily obtained.

So the Great Being having relieved his pain, was rejoiced in his heart. He took leave of the lion, and having received his thanks went his way.

Now some time after, it happened that the woodpecker flying about with his outspread wings of exquisite beauty, could nowhere get any suitable food, so that he was caught by hunger which burnt his limbs. Then he saw that same lion feasting on the flesh of a young antelope fresh killed. His mouth and claws and the lower end of his mane being tinged with the blood of that animal, he resembled a fragment of a cloud in autumn, immersed in the glow of twilight.

9. Yet, though he was his benefactor, he did not venture to address him with words of request, disagreeable to the ear; for however skilled in speech, shame imposed upon him a temporary obligation of silence.

10. Nevertheless, as his wants required satisfaction, he walked up and down before his eyes in a bashful attitude. But that scoundrel, though well aware of him, did not at all invite him to join in the repast.

11. Like seed sown on a rock, like an oblation poured out on ashes that have lost their heat, of that very nature is, at the time of fruit, a benefit bestowed on an ungrateful person, and the flower of the vidula-reed.

Then the Bodhisattva thought: 'Surely, he does not know me again,' and approaching him with a little more confidence, asked him for a share, supporting his demand with a proper benediction after the manner of mendicants.

12. 'Much good may it do thee, lord of the quadrupeds, who procurest thy livelihood by thy prowess! I beg thee to honour a mendicant, which is an instrument for thee to gather good repute and merit.'

But the lion disregarding this kind blessing, unacquainted as he was with the behaviour of the pious (ârya), owing to his habitual cruelty and selfishness, fixed a sidelong look on the Bodhisattva, as if he were willing to burn him down with the flame of the anger blazing out of his fiery eyes, and said: 'No more of this.

13. 'Is it not enough that thou art alive, after entering the mouth of a creature like me, a devourer of fresh killed deer who does not know of unmanly mercy?

14. 'Is it to insult me that thou darest molest me thus another time with a demand. Art thou weary of thy life? Thou wishest to see the world hereafter, I suppose.'

This refusal and the harsh words expressing it, filled the Bodhisattva with shame. He flew directly upward to the sky, telling him in the language of his extended wings he was a bird, and went his way.

Now some forest-deity who was indignant at this injury, or who wanted to know the extent of his virtuous constancy, mounted also to the sky, and said to the Great Being: 'Excellent one among birds, for what reason dost thou suffer this injury inflicted by that scoundrel on thee, his benefactor, though thou dost possess the power of revenge? What is the profit of overlooking that ungrateful one in this manner?

15. 'He may be ever so strong, thou art still able to blind him by a sudden assault on his face. Thou mayst also rob the flesh of his repast from between his very teeth. Why then dost thou suffer his insolence?'

At that moment the Bodhisattva, though having

been ill-treated and insulted, and notwithstanding the provocation of the forest-deity, manifested the extreme goodness of his nature, saying: 'Enough, enough of this manner of proceeding. This way is not followed by such as me.

16. 'It is out of mercy, not with the desire of gain, that the virtuous take care of a person in distress, nor do they mind whether the other understands this or not. What opportunity for anger is there in such a case?

17. 'Ingratitude cannot but tend to the deception of the ungrateful one himself. Who, indeed, wishing a service in return, will do good to him a second time?

18. 'As to the benefactor, he obtains merit and the result of it in the world hereafter in consequence of his self-restraint, and an illustrious renown still in this world.

19. 'Moreover, if the benefit has been performed in order to practise a righteous action, why should it be regretted afterwards? If done with the purpose of receiving something in return, it is a loan, not a benefit.

20. 'He who because of the ingratitude of his neighbour prepares to do him harm, such a one, in truth, after first earning a spotless reputation by his virtues, will subsequently act after the manner of elephants.

21. 'If my neighbour by the infirmity of his mind does not know how to return the benefit, he will also never obtain the lovely lustre inherent in virtues; but, say, what reason should there exist for a sentient being to destroy, on account of that, his own lofty renown?

'But this seems to me most becoming in this case.

22. 'He in whose heart a service done by a virtuous person did not rouse a friendly disposition, such a one is to be left, but gently, without harshness and anger.'

Then the deity, rejoiced at his well-said sentences, praised him, exclaiming repeatedly: 'Well said! well said!' and adding many kind words.

23. 'Though exempt from the toil caused by

matted hair and a bark garment, thou art a *Ri*shi, thou art a holy ascetic knowing the future! It is not the dress, truly, that makes the Muni, but he who is adorned by virtues is the real Muni here.'

After thus distinguishing him and honouring him, he disappeared on the spot.

In this manner, then, a virtuous person is incapable of betaking himself to wickedness, even though provoked, having never learnt to do so. [So is to be said when eulogising the virtuous. And when discoursing on forbearance, this is to be propounded : ' In this manner a man practising forbearance will rarely meet with enmity, rarely with reproach, and will be beloved and welcome to many people.' When praising adherence to tranquillity, this is to be said: ' In this manner the wise being great in preserving their tranquillity preserve their own lustre of virtues.' Likewise, when glorifying the Tathâgata and praising the cultivation of an excellent nature : ' In this manner a good nature being always striven after does not pass away, even when in the state of a beast.']

SYNOPTICAL TABLE

OF THE CORRESPONDENCE BETWEEN THE STANZAS OF THE GÂTAKAMÂLÂ AND THE SCRIPTURE VERSES OF THE PÂLI GÂTAKA.

* *Indicates a very close and partly verbal agreement.*

II. Sibigâtaka = Fausb. No. 499.

Gâtakamâlâ.	Pâli Gâtaka.
Stanza 10–12	Stanza 1–3
,, 13, 14	,, 5, 6
,, 15–18	,, 7–9
,, 21–23	,, 10, 11
,, 25	,, 12
,, 26, 27	,, 13
,, 28	,, 14
,, *32, *33	,, *20, *21
,, 35, 36	,, 23
,, 37	,, 24, 25
,, 44–49	,, 26–31

III. Kulmâshapi*ndi*gâtaka = Fausb. No. 415.

Stanza 4, 5	Stanza 1, 2
,, 6, 7	,, 3
,, 10–13	,, 4–7
,, 14–16	,, 8–10
,, 17	,, 11, 12

IV. Sresh*thi*gâtaka = Fausb. No. 40.

Stanza 18	Stanza 1

V. Avishahya*sresh*t*hi*gâtaka = Fausb. No. 340.

Stanza 9	Stanza 1
,, *11	,, *2
,, 26, 27	,, 3, 4

VI. Sa*s*agâtaka = Fausb. No. 316.

Stanza 26–29	Stanza 1–4

VII. Agastyagâtaka = Fausb. No. 480.

Stanza 12	Stanza 2
,, 14, 15	,, 4
,, 17, 18	,, 6

Gâtakamâlâ.	Pâli Gâtaka.
Stanza 20-22	Stanza 8, 9
,, 24-26	,, 10
,, 28, *29	,, 12, *13
,, 30, 31	,, 14
,, 34	,, 16, 17
,, 36-38	,, 19-21
Stanzas 13, 16, 19, 27, 32 and 33, 35 are different embellishments of one stereotyped verse	,, 3, 5, 7, 11, 15, 18

XII. Brâhma*n*agâtaka = Fausb. No. 305.

Stanza *13, 14, *15	Stanza *1, *2.

XIII. Unmâdayantîgâtaka = Fausb. No. 527.

Stanza 12	Stanza 5
,, *17, 18	,, 15
,, *19	,, 16
,, 22	,, 17
,, 26, 27	,, 18, 19
,, 29	,, 29, and cp. 24 and 26
,, 30, 31	,, 30, 32
,, 32	,, 35 and cp. 33
,, 33	,, 41
,, 34	,, 34
,, 36	,, 36
,, 39	,, 48-51

XIV. Supâragagâtaka = Fausb. No. 463.

Stanza 12, 13	Stanza 1, 2
,, 14, 15	,, 5, 6
,, 16, 17	,, 3, 4
,, 18, 19	,, 7, 8
,, 20, 21	,, 9, 10
,, 22, 23	,, 11, 12
,, *30, 31	,, 13

XV. Matsyagâtaka = Fausb. No. 75.

Stanza 14	Stanza 1, cp. *K*ariyâpi*t*aka III, 10, 6

XVI. Vartakâpotakagâtaka = Fausb. No. 35.

Stanza 7	Stanza 3 = 34 of Ekanipâta

XVII. Kumbhagâtaka = Fausb. No. 512.

Stanza 7, 11	Stanza 1-3
,, 12, 13	,, 4, 5
,, 14	,, 6 and 8
,, 15	,, 7
,, 16	,, 9 and 22
,, 18	,, 25
,, 19	,, 13 and *14
,, 22	,, 26
,, 25	,, 15-17
,, 27	,, 18
,, 30, *31	,, 28, *29
,, 32, 33	,, 30, 31

XIX. Bisagâtaka = Fausb. No. 488.

Gâtakamâlâ.	Pâli Gâtaka.
Stanza *11, *12, 13	Stanza *1, *2, 3
,, 14, 15, *16	,, 4, 5, *6
,, *17, *18	,, *7, *8
,, 19, 20	,, 9, 10
,, *21, *22, *23	,, *11, *12, *13
,, *24, 25, 26-28	,, *14, 15, 16 and 17
,, 29, 30	,, 18
,, *31	,, *19
,, *32, 33	,, 20

XX. Sreshthigâtaka = Fausb. No. 171.

Stanza *18 . Stanza *1

XXI. Kuddabodhigâtaka = Fausb. No. 443.

Stanza 9, 11	Stanza 1, 2
,, 18, 20, 21	,, 3, 4, 5
,, *22, *23, *24, *25 a	,, *6, *7, *8, *9 a
,, 25 b-d, 26	,, 9 b-d, 10, 11
,, 27, 28	,, 12, 13

XXII. Hamsagâtaka = Fausb. No. 533.

Stanza 26	Stanza 1, cp. No. 534, 1-3
,, 27, 29	,, 2, 4
,, *30, *31, *32	,, *5, *6, *7
,, *33, *34	,, *8, *9
,, *35	,, *10 identical.
,, *36, *37, *38	,, *11, *12, *13
,, 39, 40	,, 19 (read disam)
,, 43, 44	,, 20, 21, cp. No. 534, 15 and 16
,, 45-48	,, 25-28
,, *49, 50, 51	,, *29, 30, 31 (stands in a wrong place, as 31, being spoken by Sumukha, must immediately follow 30)
,, 54	,, 35 = 49
,, 55, 56	,, 37, 39
,, 57, 58	,, 41, 42
,, 59-62	,, 43, 44, 46
,, 63, 64	,, 47-53
,, 65	,, 54, 55
,, 66, 67	,, 58
,, 68	,, 60
,, 72, 73	,, 65
,, *74, 75-77	,, *66, 67-69
,, 78, 79	,, 70
,, 80	,, 72, 73
,, 83	,, 74
,, 85, 86	,, 75-77
,, *89	,, 81

XXIII. Mahâbodhigâtaka = Fausb. No. 528.
Gâtakamâlâ.   Pâli Gâtaka.
Stanza 13, 14   .   .   .   .   Stanza 7, 8
„   15   .   .   .   .   „   10
„   16   .   .   .   .   „   11, 13
„   66–69   .   .   .   .   „   53–56
„   70   .   .   .   .   „   49, 50
„   71   .   .   .   .   „   51, 52

XXIV. Mahâkapigâtaka = Fausb. No. 516.
Stanza 11   .   .   .   .   Stanza 21

XXVI. Rurugâtaka = Fausb. No. 482.
Stanza 22, 23 .   .   .   .   Stanza 5
„   24   .   .   .   .   „   7
„   26, 27 .   .   .   .   „   8
„   30   .   .   .   .   „   9

XXVII. Mahâkapigâtaka = Fausb. No. 407.
Stanza 13   .   .   .   .   Stanza 1
„   15   .   .   .   .   „   2
„   20 d, 21–23 . . .   „   3–5

XXVIII. Kshântigâtaka = Fausb. No. 313.
Stanza 59   .   .   .   .   Stanza 1
„   61, *62 .   .   .   .   „   2

XXXI. Sutasomagâtaka = Fausb. No. 537.
Stanza 47, *48, *49 .   .   .   Stanza 54, *55, *56
„   52   .   .   .   .   „   59
„   *54   .   .   .   .   „   *60
„   61–66   .   .   .   .   „   64–71
„   67   .   .   .   .   „   72
„   71, 72 .   .   .   .   „   40, 41 = 74, 75
„   74, 75 .   .   .   .   „   42, 43 = 76, 77
„   76, 77 .   .   .   .   „   78, 79
„   *78   .   .   .   .   „   *80
„   93, 94 .   .   .   .   „   102

XXXII. Ayogrihagâtaka = Fausb. No. 510.
Stanza 21, 22 .   .   .   .   Stanza 1, 2
„   23, 24 .   .   .   .   „   3, 4
„   25, 26 .   .   .   .   „   6, 7
„   27 and 33 .   .   .   „   17
„   28, 29 .   .   .   .   „   14, 15
„   30, 31 .   .   .   .   „   19, 20
„   35, 36 .   .   .   .   „   12, 13
„   37   .   .   .   .   „   18
„   38, 39 .   .   .   .   „   21, 22
„   47, 48 .   .   .   .   „   23, 24

XXXIII. Mahishagâtaka = Fausb. No. 278.
Stanza 19   .   .   .   .   Stanza 3 = Kariyâpitaka II, 5, 10

XXXIV. Satapattragâtaka = Fausb. No. 308.
Stanza *13   .   .   .   .   Stanza 2
„   *22   .   .   .   .   „   4

INDEX.

abhigñâ, page 206.
Abhipâraga, 116, 117, 118, 119, 120, 121, 122, 123.
Act of Truth, 16, 132, 136, 137, 141.
Agastya, the story of, VII. 46-55.
Agni, 140.
Agnihotra, 49.
Agnimâlin, 129.
Agita, 4.
Almsgiving, eulogy of, 24.
Andhakas, 145.
Angels, charged with the care of rain, 94, 135.
Anger, sermon on, 178-180.
Aniruddha, 164.
Annihilation, doctrine of, 207, 213.
Aṅgadinna, 269.
Aṅgas, see Vedâṅgas.
Ape, 38, 45; for the rest cp. Monkey.
  Story of the great, XXIV. 218-227.
Apsaras(as), 17, 97, 115, 117.
arghya, 271.
Arhat, 22, 105.
artha, a means for attaining dharma. 27-29.
— 9, 95, 195, 202, 253, 264, 302, 312.
Asuras, 105, 322.
Asukiruṇapa, 276.
avabhṛitha, 95, 97.
Avadânakalpalatâ, see Bodhisattvâvadânakalpalatâ.
Avadânaṡataka, 37.
Avishahya, 30, 31.
  Story of, V. 30-37.
Aviki, 147.
Ayogṛiha, story of, XXXII. 314-324.

Âdityas, 131.
Ânanda, 164, 181, 199, 291.
âpaddharma, 111, 223.
Âryasthaviriyanikâya, 139.

Bauddhakâvya, 291.
Benares, 183, 186, 187, 245.
Bodhi (proper name), 202.
Bodhi, see Buddhahood.
Bodhisattva, 1, 2, 4, 5, 6, 7, 8, 12, 18, 20, 25, 26, 27, 28, 29, 30, 31, 32, 33, 35, 39, 46, 48, 49, 50, 51, 52, 53, 54, 55, 56, 71, 74, 78, 81, 82, 83, 84, 85, 86, 87, 89, 91, 92, 93, 104, 109, 111, 112, 113, 114, 124, 125, 128, 132, 134, 136, 137, 138, 140, 141, 148, 151, 154, 156, 157, 158, 159, 162, 163, 165, 166, 167, 169, 173, 174, 175, 176, 178, 180, 181, 185, 186, 187, 188, 189, 190, 195, 197, 199, 200, 201, 202, 203, 204, 205, 207, 208, 209, 210, 219, 221, 222, 224, 227, 228, 229, 232, 234, 235, 236, 239, 240, 241, 243, 244, 245, 248, 250, 251, 253, 263, 265, 266, 267, 269, 270, 271, 273, 278, 281, 282, 291, 295, 296, 297, 299, 300, 301, 303, 304, 305, 306, 307, 308, 309, 310, 311, 312, 313, 314, 319, 325, 327, 328, 329, 331, 332, 333.
Bodhisattvas, 125, 329.
Bodhisattvâvadânakalpalatâ, 8, 19, 20, 37, 41, 71, 78, 93, 200, 268, 291.
Brahma (n.), 43, 68.
Brahmâ (m.), 98.
Brahmadatta, 182, 186, 245.
Brahmaloka, 269, 270, 271, 286, 324.
  Story of the inhabitant of the, XXIX. 268-281.
Brâhman, majestic figure of a. 143;
  Brâhmans abhor falsehood, 144:
  the Brâhman with the four well-said sentences, 293, 294, 297, 298, 299, 300; the Brâhman who asked the Bodh.'s eye, 11, 12, 13, 15; the Brâhman in

the shape of whom Sakra tried
  the hare, 42, 43, 44.
Brâhman, story of the, XII. 109–114.
Brâhmanî, A, 85.
Br*i*haspati, 123.
Brothers, the six, of the Bodhisattva,
  154, 155, 156, 157, 159, 160.
Buddha, 1, 8, 67, 218, 313, 325.
Buddhas, 21.
Buddhahood, 1, 56, 69.
Buddha-virtues, 5.
Buddhayâna, 5.
buddhi, 272.
Buffalo, story of the, XXXIII. 324–329.

Bhadra, 291.
Bhadrakalpâvadâna, 313, 314.
bhakti, doctrine of, 211.
Bharuka*kkh*a, 125, 134.
bhâvanâs, 3.

Celestials, celestial gods, see Devas.
Charity praised, 19, 24, 28, 29, 30, 31, 32, 35, 36, 45, 54, 60, 72, 73; excess of, 75.
Childless one, story of the, XVIII. 148–154.
Comrade, the, of the Bodhisattva, 156, 160.
Curse, the effect of penance-power, 176, 267; strong liquor, an embodied Curse, 146.

Dadhimâlin, 129.
Daityas, 54, 105, 186, 192, 229.
Dânavas, 105.
Delusion (= mâyâ) 259; (= moha) 301.
Demoness, 117.
Demons, 105, 106, 107, 108, 126, 128; (= g raha) 320, 321.
Destiny, 14, 123, 166.
Detachment praised, 151, 156, 253.
Devadatta, 260.
Devaputras, 55, 161, and see Angels.
Devarshi, 270.
Devas, 7, 14, 44, 63, 90, 92, 96, 97, 106, 107, 108, 119, 136, 182, 287, 322.
  City of the, 24; hall of the, 45; Lord of the, see Sakra; rank of the, 28; world of the, 38, 45, 96; sovereignty of the, 113; old, 146.
Devil, the embodied, 226.
Devî, 131.

Diti, 104.
Divyâvadâna, 8, 20, 56, 318.
dikshâ, 95, 102.
dîkshita, 95, 102.
Dog, a, 204.

Dhammapada, 21, 139, 143.
Dhanvantari, 322.
dharma, 9, 27, 69, 95, 195, 207, 211, 214, 216, 259, 263, 302, 312, 328.
Dharma (personified), 94, 177, 257.
Dh*ri*tarâsh*t*ra, 181.
dhyâna, 55, 174, 206, 257, 269, 271, 272, 324.

Elephant, 161, 162; a white, 73, 74, 75, 78.
  Story of the, XXX. 281–291.
Elephants of the world-quarters, 288.

False doctrines, 206, 207, 209–214, 216, 218.
Fear of Death, 306, 307; discourse on the, 319–323.
Fish, story of the, XV. 134–138.
Five, the (first followers of the Lord), 71.
Forbearance, praise of, 258, 259, 264, 265, 328.
Forest-deity, 333–335.

Gandharvas, 7, 92.
Ganges, 245, 315.
Ga*n*as, 17.
garbhâdhâna, 109.
Garu*d*a(s), 287, 321.
gâthâs, tetrad of, 300, 308, 309.
Goblins, 57, 58, 63, 295, 300, 315, 316.
Goldland, 125.
grahas, 321.
Gruel, story of the small portion of, 111. 20–25.
Guild, story of the head of a, IV. 25–30.
guru, the, of Âry*a*ûra, 2.

Gâlin, 82, 86.
Gâtaka, the Pâli, 8, 18, 19, 20, 21, 25, 30, 37, 46, 71, 93, 104, 109, 114, 124, 125, 126, 130, 132, 133, 134, 137, 138, 141, 154, 159, 160, 164, 172, 181, 182, 190, 195, 200, 214, 218, 227, 234, 244, 245, 253, 260, 268, 291, 314, 324, 329.
  Commentary on the, 160, 161, 162.
gâtakarma, 2, 46, 109, 316.

Gvalatkukûla, 274.

Hamsa, the supreme, 44. For the rest, cp. Swan.
Hare, story of the, VI. 37-45.
Hâlahala, the poison, 307.
Hells, description of, 274-277.
Himâlaya or Himavat, 36, 141, 186, 218, 244, 289.
Hitopadesa, 200.
Hospitality praised, 39-44, 49.

Indra, 16, 68, 196.

Îsvara, 206, 211, 212.

Jackal, the friend of the hare, 38, 42, 45.
Jar, story of the, XVII. 141-154.
Jewels (the three), or Triratna, 2.

Kailâsa, 73.
Kakangalâ, 161.
kalâs, 2, 292.
Kalmâshapâda, see the son of Sudâsa.
karma, 269, 275, 276; doctrine of, 206, 212, 325; result of, 148, 258, 270, 325; harvest of, 225, 239; evil, 239.
Kathâsaritsâgara, 20, 124, 200.
Kaumudî, 117.
Kaumudî-festival, 116, 317.
Kauravas, 291.
Kâlodâyin, 164.
kâma, 9, 95, 195, 202, 253, 264, 302.
kâmadhâtu, 269.
kâmâvakara, 269.
Kârâ, 47.
Kâsyapa, 51, 53; (another) 164.
Kâsyapa, the Buddha, 161.
King's duties, a, 216, 217, 250, 252, 278-280.
Kirîtavatsa, 118.
Kosala, 20.
Krishnâginâ, 82, 86, 87.
Krita Yuga, 9, 99, 101.
kshamâ, 259, 264.
kshânti, 253, 259.
Kshântivâdin, 253, 254, 256, 260, 261. Story of, XXVIII. 253-268.
Kshemendra, 8, 93.
Kubera, 31, 56, 68, 145.
Kubgottarâ, 164.
Kusamâlin, 130.

Khuramâlin, 128.

Kandra, 45.
Kariyâpitaka, 8, 37, 46, 71, 93, 134, 137, 138, 154, 172, 234, 291, 314, 324.
Kitra, 164.
Kuddabodhi, story of, XXI. 172-181.

Leprosy a punishment for treachery, 225, 226.
Lion, 330-333.
Lioness, 294.
Liquors, sin of drinking strong, 142, 148; discourse on the sin of drinking, 144-147.
Lokapâlas, 80, 177.
Lotus stalks, story of the, XIX. 154-164.
Love-god, 91, 117, 119, 175, 176.

Madrî, 78, 79, 81, 82, 88, 89, 90, 91, 92.
Madhudâtar, 164.
Magic, the power of, 15, 44, 207, 215.
Mahâbodhi, story of, XXIII. 200-218.
Mahâraurava, 27.
Maitribala, story of, VIII. 55-71.
Mangala Buddha, 93.
Man-eater, the, see Kalmâshapâda.
Manmatha, 7, 118.
Manu, 320.
Mare-mouth, the, 131, 132.
Maruts, 131.
Maudgalyâyana, 164.
Mânasa, Lake, 181, 183, 185, 186, 187.
Mâra, 26, 27, 29, 30, 91, 287; hosts of, 5.
Mâtali, 106, 107.
Mercy, discourse on, 243, 244.
Merit and Meritorious actions, 8, 23, 24, 25, 26, 39, 40, 45, 68, 233, 245, 279; power of, 9, 20, 30, 39, 133, 136, 200, 201, 316, 317; result of, 19, 22, 23, 94.
Meru, 4, 58, 66, 69.
Milinda Pañha, 93.
Monastery, the Great, 161.
Monkey, 43, 161, 162, 207, 208, 215, 244, 245, 247, 248, 249; the wicked, 325, 326, 327. Story of the great, XXVII. 244-253.
Monks, false, 215.
Mountain, the golden, see Meru; the snow-bright, see Himâlaya.

Muni, epitheton of the Buddha, and the Bodhisattva, 1, 55, 262, 265, 278; foremost of Munis, 266, 268, Lord of Munis, 141.
Muni, a, 23, 48, 94, 112, 116, 144. 163, 198, 254, 263, 335.

naishkrama, 47, 154.
Nalamâlin, 130, 133.
Nandana, the park of the Devas, 255. 293.
Narakântaka, 28.
naya = niti, 76.
Nirgranthas, 145.
Nirvâ*n*a, 269, 286.
Nishâda, 190, 191, 192, 193, 196.
niti, see Political wisdom.

Ogohâras, 56, 57.
Otter, 38, 42, 45.

paraloka, see World hereafter.
paramâtman, 280.
Parganya, 137.
pâramitâ, 93.
Pârileya, 164.
Pâtâla, 126.
Pisâ*k*as, 57, 61.
Pitaras, 147.
Political wisdom, the science of princes, 40, 59, 74. 75, 105. 163, 203, 207, 213, 214, 215. 250, 302, 305, 306.
poshadha, 20, 39.
pramâ*n*a, 271.
pra*n*idhâna, pra*n*idhi, 286.
prasâda, 67.
Pratyekabuddha, 26, 27, 30, 55.
Preaching of the Law, 39, 157, 159, 161, 237, 243, 330; listening with attention to the—of the Law, 8, 71, 108, 227, 253, 280, 290, 313, 329.
Pretas, 147. 226.
pu*m*savana, 109.
pu*n*ya, see Merit.
purohita, 94, 97, 98, 160, 316.
purushamedha, 97.
Pûr*n*a, 164.
Pûtana, 226.

Quail's young, story of the, XVI. 138-141.

Rakshas = Râkshasa, 294.
Rati, 115.
râgarshi, 16, 252.

Râhu, 192.
Râkshasas, 32, 57, 58, 61, 294.
Recollection of former existences, 20, 22, 23, 272, 317.
Rudras, 131.
Ruru-deer, story of the, XXVI. 234-244.

R*i*shi, 162, 163, 182, 260, 261, 262, 263, 265, 278, 323, 335.

Sabbath-days, 20, 39, 73.
Sacraments, 2, 109, 173, 316.
Sacrifice, story of the, X. 93-104.
Sacrificial fee, 122.
sa*kk*akiriyâ, see Act of Truth.
sambodhi = Supreme Wisdom, 6, 15.
Sa*m*ghâta, 275.
Sa*m*gaya, 71, 75, 76, 92.
Sa*m*sâra, 4, 24, 46, 286, 306.
sa*m*-kâra and sa*m*skr*i*ta, 324.
Sa*m*vega, 280, 314, 317.
Sangha, 25.
Sarvamitra, 142, 143.
sattra, 31, 97, 102.
Saviour of the World, 15, 286.
Sâgara, the Ocean, as a god, 131.
Sâtâgiri, 164.
sâtmîbhâva, 135, 232.
Servant, the male, and the female, of the Bodhisattva, 156, 161.
Siddhas, 77, 182.
Sister, the, of the Bodhisattva, 156, 161.
sîmantonnayana, 109.
Snakes, 7, 126, 136, 182.
Snow-mountain, see Himâlaya.
Soma, 292.
Soma-sacrifices, 97.
Southern Ocean, 47.
Stars, the, the wives of the Moon-god, 184.
strîdhana, 79.
Sudâsa, 294; the son of, 294, 295, 296, 297, 298, 299, 302, 303, 304, 305, 306, 307, 308, 309, 310, 311, 312, 313.
Sudharmâ, 45.
Sumeru, 11, 90.
Sumukha, 181, 182, 186, 187, 189, 190, 191, 192, 194, 195, 196, 197, 199.
Sunanda, 118.
Supâraga (the man), 125, 128, 129, 130, 131, 132, 133.
The story of, XIV. 124-134.
(the town), 125.
Suppâraka, 125.

Sutasoma, 292, 294, 296, 299, 305, 312, 314.
The story of, XXXI. 291-314.
Sûpâraga, 125.
svastyayana, 58.
Swans, the story of the holy, XXII. 181-200.

Sakra, the Lord of the Devas, 2, 11, 12, 14, 15, 16, 17, 18, 32, 33, 34, 35, 36, 37, 41, 42, 43, 44, 45, 48, 49, 50, 51, 52, 53, 54, 55, 58, 67, 68, 70, 83, 90, 91, 92, 103, 104, 106, 107, 131, 136, 138, 142, 144, 146, 147, 148, 153, 157, 158, 159, 162, 163, 164; the riches, (brilliancy, realm) of, 14, 68, 198; city of, 278.
Story of, XI. 104-108.
Sarabha, story of the, XXV. 227-234.
Sasâṅka, 45.
Satakratu, 103.
Satayagvan, 103.
Sâkya prince, 93.
Sâradvatî, 164.
Sâriputra, 164.
Sibis, the, 8, 9, 19, 71, 74, 75, 76, 77, 78, 85, 92, 114, 123.
Story of the king of the, II. 8-19.
Sraddhâ, 96.
Sri. 67, 115.
Sruti. praise of, 301, 302.
Sûra, 1, 93.

Tantular, 291.
Tathâgata, 19, 55, 71, 92, 104, 108, 141, 148, 181, 227, 233, 252, 290, 291, 313, 329.
Tathâgatas, 132.
Tigress, story of the, I. 1-8.
tîrtha, 254, 306.
trayî, 71.
Treasurer, story of the, XX. 164 172.
Triad of dharma, artha, kâma (trivarga), 9, 27, 76, 95, 123, 195, 217, 263, 302.
Triad of low, middle, high, 163, 258.
Trivarga, see Triad of dharma, &c.

Unmâdayantî, 115, 117, 118, 122; story of, XIII. 114-124.

Upavedas, 154, 292.
Utpalâvarnâ, 164.

Vadavâmukha, see Mare-mouth.
Vaigayanta, 45.
Vaitaranî, 276.
Vaṅka, Mount, 77, 81, 83, 93.
Vasus, 131.
Vâsava = Sakra, 52, 92.
Vedas, 46, 71, 95, 96, 109, 154, 155, 160, 292, 302, 308, 316.
Vedâṅgas, 46, 292.
Veracity, praise of, 306; power of, 17, 133, 138.
Vetâlapaṅkaviṃsati, 124.
Videha, 269.
Vidhi, 14.
Vidyâdharas, 182, 184, 219.
vinaya, 216.
Virtues, praise of, 198, 292; lover of virtues, partisan of virtues, 54, 292, 328; property of a virtuous person, 332, 334.
Visvakarman, 83.
Visvantara, 72, 73, 75, 76, 77, 78, 79, 80, 93; story of, IX. 71-93.
Vrishnayas, 145.

Wisdom, supreme, see Buddhahood.
Woodpecker, story of the, XXXIV. 329-335.
World hereafter, proof for its existence, 271-277.
World-renunciation, 3, 4, 47, 149-153, 156, 166-172, 253, 268, 319.
Worldly pleasures censured, 159-163, 173.

Yakshas, 7, 57. 61, 81, 83, 119, 136, 161, 164, 182, 327, 328, 329; the five, in story VIII. 56, 57, 58, 59, 60, 61, 62, 63, 65, 66, 67, 68, 69, 71.
Yakshinî, 315.
Yama, 275, 277, 326.
yâna, the three, 5, 6, cp. 280.
yoga, 4, 217.
Yogin, 228.
yuga, 219.

TRANSLITERATION OF ORIENTAL ALPHABETS. 347

TRANSLITERATION OF ORIENTAL ALPHABETS ADOPTED FOR THE TRANSLATIONS OF THE SACRED BOOKS OF THE BUDDHISTS.

CONSONANTS	MISSIONARY ALPHABET.			Sanskrit.	Zend.	Pehlevi.	Persian.	Arabic.	Hebrew.	Chinese.
	I Class.	II Class.	III Class.							
Gutturales.										
1 Tenuis	k			क	क	ᖋ	ڪ	ڪ	כּ ךּ	k
2 ,, aspirata	kh			ख	ᵹ	ᵹ			ח ך	kh
3 Media	g			ग	ल	ᖋ	گ			
4 ,, aspirata	gh			घ		ᖋ			ר	
5 Gutturo-labialis	q								ק	
6 Nasalis	ṅ (ng)			ङ	ɜ (ng) ᶜ(ɴ) ᵉʸ(ᶜɜ hv)					
7 Spiritus asper	h			ह				ʻ	ה	h, hs
8 ,, lenis	ʼ							ʼ	א	
9 ,, asper faucalis	ʼh							ح	ח	
10 ,, lenis faucalis	ʻh	ʻh						ع	ע	
11 ,, asper fricatus		ʻh								
12 ,, lenis fricatus		ʼh								
Gutturales modificatae (palatales, &c.)										
13 Tenuis		k		च	ᖋ	ل	ع	ع		k
14 ,, aspirata		kh		छ	ल	ᶜ	ڪ	ڪ		kh
15 Media		g		ज						
16 ,, aspirata		gh		झ						
17 ,, Nasalis		ñ		ञ						

348 TRANSLITERATION OF ORIENTAL ALPHABETS

CONSONANTS (continued)	MISSIONARY ALPHABET.			Sanskrit.	Zend.	Pehlevi.	Persian.	Arabic.	Hebrew.	Chinese.
	I Class.	II Class.	III Class.							
18 Semivocalis	y			य	ଯ	ງ	ى	ى	'	y
19 Spiritus asper					init. ३ ४ ५					
20 ,, lenis		(y)								
21 ,, asper assibilatus		(y)				?	־ّ؞	־ّ؞		z
22 ,, lenis assibilatus		s		स		ש				
		z					ت			
Dentales.										
23 Tenuis	t			त	४	ש	ט	ט	ת ת	t
24 ,, aspirata	th		TH	थ						th
25 ,, assibilata										
26 Media	d			द	५	ר	ג	د	ד ד	
27 ,, aspirata	dh		DH	ध						
28 ,, assibilata										
29 Nasalis	n			न	ר	ר	ن	ن	נ ן	n
30 Semivocalis	l		l	ल ळ	ᴧ	ا,ל,ר				
31 ,, mollis 1										
32 ,, mollis 2										
33 Spiritus asper 1	s		s	स	३	ש	س	س	ס ם	s
34 ,, asper 2							;(ق)			
35 ,, lenis	z					'	;(ق)	ز	ז	z
36 ,, asperrimus 1										z(ṣ)
37 ,, asperrimus 2										z(ṣ)

Dentales modificatae (linguales, &c.)										
38 Tenuis	...	*t*	....	ट	....	...	ط	ط	ט	...
39 „ aspirata	...	*th*	....	ठ	....	...	ظ	ظ	...	...
40 Media	...	*d*	....	ड	[illegible]	[illegible]	...	...	...	...
41 „ aspirata	...	*dh*	....	ढ	....	...	...	ض	...	..
42 Nasalis	...	*n*	....	ण	[illegible]	...	...	...	...	...
43 Semivocalis	r	...	....	र	[illegible]	[illegible]	ر	ر	ר	...
44 „ fricata	...	*r*	....	...	....	...	...	...	...	*r*
45 „ diacritica	...	...	R	...	....	...	...	...	...	...
46 Spiritus asper	sh	...	....	ष	[illegible]	[illegible]	...	...	...	sh
47 „ lenis	zh	...	....	...	....	...	...	...	...	...
Labiales.										
48 Tenuis	p	...	....	प	[illegible]	[illegible]	پ	...	פּ	p
49 „ aspirata	ph	...	....	फ	....	...	...	...	פ	ph
50 Media	b	...	....	ब	[illegible]	[illegible]	ب	ب	בּ	...
51 „ aspirata	bh	...	....	भ	....	...	...	...	ב	...
52 Tenuissima	...	*p*	....	...	....	...	...	...	...	...
53 Nasalis	m	...	....	म	[illegible]	[illegible]	م	م	מ	m
54 Semivocalis	w	...	....	...	[illegible]	...	...	...	...	w
55 „ aspirata	hw	...	....	...	....	...	...	...	...	...
56 Spiritus asper	f	...	....	...	[illegible]	[illegible]	ف	ف	...	f
57 „ lenis	v	...	....	व	»	[illegible]	و	و	ו	...
58 Anusvâra	...	*m*	....	सं	[illegible] ã	...	...	...	...	...
59 Visarga	...	*h*	....	अः	....	...	...	...	...	...

350   TRANSLITERATION OF ORIENTAL ALPHABETS.

VOWELS.	MISSIONARY ALPHABET.			Sanskrit.	Zend.	Pehlevi.	Persian.	Arabic.	Hebrew.	Chinese.
	I Class.	II Class.	III Class.							
1 Neutralis	o								͏̣	ă
2 Laryngo-palatalis	ă									
3 " labialis	ŏ									
4 Gutturalis brevis	a			फ़	ɔ		ا	ا	׀	a
5 " longa	â	(a)		फा	ɜ	) fin.	ل	ل	׀ָ	â
6 Palatalis brevis	i			क़ार	ⲅ	ᴅ init.	ا	ا	׀ֵ	ī
7 " longa	î	(î)		फे	ɔ	ᴅ	׀ֶ			ĭ
8 Dentalis brevis	ü			फै						
9 " longa	ü			टि						
10 Lingualis brevis	ri			टी						
11 " longa	rî			ता						
12 Labialis brevis	u	(u)		ता						
13 " longa	û			तॊ			ـا	ـا		u
14 Gutturo-palatalis brevis	e	(e)		ता ता	ɛ(e) ɣ(e)				׀	e
15 " longa	ê (ai)	(ai)			ɭ̇, ɭ̇					ê
16 Diphthongus gutturo-palatalis	âi									âi
17 "	ei (ĕi)									ei, êi
18 "	oi (ŏu)									
19 Gutturo-labialis brevis	o	(o)		ता ता		)	ۊ	ۊ	׀	o
20 " longa	ô (au)	(au)			↗ ↗					
21 Diphthongus gutturo-labialis	âu				ευ (au)				׀ו	âu
22 "	eu (ĕu)									
23 "	ou (ŏu)									
24 Gutturalis fracta	ä									
25 Palatalis fracta	ï									
26 Labialis fracta	ü									ü
27 Gutturo-labialis fracta	ö									

www.ingramcontent.com/pod-product-compliance
Lightning Source LLC
Chambersburg PA
CBHW020259240426
43673CB00039B/650